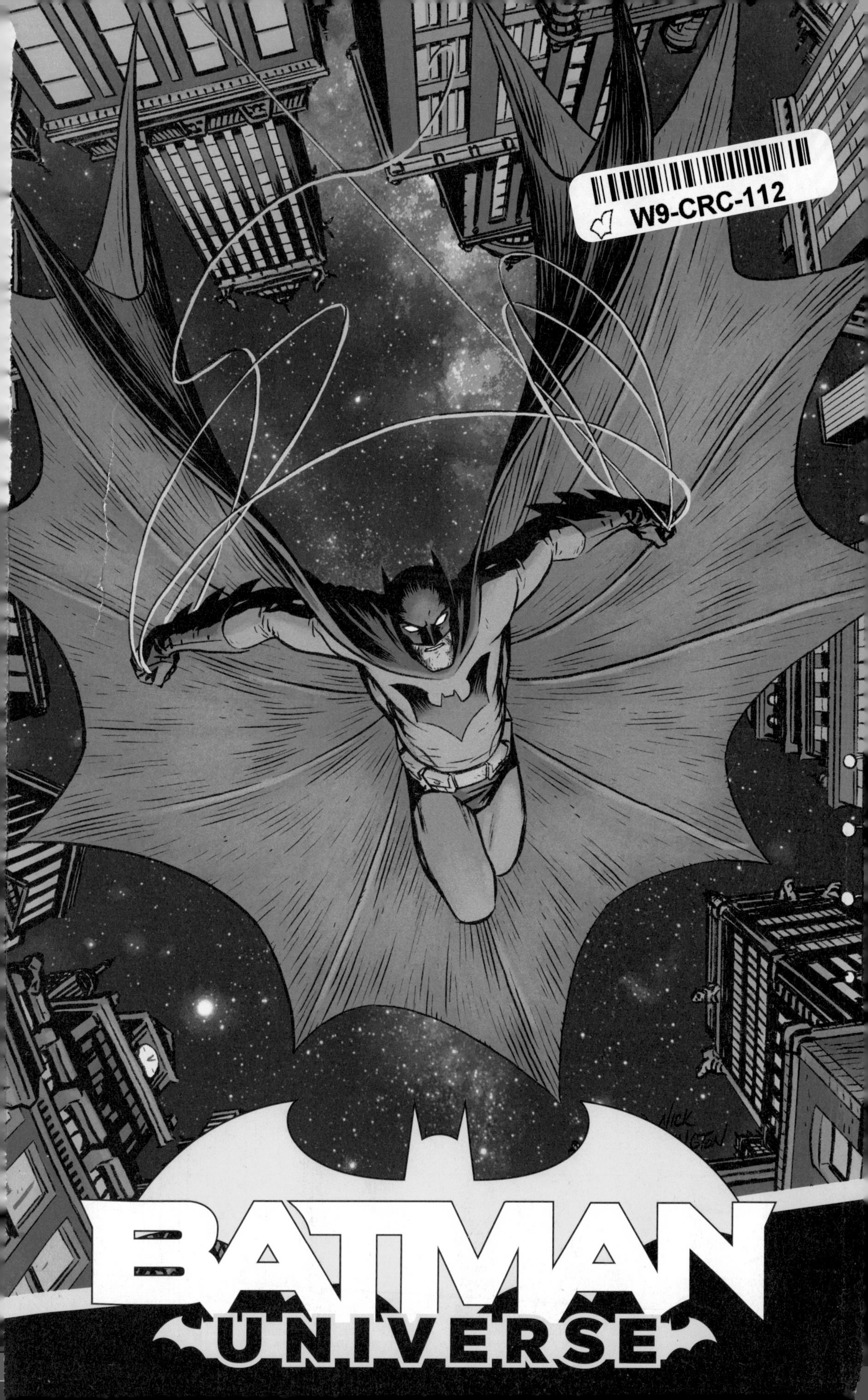
BATMAN
UNIVERSE

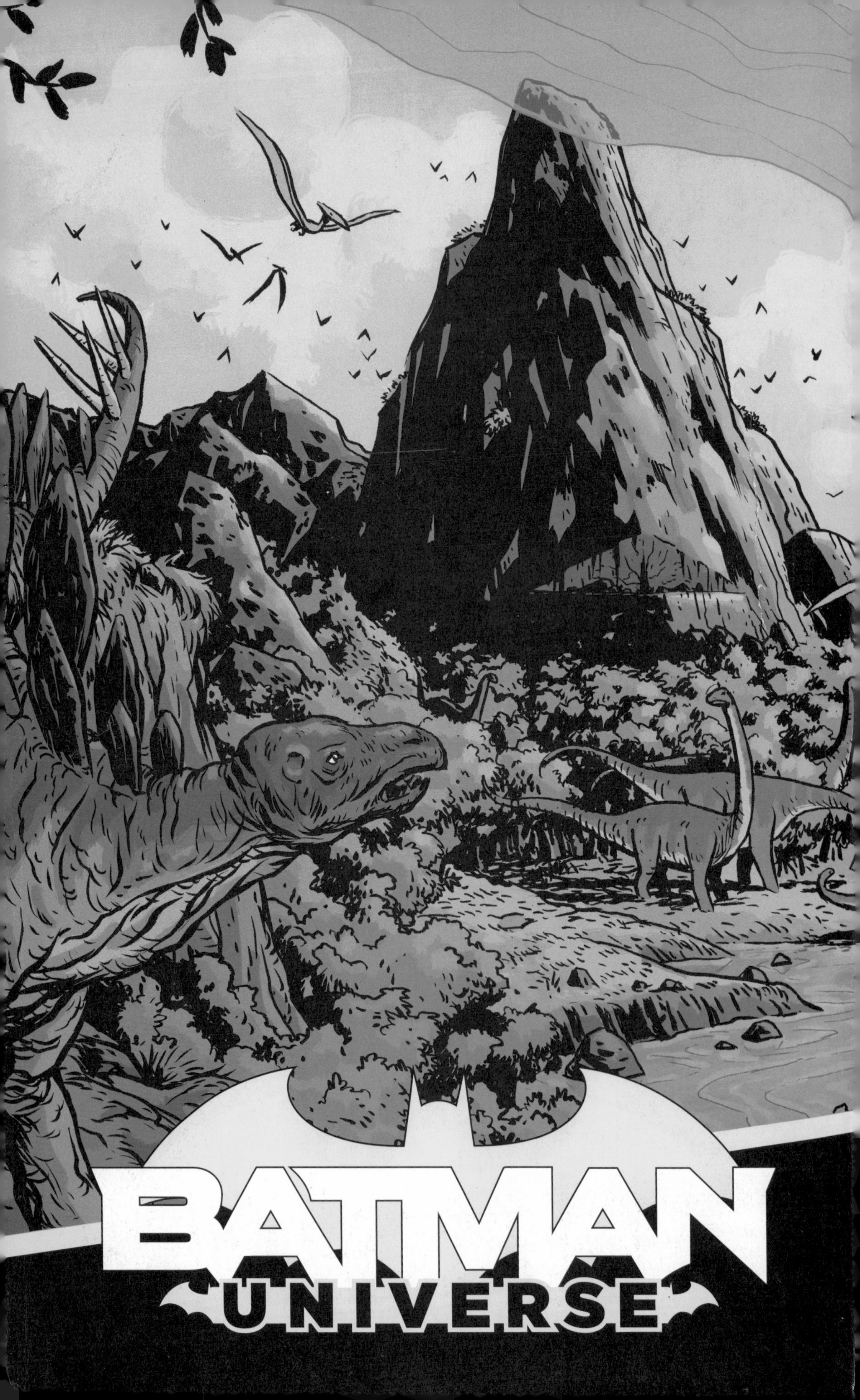
BATMAN
UNIVERSE

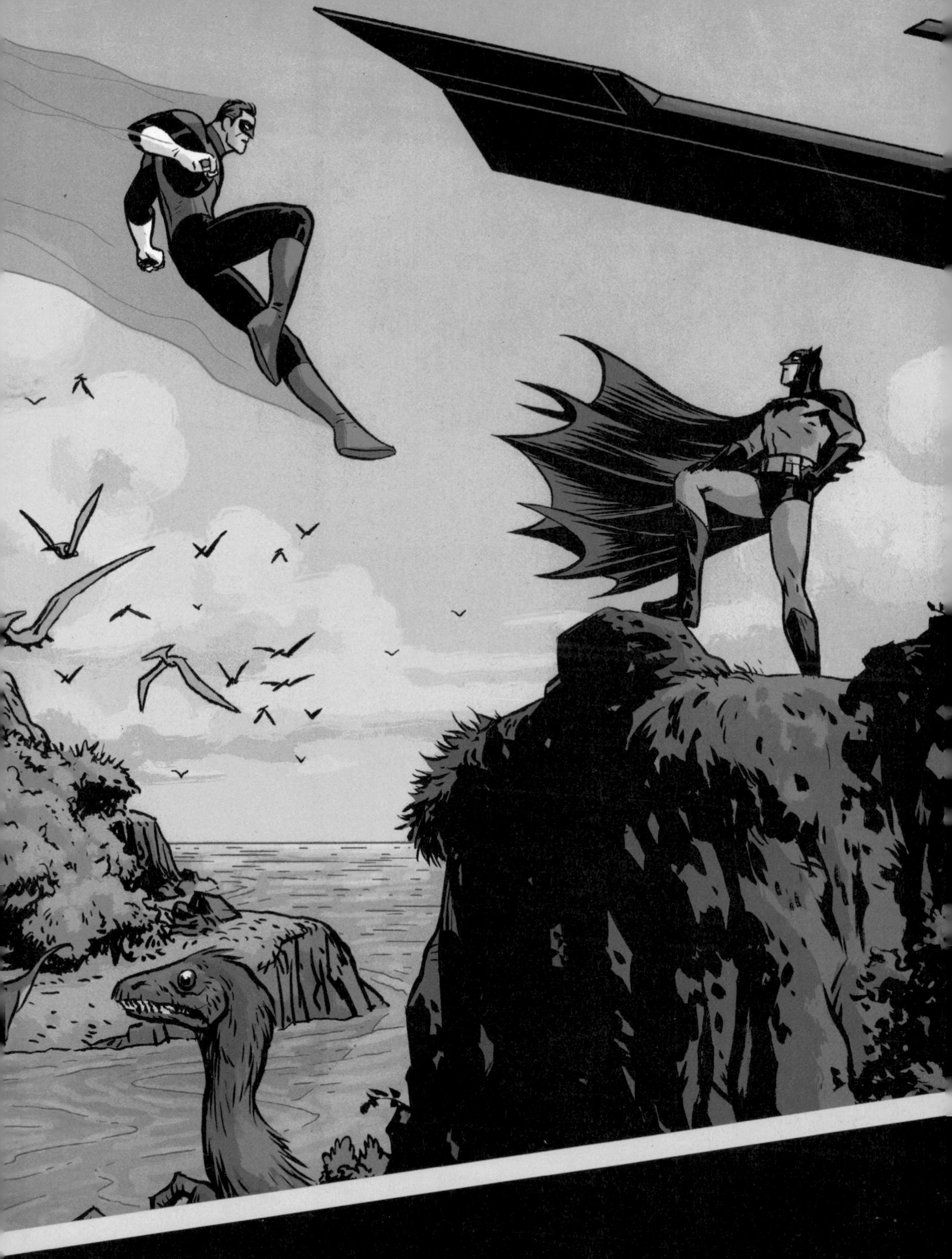

BRIAN MICHAEL BENDIS
writer

NICK DERINGTON
artist

DAVE STEWART
colorist

JOSH REED
CARLOS M. MANGUAL
TOM NAPOLITANO
ALW'S TROY PETERI
letterers

NICK DERINGTON
series and collection cover artist

BATMAN created by **BOB KANE** with **BILL FINGER**

SUPERMAN created by **JERRY SIEGEL** and **JOE SHUSTER**

PEFC Certified

This product is from
sustainably managed
forests and controlled
sources

www.pefc.org

PEFC/29-31-337

DC Comics
2900 West Alameda Ave., Burbank, CA 91505
Printed by LSC Communications,
Owensville, MO, USA. 4/2/21.
First Printing. ISBN: 978-1-77950-583-5

Library of Congress
Cataloging-in-Publication Data is available.

JAMIE S. RICH *Editor – Original Series*
BRITTANY HOLZHERR *Associate Editor – Original Series*
DAVE WIELGOSZ *Assistant Editor – Original Series*
ERIKA ROTHBERG *Editor – Collected Edition*
STEVE COOK *Design Director – Books*
CURTIS KING JR. *Publication Design*
SUZANNAH ROWNTREE *Publication Production*

MARIE JAVINS *Editor-in-Chief, DC Comics*

DANIEL CHERRY III *Senior VP – General Manager*
JIM LEE *Publisher & Chief Creative Officer*
DON FALLETTI *VP – Manufacturing Operations & Workflow Management*
LAWRENCE GANEM *VP – Talent Services*
ALISON GILL *Senior VP – Manufacturing & Operations*
NICK J. NAPOLITANO *VP – Manufacturing Administration & Design*
NANCY SPEARS *VP – Revenue*

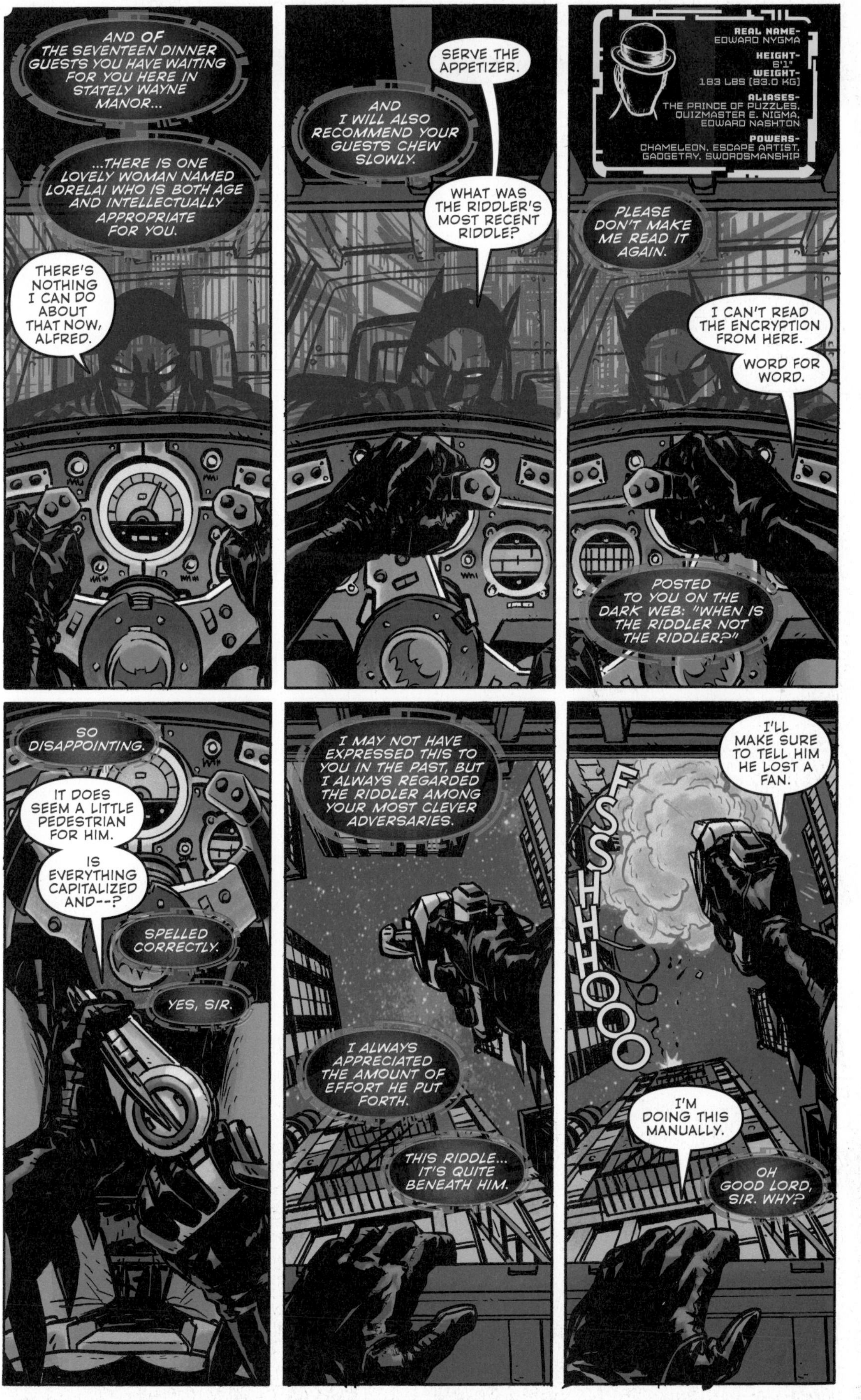
AND OF THE SEVENTEEN DINNER GUESTS YOU HAVE WAITING FOR YOU HERE IN STATELY WAYNE MANOR...
...THERE IS ONE LOVELY WOMAN NAMED LORELAI WHO IS BOTH AGE AND INTELLECTUALLY APPROPRIATE FOR YOU.
THERE'S NOTHING I CAN DO ABOUT THAT NOW, ALFRED.
SERVE THE APPETIZER.
AND I WILL ALSO RECOMMEND YOUR GUESTS CHEW SLOWLY.
WHAT WAS THE RIDDLER'S MOST RECENT RIDDLE?
REAL NAME-
EDWARD NYGMA
HEIGHT-
6'1"
WEIGHT-
183 LBS [83.0 KG]
ALIASES-
THE PRINCE OF PUZZLES, QUIZMASTER E. NIGMA, EDWARD NASHTON
POWERS-
CHAMELEON, ESCAPE ARTIST, GADGETRY, SWORDSMANSHIP
PLEASE DON'T MAKE ME READ IT AGAIN.
I CAN'T READ THE ENCRYPTION FROM HERE.
WORD FOR WORD.
POSTED TO YOU ON THE DARK WEB: "WHEN IS THE RIDDLER NOT THE RIDDLER?"
SO DISAPPOINTING.
IT DOES SEEM A LITTLE PEDESTRIAN FOR HIM.
IS EVERYTHING CAPITALIZED AND--?
SPELLED CORRECTLY.
YES, SIR.
I MAY NOT HAVE EXPRESSED THIS TO YOU IN THE PAST, BUT I ALWAYS REGARDED THE RIDDLER AMONG YOUR MOST CLEVER ADVERSARIES.
I ALWAYS APPRECIATED THE AMOUNT OF EFFORT HE PUT FORTH.
THIS RIDDLE... IT'S QUITE BENEATH HIM.
FSSHHHOOOO
I'LL MAKE SURE TO TELL HIM HE LOST A FAN.
I'M DOING THIS MANUALLY.
OH GOOD LORD, SIR. WHY?

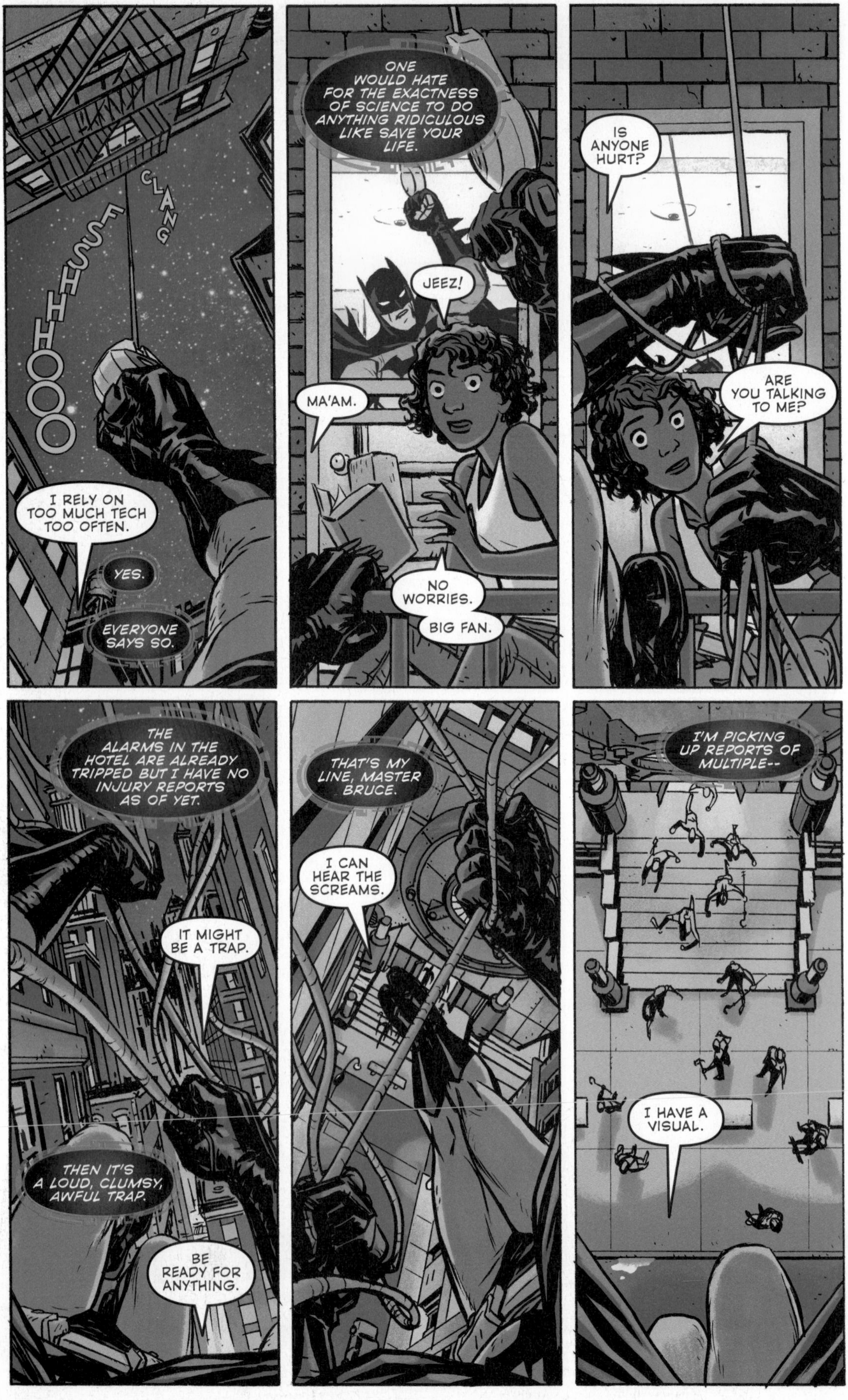
CLANG
FSHHHOOOO
I RELY ON TOO MUCH TECH TOO OFTEN.
YES.
EVERYONE SAYS SO.
ONE WOULD HATE FOR THE EXACTNESS OF SCIENCE TO DO ANYTHING RIDICULOUS LIKE SAVE YOUR LIFE.
JEEZ!
MA'AM.
NO WORRIES.
BIG FAN.
IS ANYONE HURT?
ARE YOU TALKING TO ME?
THE ALARMS IN THE HOTEL ARE ALREADY TRIPPED BUT I HAVE NO INJURY REPORTS AS OF YET.
IT MIGHT BE A TRAP.
THEN IT'S A LOUD, CLUMSY, AWFUL TRAP.
BE READY FOR ANYTHING.
THAT'S MY LINE, MASTER BRUCE.
I CAN HEAR THE SCREAMS.
I'M PICKING UP REPORTS OF MULTIPLE--
I HAVE A VISUAL.

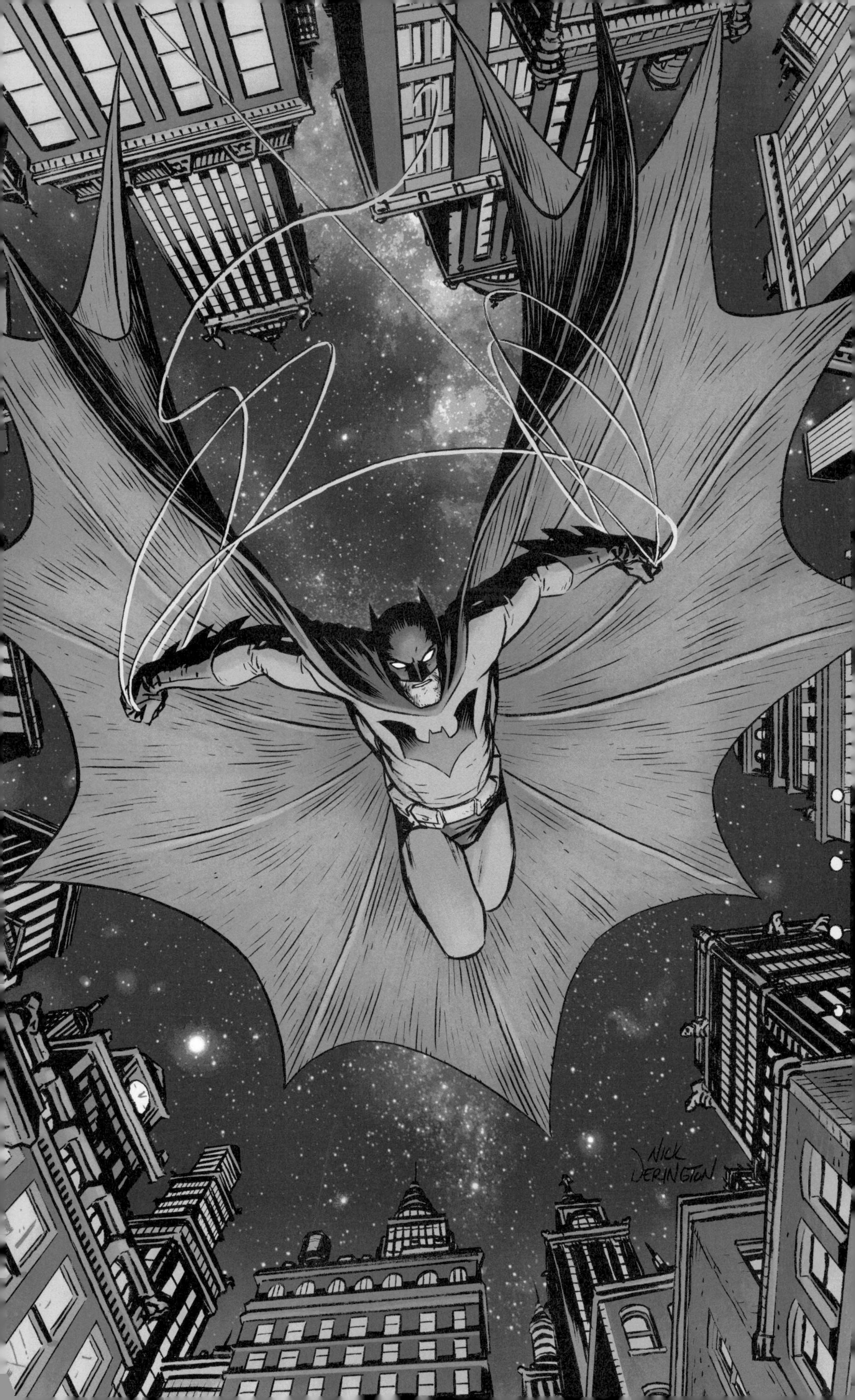
NICK DERINGTON

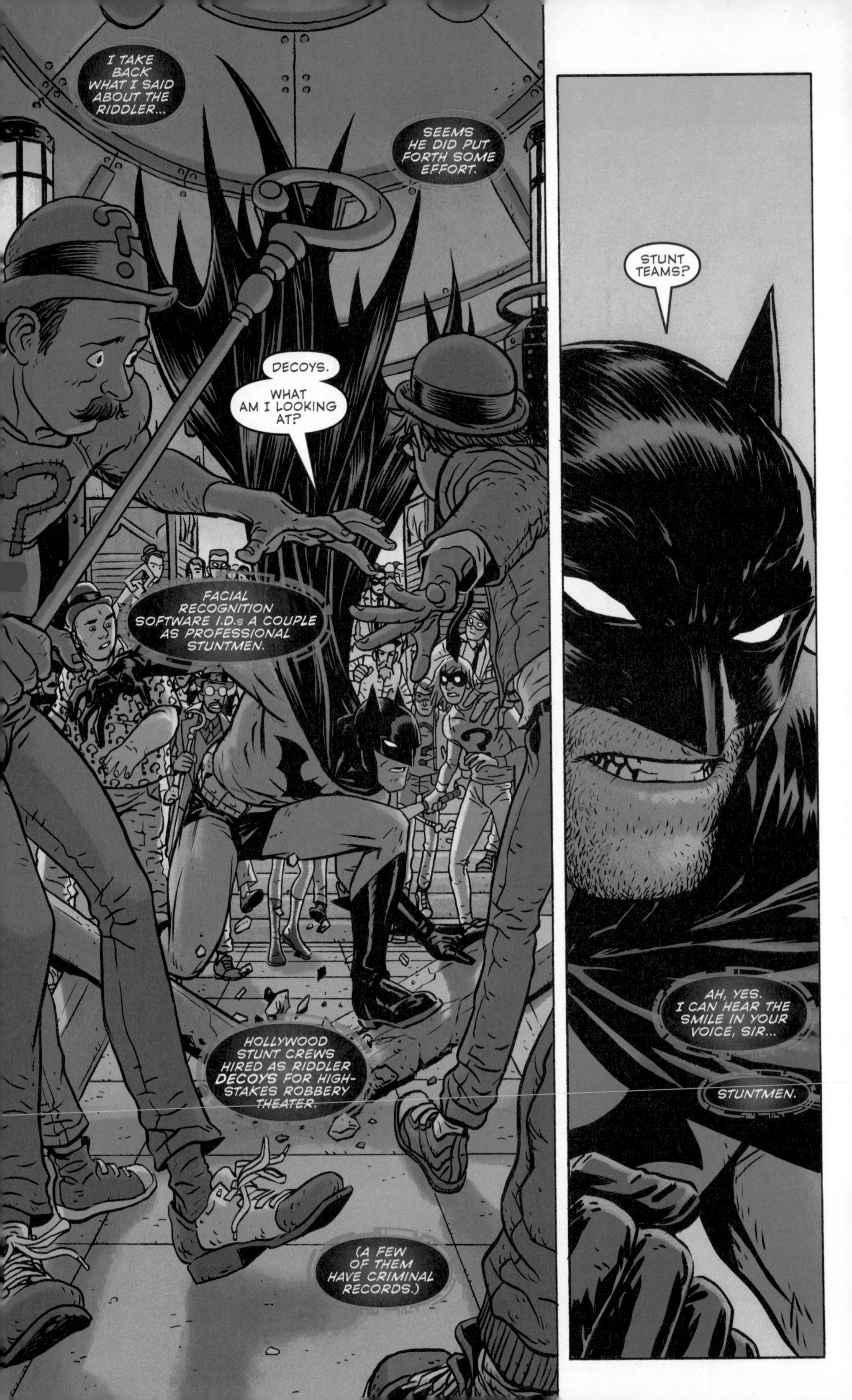
I TAKE BACK WHAT I SAID ABOUT THE RIDDLER...
SEEMS HE DID PUT FORTH SOME EFFORT.
DECOYS.
WHAT AM I LOOKING AT?
FACIAL RECOGNITION SOFTWARE I.D.s A COUPLE AS PROFESSIONAL STUNTMEN.
HOLLYWOOD STUNT CREWS HIRED AS RIDDLER DECOYS FOR HIGH-STAKES ROBBERY THEATER.
(A FEW OF THEM HAVE CRIMINAL RECORDS.)
STUNT TEAMS?
AH, YES. I CAN HEAR THE SMILE IN YOUR VOICE, SIR...
STUNTMEN.

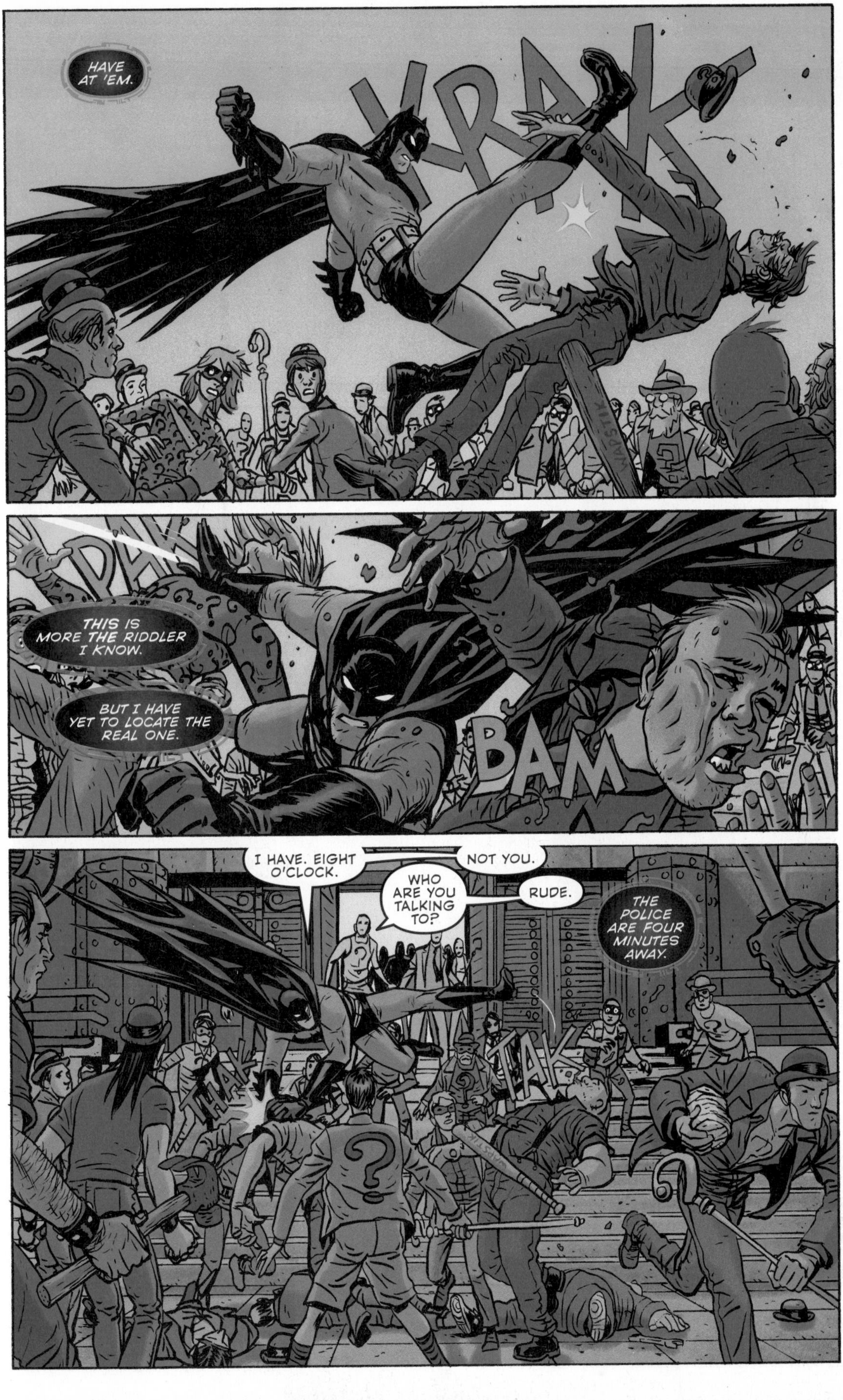
HAVE AT 'EM.
VRAK
THIS IS MORE THE RIDDLER I KNOW.
BUT I HAVE YET TO LOCATE THE REAL ONE.
BAM
THE POLICE ARE FOUR MINUTES AWAY.
I HAVE. EIGHT O'CLOCK.
WHO ARE YOU TALKING TO?
NOT YOU.
RUDE.
THAK
TAK

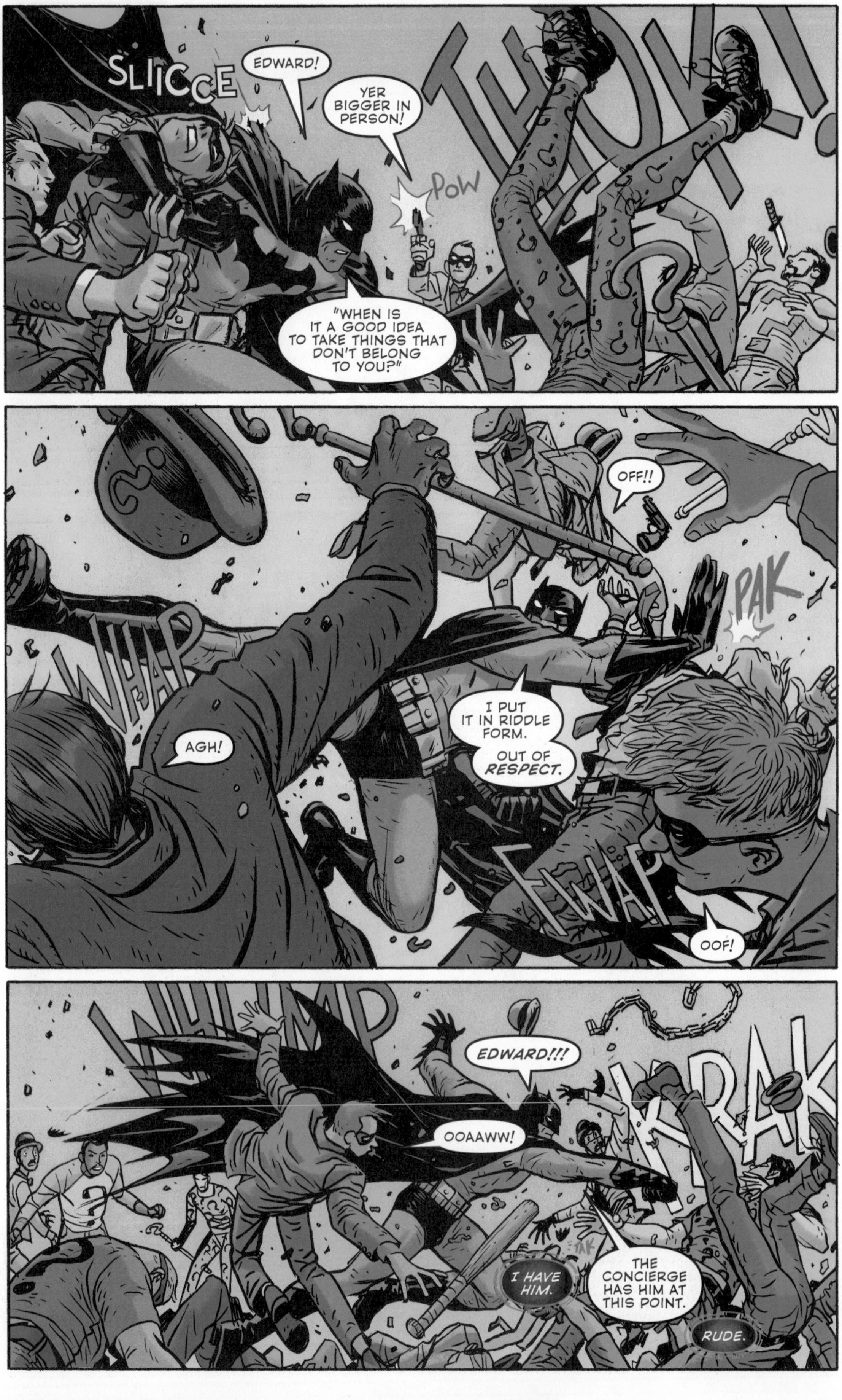
SLIICCE
EDWARD!
YER BIGGER IN PERSON!
POW
"WHEN IS IT A GOOD IDEA TO TAKE THINGS THAT DON'T BELONG TO YOU?"
OFF!!
PAK
WHAP
I PUT IT IN RIDDLE FORM.
OUT OF *RESPECT*.
AGH!
FWAP
OOF!
EDWARD!!!
KRAK
OOAAWW!
I HAVE HIM.
THE CONCIERGE HAS HIM AT THIS POINT.
RUDE.

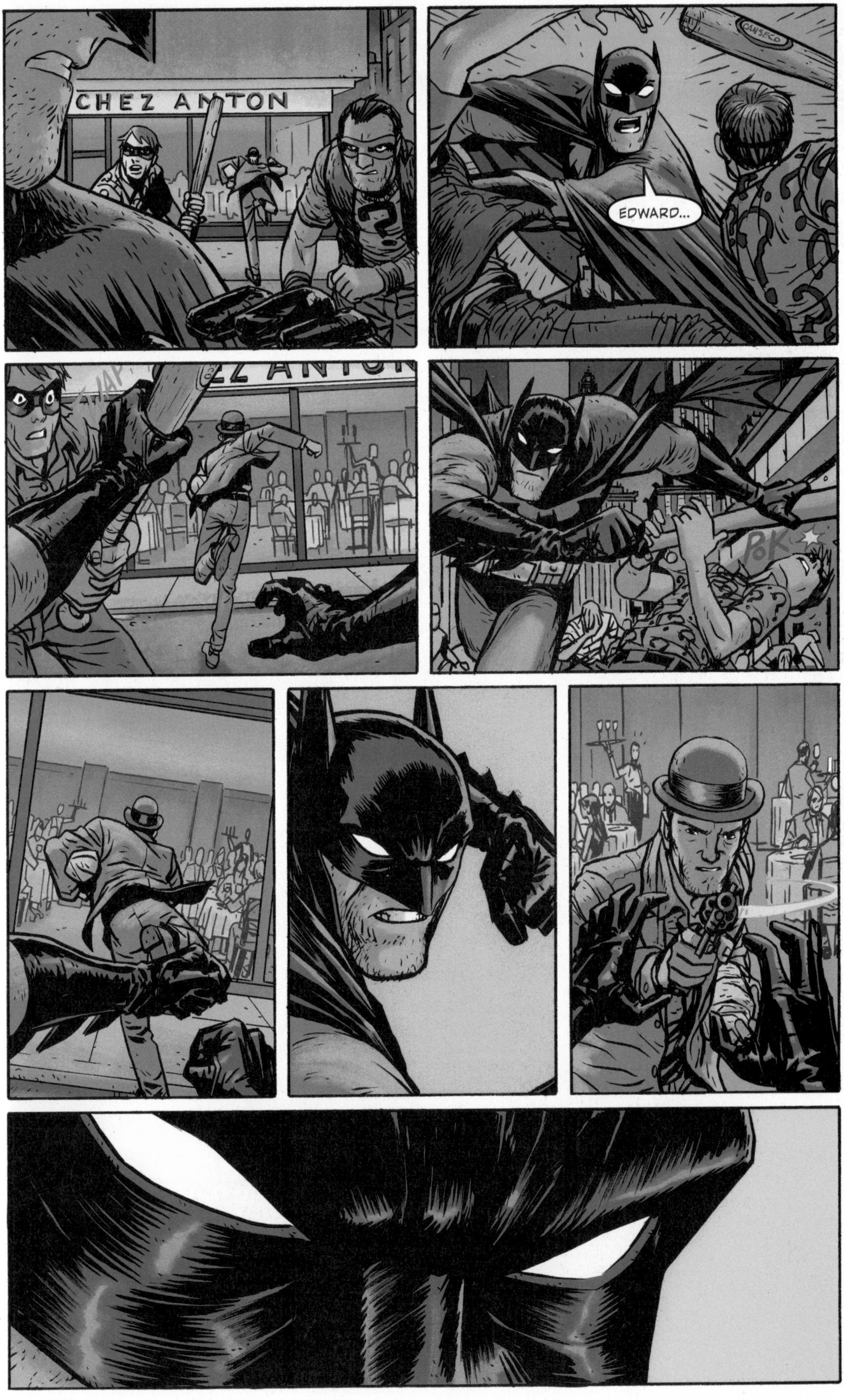
CHEZ ANTON
CANSECO
EDWARD...
POK

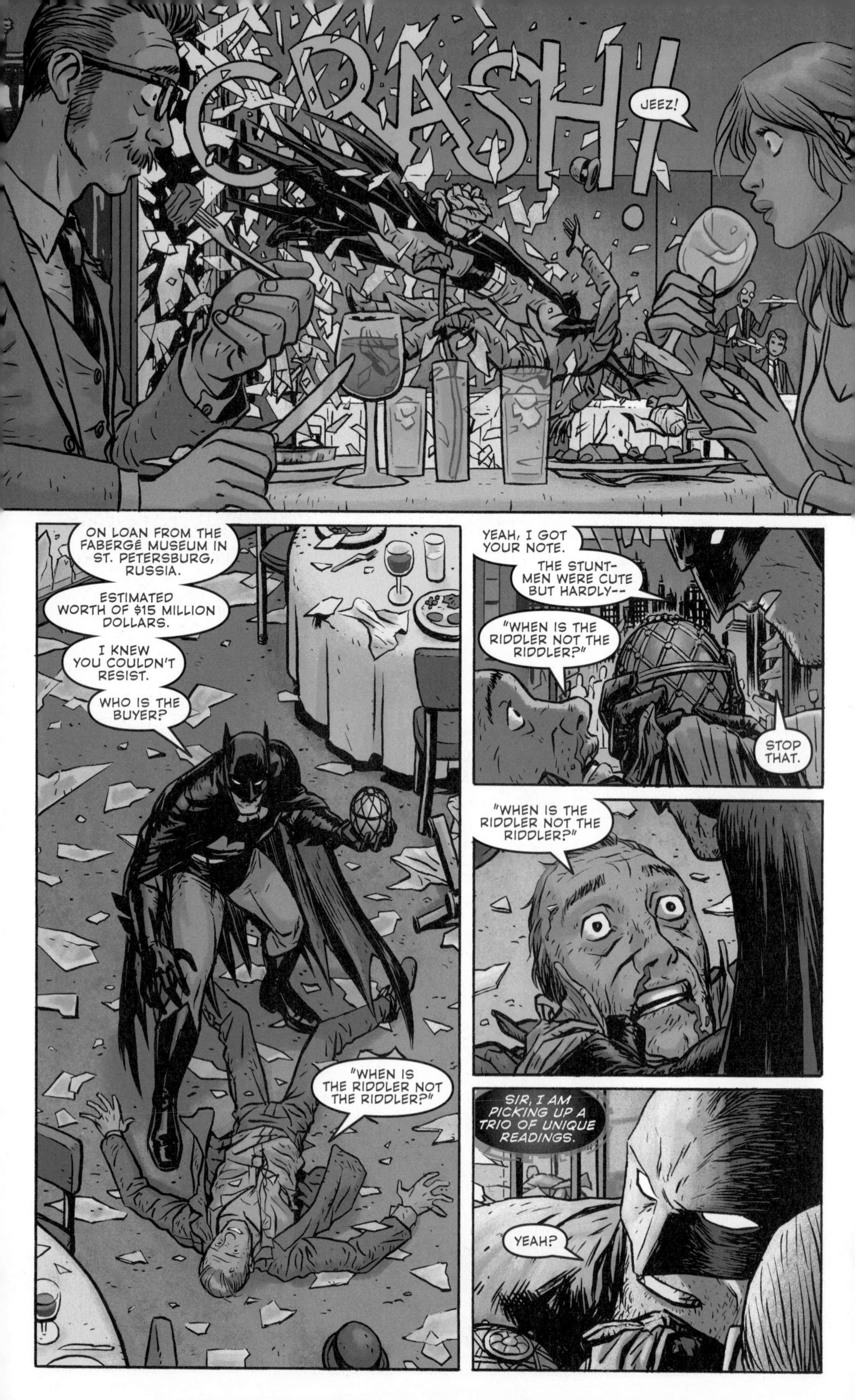
CRASH!
JEEZ!
ON LOAN FROM THE FABERGÉ MUSEUM IN ST. PETERSBURG, RUSSIA.
ESTIMATED WORTH OF $15 MILLION DOLLARS.
I KNEW YOU COULDN'T RESIST.
WHO IS THE BUYER?
"WHEN IS THE RIDDLER NOT THE RIDDLER?"
YEAH, I GOT YOUR NOTE.
THE STUNT-MEN WERE CUTE BUT HARDLY--
"WHEN IS THE RIDDLER NOT THE RIDDLER?"
STOP THAT.
"WHEN IS THE RIDDLER NOT THE RIDDLER?"
SIR, I AM PICKING UP A TRIO OF UNIQUE READINGS.
YEAH?

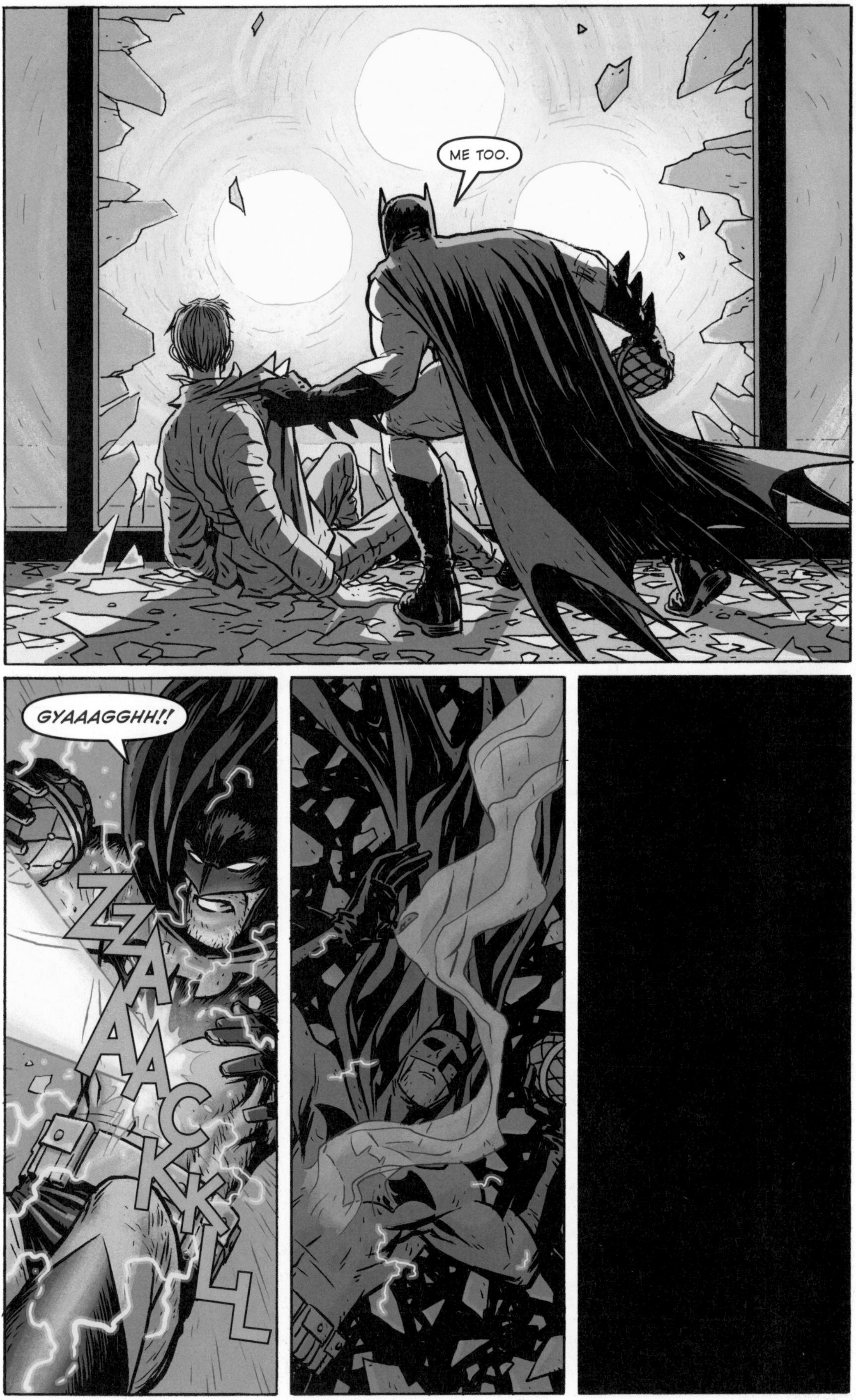
ME TOO.
GYAAAGGHH!!
ZZAAACKKLL

GO AHEAD.

BE MY GUEST.

MAYBE HE CAN'T BREATHE.

SURE, KID.

TAKE OFF HIS MASK.

HE WON'T MIND.

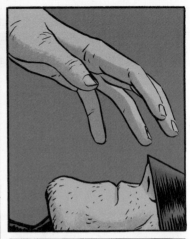

PLEASE DON'T.

WHERE'S THE EGG?

YOU ORDERED EGGS?

WHERE'S THE RIDDLER?

ALL THE RIDDLERS ARE BEING LOADED INTO THE PADDY WAGON.

NO.

THE REAL ONE.

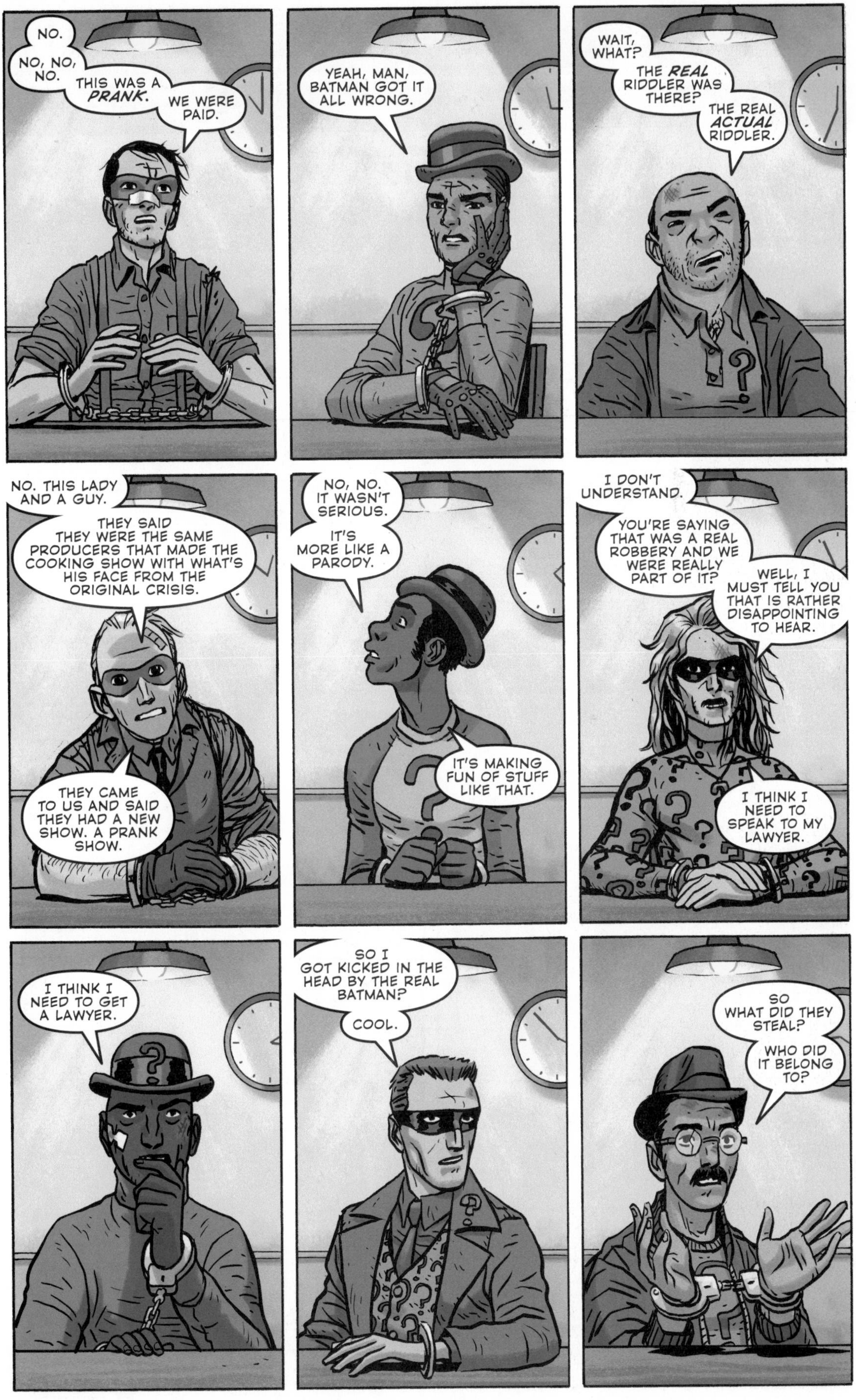
NO.
NO, NO, NO.
THIS WAS A *PRANK.*
WE WERE PAID.
YEAH, MAN, BATMAN GOT IT ALL WRONG.
WAIT, WHAT?
THE *REAL* RIDDLER WAS THERE?
THE REAL *ACTUAL* RIDDLER.
NO. THIS LADY AND A GUY.
THEY SAID THEY WERE THE SAME PRODUCERS THAT MADE THE COOKING SHOW WITH WHAT'S HIS FACE FROM THE ORIGINAL CRISIS.
THEY CAME TO US AND SAID THEY HAD A NEW SHOW. A PRANK SHOW.
NO, NO. IT WASN'T SERIOUS.
IT'S MORE LIKE A PARODY.
IT'S MAKING FUN OF STUFF LIKE THAT.
I DON'T UNDERSTAND.
YOU'RE SAYING THAT WAS A REAL ROBBERY AND WE WERE REALLY PART OF IT?
WELL, I MUST TELL YOU THAT IS RATHER DISAPPOINTING TO HEAR.
I THINK I NEED TO SPEAK TO MY LAWYER.
I THINK I NEED TO GET A LAWYER.
SO I GOT KICKED IN THE HEAD BY THE REAL BATMAN?
COOL.
SO WHAT DID THEY STEAL?
WHO DID IT BELONG TO?

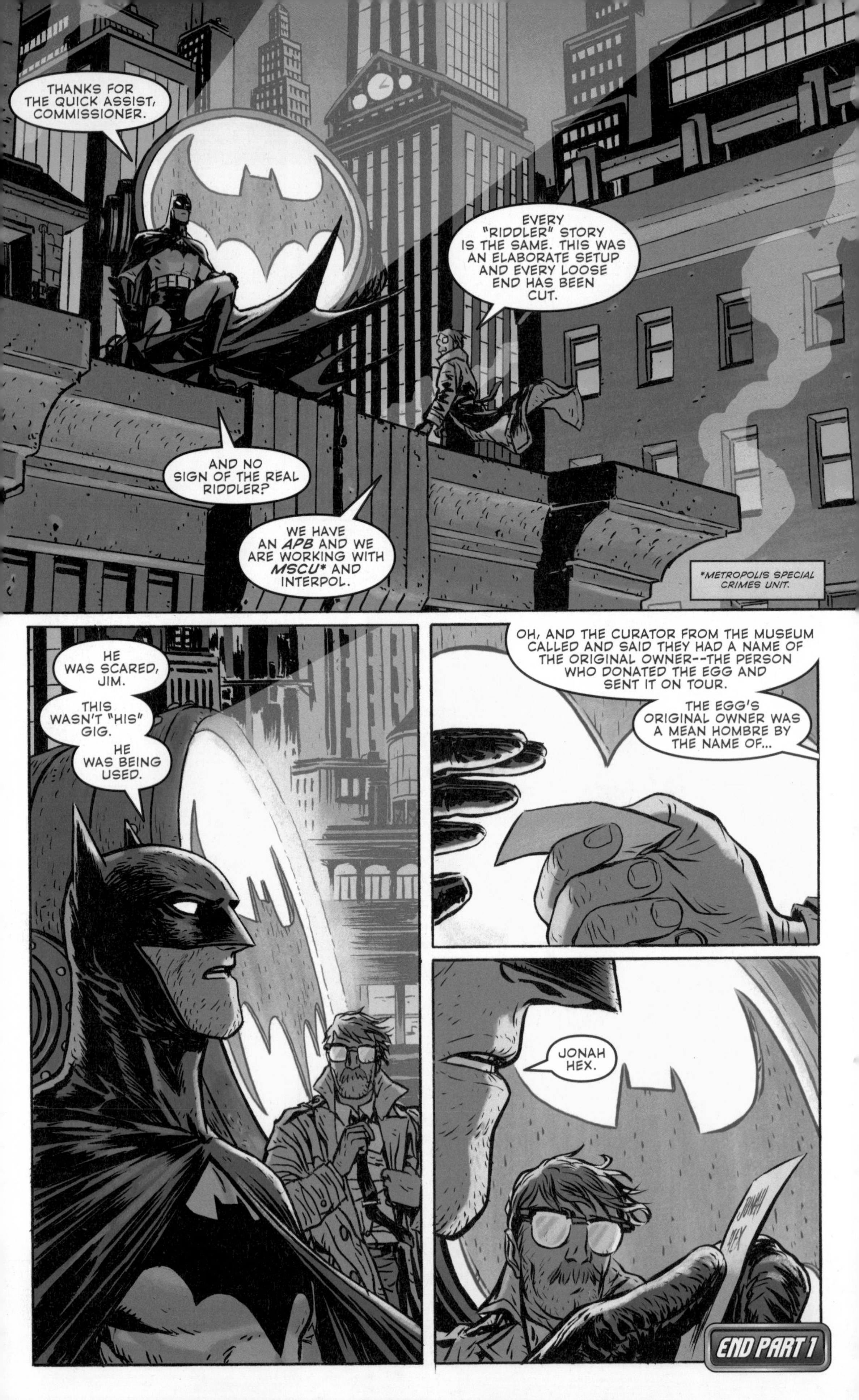
THANKS FOR THE QUICK ASSIST, COMMISSIONER.
EVERY "RIDDLER" STORY IS THE SAME. THIS WAS AN ELABORATE SETUP AND EVERY LOOSE END HAS BEEN CUT.
AND NO SIGN OF THE REAL RIDDLER?
WE HAVE AN *APB* AND WE ARE WORKING WITH *MSCU** AND INTERPOL.
*METROPOLIS SPECIAL CRIMES UNIT.
HE WAS SCARED, JIM.
THIS WASN'T "HIS" GIG.
HE WAS BEING USED.
OH, AND THE CURATOR FROM THE MUSEUM CALLED AND SAID THEY HAD A NAME OF THE ORIGINAL OWNER--THE PERSON WHO DONATED THE EGG AND SENT IT ON TOUR.
THE EGG'S ORIGINAL OWNER WAS A MEAN HOMBRE BY THE NAME OF...
JONAH HEX.
END PART 1

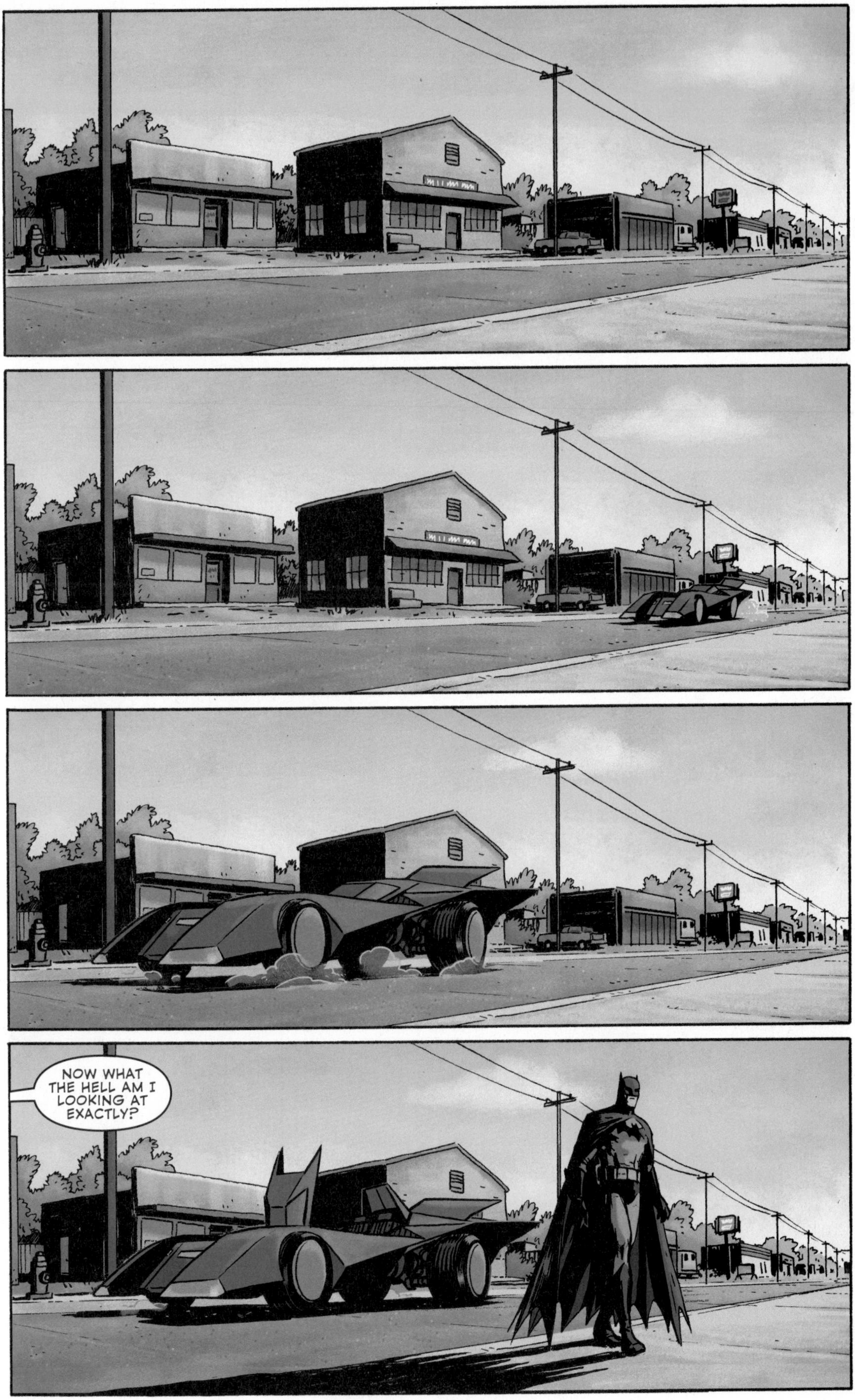
NOW WHAT THE HELL AM I LOOKING AT EXACTLY?

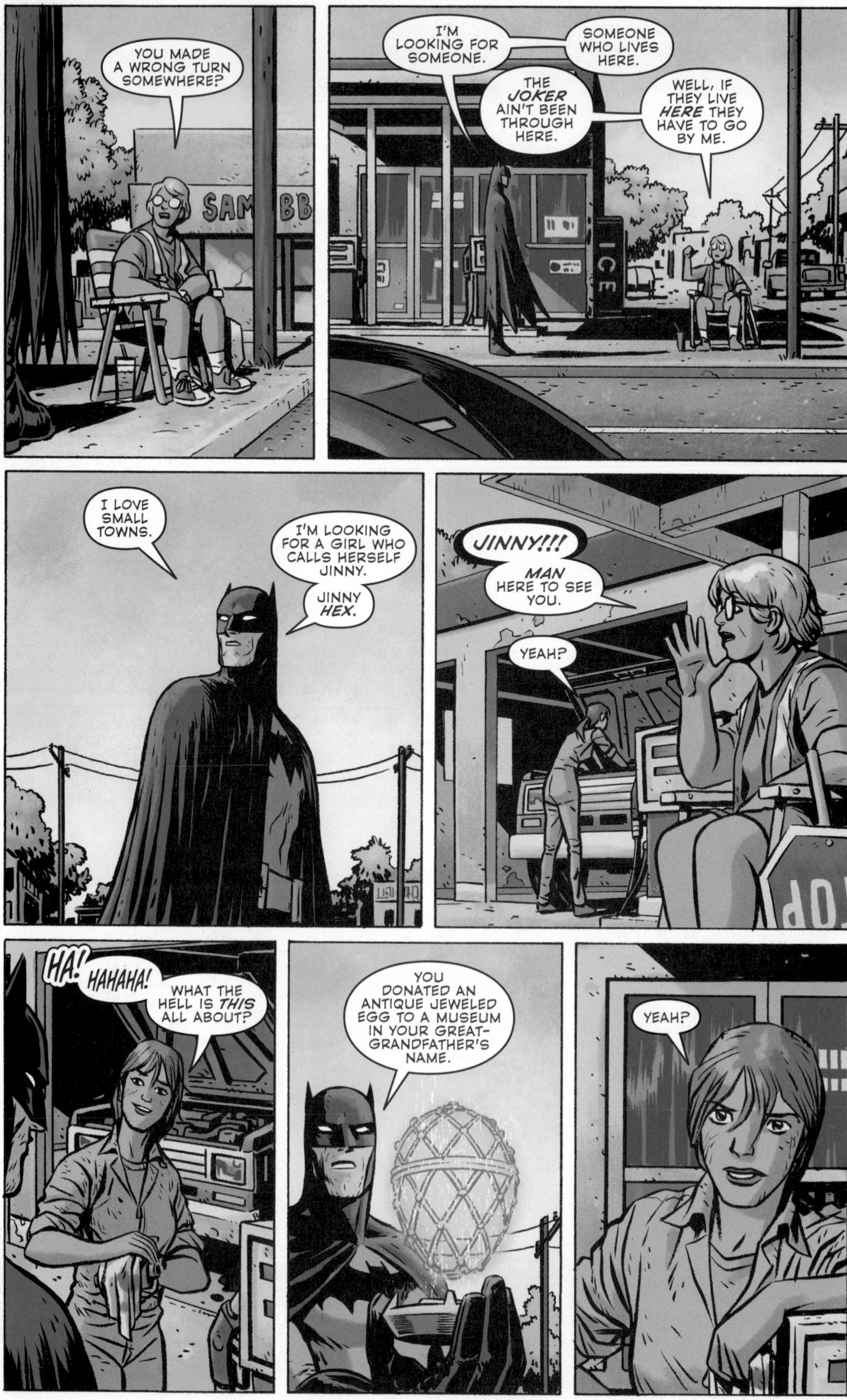
YOU MADE A WRONG TURN SOMEWHERE?
I'M LOOKING FOR SOMEONE.
SOMEONE WHO LIVES HERE.
THE JOKER AIN'T BEEN THROUGH HERE.
WELL, IF THEY LIVE HERE THEY HAVE TO GO BY ME.
ICE
I LOVE SMALL TOWNS.
I'M LOOKING FOR A GIRL WHO CALLS HERSELF JINNY.
JINNY HEX.
JINNY!!!
MAN HERE TO SEE YOU.
YEAH?
HA! HAHAHA!
WHAT THE HELL IS THIS ALL ABOUT?
YOU DONATED AN ANTIQUE JEWELED EGG TO A MUSEUM IN YOUR GREAT-GRANDFATHER'S NAME.
YEAH?

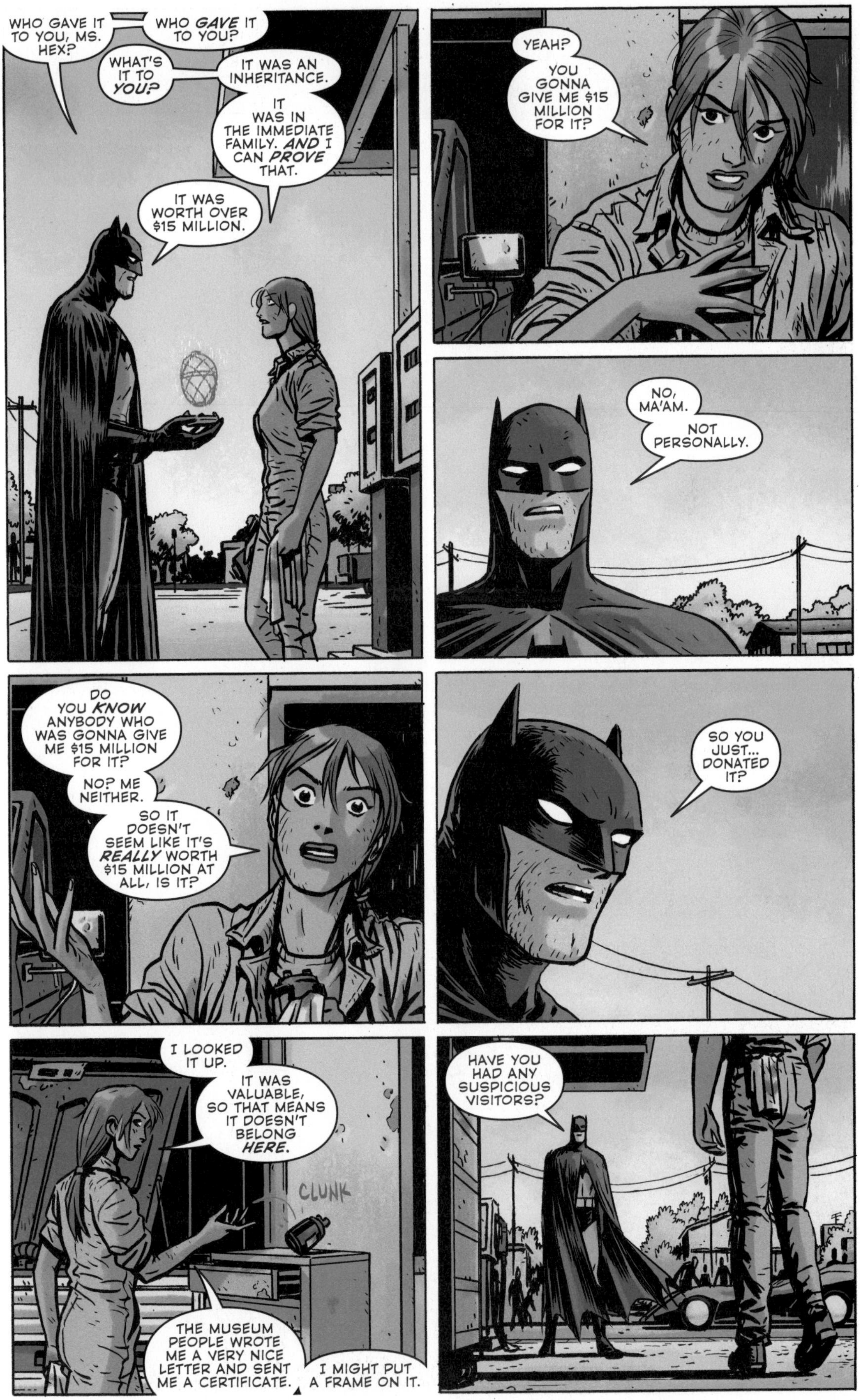

WHO GAVE IT TO YOU, MS. HEX?
WHO GAVE IT TO YOU?
WHAT'S IT TO YOU?
IT WAS AN INHERITANCE.
IT WAS IN THE IMMEDIATE FAMILY. AND I CAN PROVE THAT.
IT WAS WORTH OVER \$15 MILLION.
YEAH?
YOU GONNA GIVE ME \$15 MILLION FOR IT?
NO, MA'AM.
NOT PERSONALLY.
DO YOU KNOW ANYBODY WHO WAS GONNA GIVE ME \$15 MILLION FOR IT?
NO? ME NEITHER.
SO IT DOESN'T SEEM LIKE IT'S REALLY WORTH \$15 MILLION AT ALL, IS IT?
SO YOU JUST... DONATED IT?
I LOOKED IT UP.
IT WAS VALUABLE, SO THAT MEANS IT DOESN'T BELONG HERE.
CLUNK
THE MUSEUM PEOPLE WROTE ME A VERY NICE LETTER AND SENT ME A CERTIFICATE.
I MIGHT PUT A FRAME ON IT.
HAVE YOU HAD ANY SUSPICIOUS VISITORS?

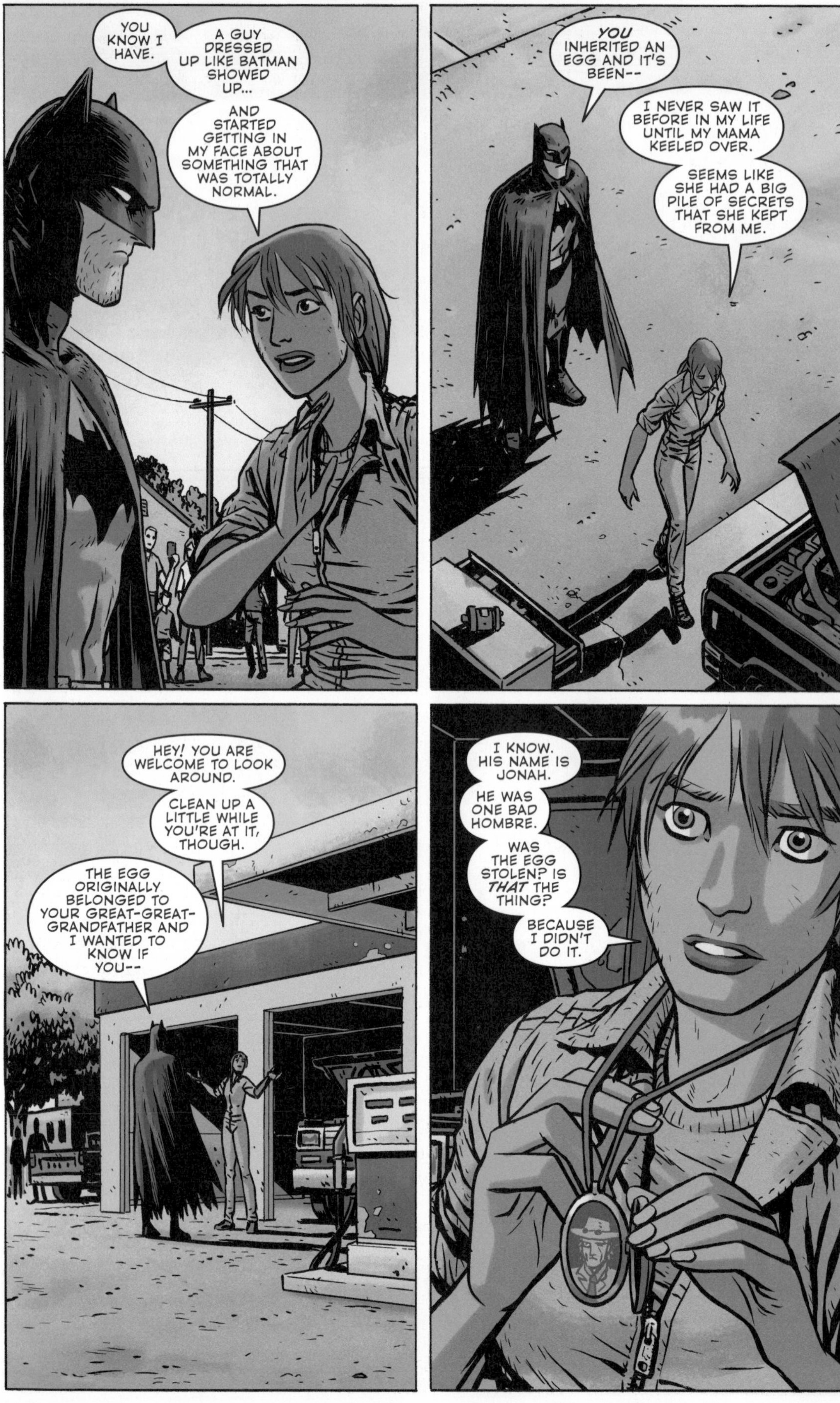

YOU KNOW I HAVE.
A GUY DRESSED UP LIKE BATMAN SHOWED UP...
AND STARTED GETTING IN MY FACE ABOUT SOMETHING THAT WAS TOTALLY NORMAL.
YOU INHERITED AN EGG AND IT'S BEEN--
I NEVER SAW IT BEFORE IN MY LIFE UNTIL MY MAMA KEELED OVER.
SEEMS LIKE SHE HAD A BIG PILE OF SECRETS THAT SHE KEPT FROM ME.
HEY! YOU ARE WELCOME TO LOOK AROUND.
CLEAN UP A LITTLE WHILE YOU'RE AT IT, THOUGH.
THE EGG ORIGINALLY BELONGED TO YOUR GREAT-GREAT-GRANDFATHER AND I WANTED TO KNOW IF YOU--
I KNOW. HIS NAME IS JONAH.
HE WAS ONE BAD HOMBRE.
WAS THE EGG STOLEN? IS *THAT* THE THING?
BECAUSE I DIDN'T DO IT.

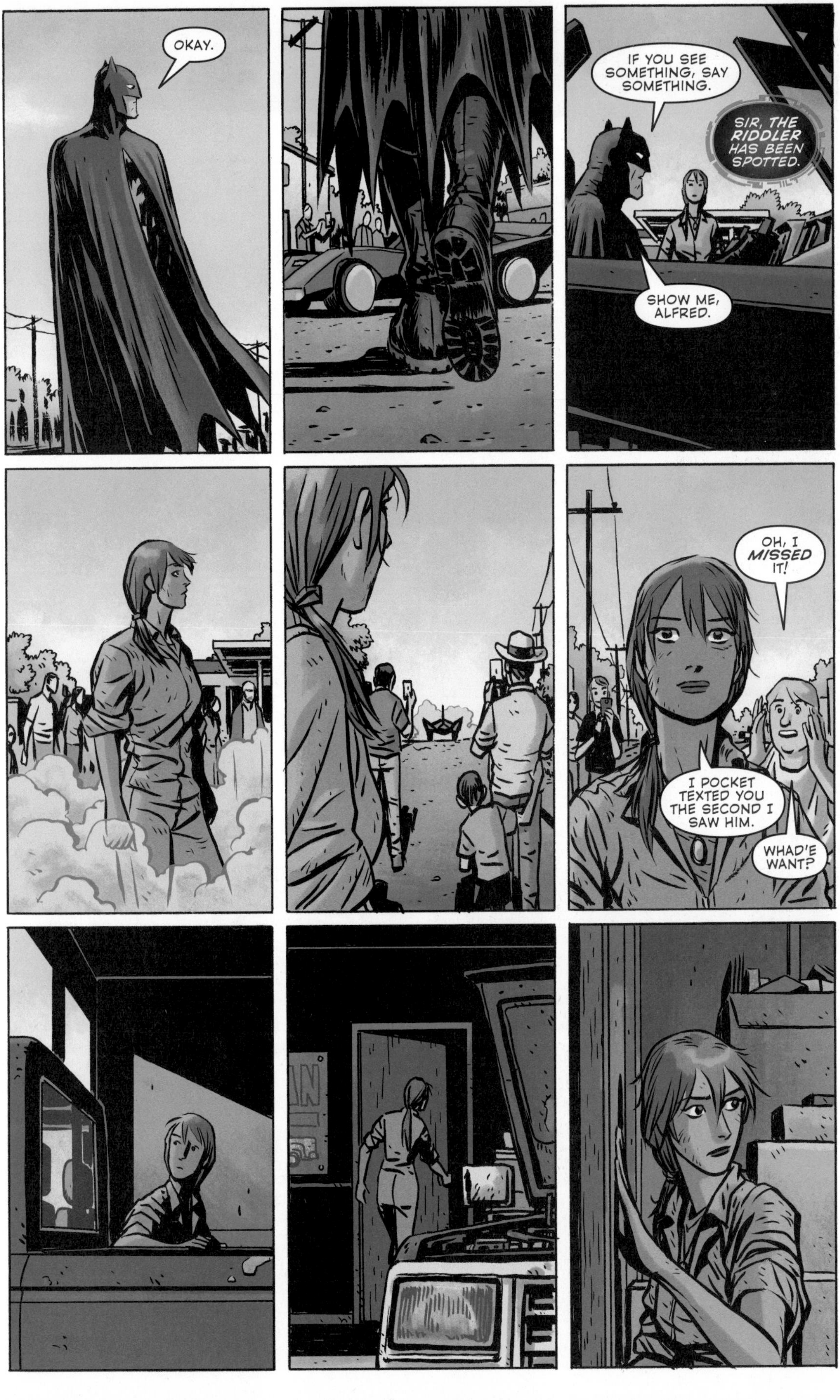
OKAY.
IF YOU SEE SOMETHING, SAY SOMETHING.
SIR, THE RIDDLER HAS BEEN SPOTTED.
SHOW ME, ALFRED.
OH, I MISSED IT!
I POCKET TEXTED YOU THE SECOND I SAW HIM.
WHAD'E WANT?

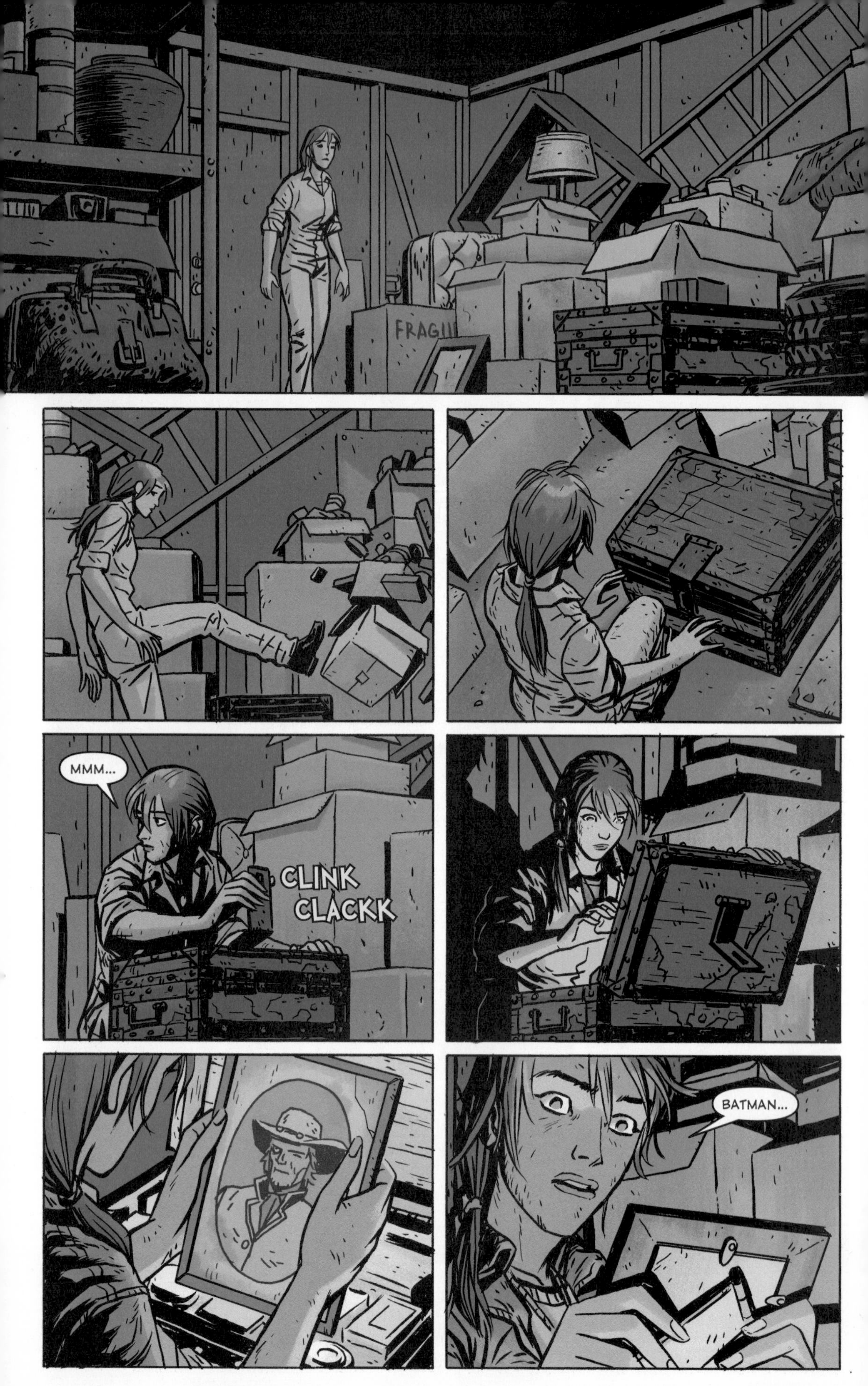
FRAGIL
MMM...
CLINK
CLACKK
BATMAN...

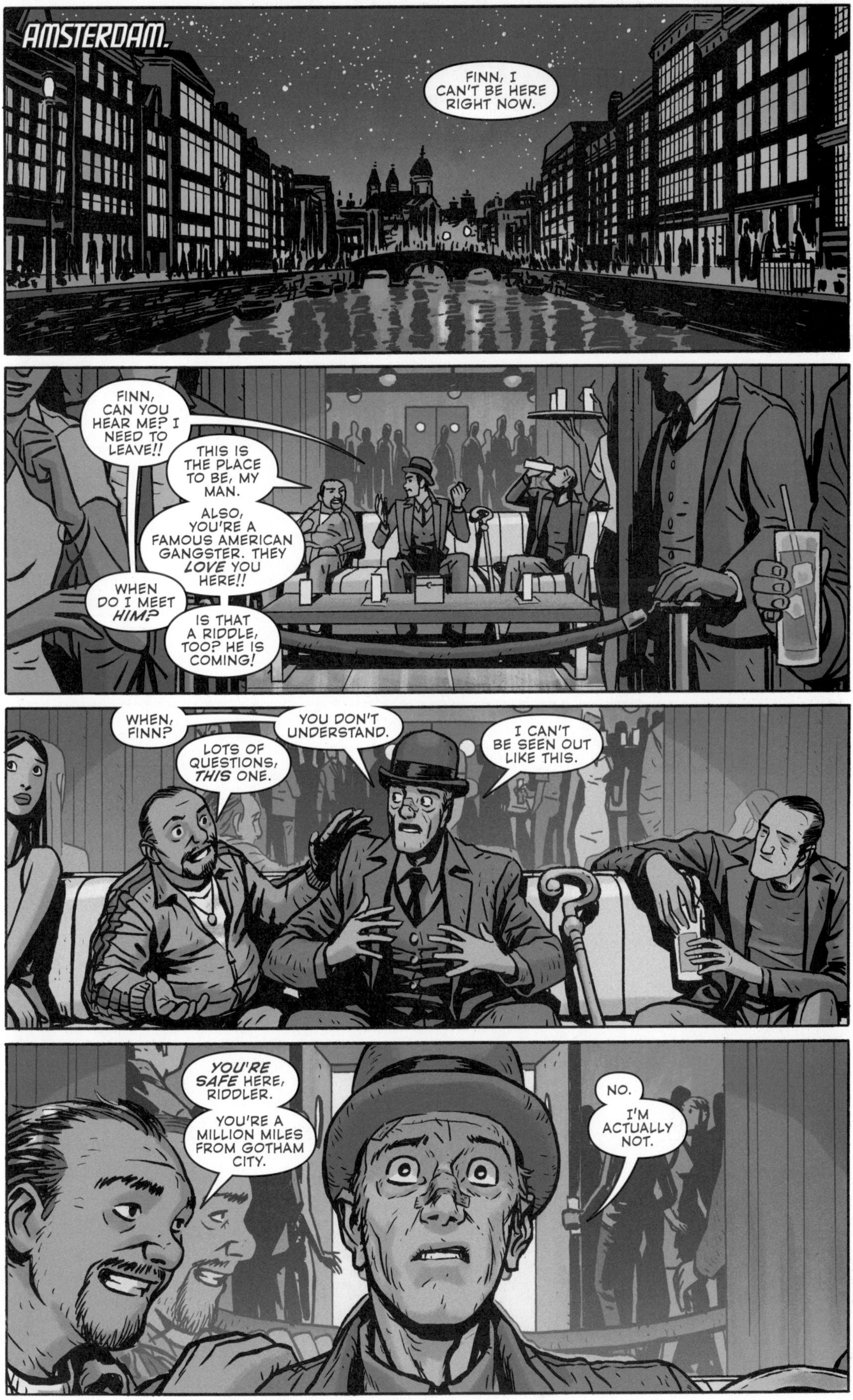
AMSTERDAM.
FINN, I CAN'T BE HERE RIGHT NOW.
FINN, CAN YOU HEAR ME? I NEED TO LEAVE!!
THIS IS THE PLACE TO BE, MY MAN.
ALSO, YOU'RE A FAMOUS AMERICAN GANGSTER. THEY LOVE YOU HERE!!
WHEN DO I MEET HIM?
IS THAT A RIDDLE, TOO? HE IS COMING!
WHEN, FINN?
YOU DON'T UNDERSTAND.
LOTS OF QUESTIONS, THIS ONE.
I CAN'T BE SEEN OUT LIKE THIS.
YOU'RE SAFE HERE, RIDDLER.
YOU'RE A MILLION MILES FROM GOTHAM CITY.
NO.
I'M ACTUALLY NOT.

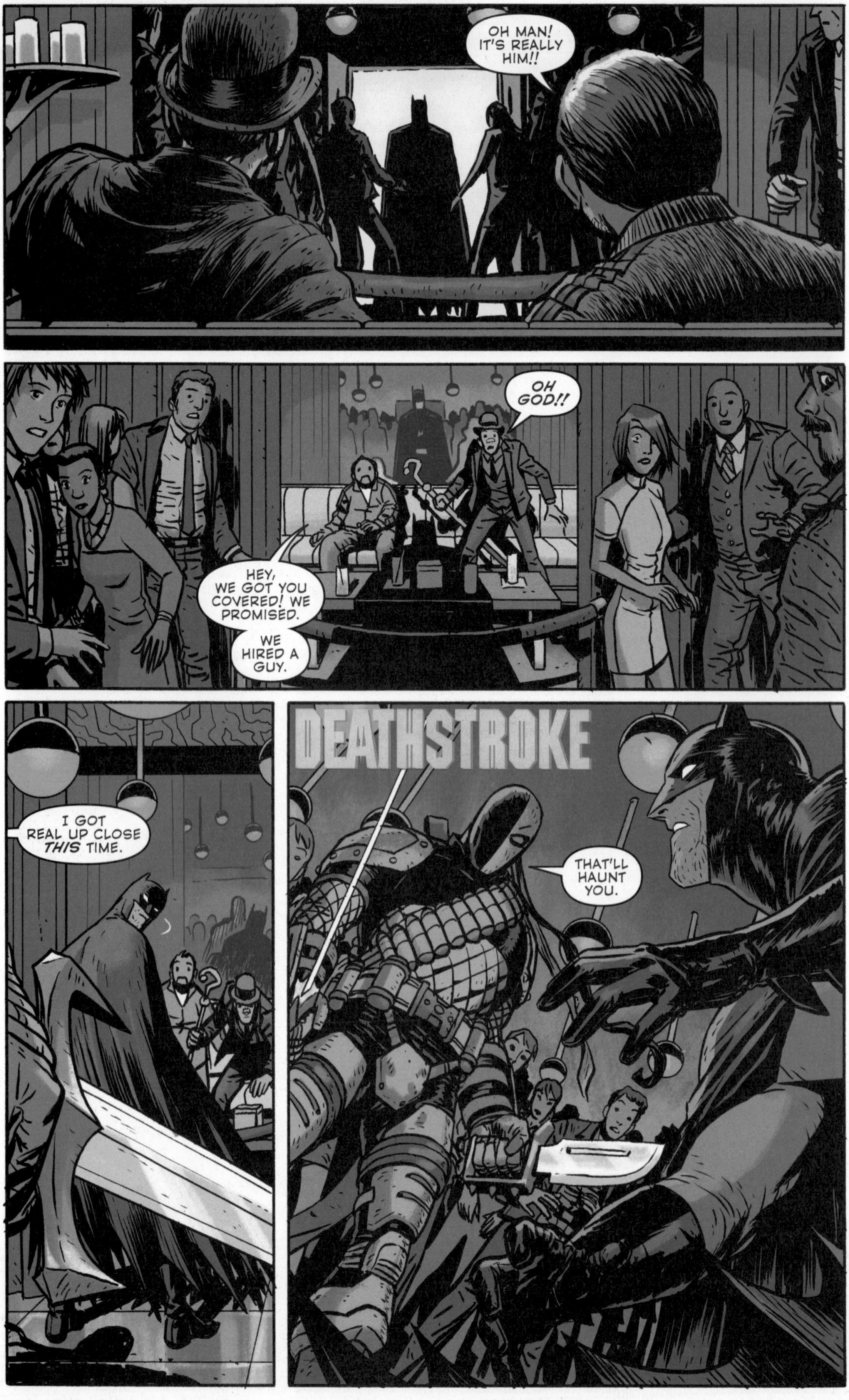

OH MAN! IT'S REALLY HIM!!
OH GOD!!
HEY, WE GOT YOU COVERED! WE PROMISED.
WE HIRED A GUY.
I GOT REAL UP CLOSE THIS TIME.
DEATHSTROKE
THAT'LL HAUNT YOU.

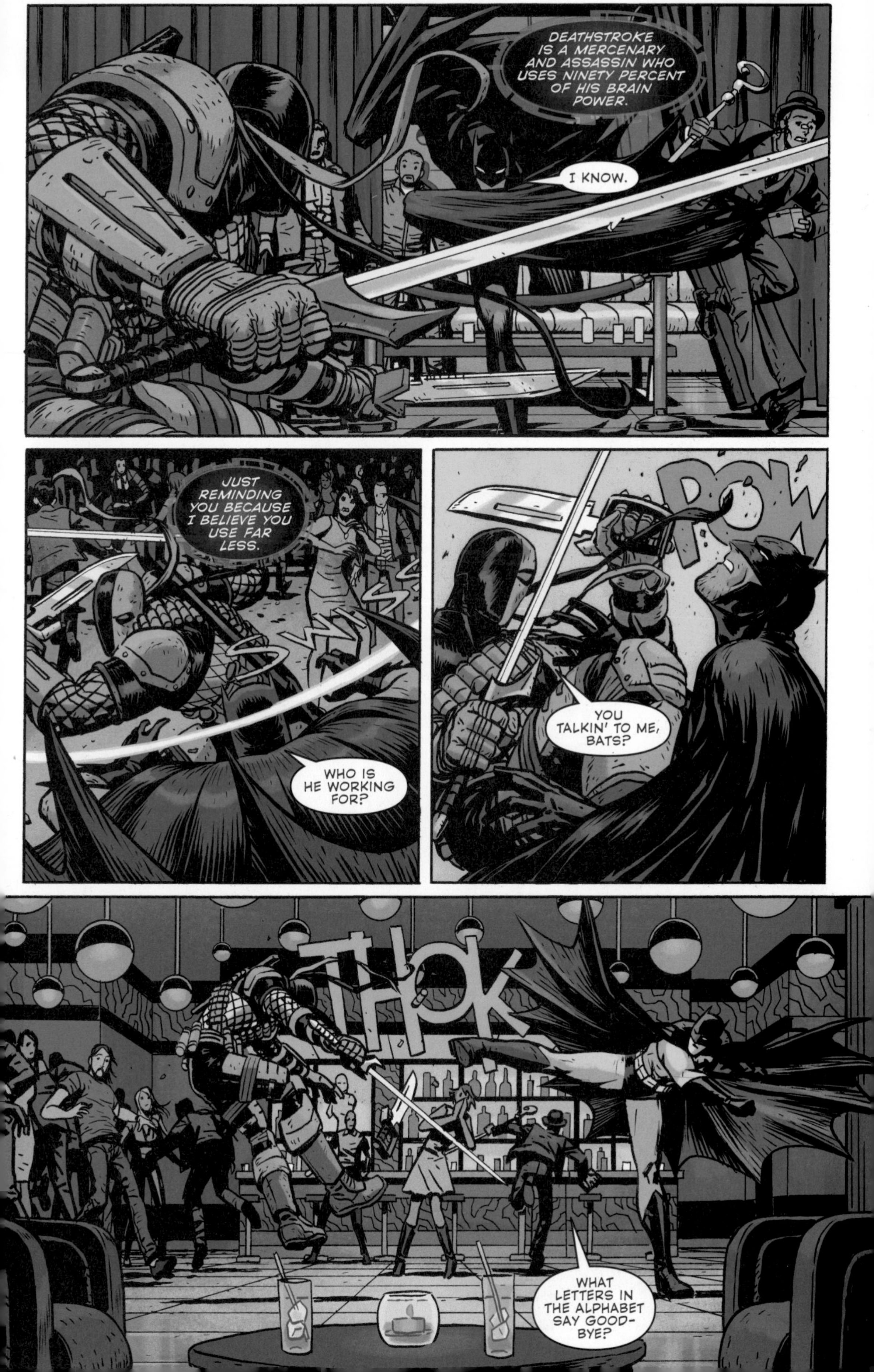
DEATHSTROKE IS A MERCENARY AND ASSASSIN WHO USES NINETY PERCENT OF HIS BRAIN POWER.
I KNOW.
JUST REMINDING YOU BECAUSE I BELIEVE YOU USE FAR LESS.
WHO IS HE WORKING FOR?
POW
YOU TALKIN' TO ME, BATS?
THOK
WHAT LETTERS IN THE ALPHABET SAY GOOD-BYE?

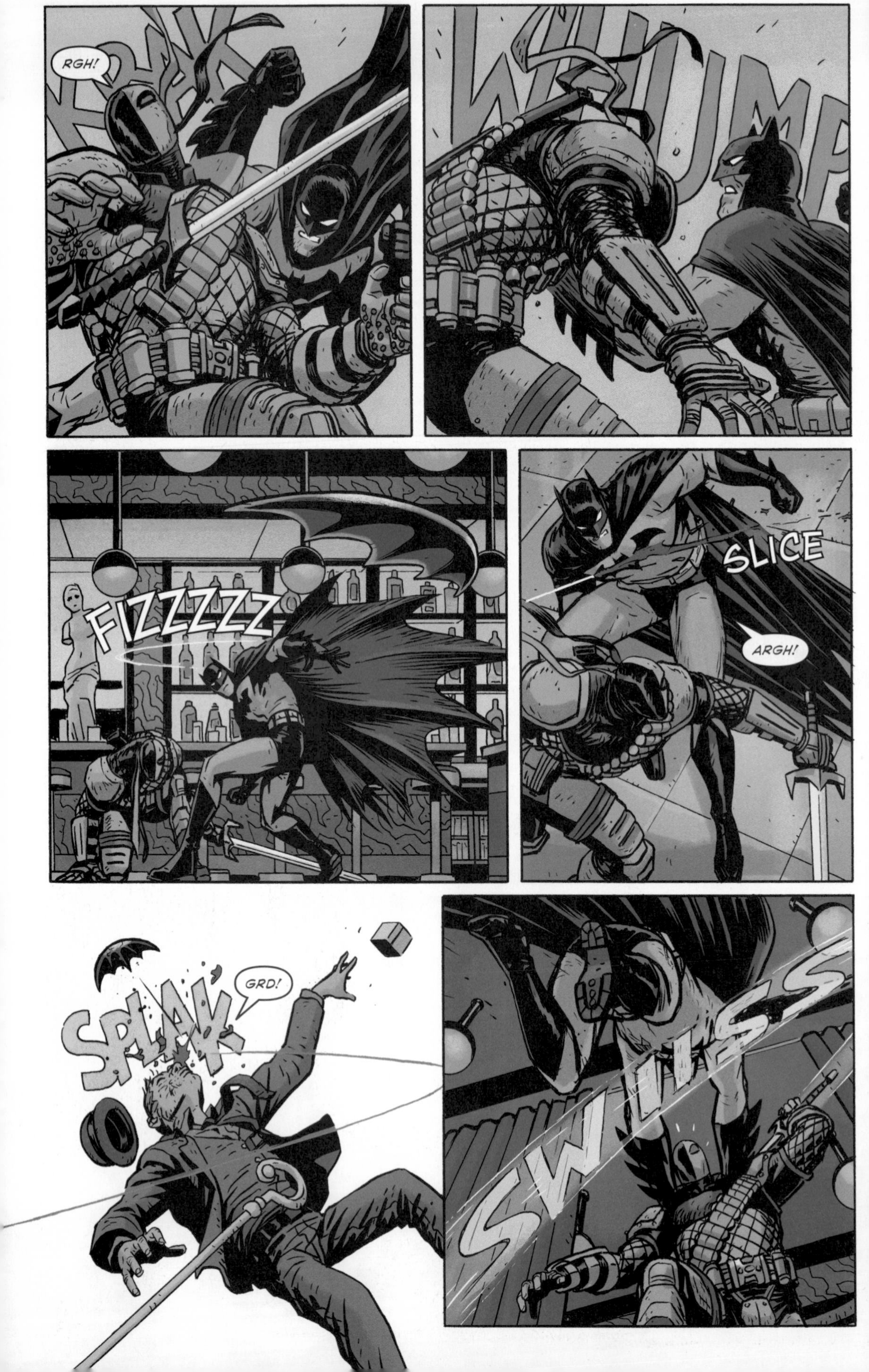
RGH!
WHUMP
FIZZZZZ
SLICE
ARGH!
SPLAK
GRD!

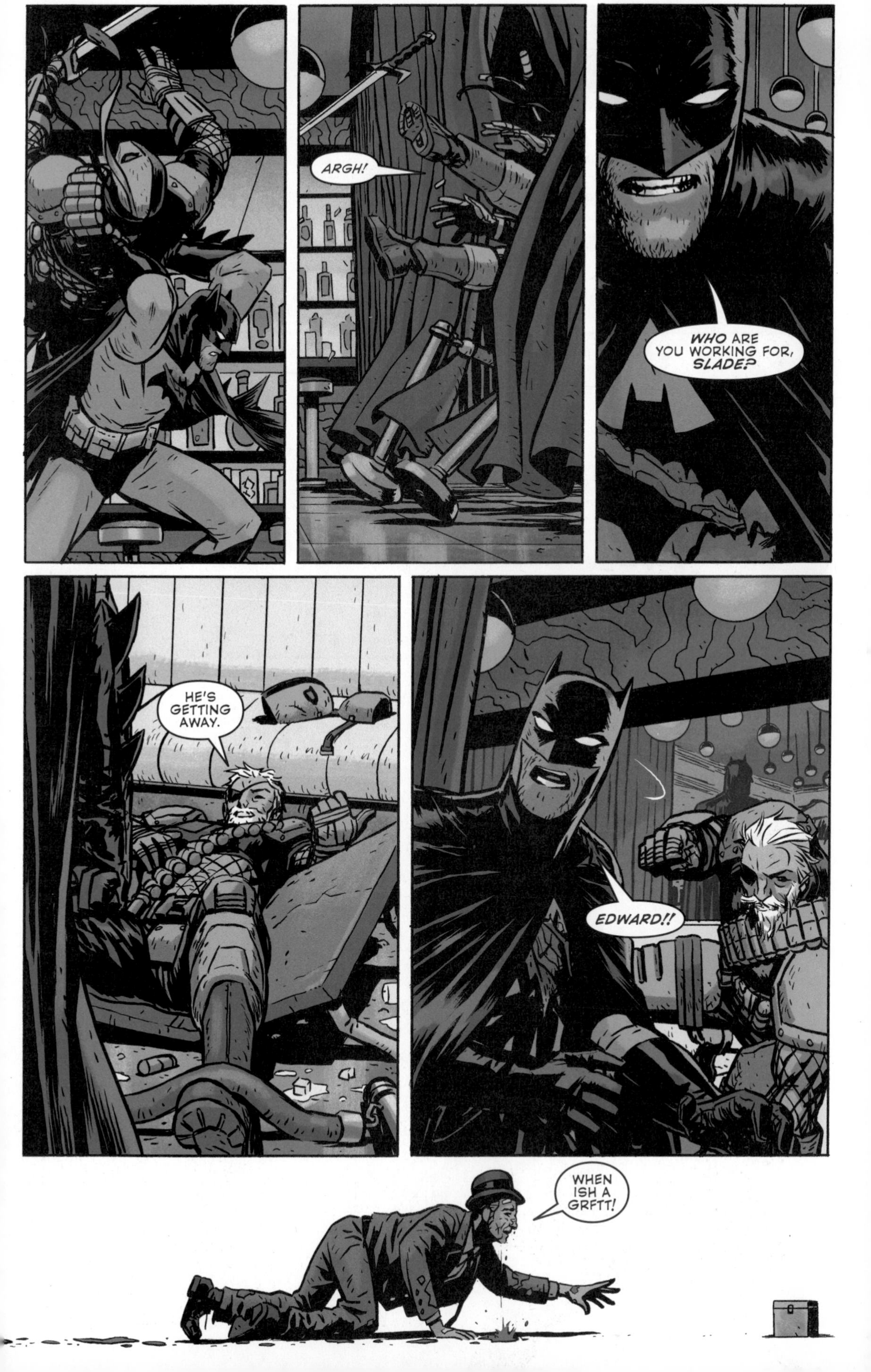
ARGH!
WHO ARE YOU WORKING FOR, SLADE?
HE'S GETTING AWAY.
EDWARD!!
WHEN ISH A GRFTT!

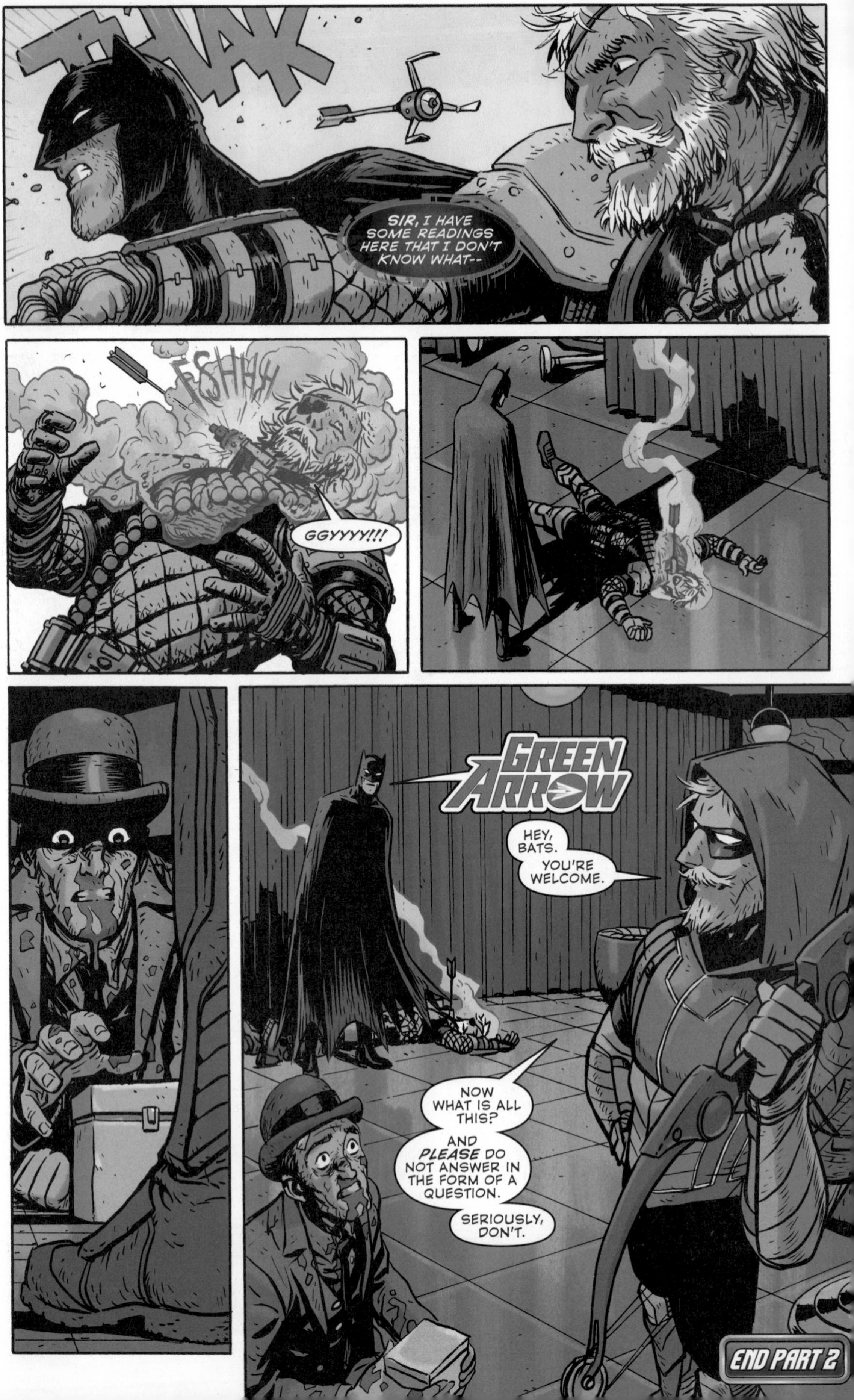
THAK
SIR, I HAVE SOME READINGS HERE THAT I DON'T KNOW WHAT--
FSHHH
GGYYYY!!!
GREEN ARROW
HEY, BATS.
YOU'RE WELCOME.
NOW WHAT IS ALL THIS?
AND PLEASE DO NOT ANSWER IN THE FORM OF A QUESTION.
SERIOUSLY, DON'T.
END PART 2

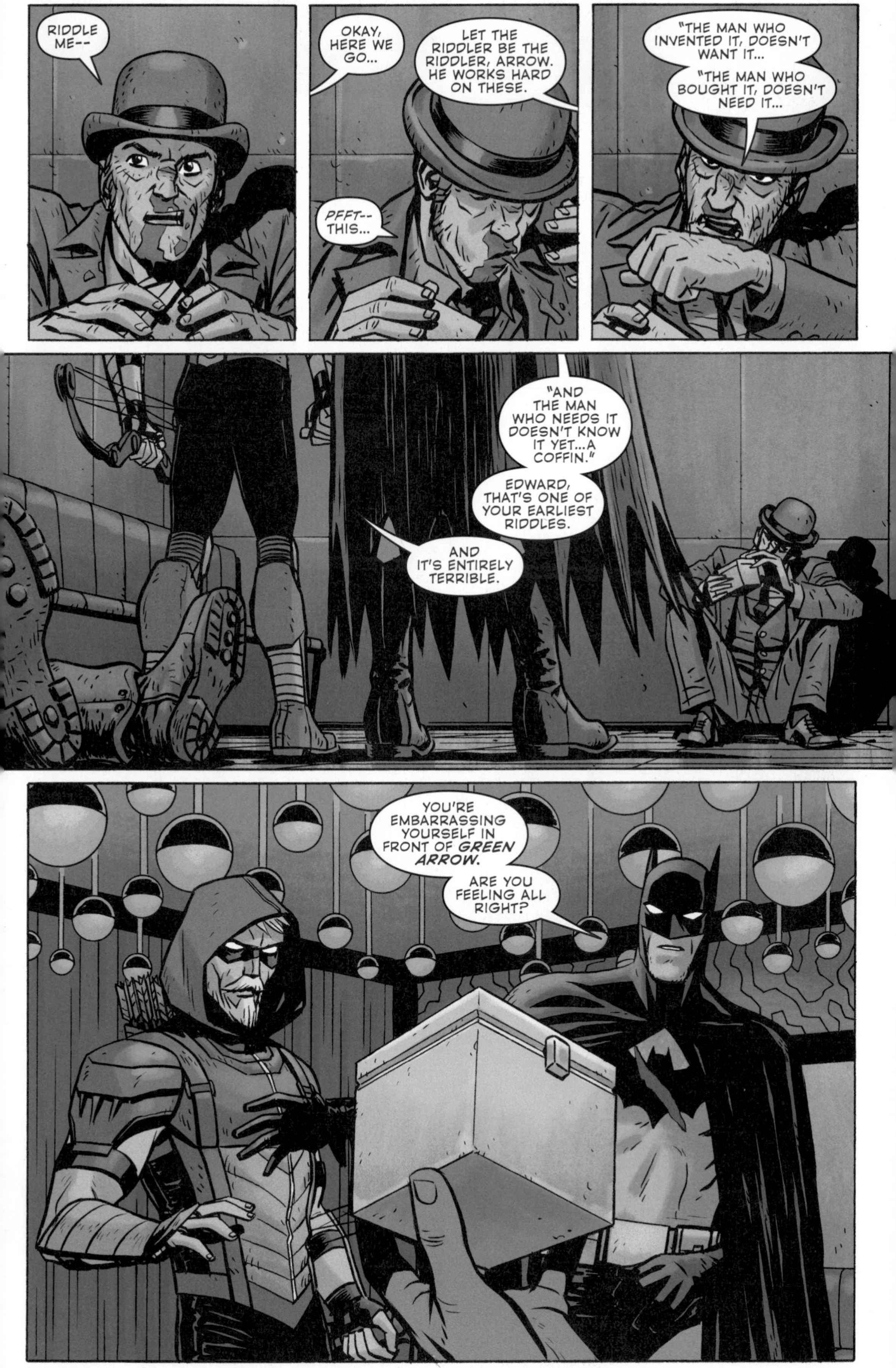
RIDDLE ME--
OKAY, HERE WE GO...
LET THE RIDDLER BE THE RIDDLER, ARROW. HE WORKS HARD ON THESE.
PFFT-- THIS...
"THE MAN WHO INVENTED IT, DOESN'T WANT IT...
"THE MAN WHO BOUGHT IT, DOESN'T NEED IT...
"AND THE MAN WHO NEEDS IT DOESN'T KNOW IT YET...A COFFIN."
EDWARD, THAT'S ONE OF YOUR EARLIEST RIDDLES.
AND IT'S ENTIRELY TERRIBLE.
YOU'RE EMBARRASSING YOURSELF IN FRONT OF GREEN ARROW.
ARE YOU FEELING ALL RIGHT?

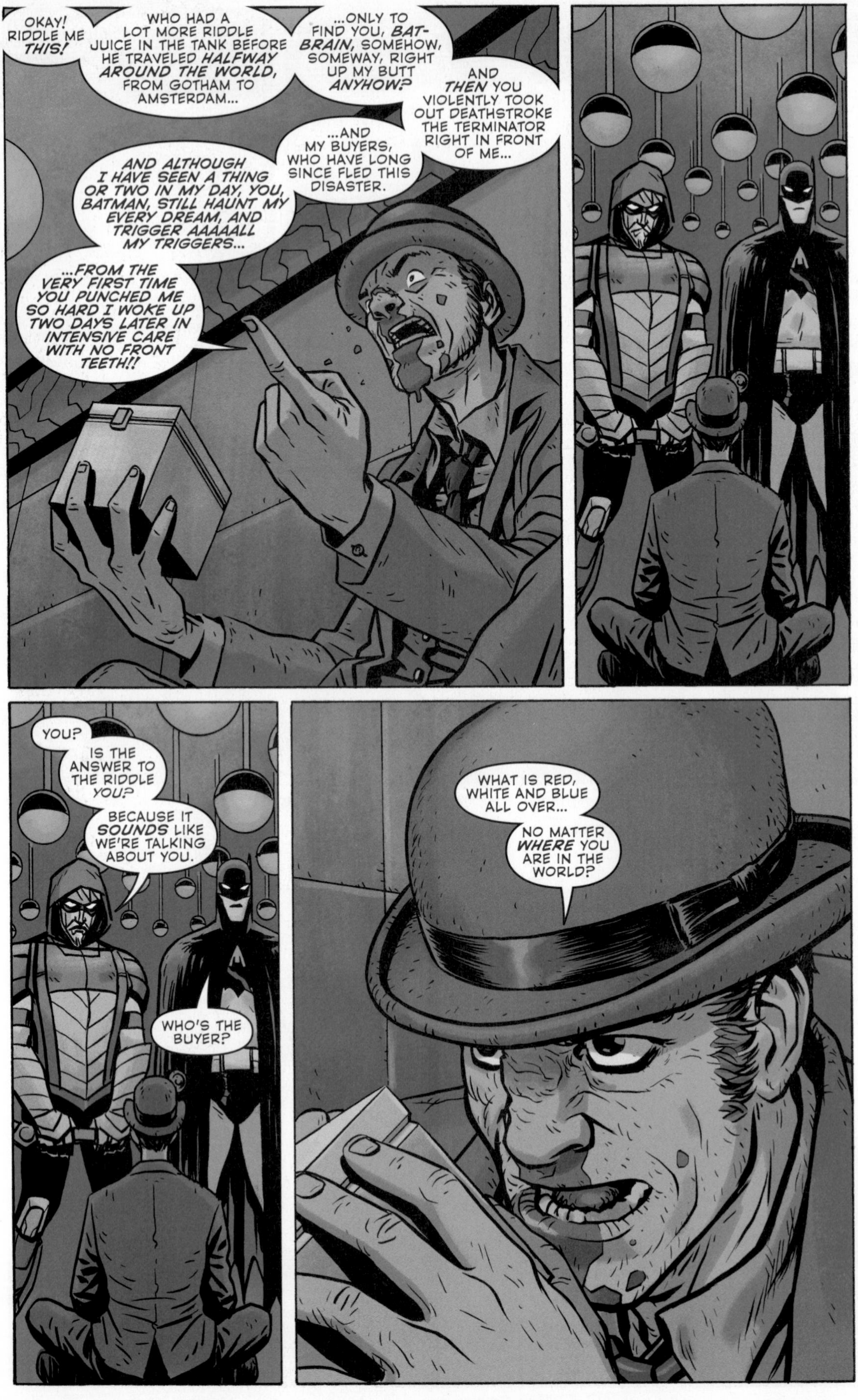
OKAY! RIDDLE ME THIS!
WHO HAD A LOT MORE RIDDLE JUICE IN THE TANK BEFORE HE TRAVELED HALFWAY AROUND THE WORLD, FROM GOTHAM TO AMSTERDAM...
...ONLY TO FIND YOU, BAT-BRAIN, SOMEHOW, SOMEWAY, RIGHT UP MY BUTT ANYHOW?
AND THEN YOU VIOLENTLY TOOK OUT DEATHSTROKE THE TERMINATOR RIGHT IN FRONT OF ME...
...AND MY BUYERS, WHO HAVE LONG SINCE FLED THIS DISASTER.
AND ALTHOUGH I HAVE SEEN A THING OR TWO IN MY DAY, YOU, BATMAN, STILL HAUNT MY EVERY DREAM, AND TRIGGER AAAAALL MY TRIGGERS...
...FROM THE VERY FIRST TIME YOU PUNCHED ME SO HARD I WOKE UP TWO DAYS LATER IN INTENSIVE CARE WITH NO FRONT TEETH!!
YOU?
IS THE ANSWER TO THE RIDDLE YOU?
BECAUSE IT SOUNDS LIKE WE'RE TALKING ABOUT YOU.
WHO'S THE BUYER?
WHAT IS RED, WHITE AND BLUE ALL OVER...
NO MATTER WHERE YOU ARE IN THE WORLD?

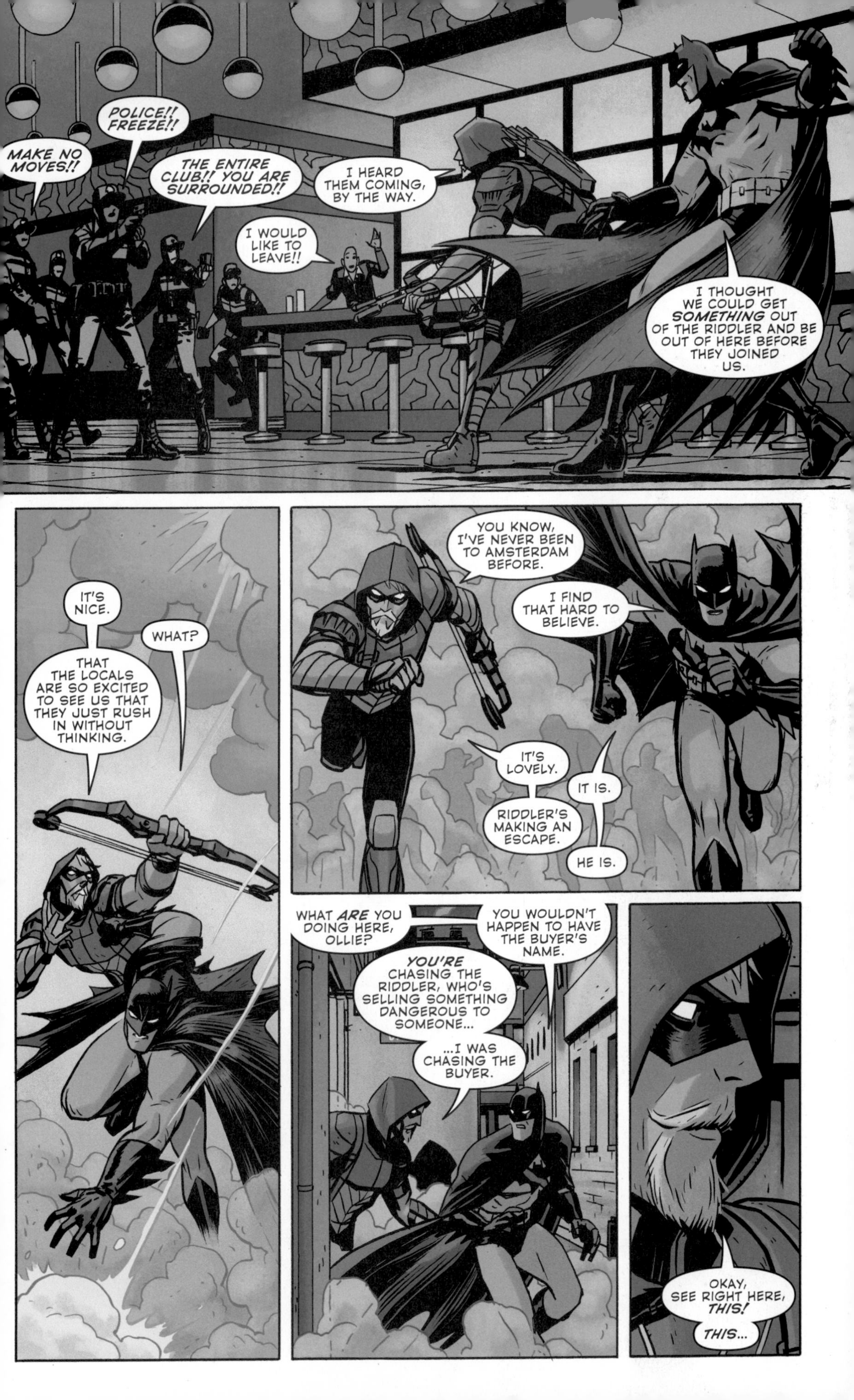

MAKE NO MOVES!!
POLICE!! FREEZE!!
THE ENTIRE CLUB!! YOU ARE SURROUNDED!!
I WOULD LIKE TO LEAVE!!
I HEARD THEM COMING, BY THE WAY.
I THOUGHT WE COULD GET SOMETHING OUT OF THE RIDDLER AND BE OUT OF HERE BEFORE THEY JOINED US.
IT'S NICE.
WHAT?
THAT THE LOCALS ARE SO EXCITED TO SEE US THAT THEY JUST RUSH IN WITHOUT THINKING.
YOU KNOW, I'VE NEVER BEEN TO AMSTERDAM BEFORE.
I FIND THAT HARD TO BELIEVE.
IT'S LOVELY.
IT IS.
RIDDLER'S MAKING AN ESCAPE.
HE IS.
WHAT ARE YOU DOING HERE, OLLIE?
YOU WOULDN'T HAPPEN TO HAVE THE BUYER'S NAME.
YOU'RE CHASING THE RIDDLER, WHO'S SELLING SOMETHING DANGEROUS TO SOMEONE...
...I WAS CHASING THE BUYER.
OKAY, SEE RIGHT HERE, THIS!
THIS...

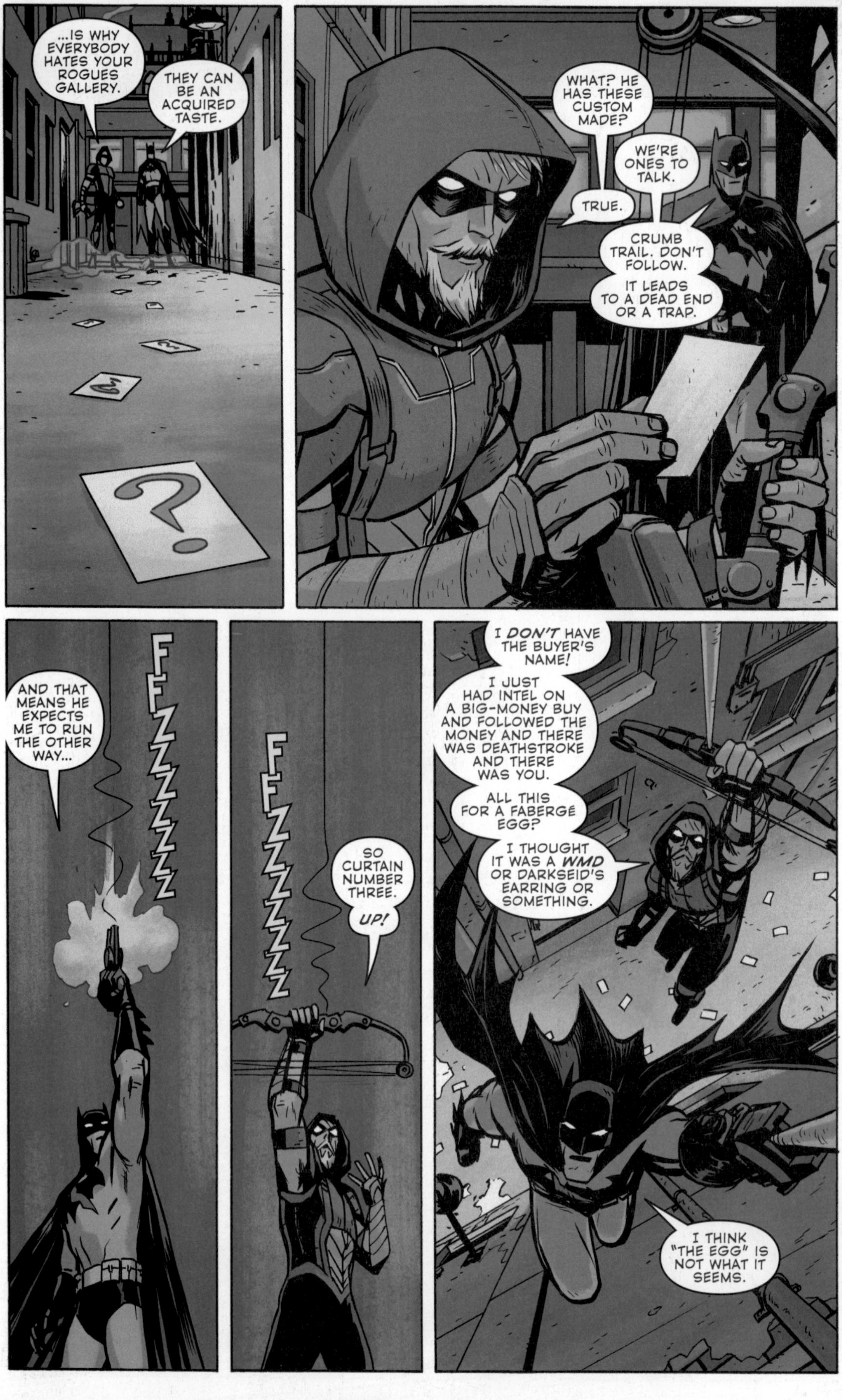

...IS WHY EVERYBODY HATES YOUR ROGUES GALLERY.
THEY CAN BE AN ACQUIRED TASTE.
WHAT? HE HAS THESE CUSTOM MADE?
WE'RE ONES TO TALK.
TRUE.
CRUMB TRAIL. DON'T FOLLOW.
IT LEADS TO A DEAD END OR A TRAP.
AND THAT MEANS HE EXPECTS ME TO RUN THE OTHER WAY...
FFZZZZZZZZ
FFZZZZZZZZ
SO CURTAIN NUMBER THREE.
UP!
I DON'T HAVE THE BUYER'S NAME!
I JUST HAD INTEL ON A BIG-MONEY BUY AND FOLLOWED THE MONEY AND THERE WAS DEATHSTROKE AND THERE WAS YOU.
ALL THIS FOR A FABERGÉ EGG?
I THOUGHT IT WAS A WMD OR DARKSEID'S EARRING OR SOMETHING.
I THINK "THE EGG" IS NOT WHAT IT SEEMS.

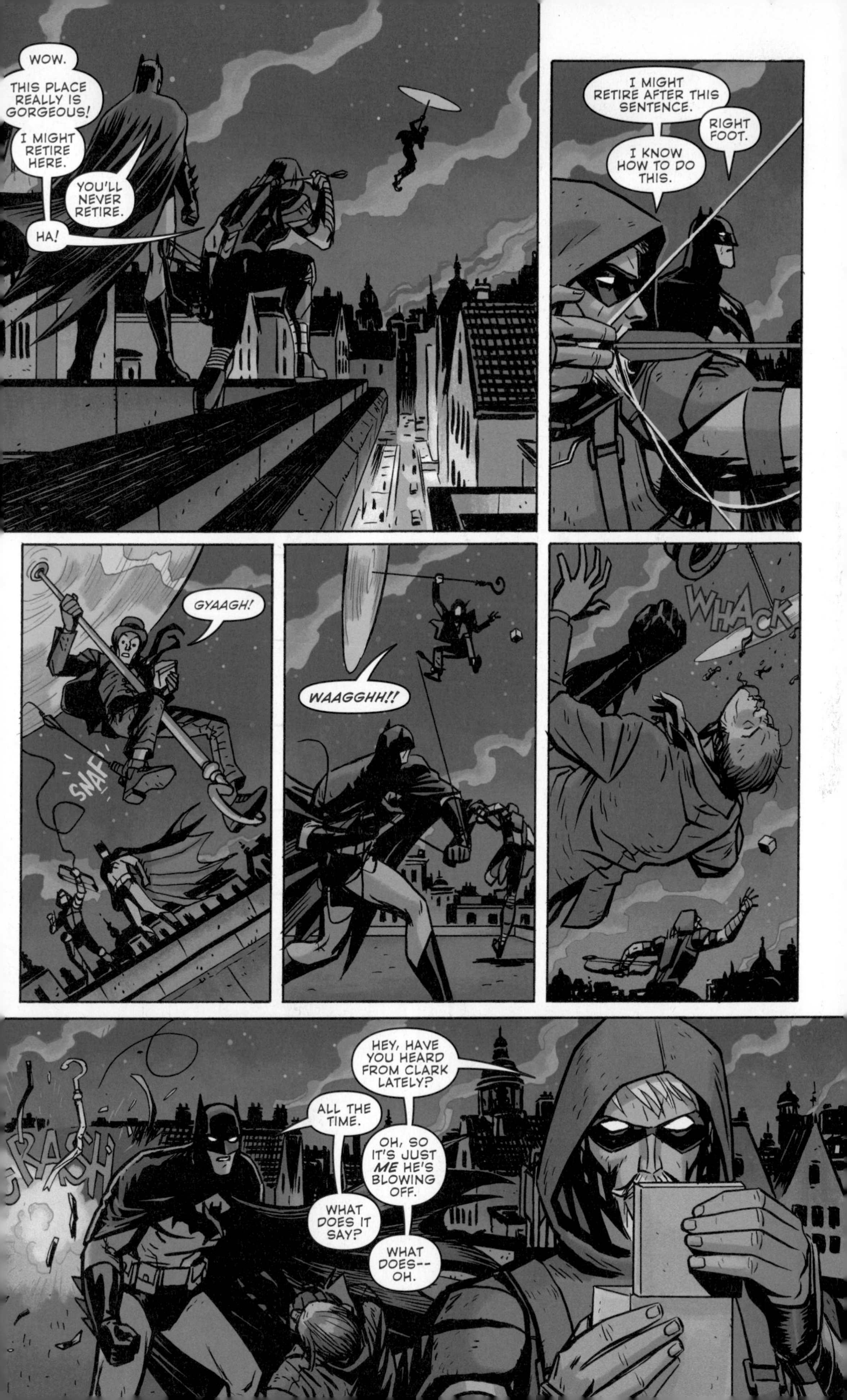
WOW.
THIS PLACE REALLY IS GORGEOUS!
I MIGHT RETIRE HERE.
YOU'LL NEVER RETIRE.
HA!
I MIGHT RETIRE AFTER THIS SENTENCE.
I KNOW HOW TO DO THIS.
RIGHT FOOT.
GYAAGH!
SNAF
WAAGGHH!!
WHACK
HEY, HAVE YOU HEARD FROM CLARK LATELY?
ALL THE TIME.
OH, SO IT'S JUST ME HE'S BLOWING OFF.
WHAT DOES IT SAY?
WHAT DOES-- OH.
CRASH

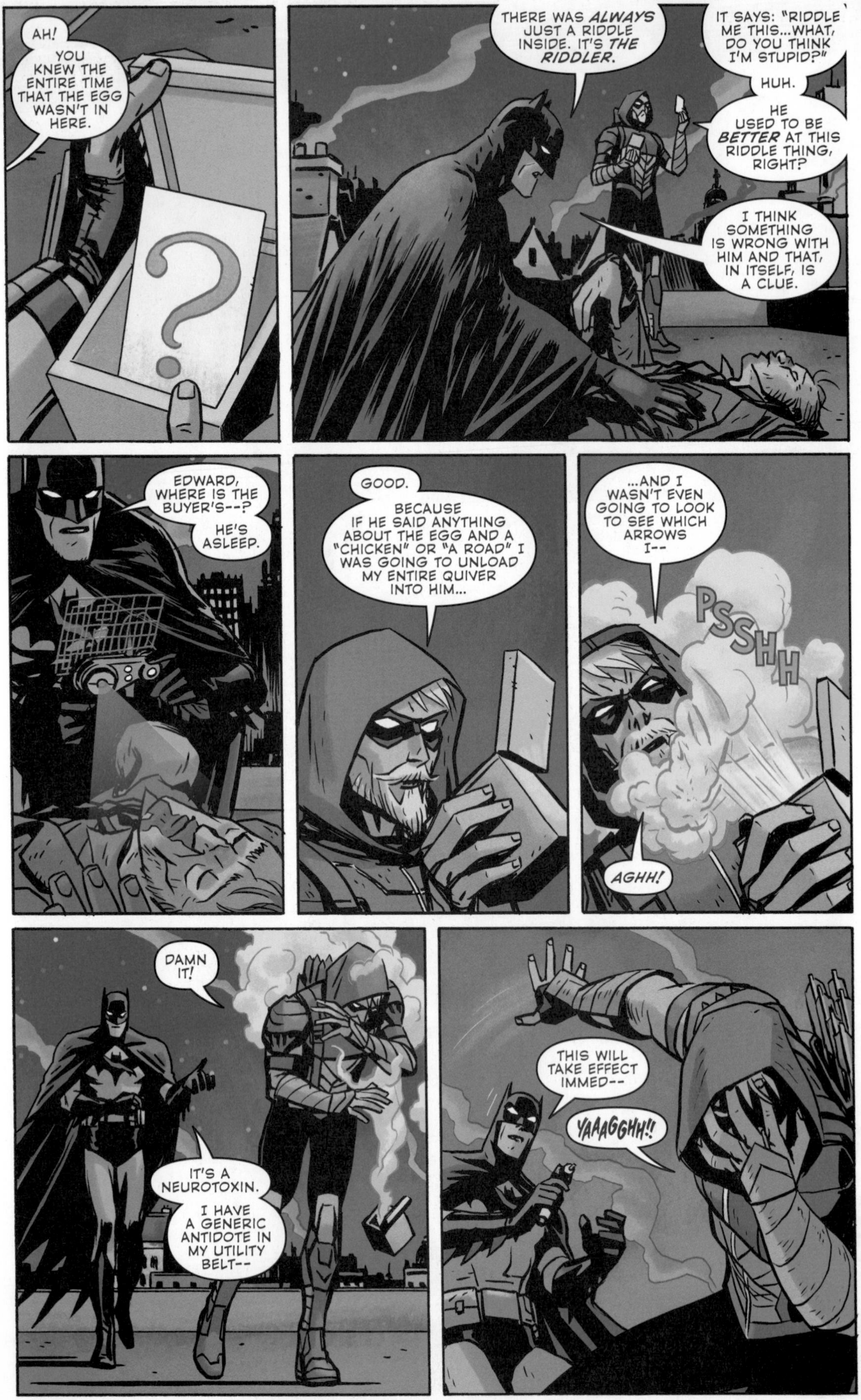
AH!
YOU KNEW THE ENTIRE TIME THAT THE EGG WASN'T IN HERE.
THERE WAS *ALWAYS* JUST A RIDDLE INSIDE. IT'S *THE RIDDLER*.
IT SAYS: "RIDDLE ME THIS...WHAT, DO YOU THINK I'M STUPID?"
HUH.
HE USED TO BE *BETTER* AT THIS RIDDLE THING, RIGHT?
I THINK SOMETHING IS WRONG WITH HIM AND THAT, IN ITSELF, IS A CLUE.
EDWARD, WHERE IS THE BUYER'S--?
HE'S ASLEEP.
GOOD.
BECAUSE IF HE SAID ANYTHING ABOUT THE EGG AND A "CHICKEN" OR "A ROAD" I WAS GOING TO UNLOAD MY ENTIRE QUIVER INTO HIM...
...AND I WASN'T EVEN GOING TO LOOK TO SEE WHICH ARROWS I--
PSSHH
AGHH!
DAMN IT!
IT'S A NEUROTOXIN.
I HAVE A GENERIC ANTIDOTE IN MY UTILITY BELT--
THIS WILL TAKE EFFECT IMMED--
YAAAGGHH!!

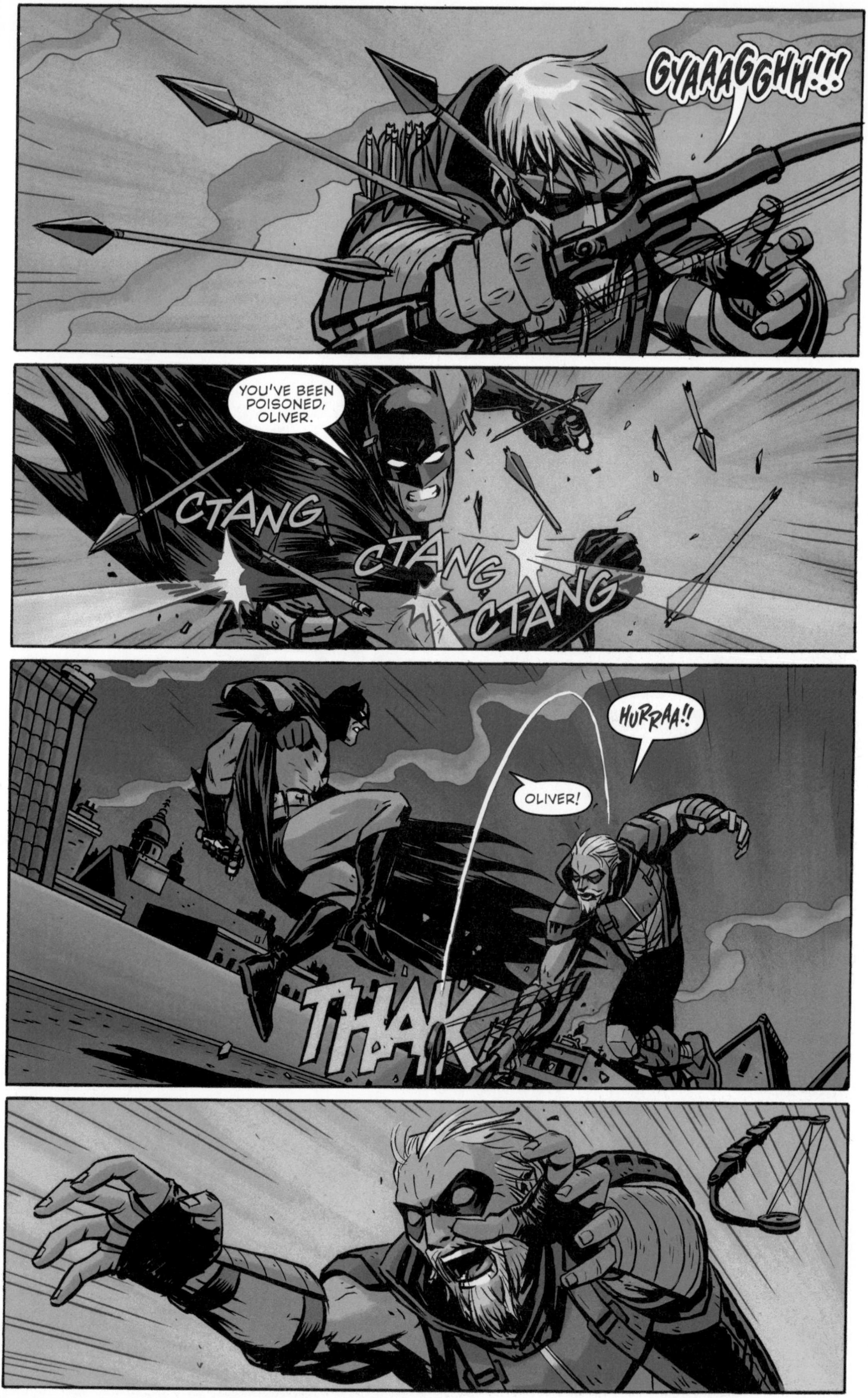
GYAAAGGHH!!!
YOU'VE BEEN POISONED, OLIVER.
CTANG
CTANG
CTANG
CTANG
HURRAA!!
OLIVER!
THAK

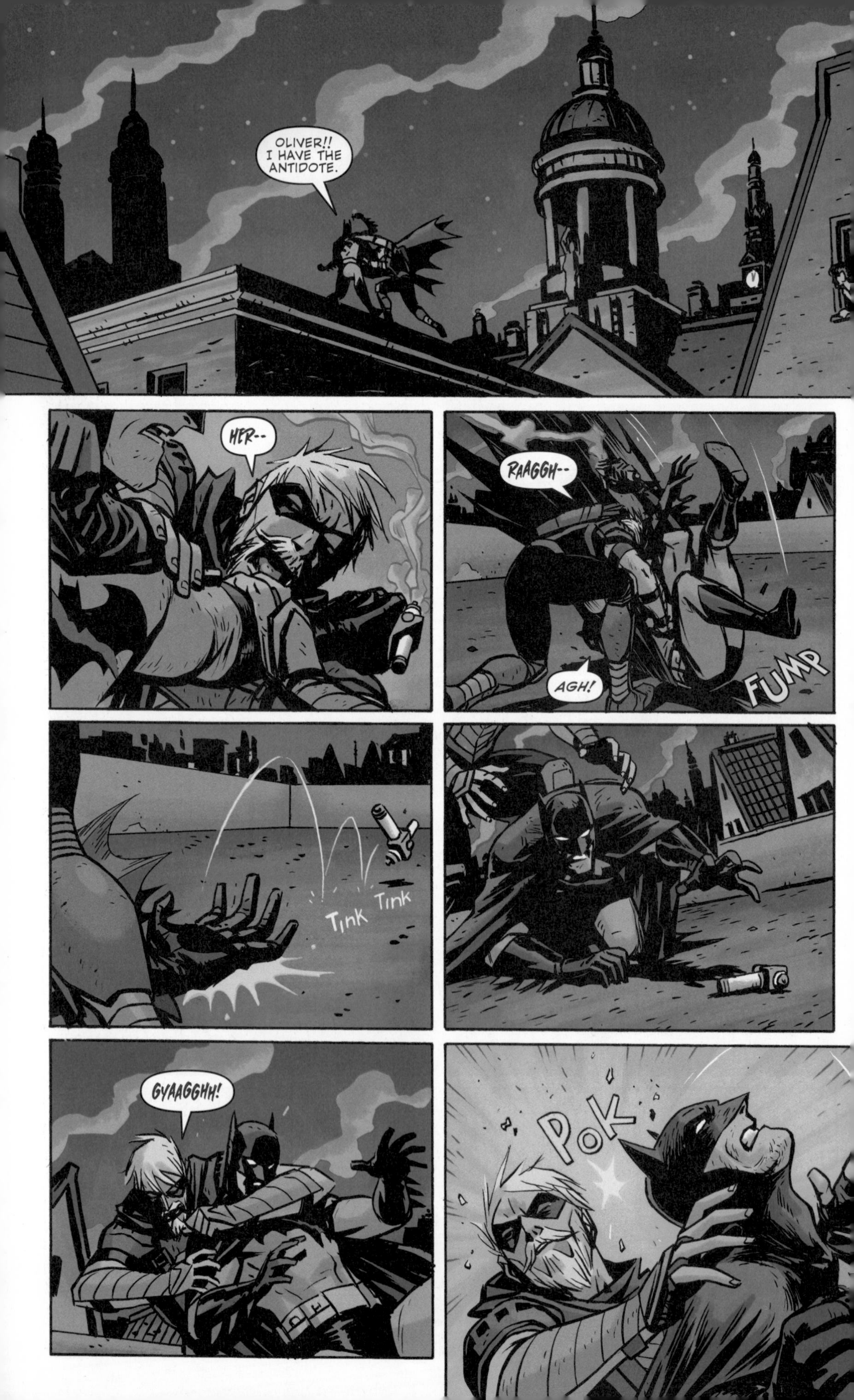
OLIVER!! I HAVE THE ANTIDOTE.
HER--
RAAGGH--
AGH!
FUMP
Tink Tink
GYAAGGHH!
POK

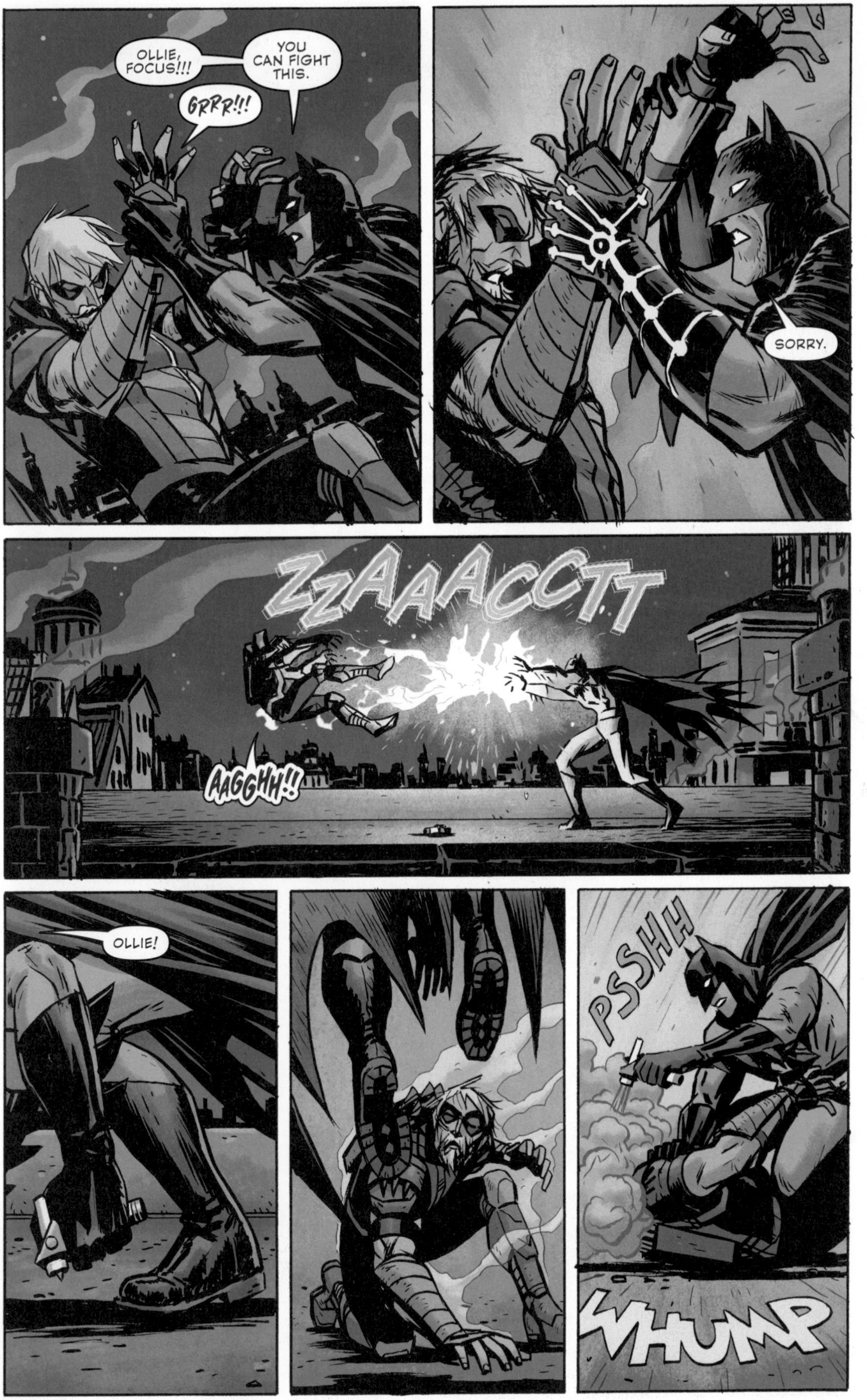
OLLIE, FOCUS!!!
YOU CAN FIGHT THIS.
GRRR!!!
SORRY.
ZzAAACCTT
AAGGHH!!
OLLIE!
PSSHH
WHUMP

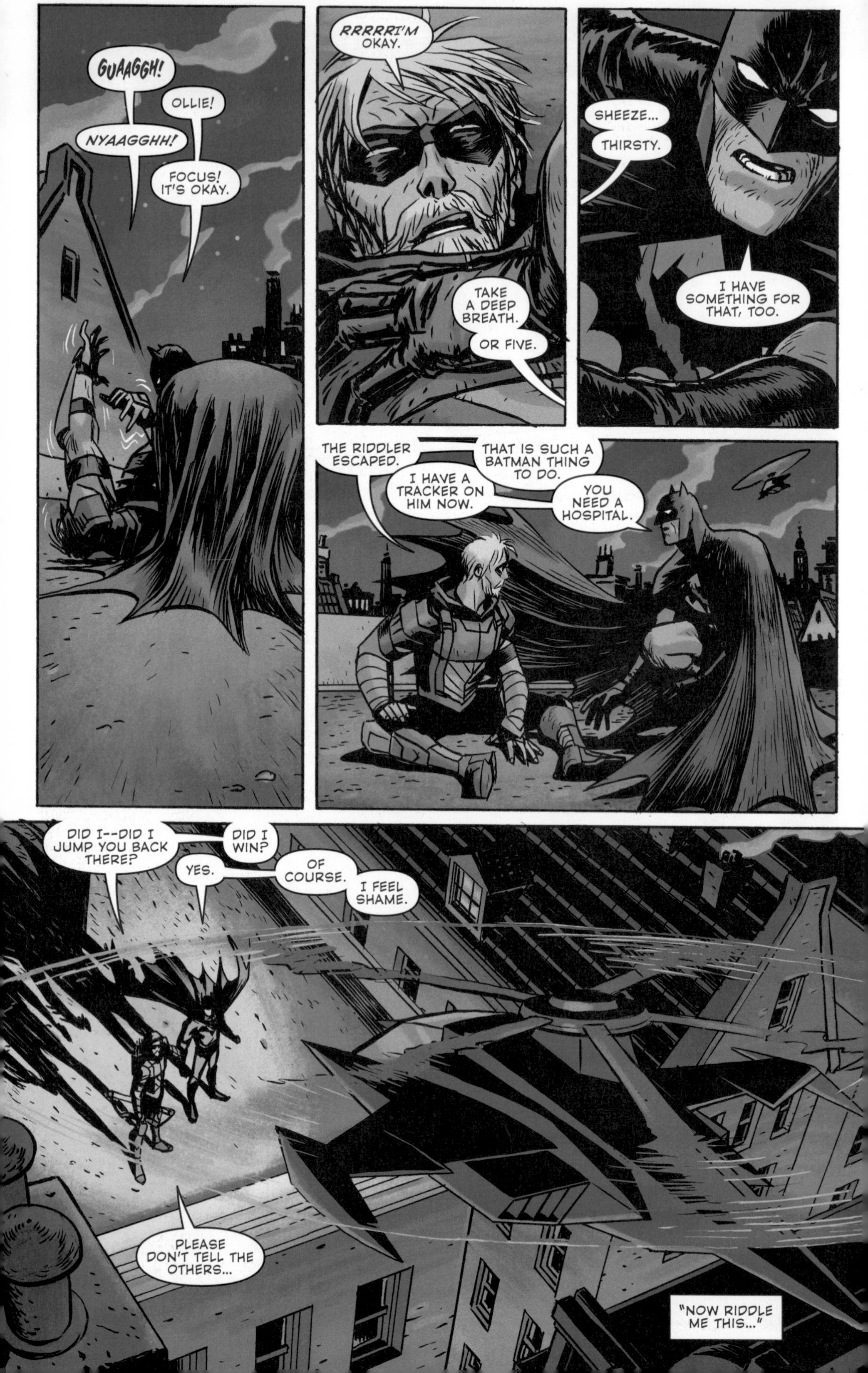
GUAAGGH!
OLLIE!
NYAAGGHH!
FOCUS! IT'S OKAY.
RRRRRI'M OKAY.
TAKE A DEEP BREATH.
OR FIVE.
SHEEZE...
THIRSTY.
I HAVE SOMETHING FOR THAT, TOO.
THE RIDDLER ESCAPED.
THAT IS SUCH A BATMAN THING TO DO.
I HAVE A TRACKER ON HIM NOW.
YOU NEED A HOSPITAL.
DID I--DID I JUMP YOU BACK THERE?
DID I WIN?
YES.
OF COURSE.
I FEEL SHAME.
PLEASE DON'T TELL THE OTHERS...
"NOW RIDDLE ME THIS..."

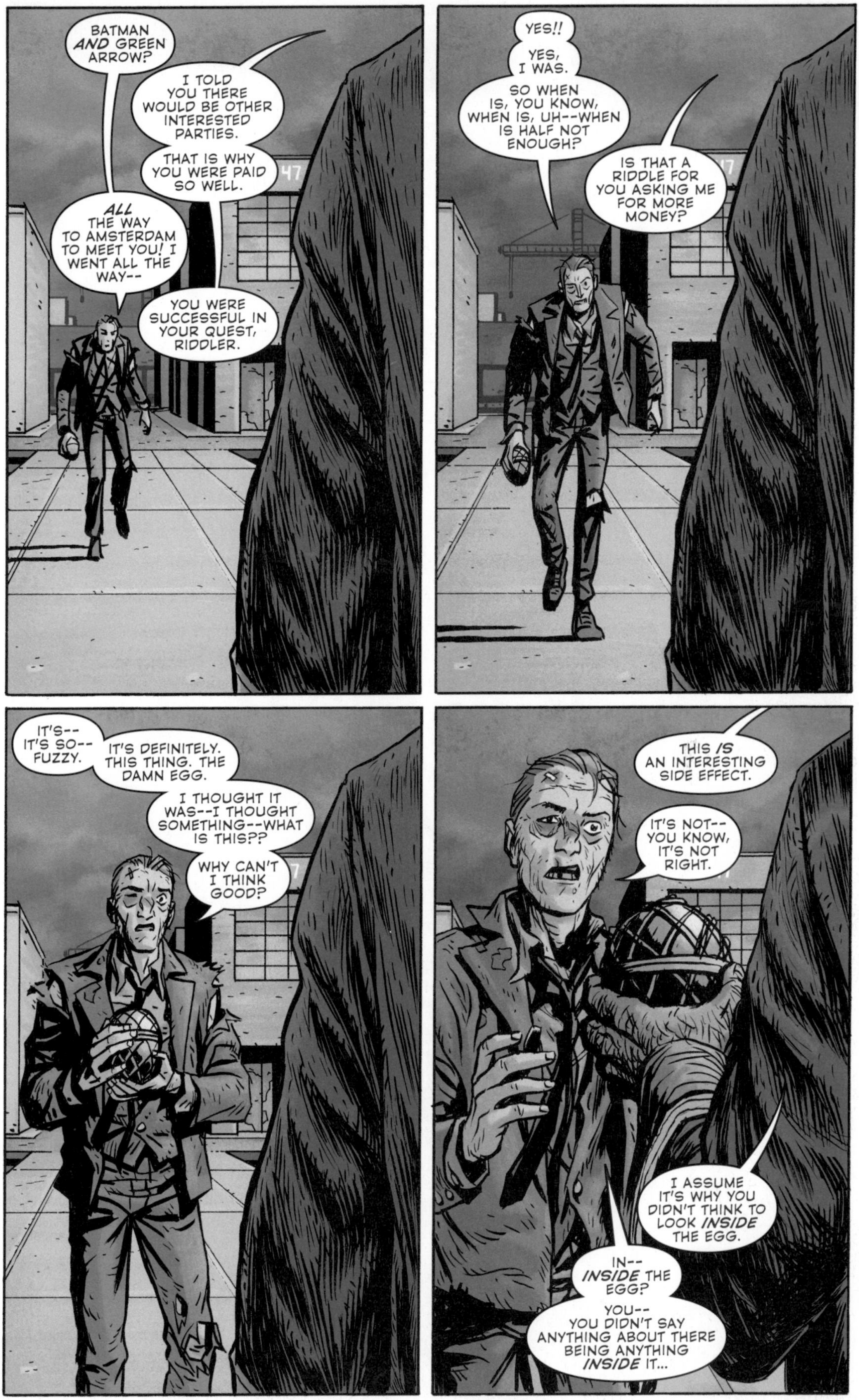
BATMAN *AND* GREEN ARROW?
I TOLD YOU THERE WOULD BE OTHER INTERESTED PARTIES.
THAT IS WHY YOU WERE PAID SO WELL.
ALL THE WAY TO AMSTERDAM TO MEET YOU! I WENT ALL THE WAY--
YOU WERE SUCCESSFUL IN YOUR QUEST, RIDDLER.
YES!!
YES, I WAS.
SO WHEN IS, YOU KNOW, WHEN IS, UH--WHEN IS HALF NOT ENOUGH?
IS THAT A RIDDLE FOR YOU ASKING ME FOR MORE MONEY?
IT'S-- IT'S SO-- FUZZY.
IT'S DEFINITELY. THIS THING. THE DAMN EGG.
I THOUGHT IT WAS--I THOUGHT SOMETHING--WHAT IS THIS??
WHY CAN'T I THINK GOOD?
THIS *IS* AN INTERESTING SIDE EFFECT.
IT'S NOT-- YOU KNOW, IT'S NOT RIGHT.
I ASSUME IT'S WHY YOU DIDN'T THINK TO LOOK *INSIDE* THE EGG.
IN-- *INSIDE* THE EGG?
YOU-- YOU DIDN'T SAY ANYTHING ABOUT THERE BEING ANYTHING *INSIDE* IT...

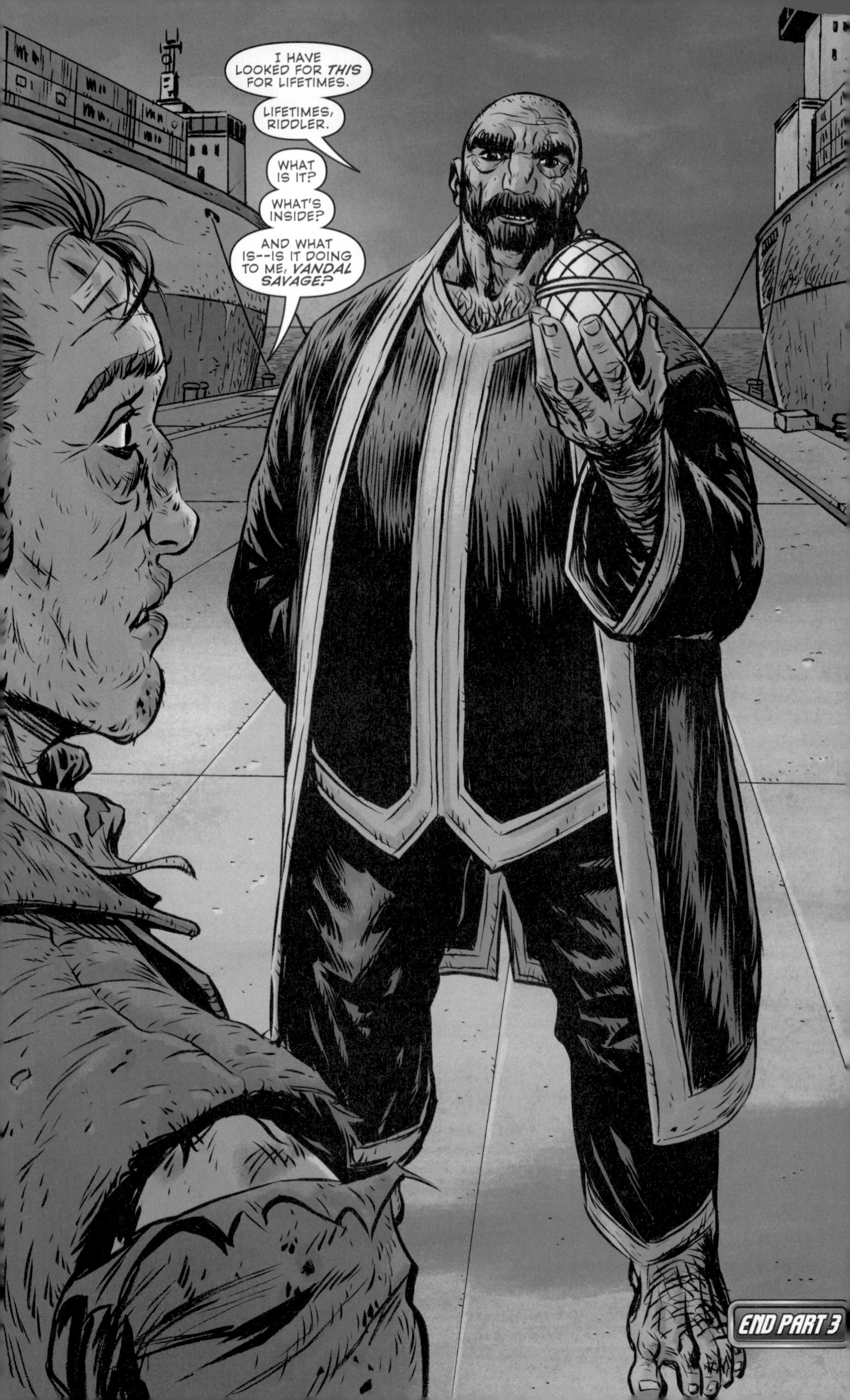
I HAVE LOOKED FOR *THIS* FOR LIFETIMES.
LIFETIMES, RIDDLER.
WHAT IS IT?
WHAT'S INSIDE?
AND WHAT IS--IS IT DOING TO ME, *VANDAL SAVAGE?*
END PART 3

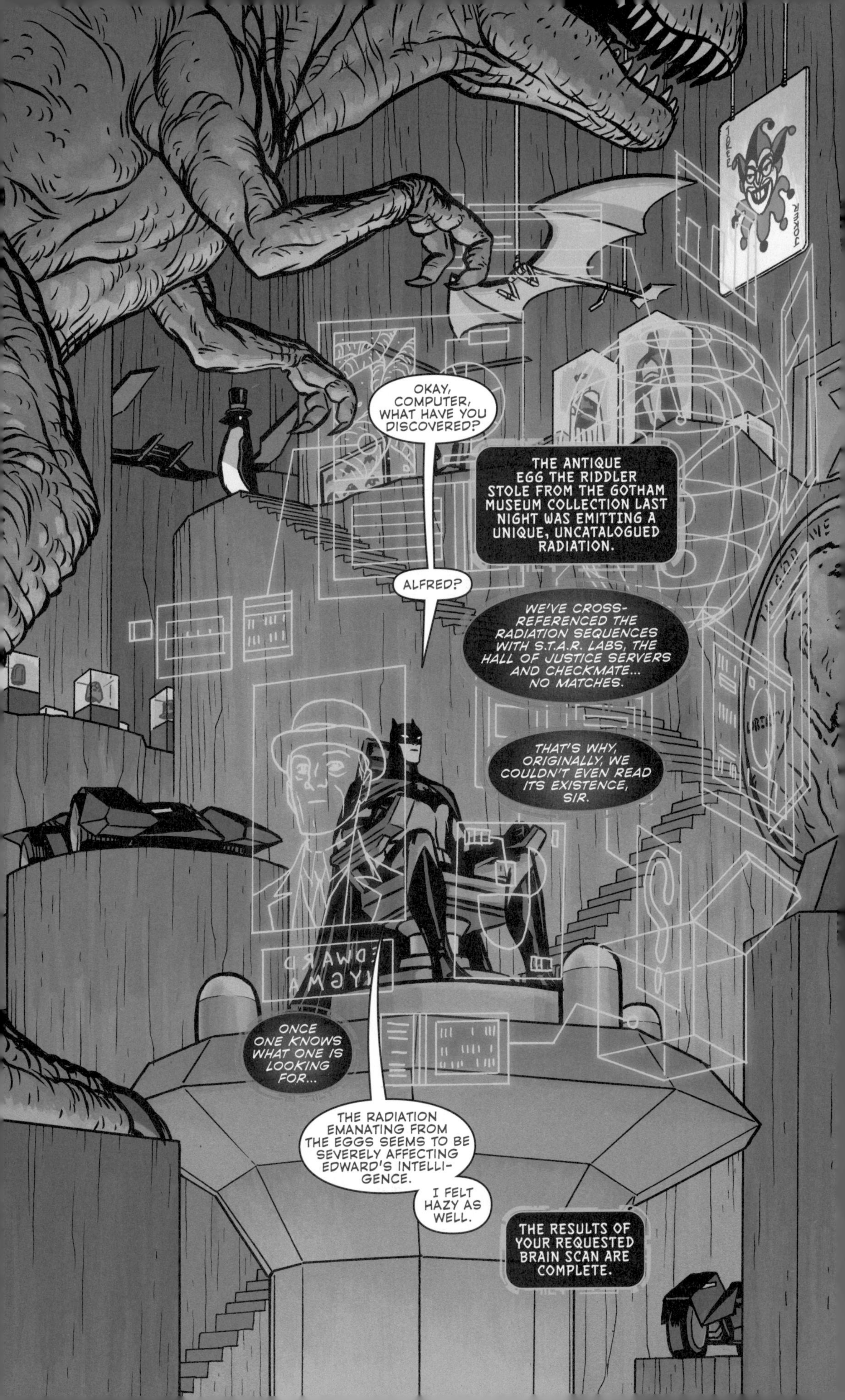
OKAY, COMPUTER, WHAT HAVE YOU DISCOVERED?
THE ANTIQUE EGG THE RIDDLER STOLE FROM THE GOTHAM MUSEUM COLLECTION LAST NIGHT WAS EMITTING A UNIQUE, UNCATALOGUED RADIATION.
ALFRED?
WE'VE CROSS-REFERENCED THE RADIATION SEQUENCES WITH S.T.A.R. LABS, THE HALL OF JUSTICE SERVERS AND CHECKMATE... NO MATCHES.
THAT'S WHY, ORIGINALLY, WE COULDN'T EVEN READ ITS EXISTENCE, SIR.
EDWARD NYGMA
ONCE ONE KNOWS WHAT ONE IS LOOKING FOR...
THE RADIATION EMANATING FROM THE EGGS SEEMS TO BE SEVERELY AFFECTING EDWARD'S INTELLI-GENCE.
I FELT HAZY AS WELL.
THE RESULTS OF YOUR REQUESTED BRAIN SCAN ARE COMPLETE.

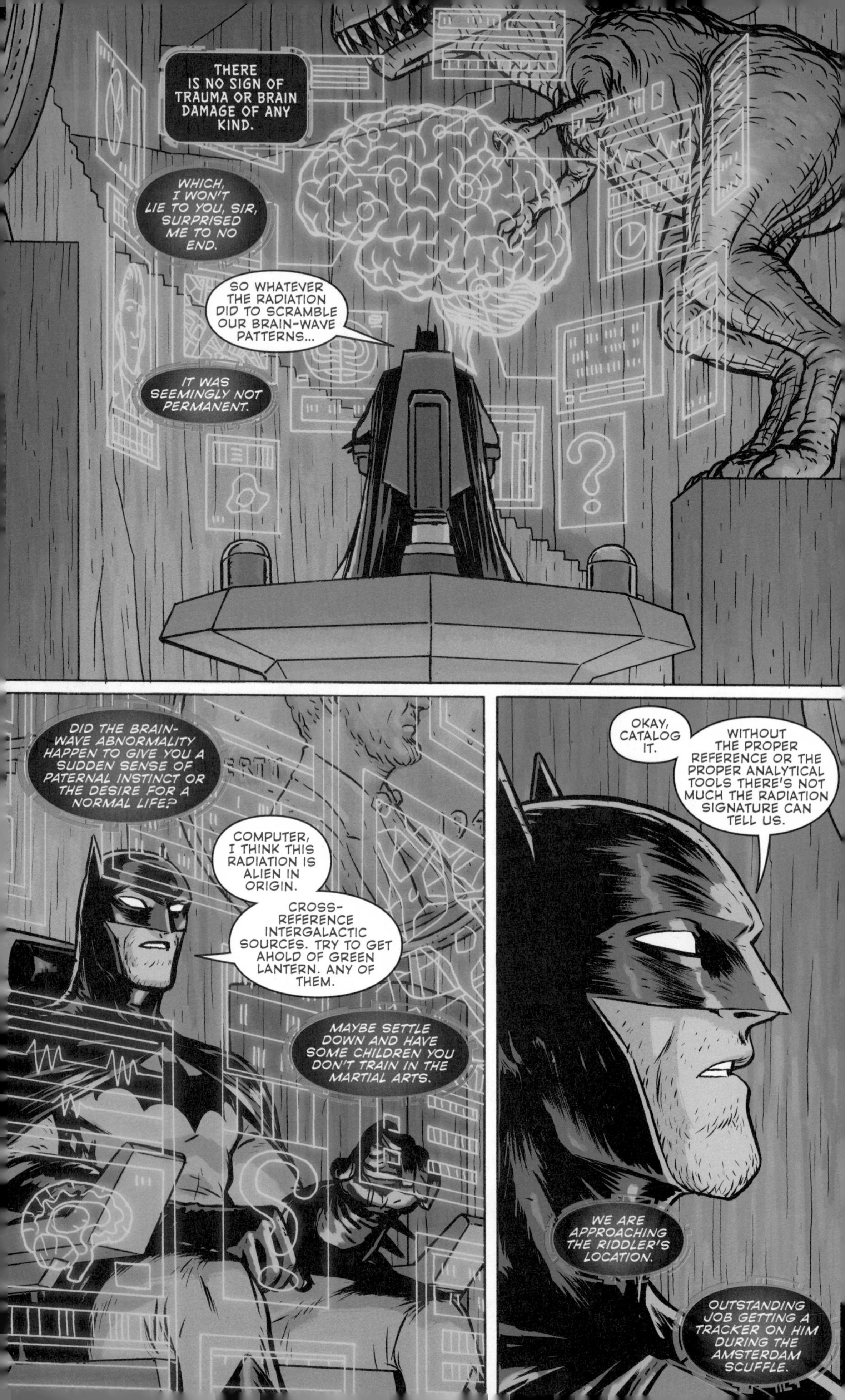
THERE IS NO SIGN OF TRAUMA OR BRAIN DAMAGE OF ANY KIND.
WHICH, I WON'T LIE TO YOU, SIR, SURPRISED ME TO NO END.
SO WHATEVER THE RADIATION DID TO SCRAMBLE OUR BRAIN-WAVE PATTERNS...
IT WAS SEEMINGLY NOT PERMANENT.
DID THE BRAIN-WAVE ABNORMALITY HAPPEN TO GIVE YOU A SUDDEN SENSE OF PATERNAL INSTINCT OR THE DESIRE FOR A NORMAL LIFE?
COMPUTER, I THINK THIS RADIATION IS ALIEN IN ORIGIN.
CROSS-REFERENCE INTERGALACTIC SOURCES. TRY TO GET AHOLD OF GREEN LANTERN. ANY OF THEM.
MAYBE SETTLE DOWN AND HAVE SOME CHILDREN YOU DON'T TRAIN IN THE MARTIAL ARTS.
OKAY, CATALOG IT.
WITHOUT THE PROPER REFERENCE OR THE PROPER ANALYTICAL TOOLS THERE'S NOT MUCH THE RADIATION SIGNATURE CAN TELL US.
WE ARE APPROACHING THE RIDDLER'S LOCATION.
OUTSTANDING JOB GETTING A TRACKER ON HIM DURING THE AMSTERDAM SCUFFLE.

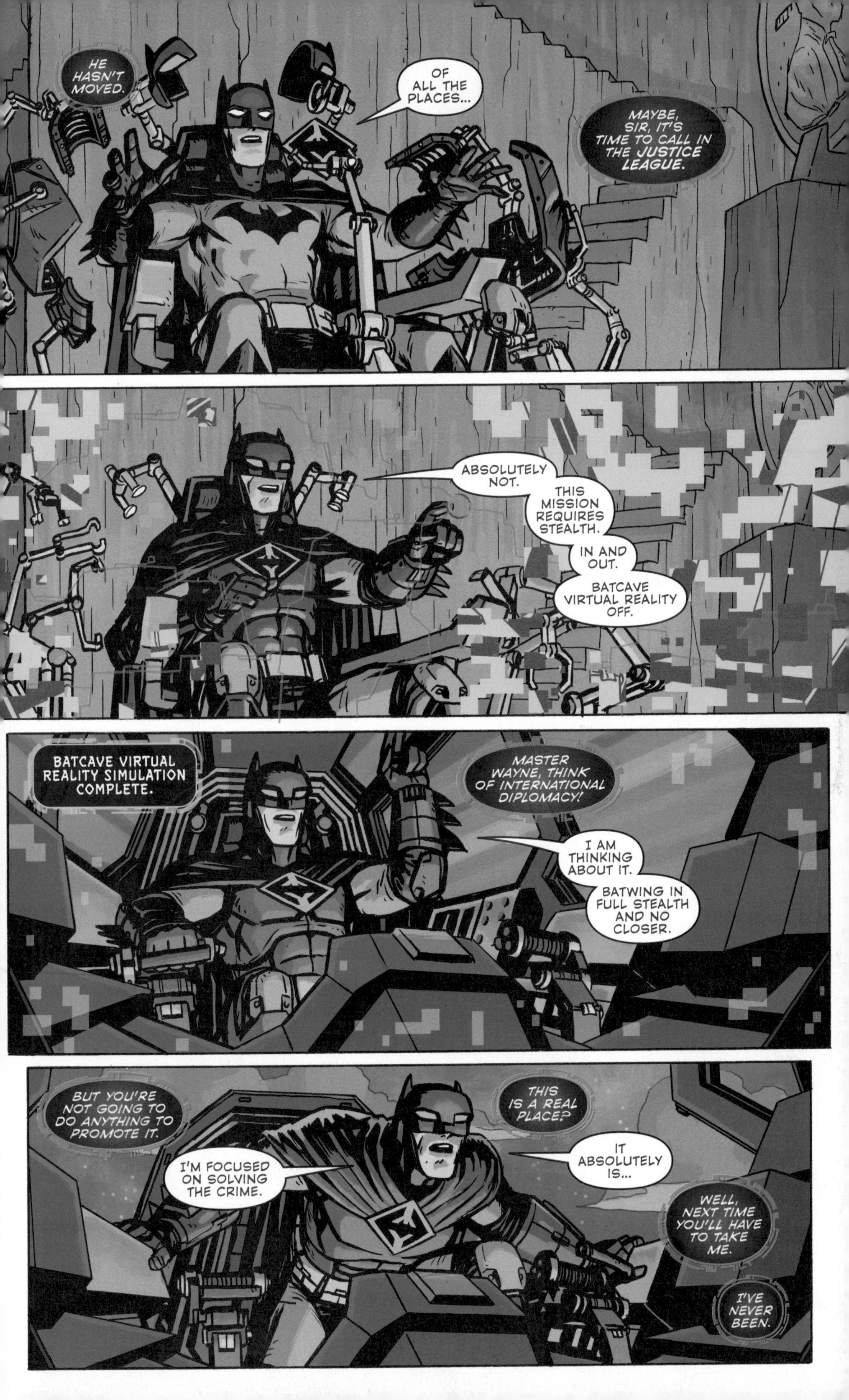
HE HASN'T MOVED.
OF ALL THE PLACES...
MAYBE, SIR, IT'S TIME TO CALL IN THE JUSTICE LEAGUE.
ABSOLUTELY NOT.
THIS MISSION REQUIRES STEALTH.
IN AND OUT.
BATCAVE VIRTUAL REALITY OFF.
BATCAVE VIRTUAL REALITY SIMULATION COMPLETE.
MASTER WAYNE, THINK OF INTERNATIONAL DIPLOMACY!
I AM THINKING ABOUT IT.
BATWING IN FULL STEALTH AND NO CLOSER.
BUT YOU'RE NOT GOING TO DO ANYTHING TO PROMOTE IT.
I'M FOCUSED ON SOLVING THE CRIME.
THIS IS A REAL PLACE?
IT ABSOLUTELY IS...
WELL, NEXT TIME YOU'LL HAVE TO TAKE ME.
I'VE NEVER BEEN.

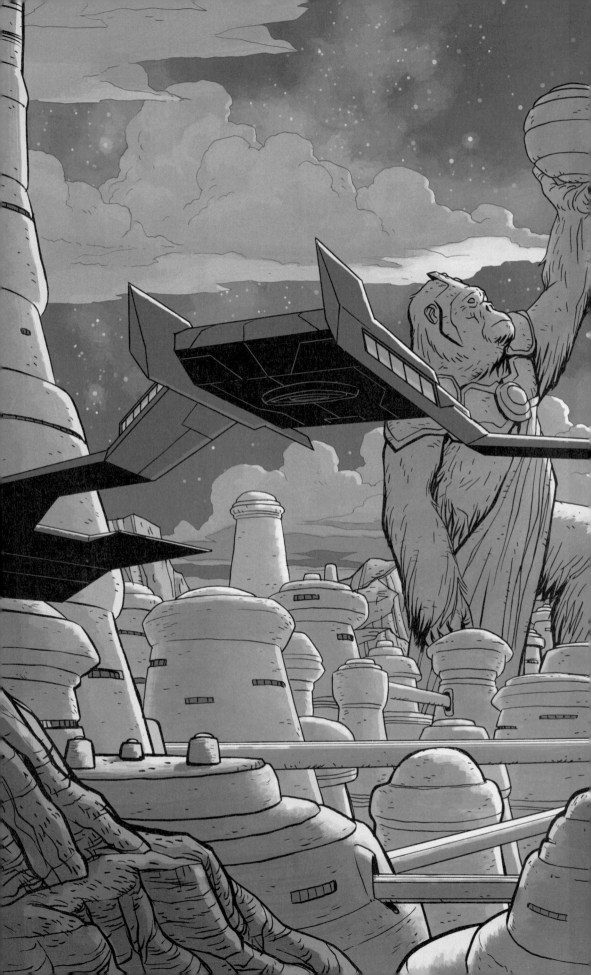

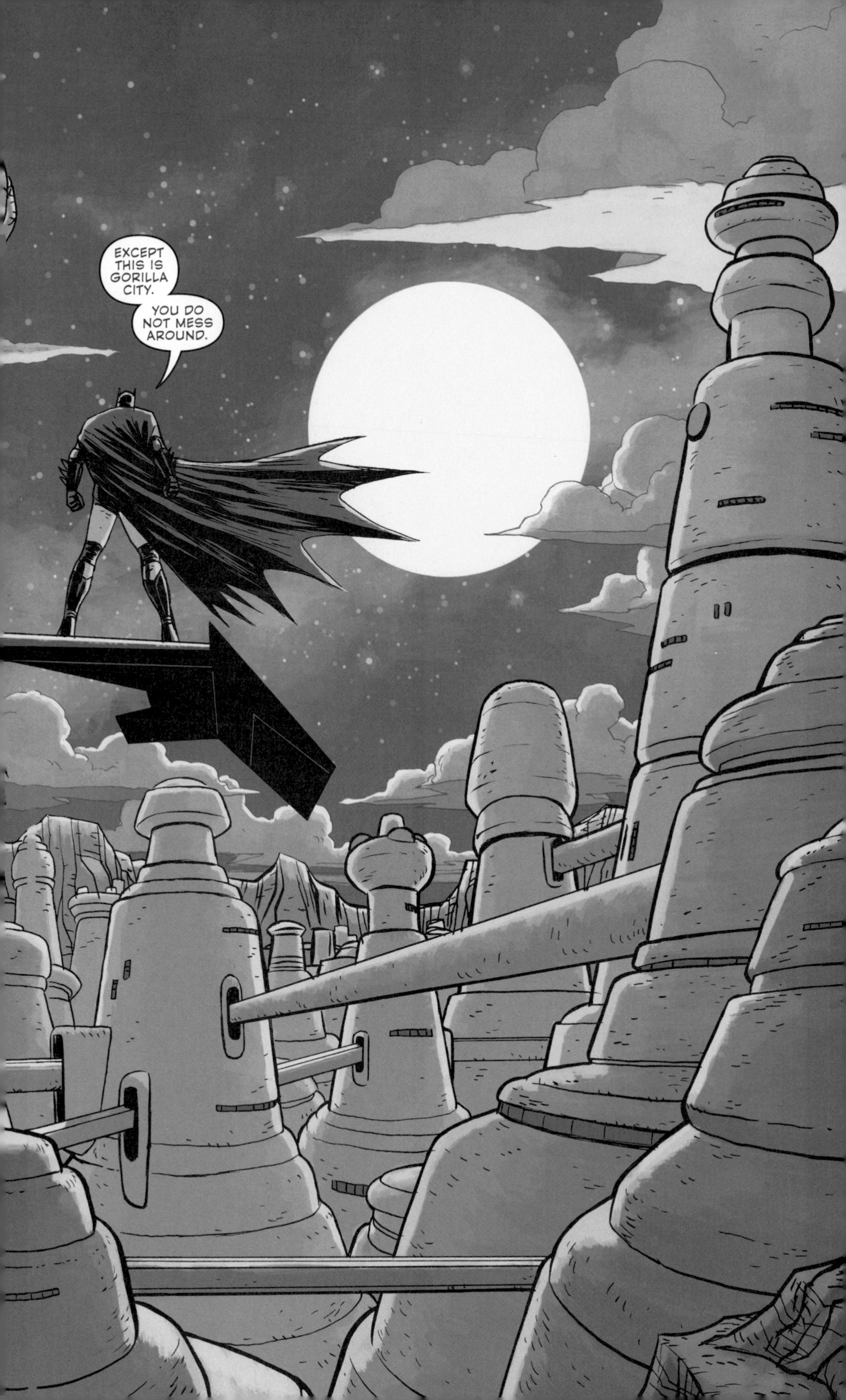
EXCEPT THIS IS GORILLA CITY.
YOU DO NOT MESS AROUND.

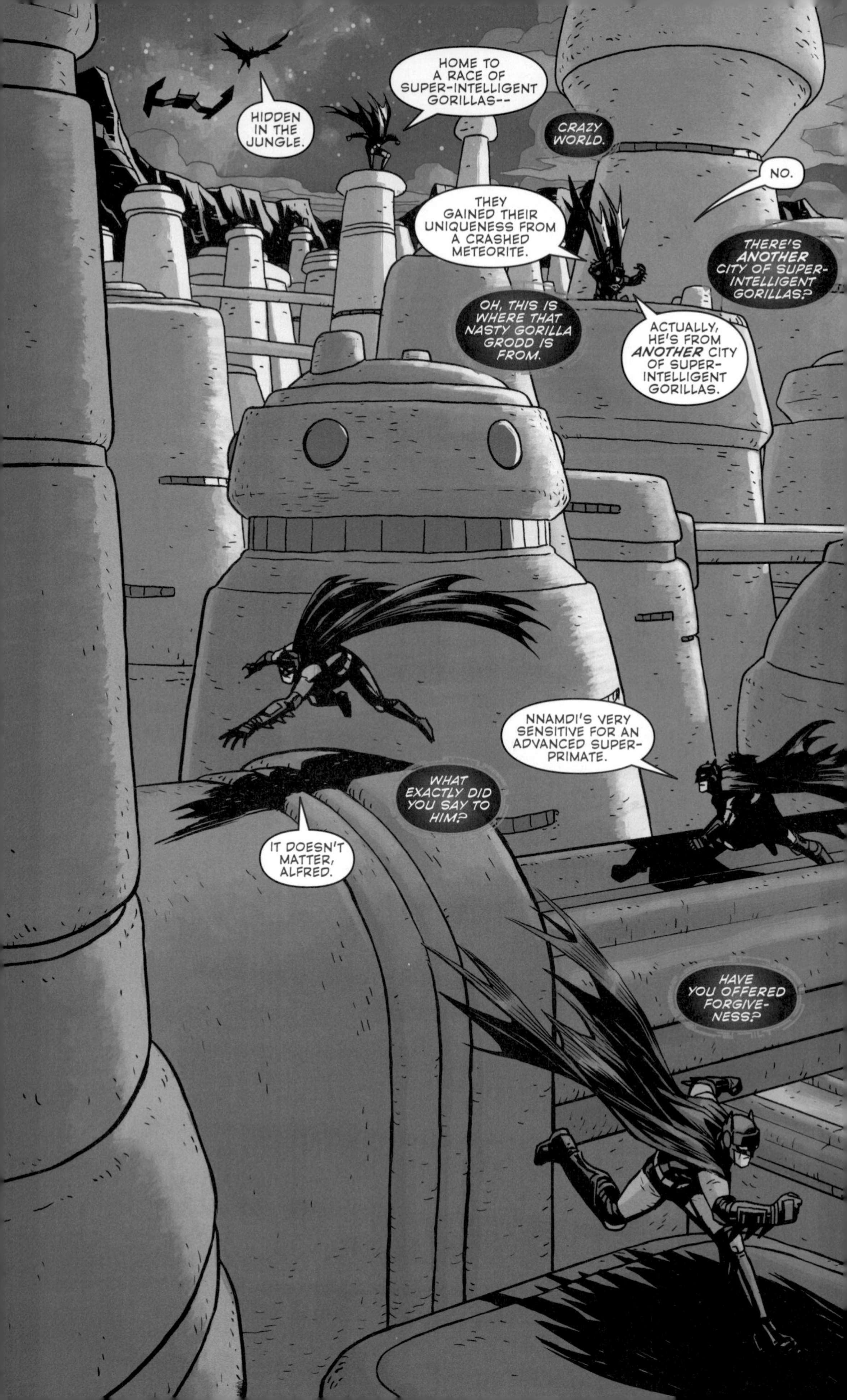
HIDDEN IN THE JUNGLE.
HOME TO A RACE OF SUPER-INTELLIGENT GORILLAS--
CRAZY WORLD.
NO.
THEY GAINED THEIR UNIQUENESS FROM A CRASHED METEORITE.
THERE'S ANOTHER CITY OF SUPER-INTELLIGENT GORILLAS?
OH, THIS IS WHERE THAT NASTY GORILLA GRODD IS FROM.
ACTUALLY, HE'S FROM ANOTHER CITY OF SUPER-INTELLIGENT GORILLAS.
NNAMDI'S VERY SENSITIVE FOR AN ADVANCED SUPER-PRIMATE.
WHAT EXACTLY DID YOU SAY TO HIM?
IT DOESN'T MATTER, ALFRED.
HAVE YOU OFFERED FORGIVE-NESS?

THESE GORILLAS ARE HYPER-INTELLIGENT AND SOME ARE TELEPATHIC.
I HAVE THE TELEPATHY SCRAMBLER ON MY BAT-COWL BUT I HAVE NO IDEA IF IT WILL WORK WITH THIS MANY TELEPATHS.
AND THEIR TECHNOLOGY...
FAR BEYOND OURS.
IT'S GORGEOUS.
ARCHITECTURE AND TECH HIDDEN AWAY FROM HUMAN SOCIETY.
BECAUSE, FRANKLY, FROM THE LOOKS OF IT, HUMANS DON'T DESERVE THIS YET.
WELL, WE CERTAINLY HAVEN'T EARNED IT.
SIR, I KNOW IT IS IN YOUR FIRST NATURE TO GO INTO STEALTH MODE AND TIPTOE AROUND...
BUT HAVE YOU CONSIDERED KNOCKING ON THE FRONT DOOR AND ASKING THE KING FOR HIS HELP?
IS HE STILL MAD AT YOU?
HE'S VERY SENSITIVE.

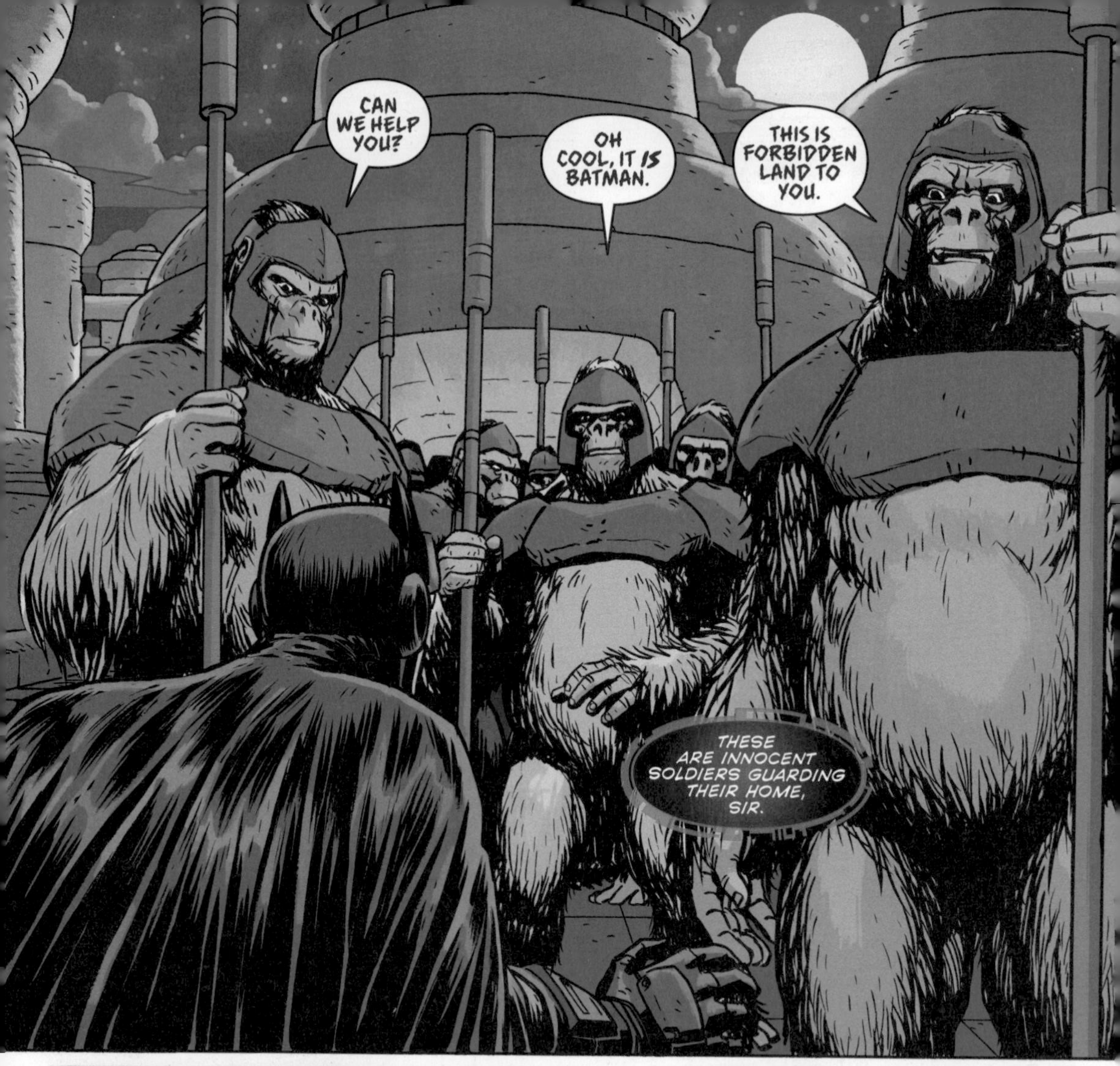
CAN WE HELP YOU?
OH COOL, IT IS BATMAN.
THIS IS FORBIDDEN LAND TO YOU.
THESE ARE INNOCENT SOLDIERS GUARDING THEIR HOME, SIR.

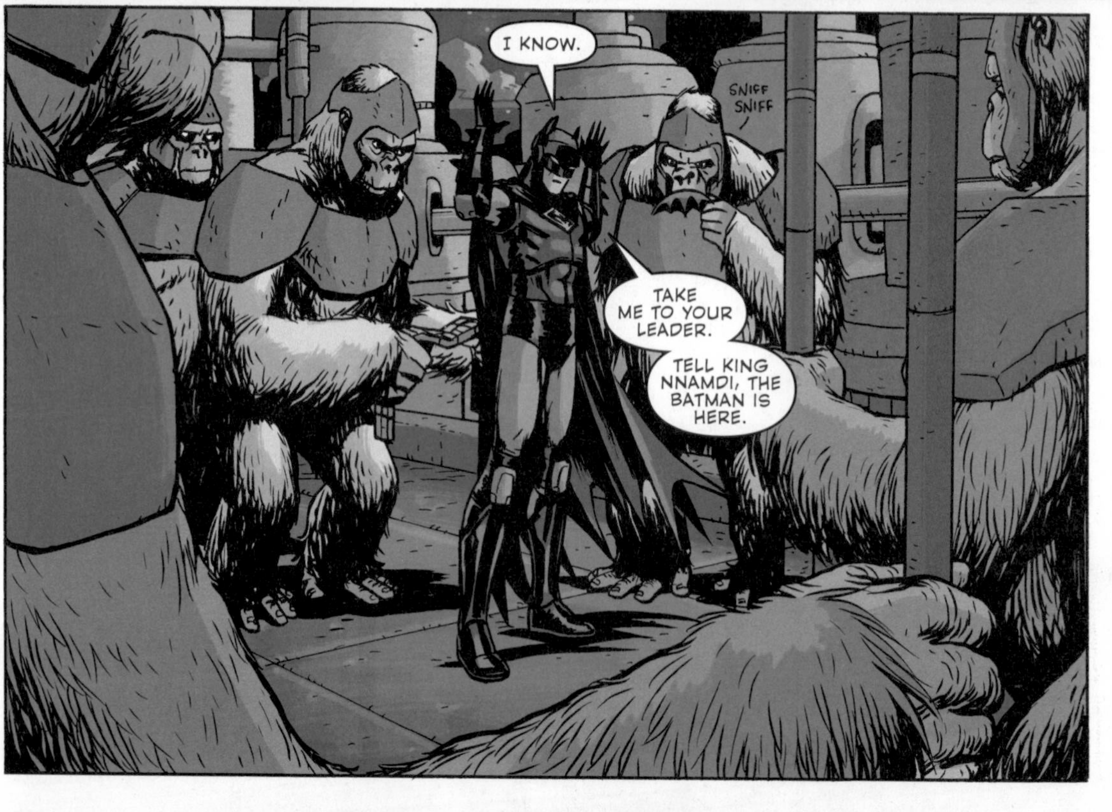
I KNOW.
SNIFF SNIFF
TAKE ME TO YOUR LEADER.
TELL KING NNAMDI, THE BATMAN IS HERE.

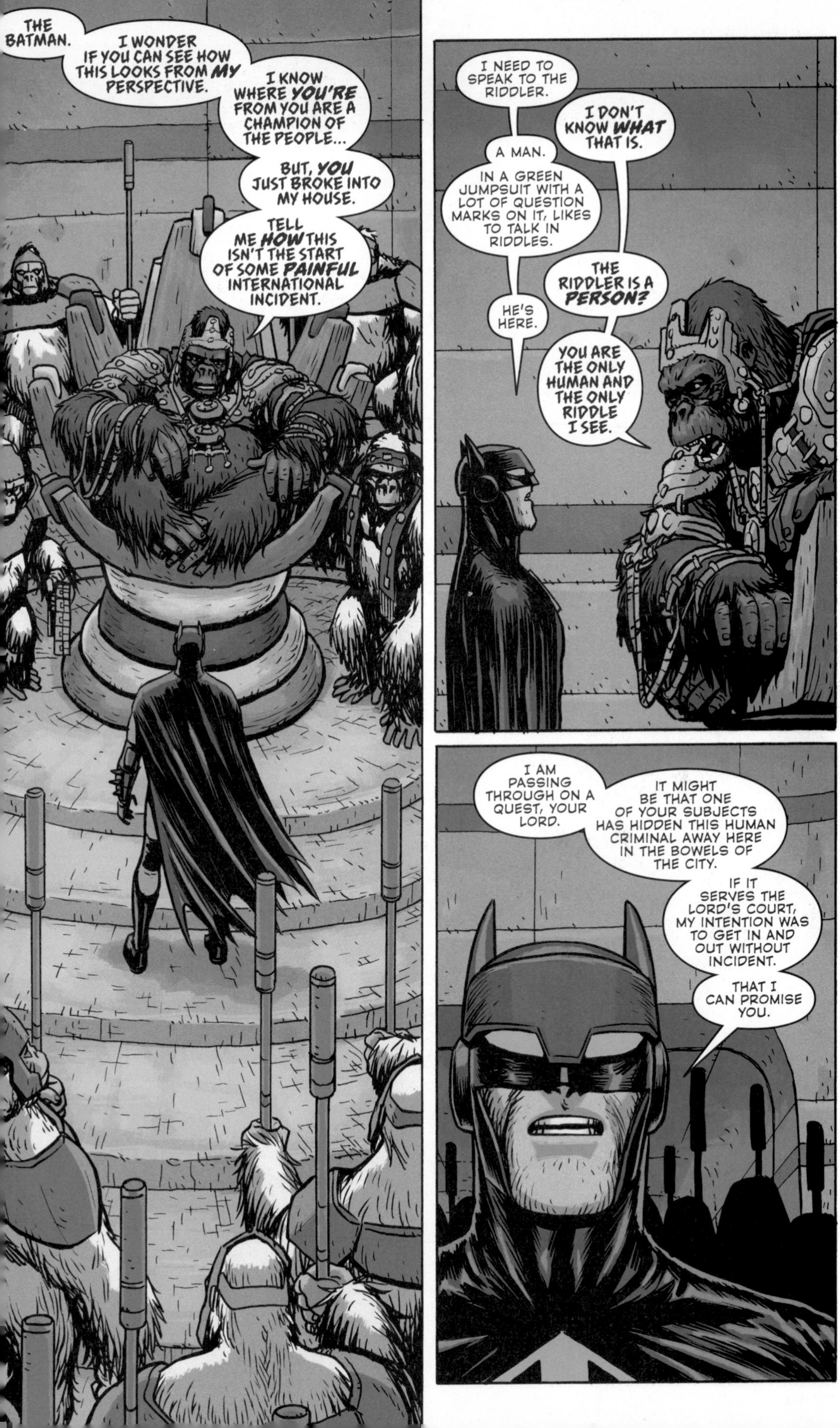
THE BATMAN.
I WONDER IF YOU CAN SEE HOW THIS LOOKS FROM MY PERSPECTIVE.
I KNOW WHERE YOU'RE FROM YOU ARE A CHAMPION OF THE PEOPLE...
BUT, YOU JUST BROKE INTO MY HOUSE.
TELL ME HOW THIS ISN'T THE START OF SOME PAINFUL INTERNATIONAL INCIDENT.
I NEED TO SPEAK TO THE RIDDLER.
I DON'T KNOW WHAT THAT IS.
A MAN.
IN A GREEN JUMPSUIT WITH A LOT OF QUESTION MARKS ON IT, LIKES TO TALK IN RIDDLES.
THE RIDDLER IS A PERSON?
HE'S HERE.
YOU ARE THE ONLY HUMAN AND THE ONLY RIDDLE I SEE.
I AM PASSING THROUGH ON A QUEST, YOUR LORD.
IT MIGHT BE THAT ONE OF YOUR SUBJECTS HAS HIDDEN THIS HUMAN CRIMINAL AWAY HERE IN THE BOWELS OF THE CITY.
IF IT SERVES THE LORD'S COURT, MY INTENTION WAS TO GET IN AND OUT WITHOUT INCIDENT.
THAT I CAN PROMISE YOU.

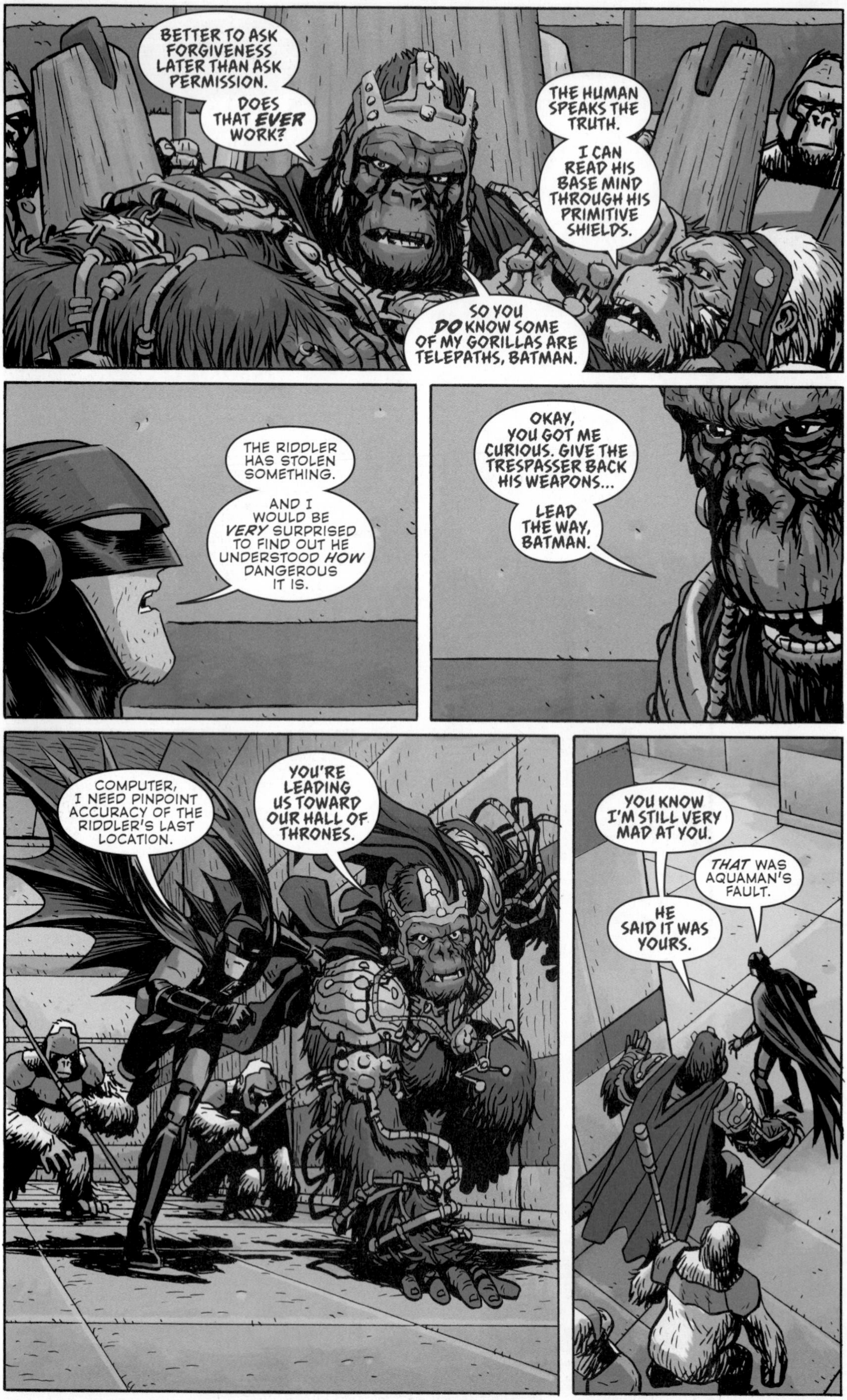
BETTER TO ASK FORGIVENESS LATER THAN ASK PERMISSION.
DOES THAT EVER WORK?
THE HUMAN SPEAKS THE TRUTH.
I CAN READ HIS BASE MIND THROUGH HIS PRIMITIVE SHIELDS.
SO YOU DO KNOW SOME OF MY GORILLAS ARE TELEPATHS, BATMAN.
THE RIDDLER HAS STOLEN SOMETHING.
AND I WOULD BE VERY SURPRISED TO FIND OUT HE UNDERSTOOD HOW DANGEROUS IT IS.
OKAY, YOU GOT ME CURIOUS. GIVE THE TRESPASSER BACK HIS WEAPONS...
LEAD THE WAY, BATMAN.
COMPUTER, I NEED PINPOINT ACCURACY OF THE RIDDLER'S LAST LOCATION.
YOU'RE LEADING US TOWARD OUR HALL OF THRONES.
YOU KNOW I'M STILL VERY MAD AT YOU.
THAT WAS AQUAMAN'S FAULT.
HE SAID IT WAS YOURS.

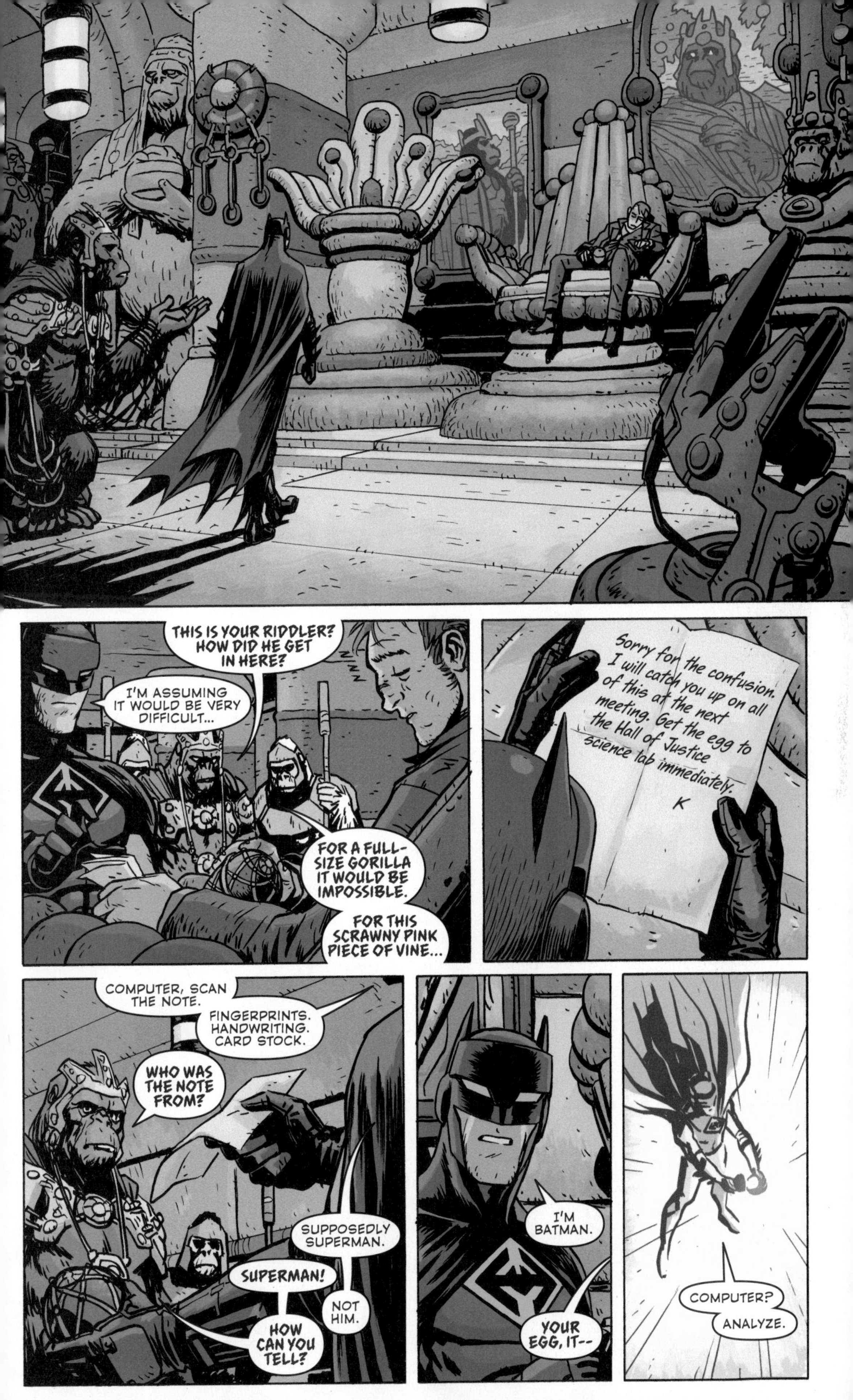

THIS IS YOUR RIDDLER? HOW DID HE GET IN HERE?
I'M ASSUMING IT WOULD BE VERY DIFFICULT...
FOR A FULL-SIZE GORILLA IT WOULD BE IMPOSSIBLE.
FOR THIS SCRAWNY PINK PIECE OF VINE...
Sorry for the confusion. I will catch you up on all of this at the next meeting. Get the egg to the Hall of Justice science lab immediately.
K
COMPUTER, SCAN THE NOTE.
FINGERPRINTS. HANDWRITING. CARD STOCK.
WHO WAS THE NOTE FROM?
SUPPOSEDLY SUPERMAN.
SUPERMAN!
NOT HIM.
HOW CAN YOU TELL?
I'M BATMAN.
YOUR EGG, IT--
COMPUTER?
ANALYZE.

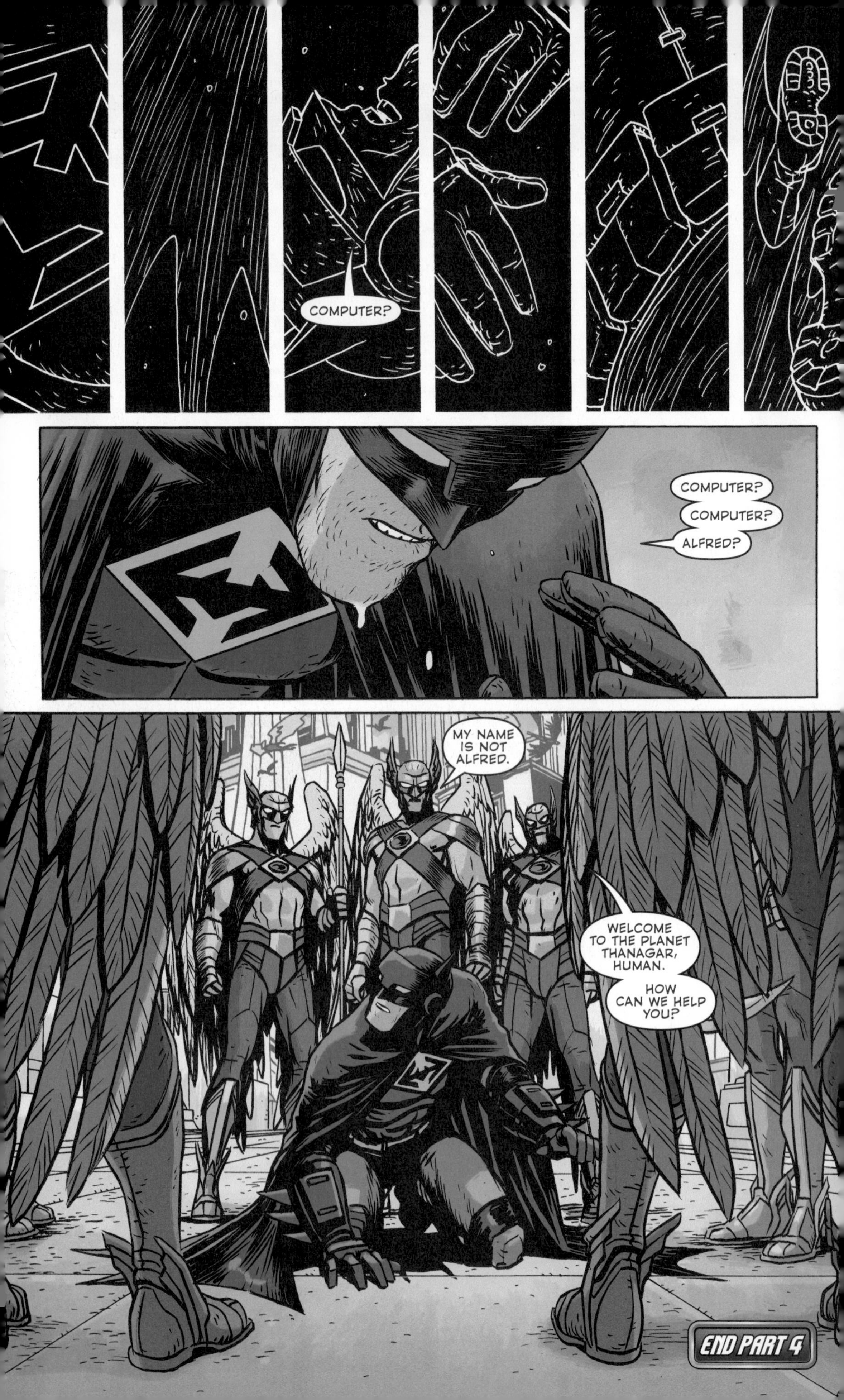
COMPUTER?
COMPUTER?
COMPUTER?
ALFRED?
MY NAME IS NOT ALFRED.
WELCOME TO THE PLANET THANAGAR, HUMAN.
HOW CAN WE HELP YOU?
END PART 4

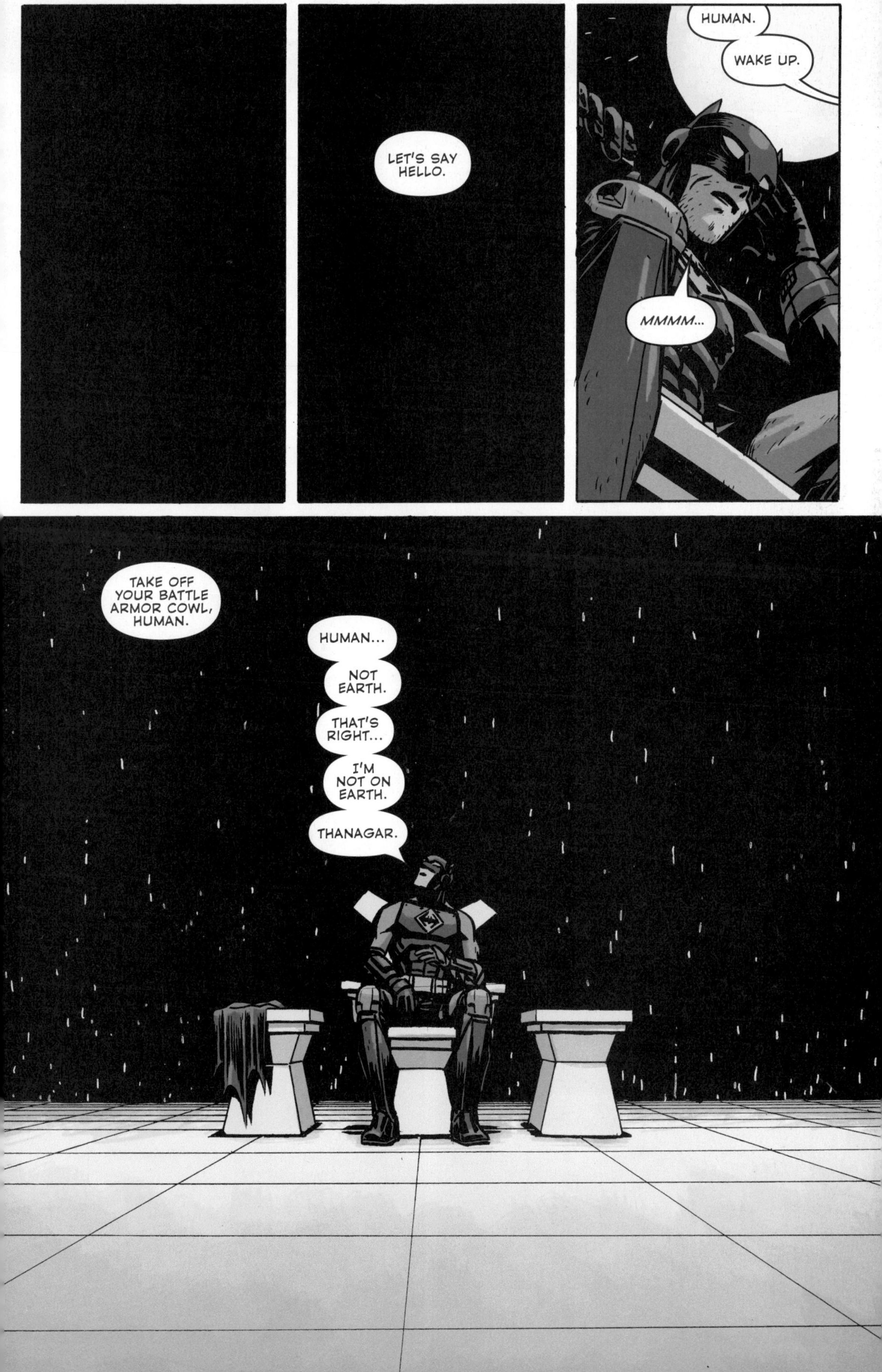
LET'S SAY HELLO.
HUMAN.
WAKE UP.
MMMM...
TAKE OFF YOUR BATTLE ARMOR COWL, HUMAN.
HUMAN...
NOT EARTH.
THAT'S RIGHT...
I'M NOT ON EARTH.
THANAGAR.

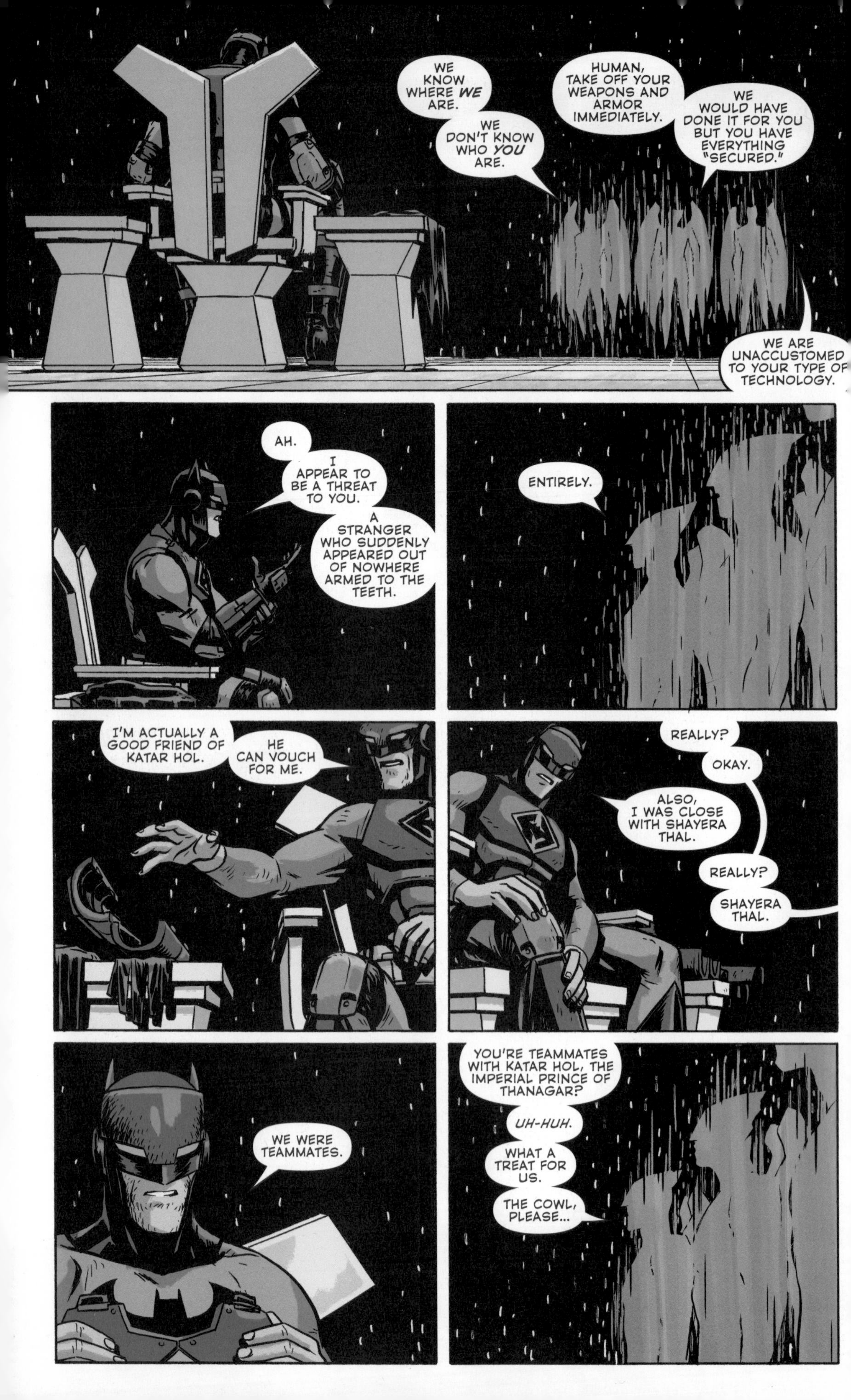
WE KNOW WHERE *WE* ARE.
WE DON'T KNOW WHO *YOU* ARE.
HUMAN, TAKE OFF YOUR WEAPONS AND ARMOR IMMEDIATELY.
WE WOULD HAVE DONE IT FOR YOU BUT YOU HAVE EVERYTHING "SECURED."
WE ARE UNACCUSTOMED TO YOUR TYPE OF TECHNOLOGY.
AH.
I APPEAR TO BE A THREAT TO YOU.
A STRANGER WHO SUDDENLY APPEARED OUT OF NOWHERE ARMED TO THE TEETH.
ENTIRELY.
I'M ACTUALLY A GOOD FRIEND OF KATAR HOL.
HE CAN VOUCH FOR ME.
REALLY?
OKAY.
ALSO, I WAS CLOSE WITH SHAYERA THAL.
REALLY?
SHAYERA THAL.
WE WERE TEAMMATES.
YOU'RE TEAMMATES WITH KATAR HOL, THE IMPERIAL PRINCE OF THANAGAR?
UH-HUH.
WHAT A TREAT FOR US.
THE COWL, PLEASE...

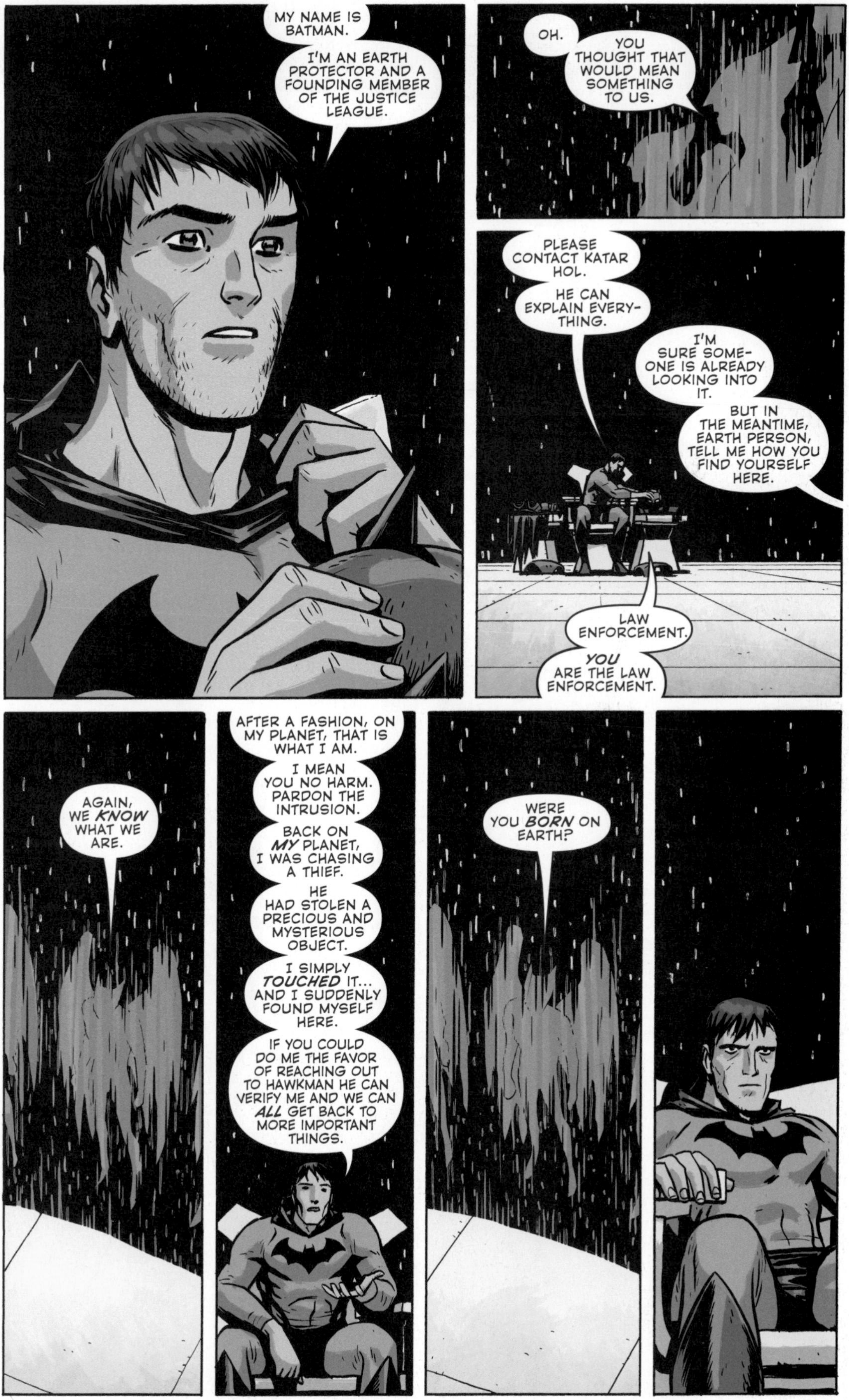
MY NAME IS BATMAN.
I'M AN EARTH PROTECTOR AND A FOUNDING MEMBER OF THE JUSTICE LEAGUE.
OH.
YOU THOUGHT THAT WOULD MEAN SOMETHING TO US.
PLEASE CONTACT KATAR HOL.
HE CAN EXPLAIN EVERY-THING.
I'M SURE SOME-ONE IS ALREADY LOOKING INTO IT.
BUT IN THE MEANTIME, EARTH PERSON, TELL ME HOW YOU FIND YOURSELF HERE.
LAW ENFORCEMENT.
YOU ARE THE LAW ENFORCEMENT.
AGAIN, WE KNOW WHAT WE ARE.
AFTER A FASHION, ON MY PLANET, THAT IS WHAT I AM.
I MEAN YOU NO HARM. PARDON THE INTRUSION.
BACK ON MY PLANET, I WAS CHASING A THIEF.
HE HAD STOLEN A PRECIOUS AND MYSTERIOUS OBJECT.
I SIMPLY TOUCHED IT... AND I SUDDENLY FOUND MYSELF HERE.
IF YOU COULD DO ME THE FAVOR OF REACHING OUT TO HAWKMAN HE CAN VERIFY ME AND WE CAN ALL GET BACK TO MORE IMPORTANT THINGS.
WERE YOU BORN ON EARTH?

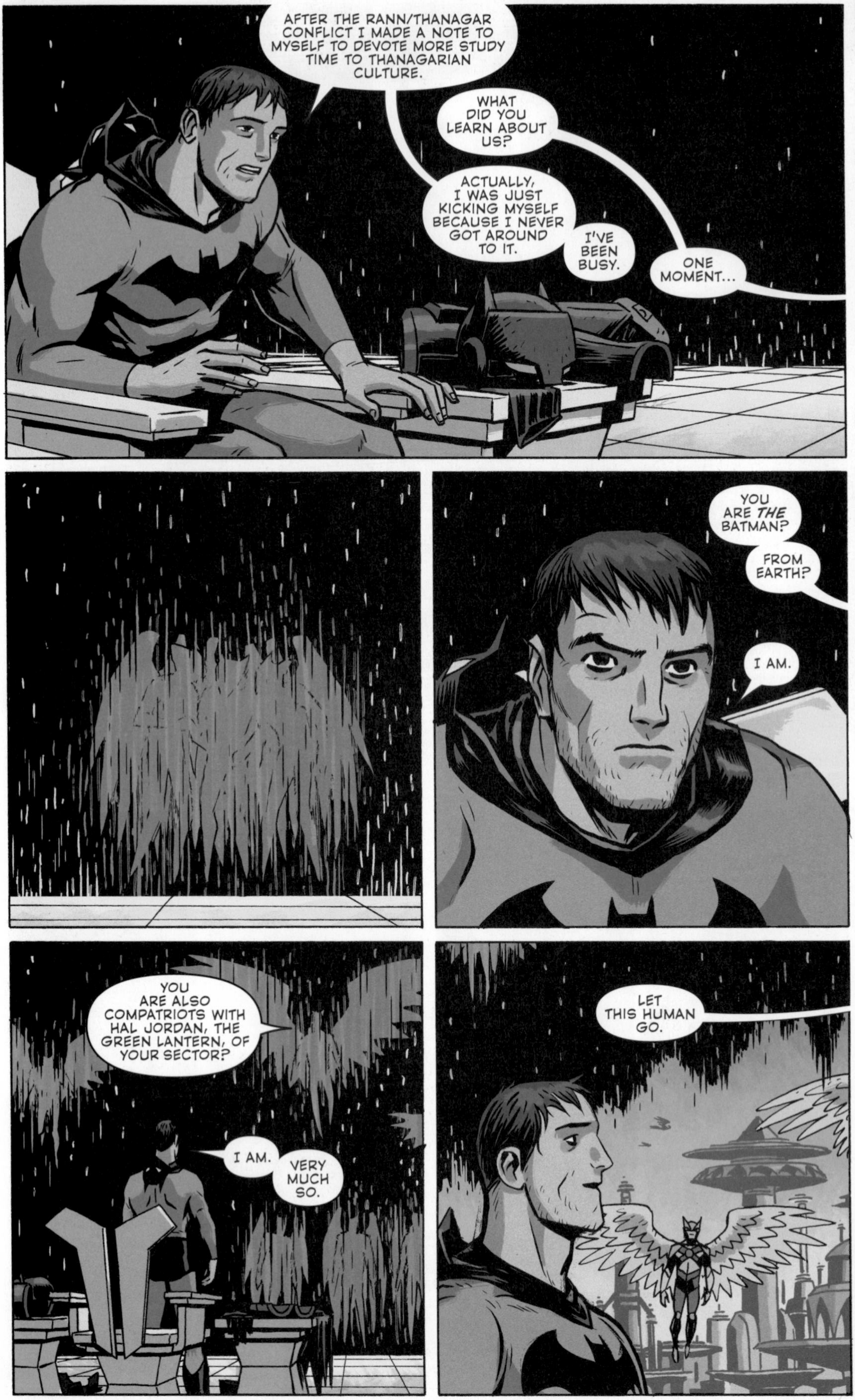

AFTER THE RANN/THANAGAR CONFLICT I MADE A NOTE TO MYSELF TO DEVOTE MORE STUDY TIME TO THANAGARIAN CULTURE.
WHAT DID YOU LEARN ABOUT US?
ACTUALLY, I WAS JUST KICKING MYSELF BECAUSE I NEVER GOT AROUND TO IT.
I'VE BEEN BUSY.
ONE MOMENT...
YOU ARE *THE* BATMAN?
FROM EARTH?
I AM.
YOU ARE ALSO COMPATRIOTS WITH HAL JORDAN, THE GREEN LANTERN, OF YOUR SECTOR?
I AM.
VERY MUCH SO.
LET THIS HUMAN GO.

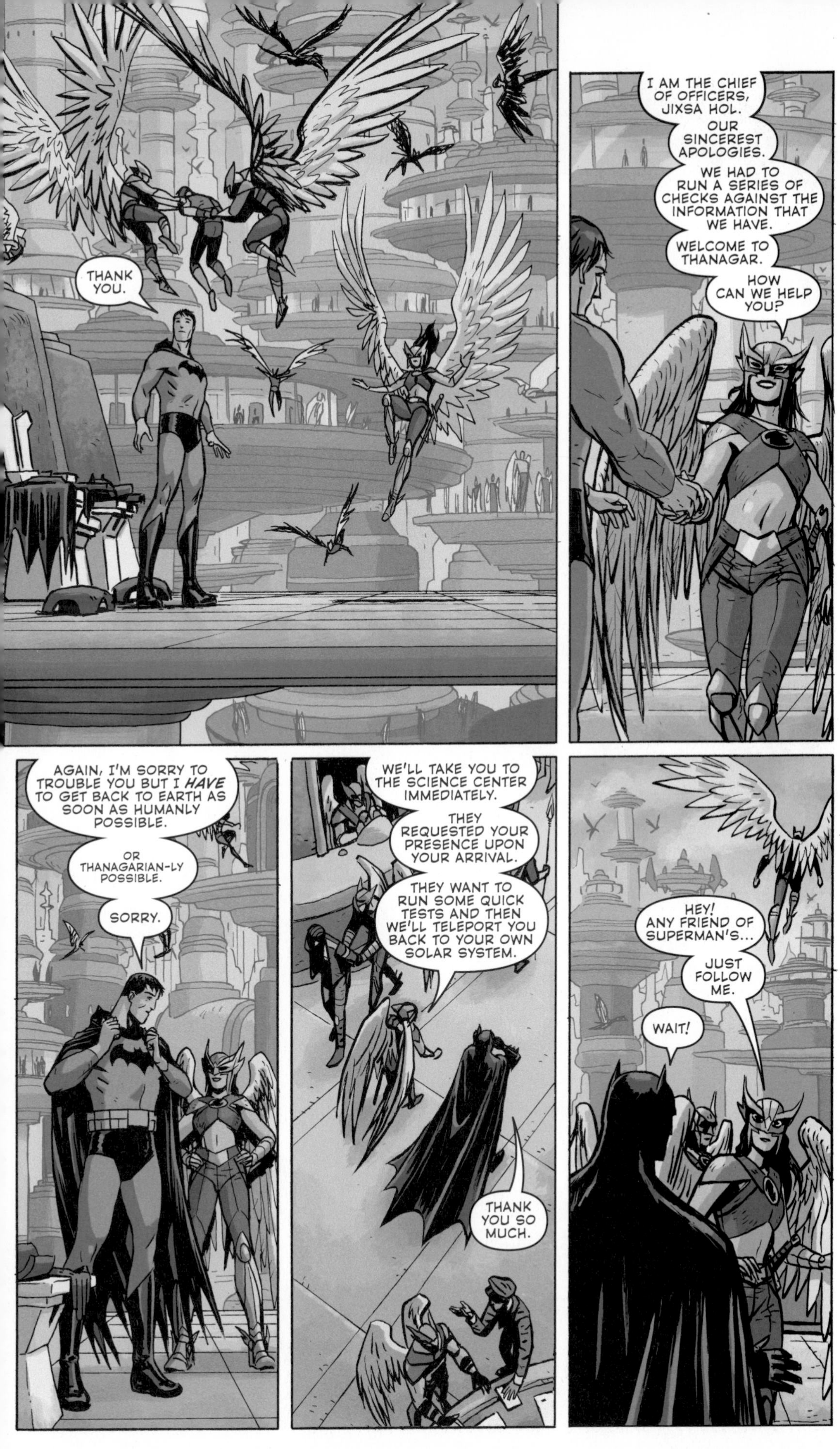
THANK YOU.
I AM THE CHIEF OF OFFICERS, JIXSA HOL.
OUR SINCEREST APOLOGIES.
WE HAD TO RUN A SERIES OF CHECKS AGAINST THE INFORMATION THAT WE HAVE.
WELCOME TO THANAGAR.
HOW CAN WE HELP YOU?
AGAIN, I'M SORRY TO TROUBLE YOU BUT I *HAVE* TO GET BACK TO EARTH AS SOON AS HUMANLY POSSIBLE.
OR THANAGARIAN-LY POSSIBLE.
SORRY.
WE'LL TAKE YOU TO THE SCIENCE CENTER IMMEDIATELY.
THEY REQUESTED YOUR PRESENCE UPON YOUR ARRIVAL.
THEY WANT TO RUN SOME QUICK TESTS AND THEN WE'LL TELEPORT YOU BACK TO YOUR OWN SOLAR SYSTEM.
THANK YOU SO MUCH.
HEY! ANY FRIEND OF SUPERMAN'S...
JUST FOLLOW ME.
WAIT!

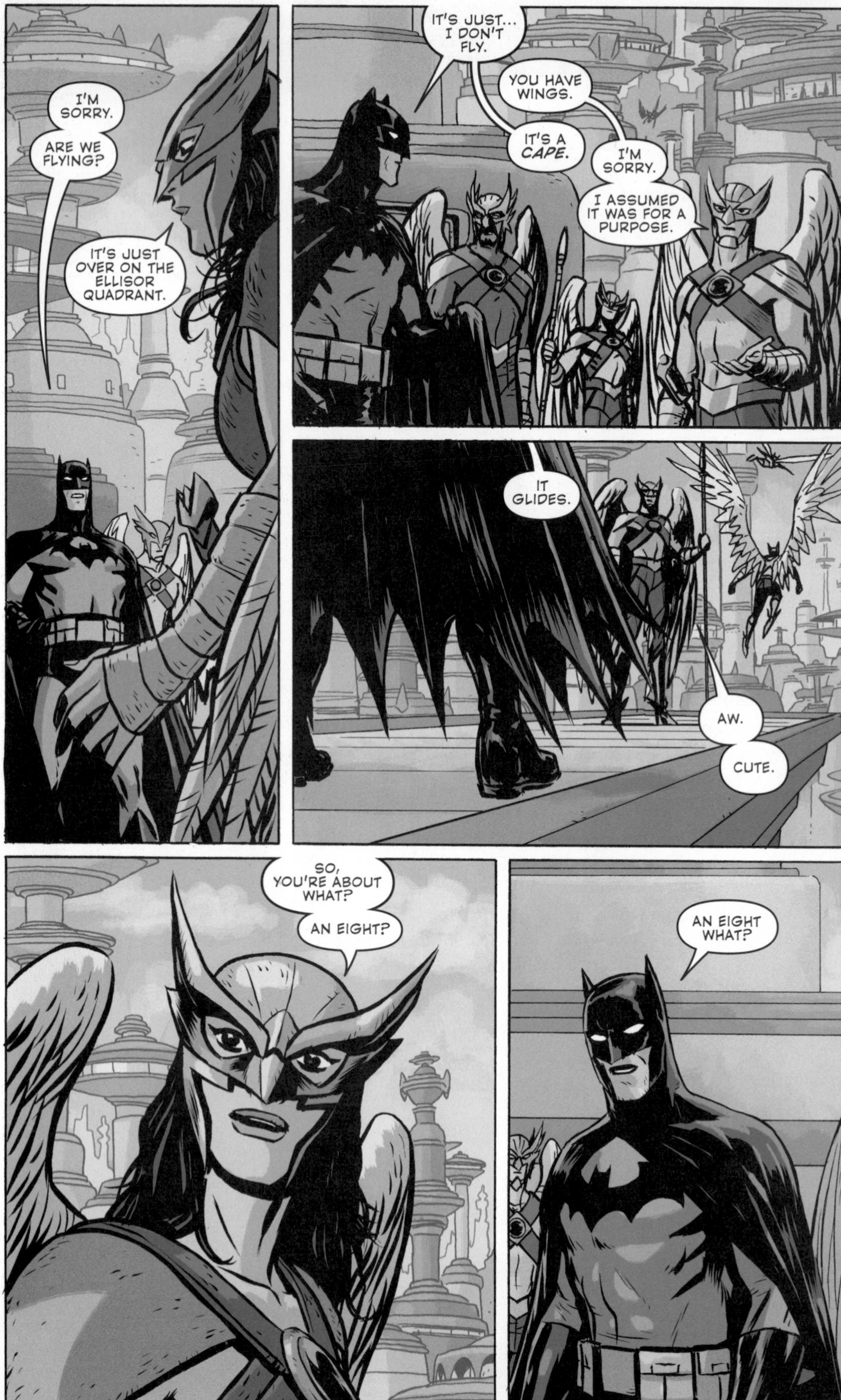
I'M SORRY.
ARE WE FLYING?
IT'S JUST OVER ON THE ELLISOR QUADRANT.
IT'S JUST... I DON'T FLY.
YOU HAVE WINGS.
IT'S A *CAPE.*
I'M SORRY.
I ASSUMED IT WAS FOR A PURPOSE.
IT GLIDES.
AW.
CUTE.
SO, YOU'RE ABOUT WHAT?
AN EIGHT?
AN EIGHT WHAT?

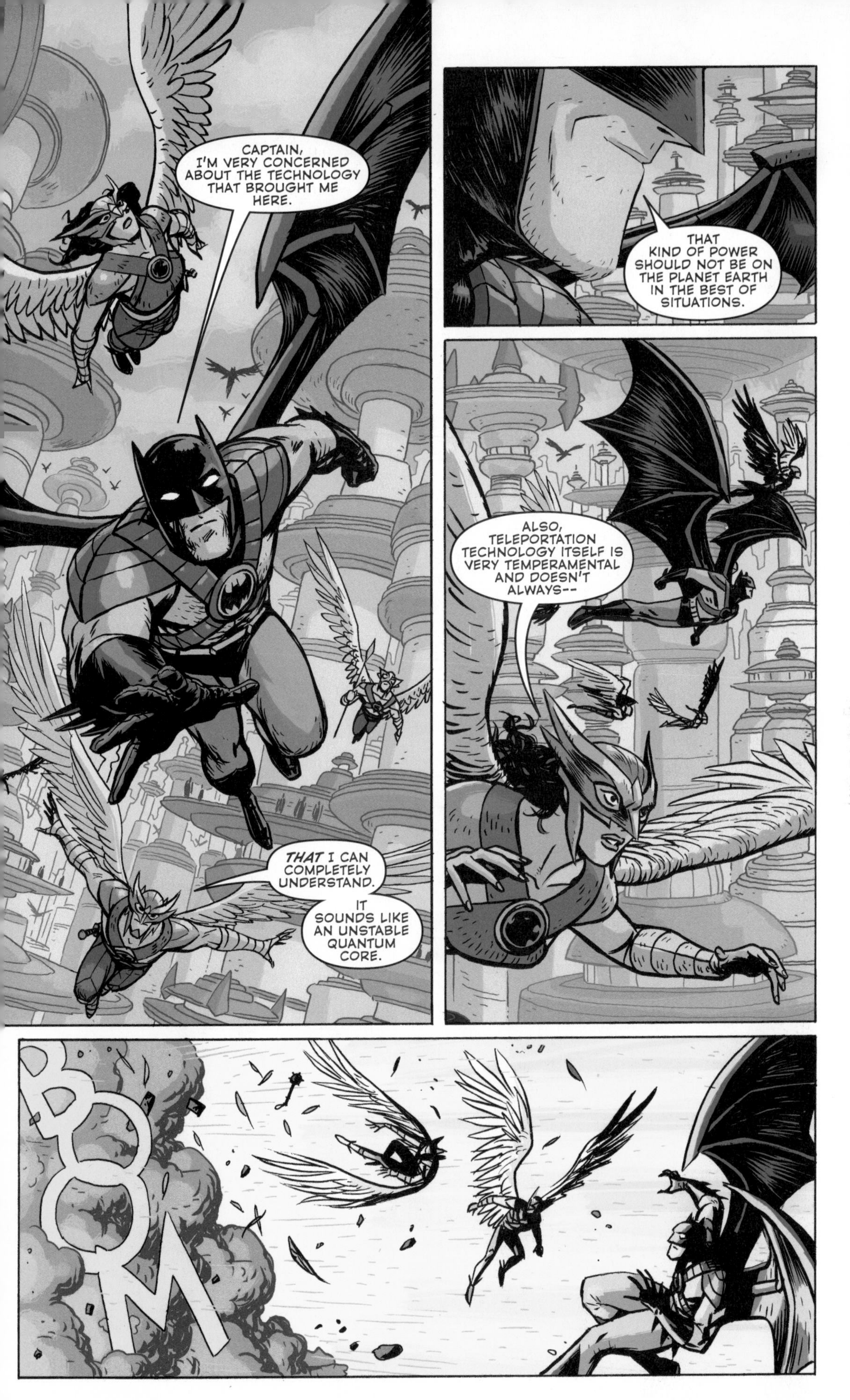
CAPTAIN, I'M VERY CONCERNED ABOUT THE TECHNOLOGY THAT BROUGHT ME HERE.
THAT KIND OF POWER SHOULD NOT BE ON THE PLANET EARTH IN THE BEST OF SITUATIONS.
THAT I CAN COMPLETELY UNDERSTAND.
IT SOUNDS LIKE AN UNSTABLE QUANTUM CORE.
ALSO, TELEPORTATION TECHNOLOGY ITSELF IS VERY TEMPERAMENTAL AND DOESN'T ALWAYS--
BOOM

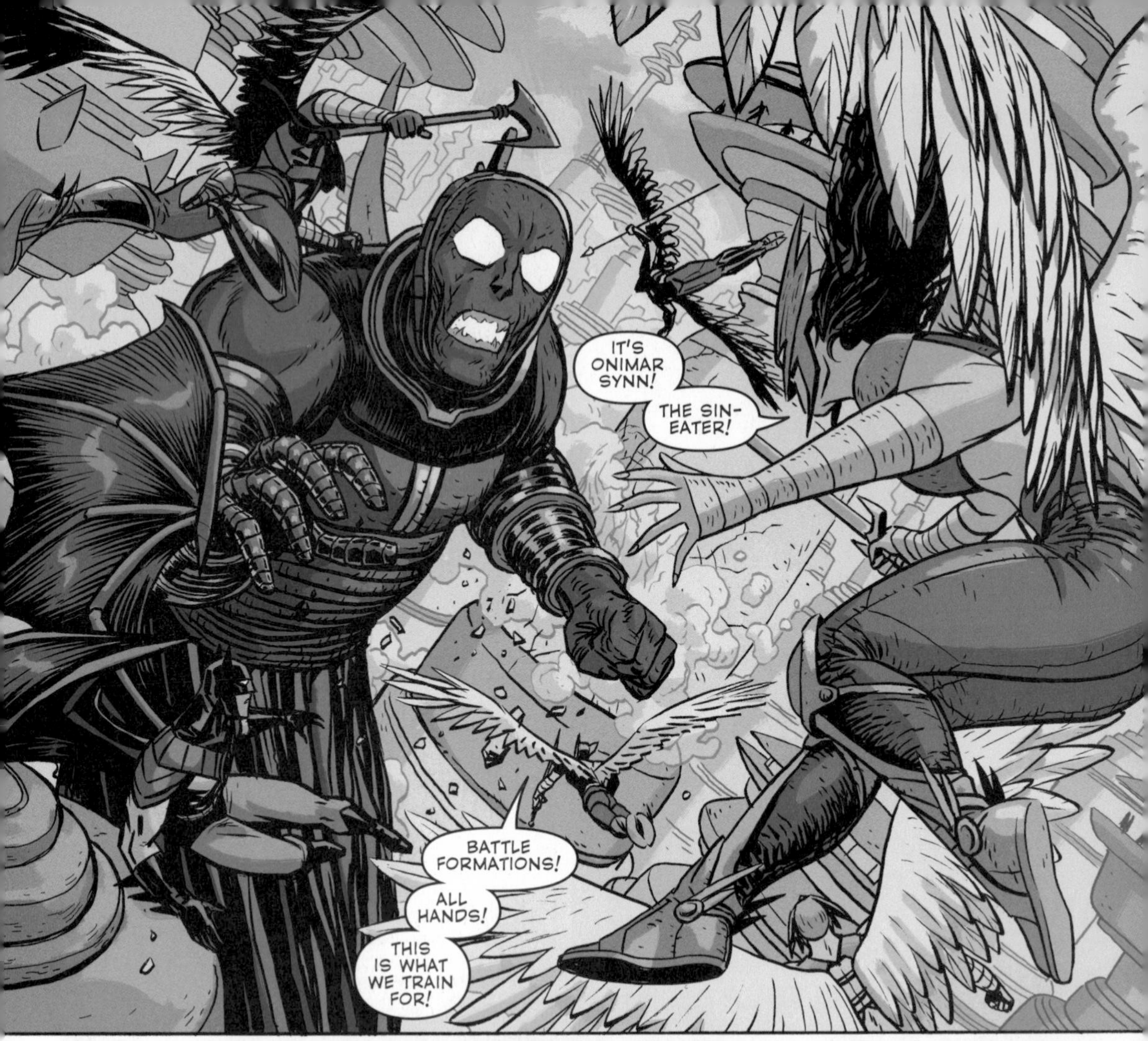
IT'S ONIMAR SYNN!
THE SIN-EATER!
BATTLE FORMATIONS!
ALL HANDS!
THIS IS WHAT WE TRAIN FOR!

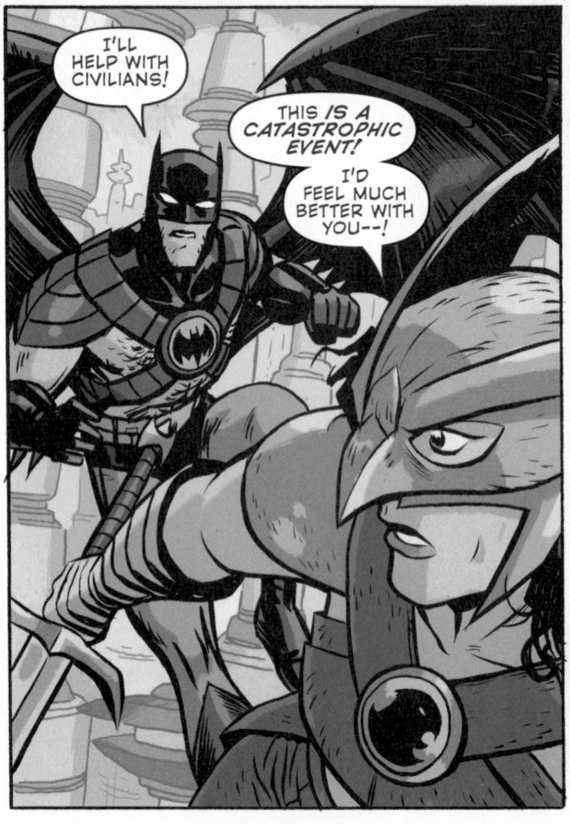
I'LL HELP WITH CIVILIANS!
THIS *IS A CATASTROPHIC EVENT!*
I'D FEEL MUCH BETTER WITH YOU--!

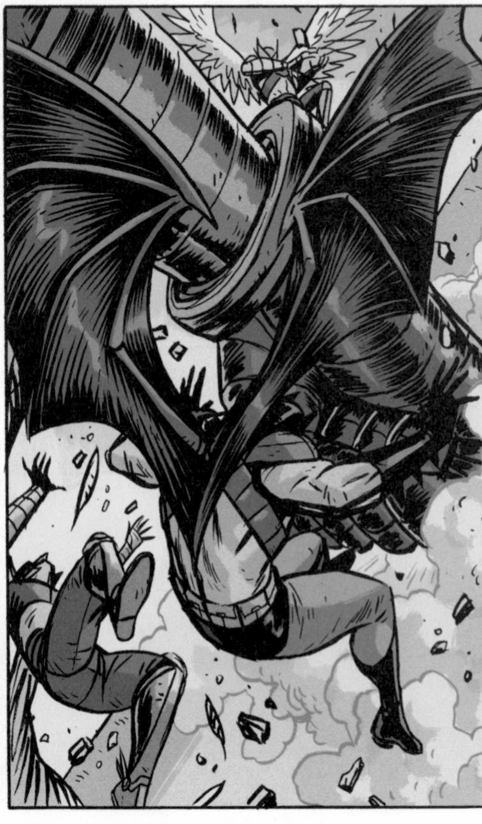

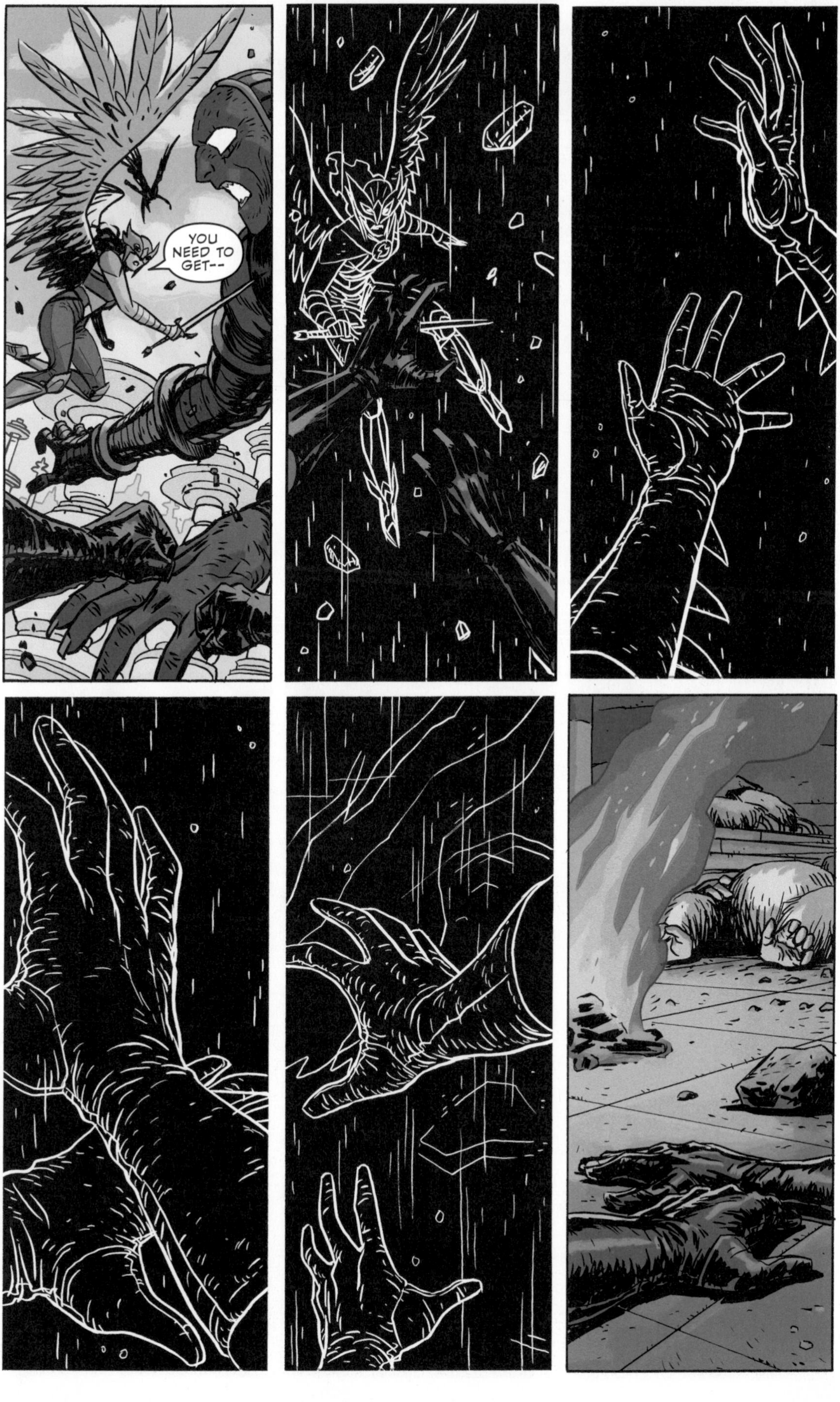
YOU NEED TO GET--

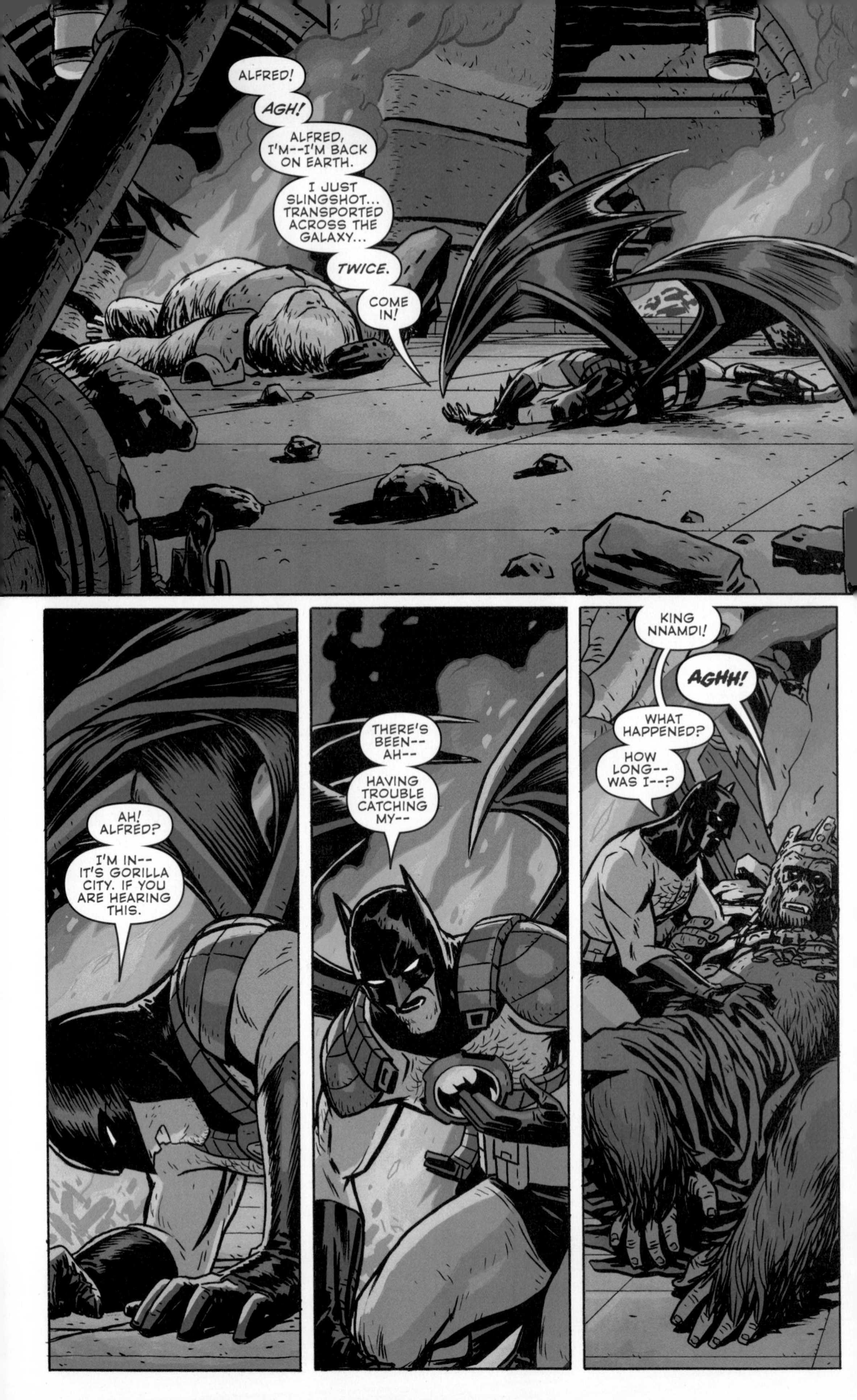
ALFRED!
AGH!
ALFRED, I'M--I'M BACK ON EARTH.
I JUST SLINGSHOT... TRANSPORTED ACROSS THE GALAXY...
TWICE.
COME IN!
AH! ALFRED?
I'M IN-- IT'S GORILLA CITY. IF YOU ARE HEARING THIS.
THERE'S BEEN-- AH--
HAVING TROUBLE CATCHING MY--
KING NNAMDI!
AGHH!
WHAT HAPPENED?
HOW LONG-- WAS I--?

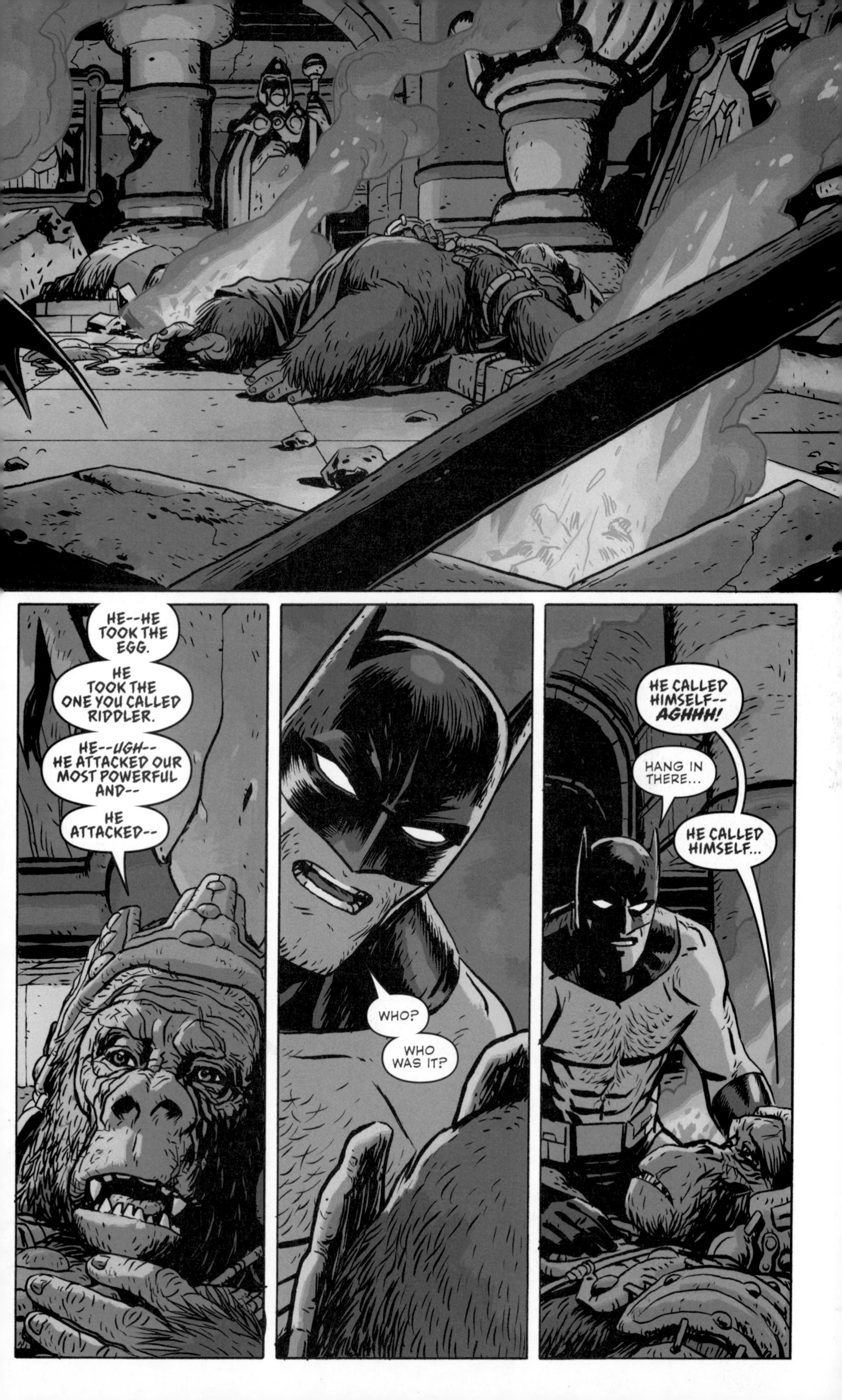
HE--HE TOOK THE EGG.
HE TOOK THE ONE YOU CALLED RIDDLER.
HE--UGH--HE ATTACKED OUR MOST POWERFUL AND--
HE ATTACKED--
WHO?
WHO WAS IT?
HE CALLED HIMSELF--AGHHH!
HANG IN THERE...
HE CALLED HIMSELF...

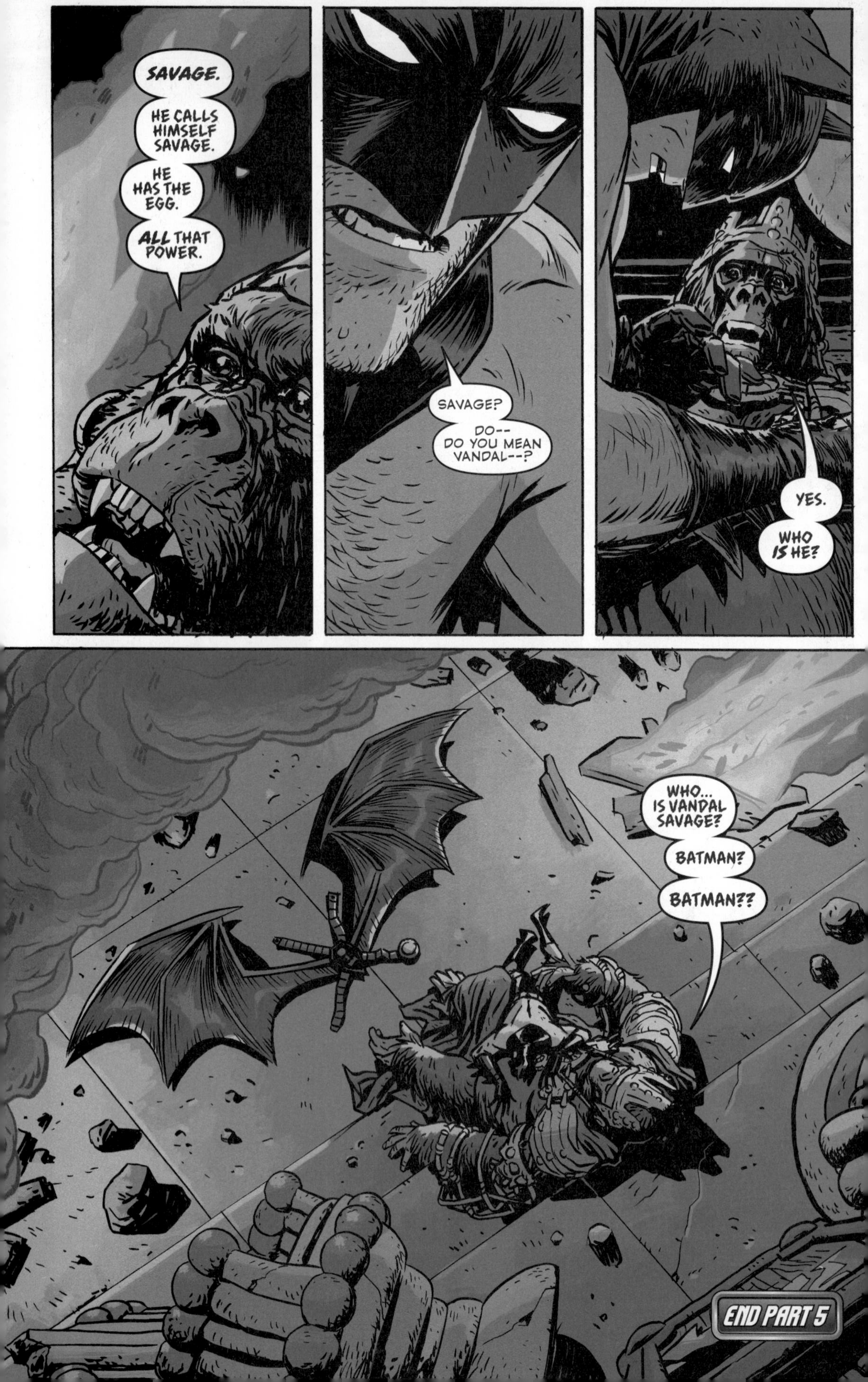
SAVAGE.
HE CALLS HIMSELF SAVAGE.
HE HAS THE EGG.
ALL THAT POWER.
SAVAGE?
DO-- DO YOU MEAN VANDAL--?
YES.
WHO IS HE?
WHO... IS VANDAL SAVAGE?
BATMAN?
BATMAN??
END PART 5

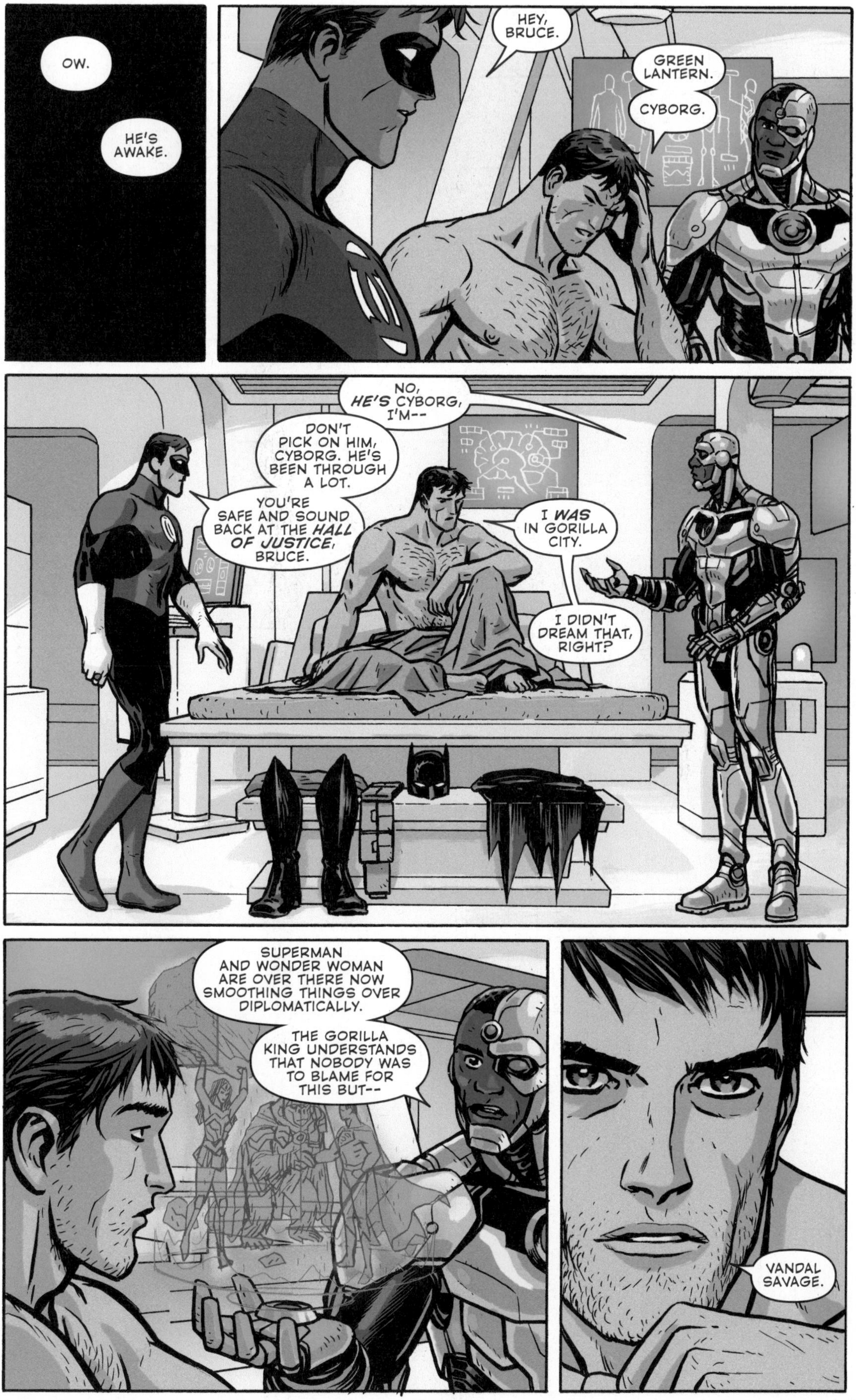
OW.
HE'S AWAKE.
HEY, BRUCE.
GREEN LANTERN.
CYBORG.
NO, *HE'S* CYBORG, I'M--
DON'T PICK ON HIM, CYBORG. HE'S BEEN THROUGH A LOT.
YOU'RE SAFE AND SOUND BACK AT THE *HALL OF JUSTICE*, BRUCE.
I *WAS* IN GORILLA CITY.
I DIDN'T DREAM THAT, RIGHT?
SUPERMAN AND WONDER WOMAN ARE OVER THERE NOW SMOOTHING THINGS OVER DIPLOMATICALLY.
THE GORILLA KING UNDERSTANDS THAT NOBODY WAS TO BLAME FOR THIS BUT--
VANDAL SAVAGE.

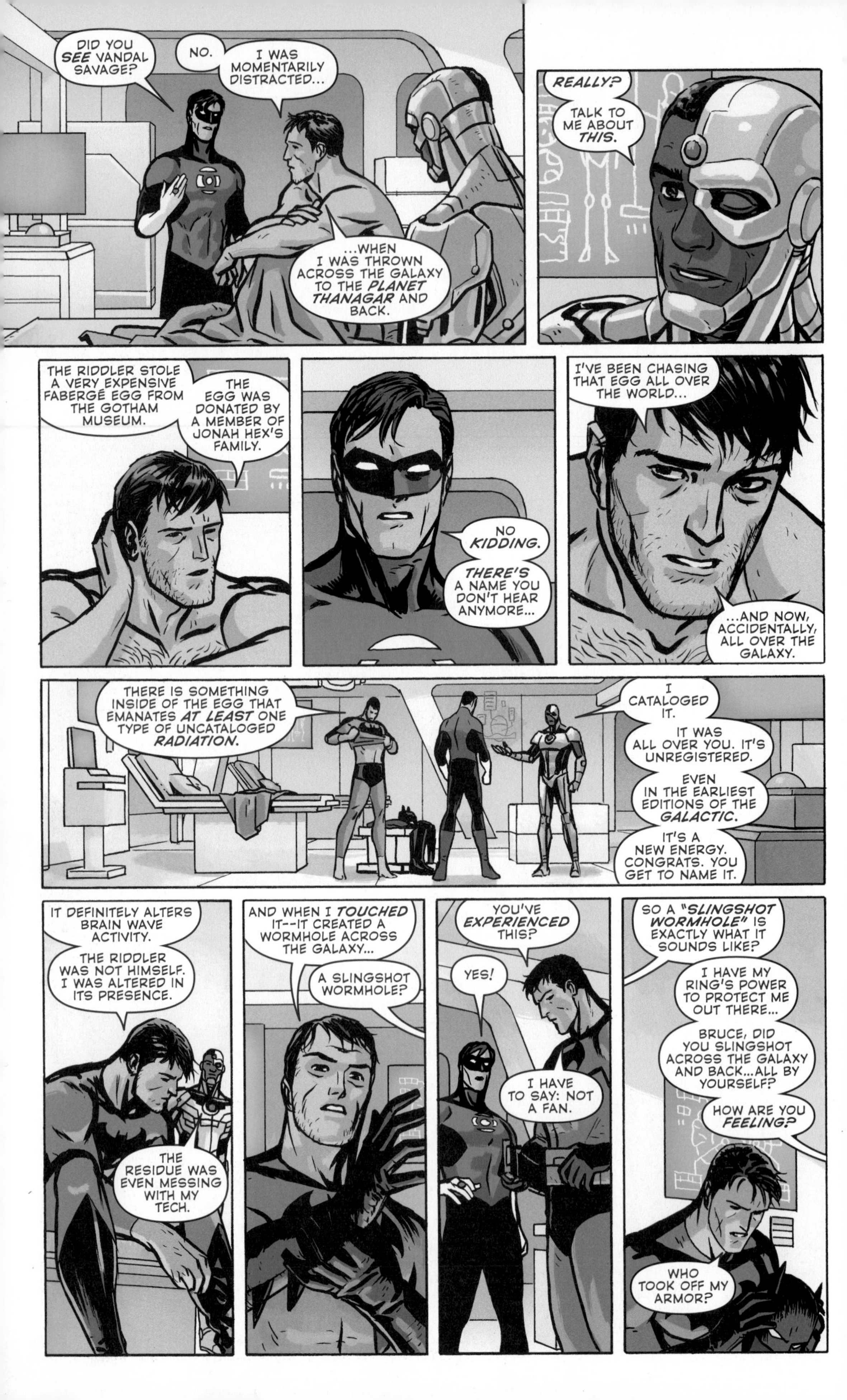
DID YOU SEE VANDAL SAVAGE?
NO.
I WAS MOMENTARILY DISTRACTED...
...WHEN I WAS THROWN ACROSS THE GALAXY TO THE PLANET THANAGAR AND BACK.
REALLY?
TALK TO ME ABOUT THIS.
THE RIDDLER STOLE A VERY EXPENSIVE FABERGÉ EGG FROM THE GOTHAM MUSEUM.
THE EGG WAS DONATED BY A MEMBER OF JONAH HEX'S FAMILY.
NO KIDDING.
THERE'S A NAME YOU DON'T HEAR ANYMORE...
I'VE BEEN CHASING THAT EGG ALL OVER THE WORLD...
...AND NOW, ACCIDENTALLY, ALL OVER THE GALAXY.
THERE IS SOMETHING INSIDE OF THE EGG THAT EMANATES AT LEAST ONE TYPE OF UNCATALOGED RADIATION.
I CATALOGED IT.
IT WAS ALL OVER YOU. IT'S UNREGISTERED.
EVEN IN THE EARLIEST EDITIONS OF THE GALACTIC.
IT'S A NEW ENERGY. CONGRATS. YOU GET TO NAME IT.
IT DEFINITELY ALTERS BRAIN WAVE ACTIVITY.
THE RIDDLER WAS NOT HIMSELF. I WAS ALTERED IN ITS PRESENCE.
THE RESIDUE WAS EVEN MESSING WITH MY TECH.
AND WHEN I TOUCHED IT--IT CREATED A WORMHOLE ACROSS THE GALAXY...
A SLINGSHOT WORMHOLE?
YOU'VE EXPERIENCED THIS?
YES!
I HAVE TO SAY: NOT A FAN.
SO A "SLINGSHOT WORMHOLE" IS EXACTLY WHAT IT SOUNDS LIKE?
I HAVE MY RING'S POWER TO PROTECT ME OUT THERE...
BRUCE, DID YOU SLINGSHOT ACROSS THE GALAXY AND BACK...ALL BY YOURSELF?
HOW ARE YOU FEELING?
WHO TOOK OFF MY ARMOR?

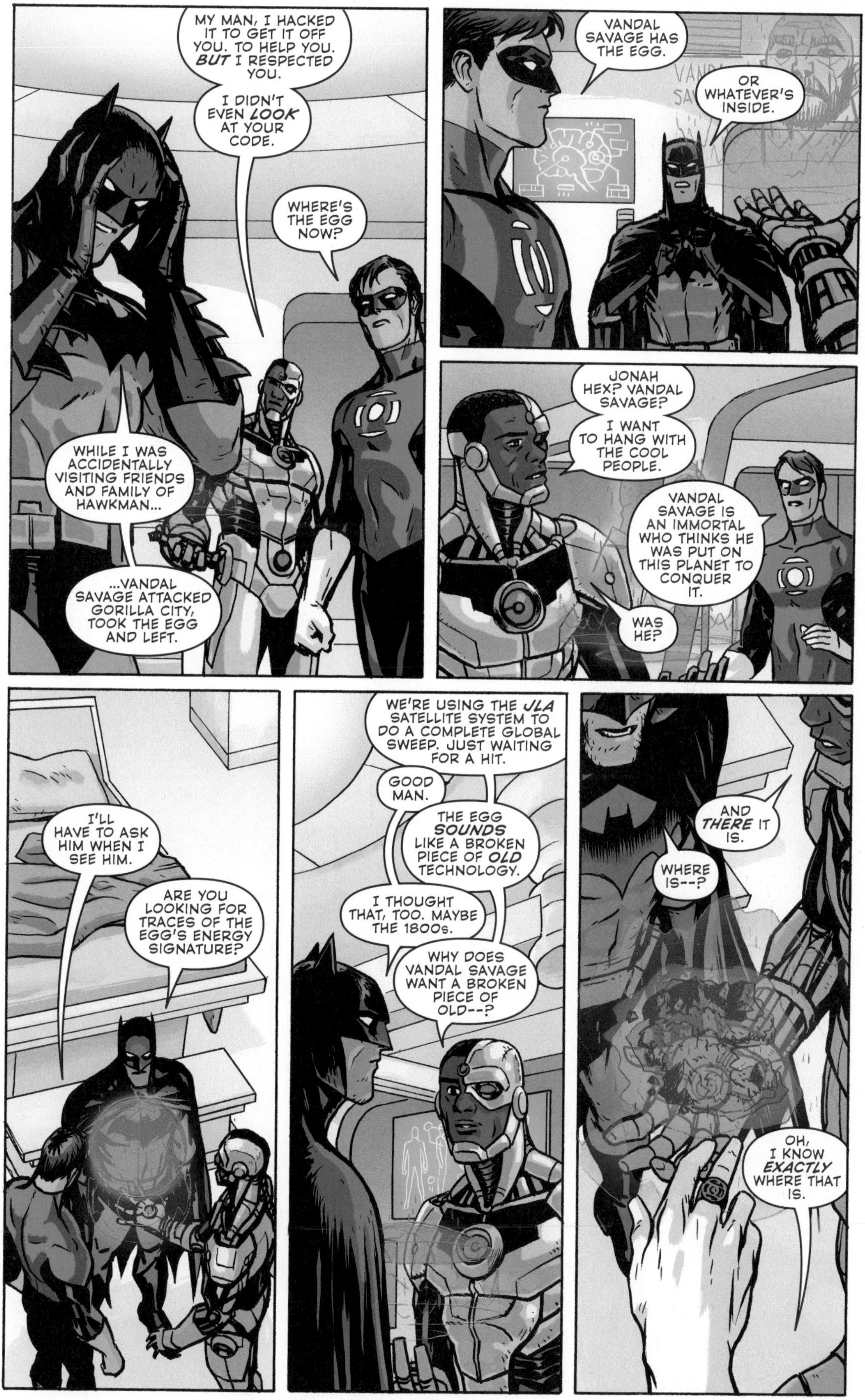
MY MAN, I HACKED IT TO GET IT OFF YOU. TO HELP YOU. BUT I RESPECTED YOU.
I DIDN'T EVEN LOOK AT YOUR CODE.
WHERE'S THE EGG NOW?
WHILE I WAS ACCIDENTALLY VISITING FRIENDS AND FAMILY OF HAWKMAN...
...VANDAL SAVAGE ATTACKED GORILLA CITY, TOOK THE EGG AND LEFT.
VANDAL SAVAGE HAS THE EGG.
OR WHATEVER'S INSIDE.
JONAH HEX? VANDAL SAVAGE?
I WANT TO HANG WITH THE COOL PEOPLE.
VANDAL SAVAGE IS AN IMMORTAL WHO THINKS HE WAS PUT ON THIS PLANET TO CONQUER IT.
WAS HE?
I'LL HAVE TO ASK HIM WHEN I SEE HIM.
ARE YOU LOOKING FOR TRACES OF THE EGG'S ENERGY SIGNATURE?
WE'RE USING THE JLA SATELLITE SYSTEM TO DO A COMPLETE GLOBAL SWEEP. JUST WAITING FOR A HIT.
GOOD MAN.
THE EGG SOUNDS LIKE A BROKEN PIECE OF OLD TECHNOLOGY.
I THOUGHT THAT, TOO. MAYBE THE 1800s.
WHY DOES VANDAL SAVAGE WANT A BROKEN PIECE OF OLD--?
AND THERE IT IS.
WHERE IS--?
OH, I KNOW EXACTLY WHERE THAT IS.

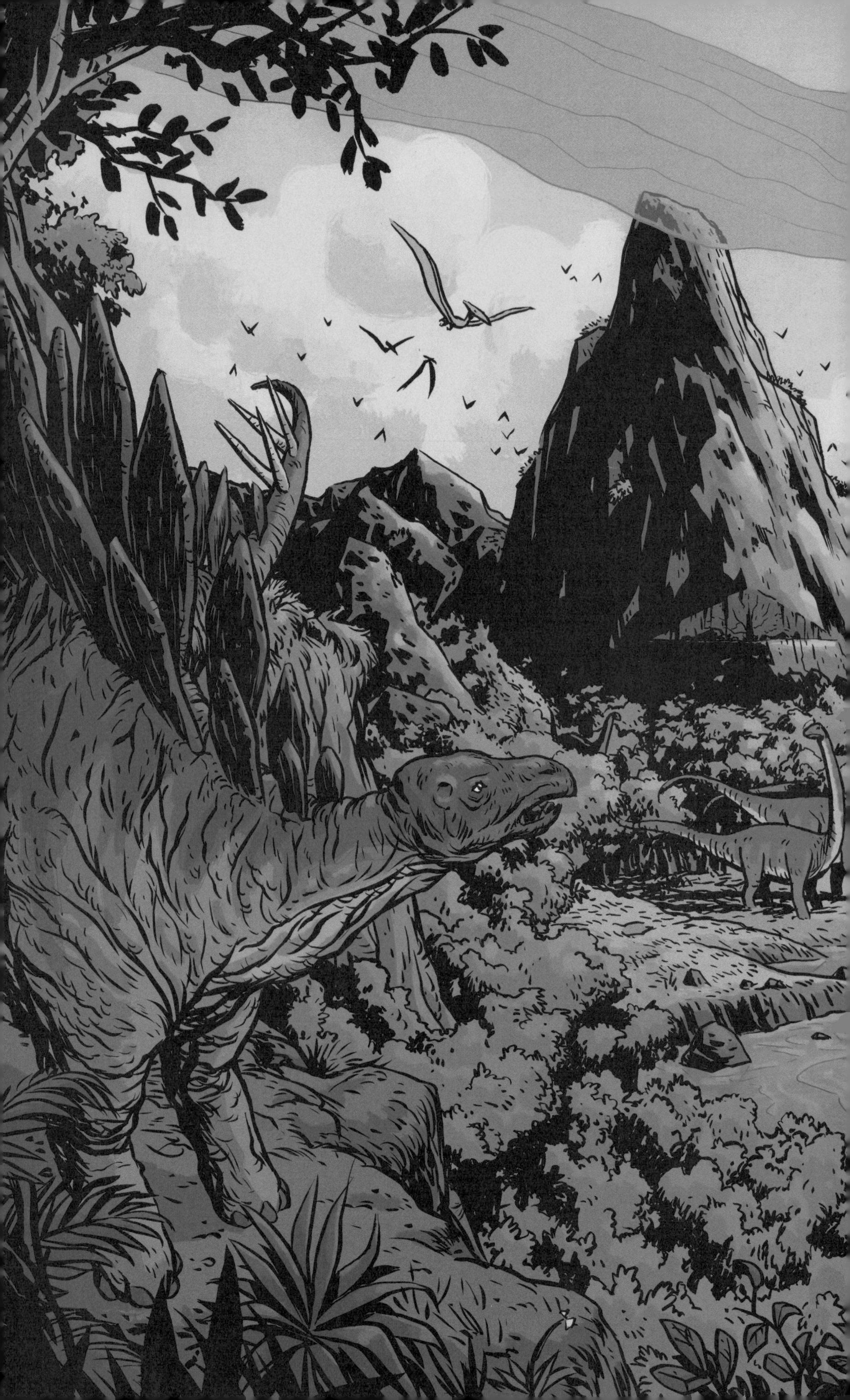

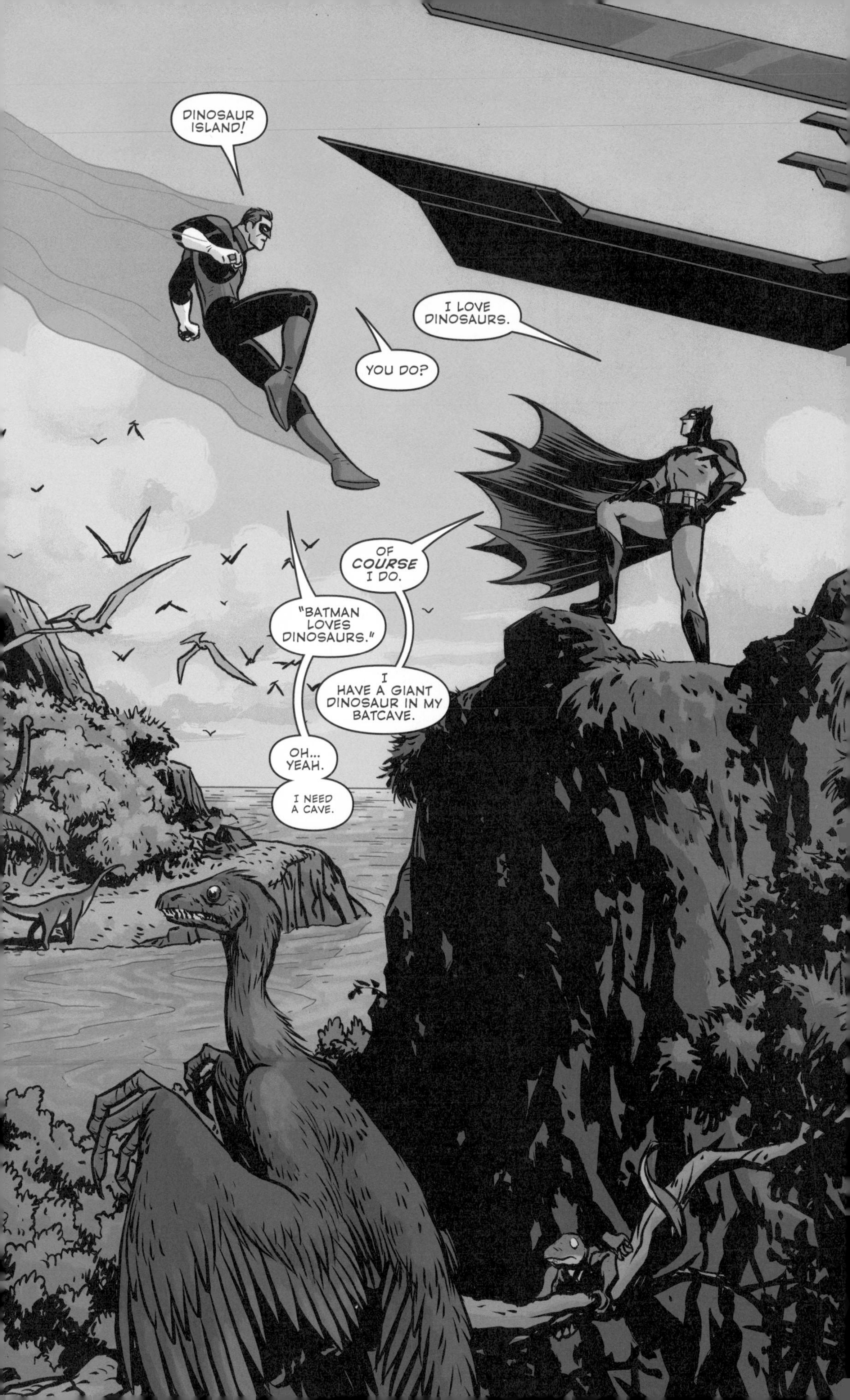
DINOSAUR ISLAND!
I LOVE DINOSAURS.
YOU DO?
OF COURSE I DO.
"BATMAN LOVES DINOSAURS."
I HAVE A GIANT DINOSAUR IN MY BATCAVE.
OH... YEAH.
I NEED A CAVE.

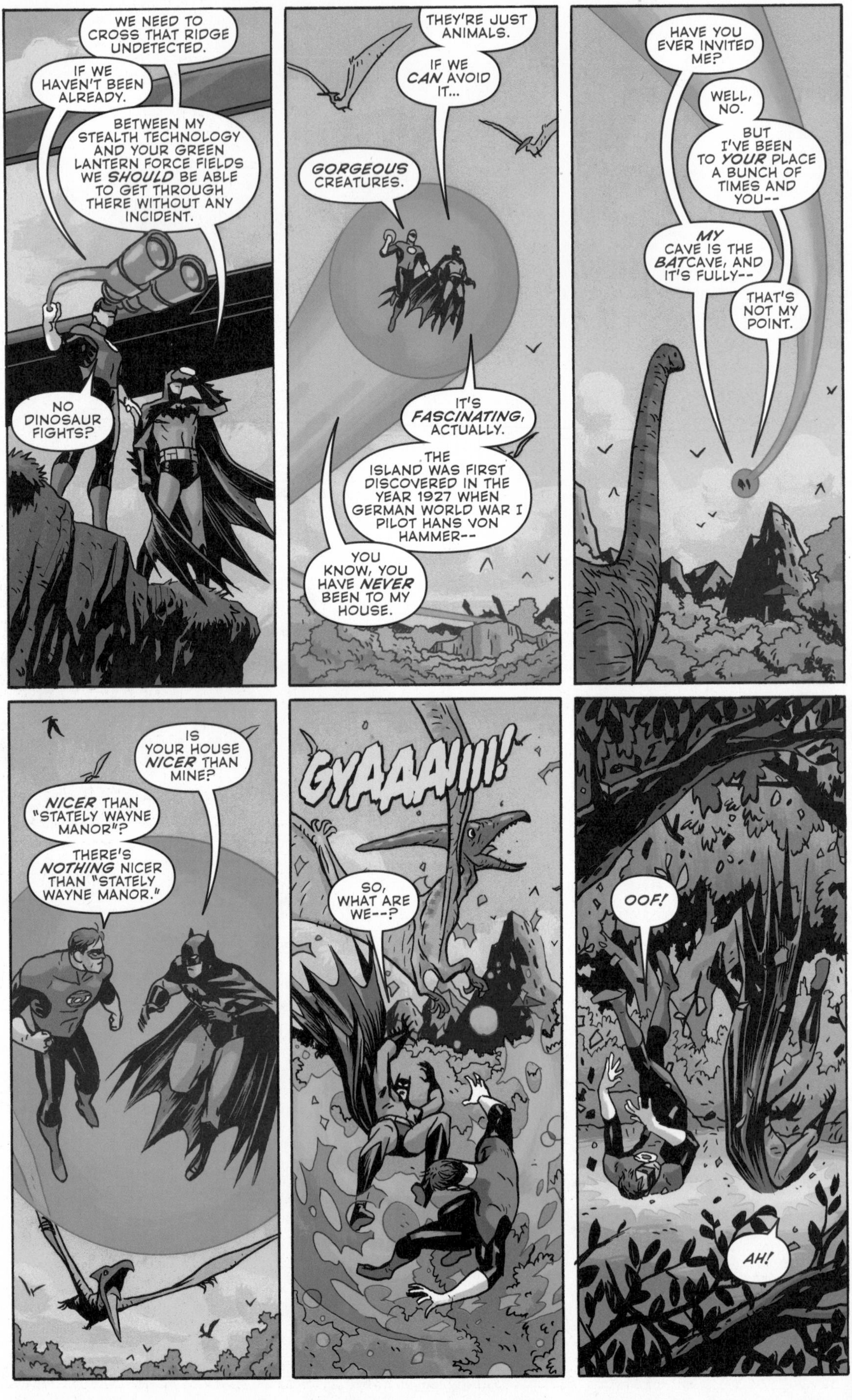

WE NEED TO CROSS THAT RIDGE UNDETECTED.
IF WE HAVEN'T BEEN ALREADY.
BETWEEN MY STEALTH TECHNOLOGY AND YOUR GREEN LANTERN FORCE FIELDS WE SHOULD BE ABLE TO GET THROUGH THERE WITHOUT ANY INCIDENT.
NO DINOSAUR FIGHTS?
THEY'RE JUST ANIMALS.
IF WE CAN AVOID IT...
GORGEOUS CREATURES.
IT'S FASCINATING, ACTUALLY.
THE ISLAND WAS FIRST DISCOVERED IN THE YEAR 1927 WHEN GERMAN WORLD WAR I PILOT HANS VON HAMMER--
YOU KNOW, YOU HAVE NEVER BEEN TO MY HOUSE.
HAVE YOU EVER INVITED ME?
WELL, NO.
BUT I'VE BEEN TO YOUR PLACE A BUNCH OF TIMES AND YOU--
MY CAVE IS THE BATCAVE, AND IT'S FULLY--
THAT'S NOT MY POINT.
IS YOUR HOUSE NICER THAN MINE?
NICER THAN "STATELY WAYNE MANOR"?
THERE'S NOTHING NICER THAN "STATELY WAYNE MANOR."
GYAAAIIII!
SO, WHAT ARE WE--?
OOF!
AH!

WHACK

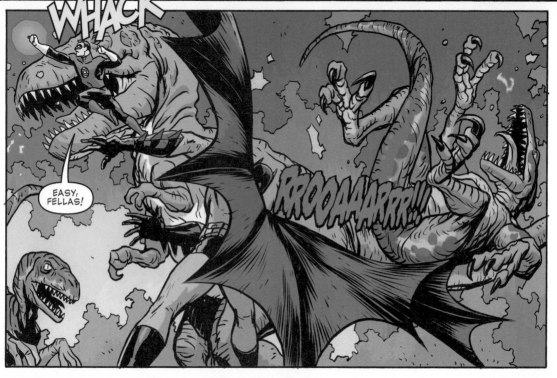

EASY, FELLAS!

IRROOAAARRR!!

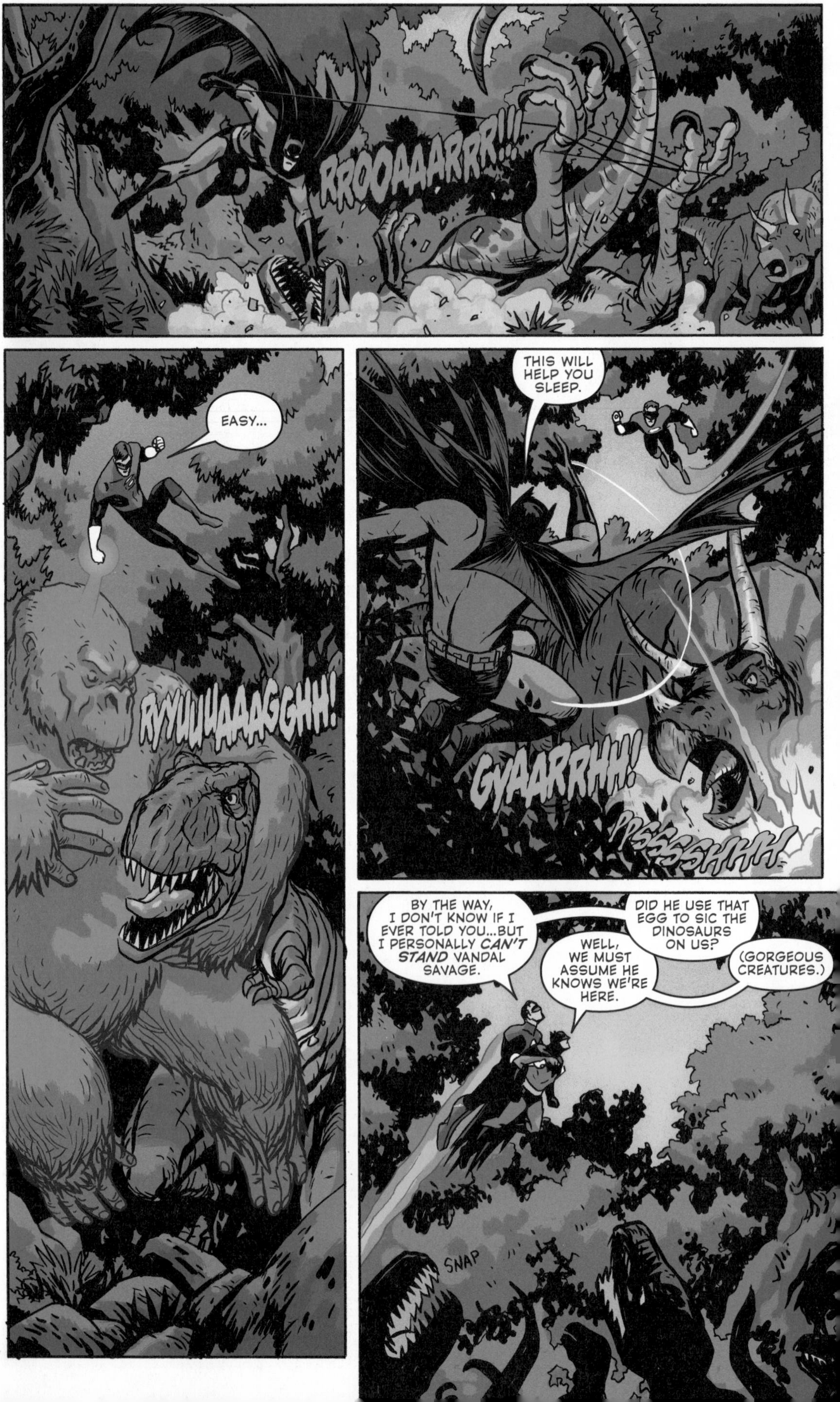

RROOAAARRR!!!
EASY...
RYYUUUAAAGGHH!
THIS WILL HELP YOU SLEEP.
GYAARRHH!
PSSSSHHH
BY THE WAY, I DON'T KNOW IF I EVER TOLD YOU...BUT I PERSONALLY *CAN'T STAND* VANDAL SAVAGE.
DID HE USE THAT EGG TO SIC THE DINOSAURS ON US?
WELL, WE MUST ASSUME HE KNOWS WE'RE HERE.
(GORGEOUS CREATURES.)
SNAP

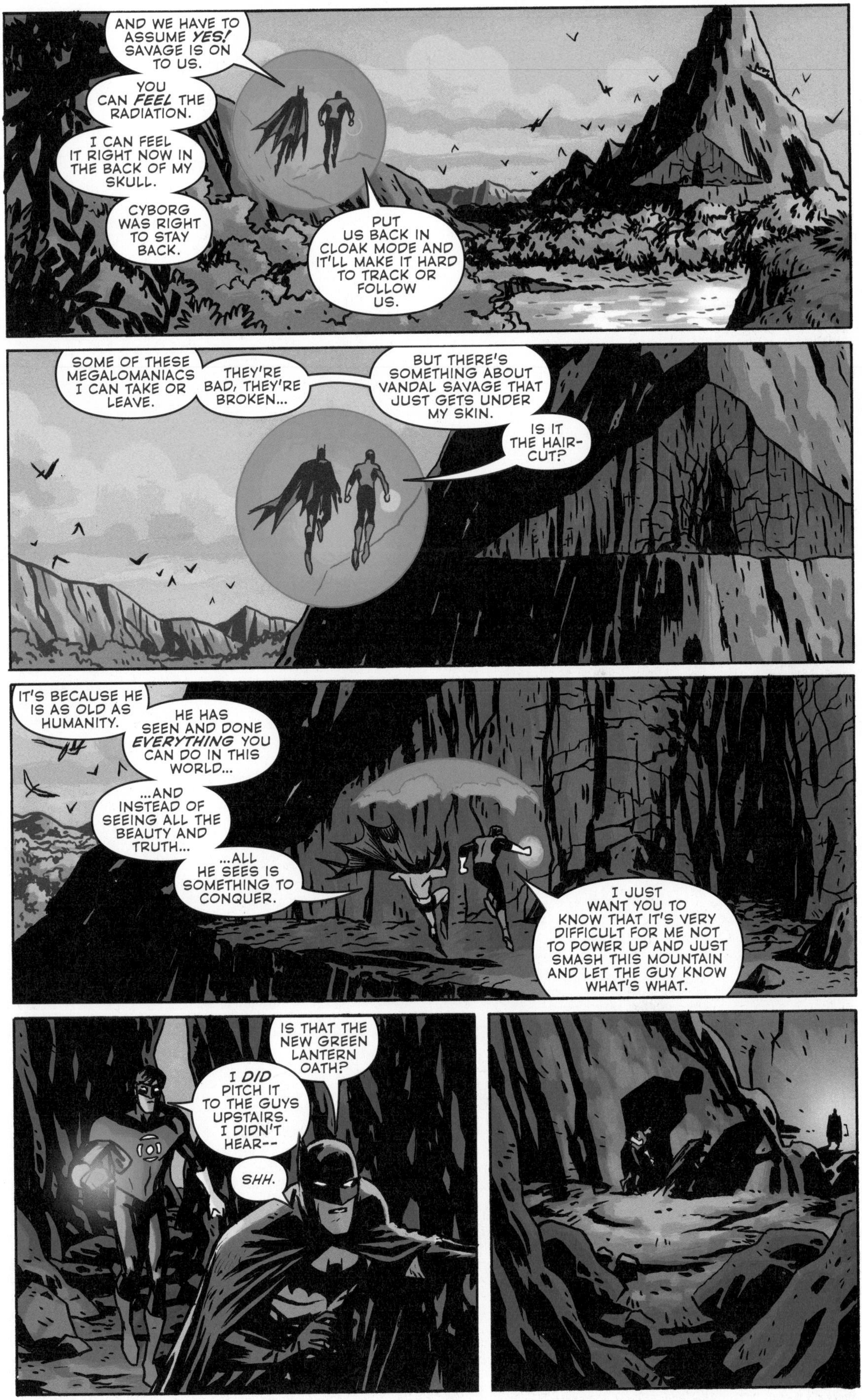
AND WE HAVE TO ASSUME YES! SAVAGE IS ON TO US.
YOU CAN FEEL THE RADIATION.
I CAN FEEL IT RIGHT NOW IN THE BACK OF MY SKULL.
CYBORG WAS RIGHT TO STAY BACK.
PUT US BACK IN CLOAK MODE AND IT'LL MAKE IT HARD TO TRACK OR FOLLOW US.
SOME OF THESE MEGALOMANIACS I CAN TAKE OR LEAVE.
THEY'RE BAD, THEY'RE BROKEN...
BUT THERE'S SOMETHING ABOUT VANDAL SAVAGE THAT JUST GETS UNDER MY SKIN.
IS IT THE HAIR-CUT?
IT'S BECAUSE HE IS AS OLD AS HUMANITY.
HE HAS SEEN AND DONE EVERYTHING YOU CAN DO IN THIS WORLD...
...AND INSTEAD OF SEEING ALL THE BEAUTY AND TRUTH...
...ALL HE SEES IS SOMETHING TO CONQUER.
I JUST WANT YOU TO KNOW THAT IT'S VERY DIFFICULT FOR ME NOT TO POWER UP AND JUST SMASH THIS MOUNTAIN AND LET THE GUY KNOW WHAT'S WHAT.
IS THAT THE NEW GREEN LANTERN OATH?
I DID PITCH IT TO THE GUYS UPSTAIRS. I DIDN'T HEAR--
SHH.

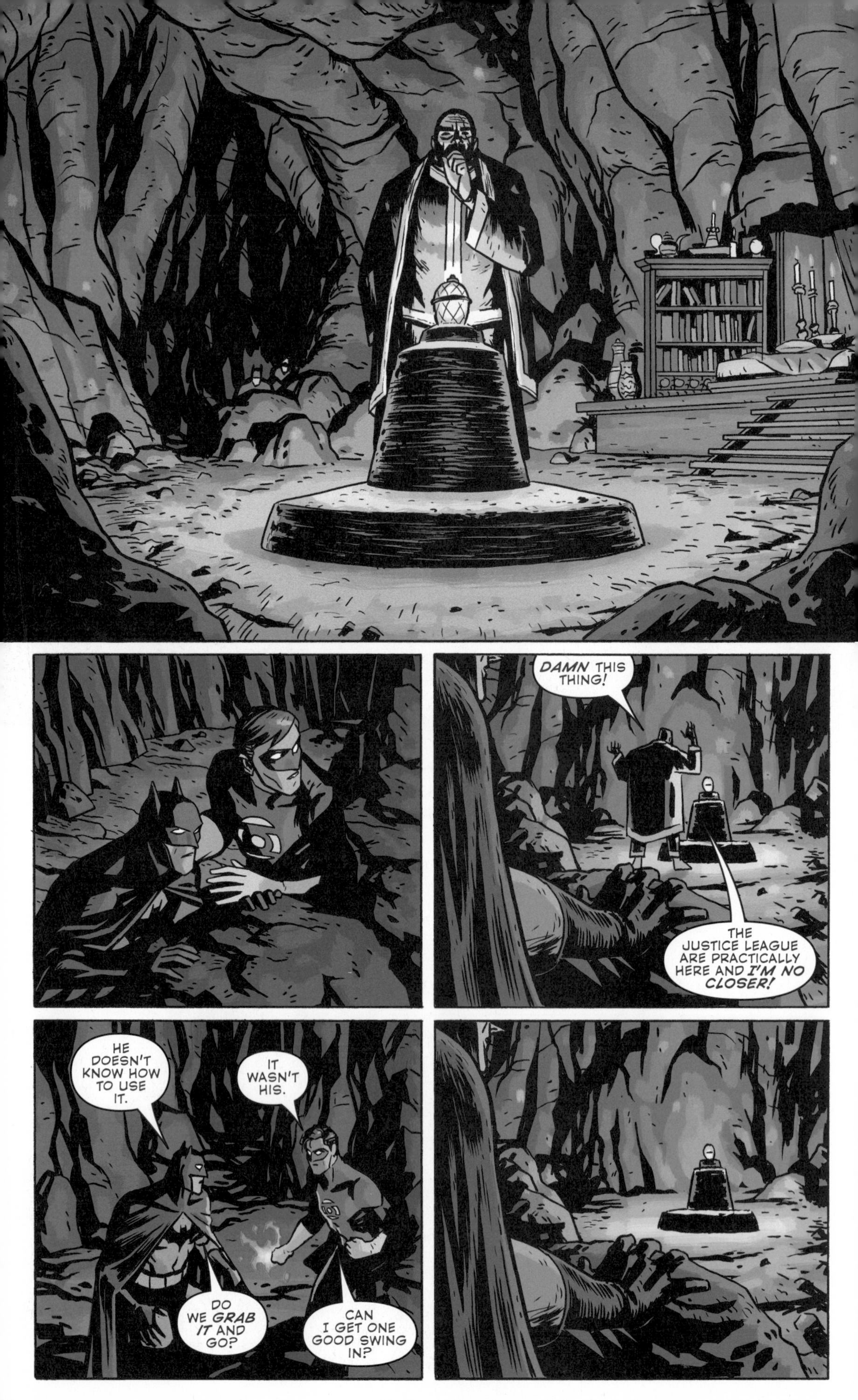
DAMN THIS THING!
THE JUSTICE LEAGUE ARE PRACTICALLY HERE AND I'M NO CLOSER!
HE DOESN'T KNOW HOW TO USE IT.
IT WASN'T HIS.
DO WE GRAB IT AND GO?
CAN I GET ONE GOOD SWING IN?

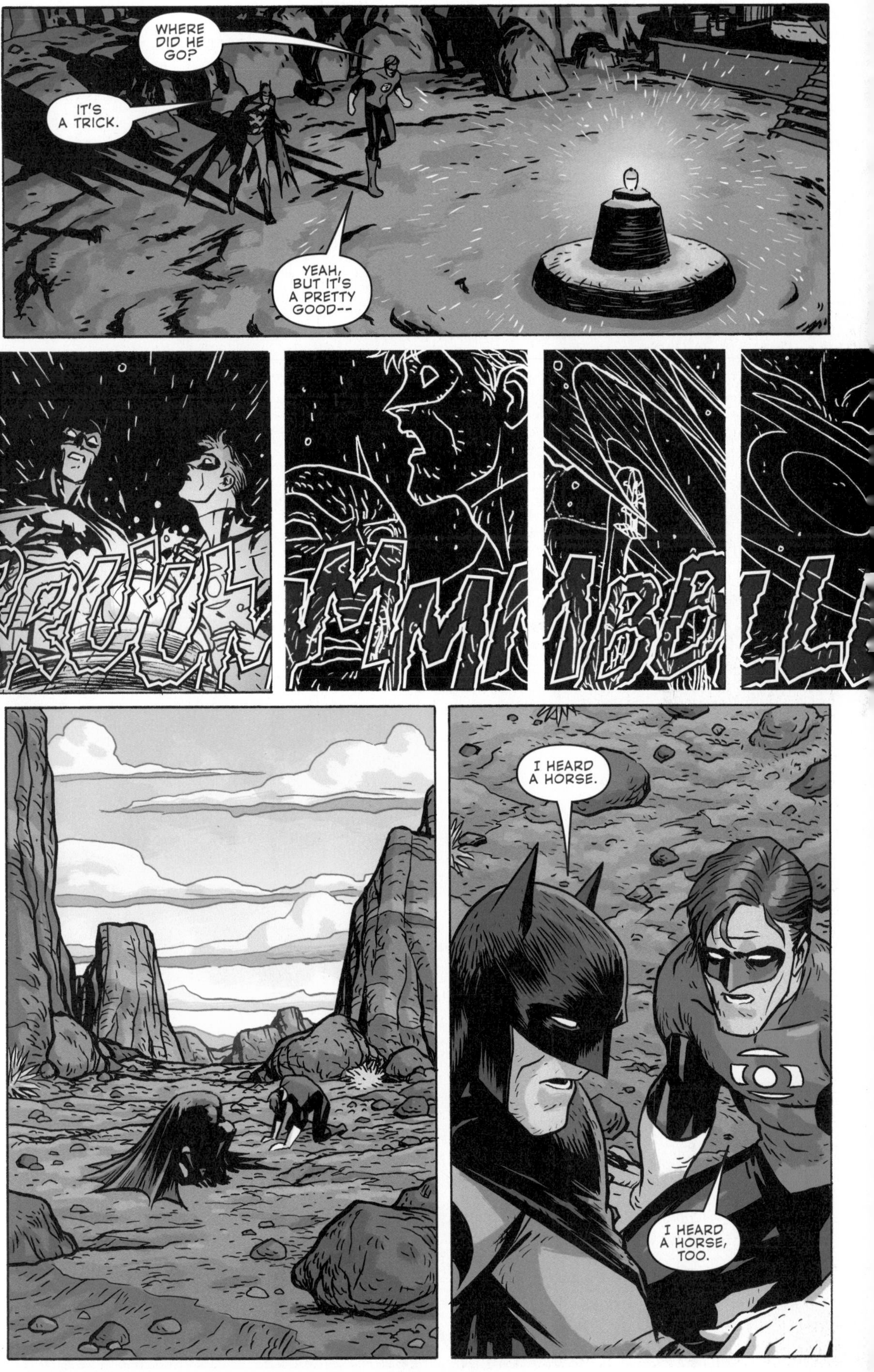
WHERE DID HE GO?
IT'S A TRICK.
YEAH, BUT IT'S A PRETTY GOOD--
I HEARD A HORSE.
I HEARD A HORSE, TOO.

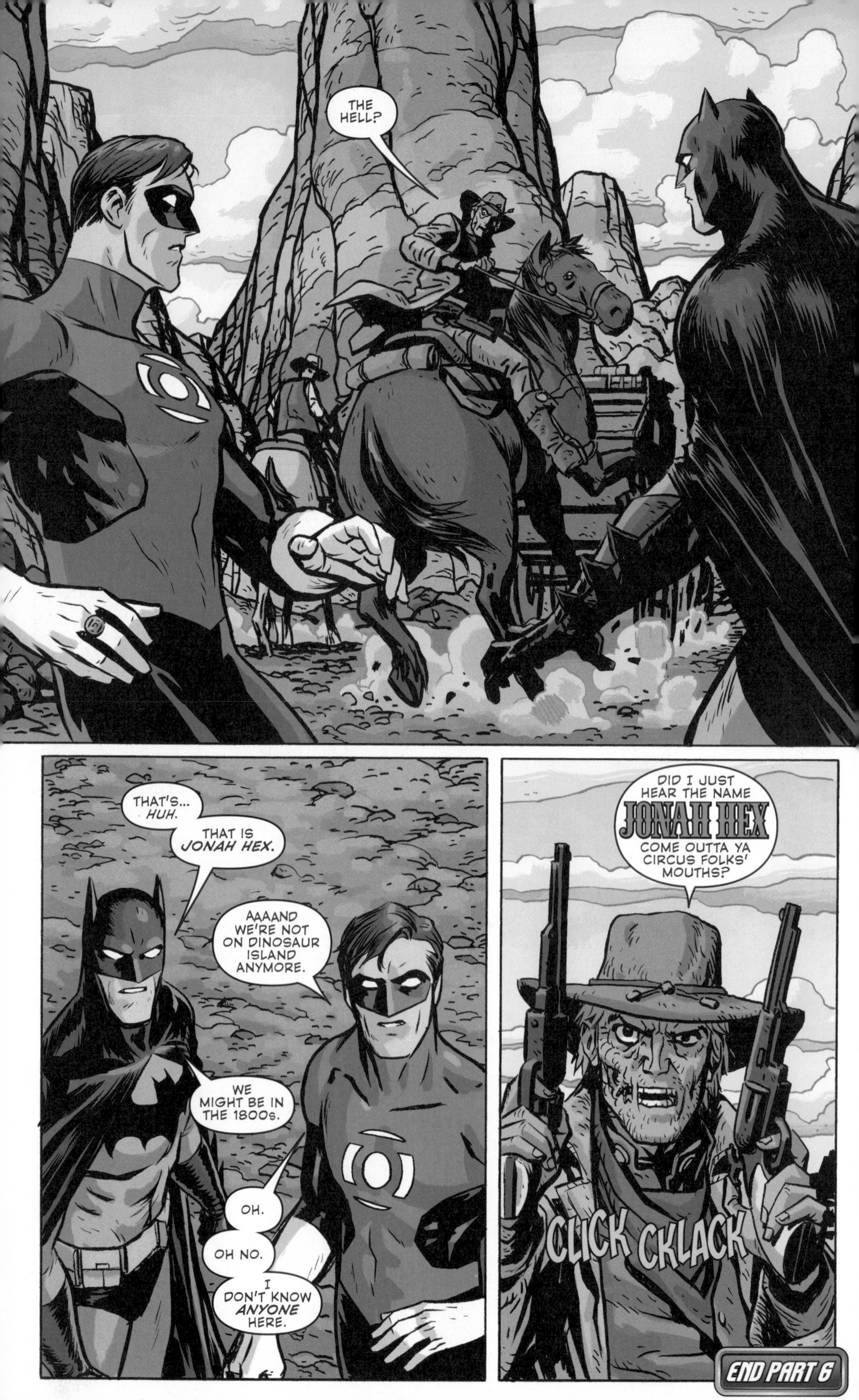
THE HELL?
THAT'S... *HUH.*
THAT IS *JONAH HEX.*
AAAAND WE'RE NOT ON DINOSAUR ISLAND ANYMORE.
WE MIGHT BE IN THE 1800s.
OH.
OH NO.
I DON'T KNOW *ANYONE* HERE.
DID I JUST HEAR THE NAME JONAH HEX COME OUTTA YA CIRCUS FOLKS' MOUTHS?
CLICK CKLACK
END PART 6

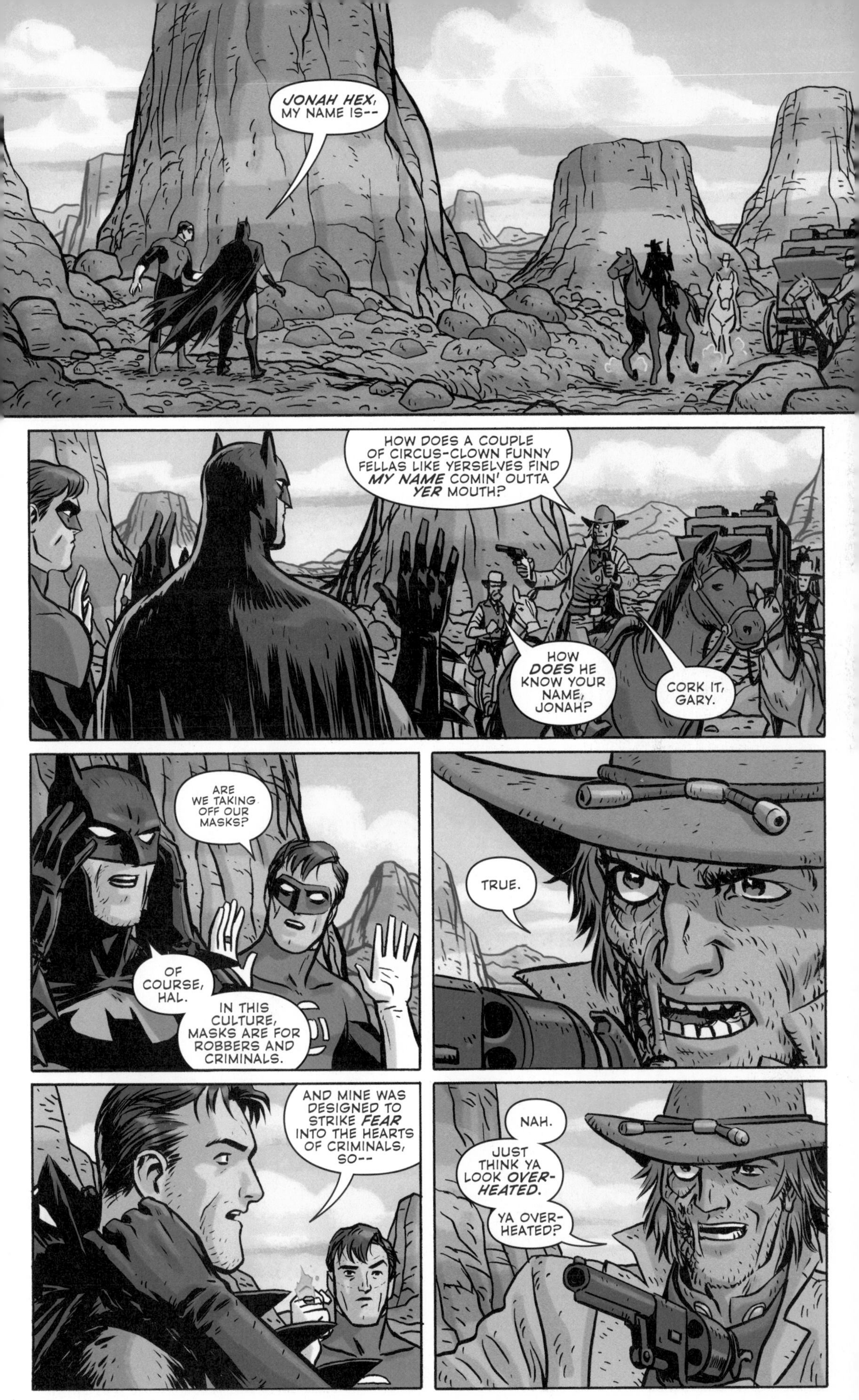
JONAH HEX, MY NAME IS--
HOW DOES A COUPLE OF CIRCUS-CLOWN FUNNY FELLAS LIKE YERSELVES FIND MY NAME COMIN' OUTTA YER MOUTH?
HOW DOES HE KNOW YOUR NAME, JONAH?
CORK IT, GARY.
ARE WE TAKING OFF OUR MASKS?
OF COURSE, HAL.
IN THIS CULTURE, MASKS ARE FOR ROBBERS AND CRIMINALS.
TRUE.
AND MINE WAS DESIGNED TO STRIKE FEAR INTO THE HEARTS OF CRIMINALS, SO--
NAH.
JUST THINK YA LOOK OVER-HEATED.
YA OVER-HEATED?

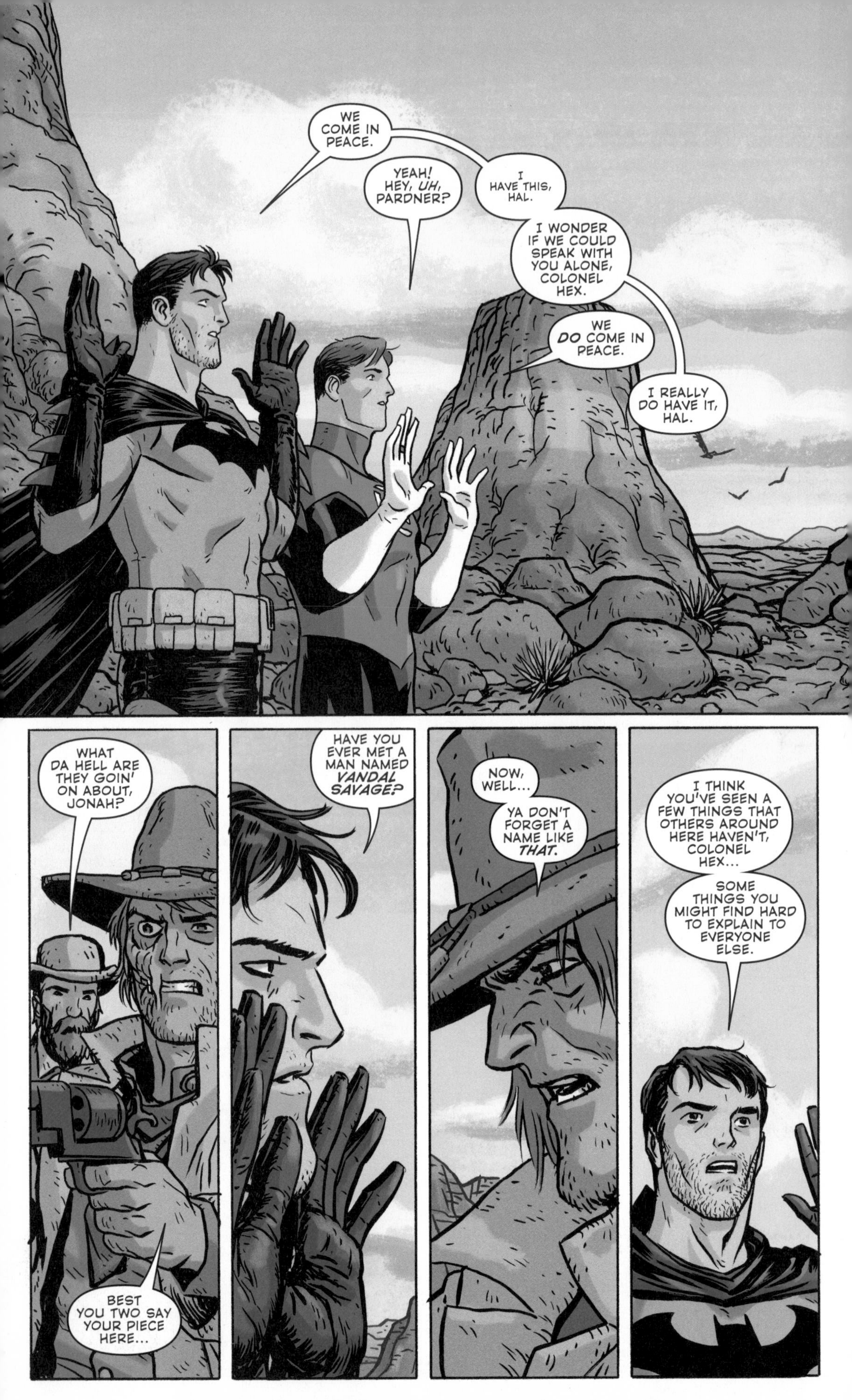
WE COME IN PEACE.
YEAH! HEY, UH, PARDNER?
I HAVE THIS, HAL.
I WONDER IF WE COULD SPEAK WITH YOU ALONE, COLONEL HEX.
WE DO COME IN PEACE.
I REALLY DO HAVE IT, HAL.
WHAT DA HELL ARE THEY GOIN' ON ABOUT, JONAH?
BEST YOU TWO SAY YOUR PIECE HERE...
HAVE YOU EVER MET A MAN NAMED VANDAL SAVAGE?
NOW, WELL...
YA DON'T FORGET A NAME LIKE THAT.
I THINK YOU'VE SEEN A FEW THINGS THAT OTHERS AROUND HERE HAVEN'T, COLONEL HEX...
SOME THINGS YOU MIGHT FIND HARD TO EXPLAIN TO EVERYONE ELSE.

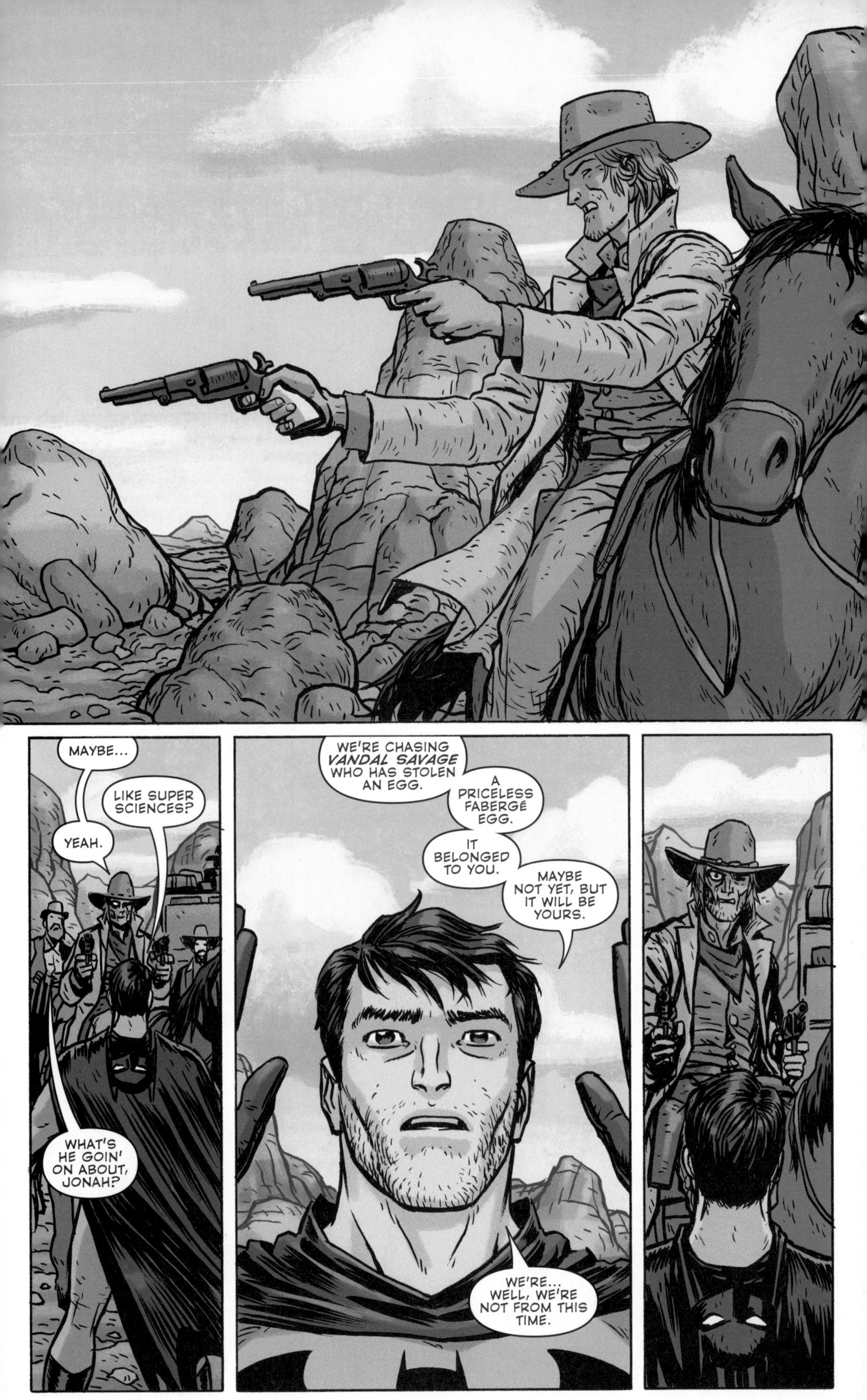
MAYBE...
LIKE SUPER SCIENCES?
YEAH.
WHAT'S HE GOIN' ON ABOUT, JONAH?
WE'RE CHASING *VANDAL SAVAGE* WHO HAS STOLEN AN EGG.
A PRICELESS FABERGÉ EGG.
IT BELONGED TO YOU.
MAYBE NOT YET, BUT IT WILL BE YOURS.
WE'RE... WELL, WE'RE NOT FROM THIS TIME.

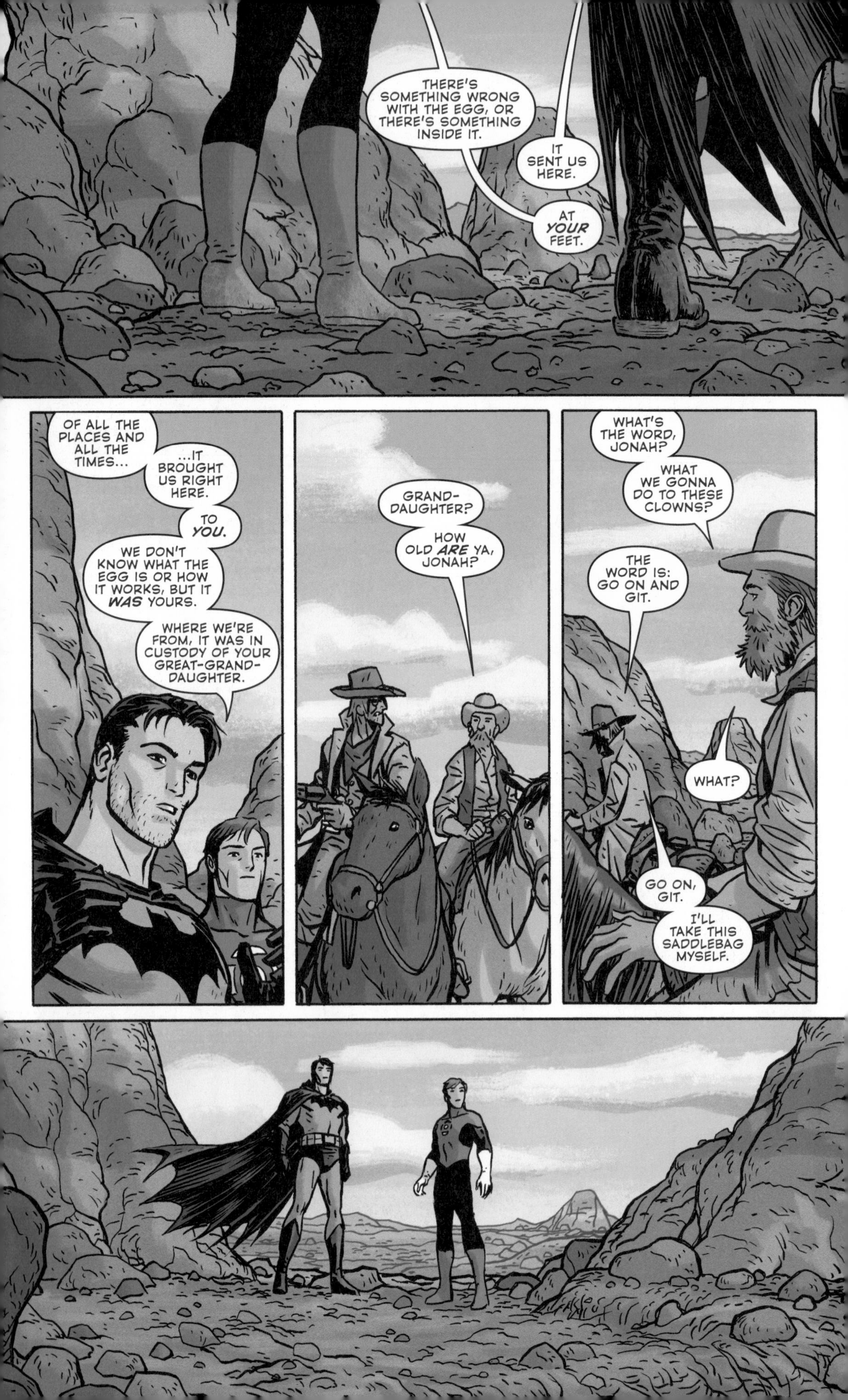

THERE'S SOMETHING WRONG WITH THE EGG, OR THERE'S SOMETHING INSIDE IT.
IT SENT US HERE.
AT YOUR FEET.
OF ALL THE PLACES AND ALL THE TIMES...
...IT BROUGHT US RIGHT HERE.
TO YOU.
WE DON'T KNOW WHAT THE EGG IS OR HOW IT WORKS, BUT IT WAS YOURS.
WHERE WE'RE FROM, IT WAS IN CUSTODY OF YOUR GREAT-GRAND-DAUGHTER.
GRAND-DAUGHTER?
HOW OLD ARE YA, JONAH?
WHAT'S THE WORD, JONAH?
WHAT WE GONNA DO TO THESE CLOWNS?
THE WORD IS: GO ON AND GIT.
WHAT?
GO ON, GIT.
I'LL TAKE THIS SADDLEBAG MYSELF.

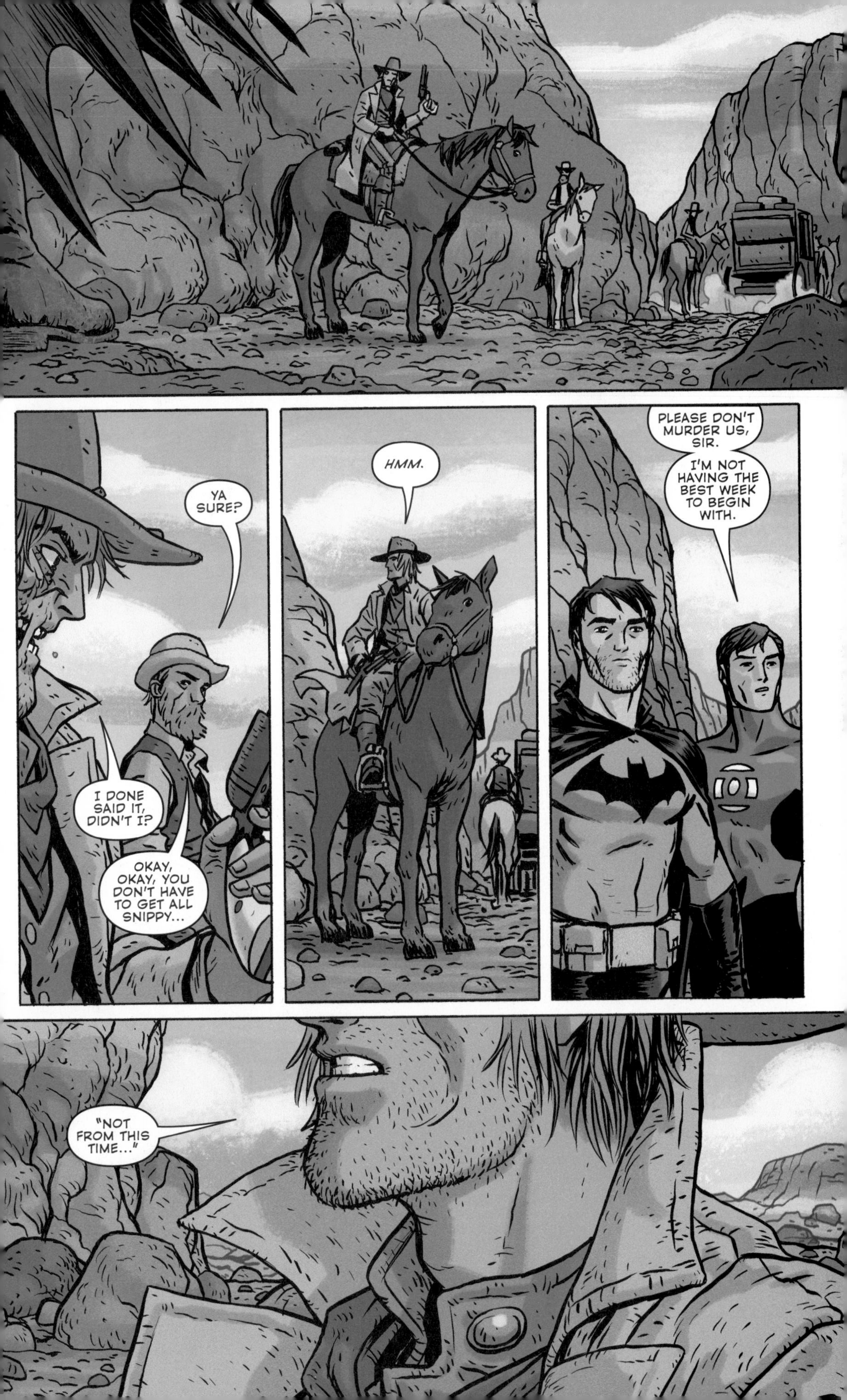
YA SURE?
I DONE SAID IT, DIDN'T I?
OKAY, OKAY, YOU DON'T HAVE TO GET ALL SNIPPY...
HMM.
PLEASE DON'T MURDER US, SIR.
I'M NOT HAVING THE BEST WEEK TO BEGIN WITH.
"NOT FROM THIS TIME..."

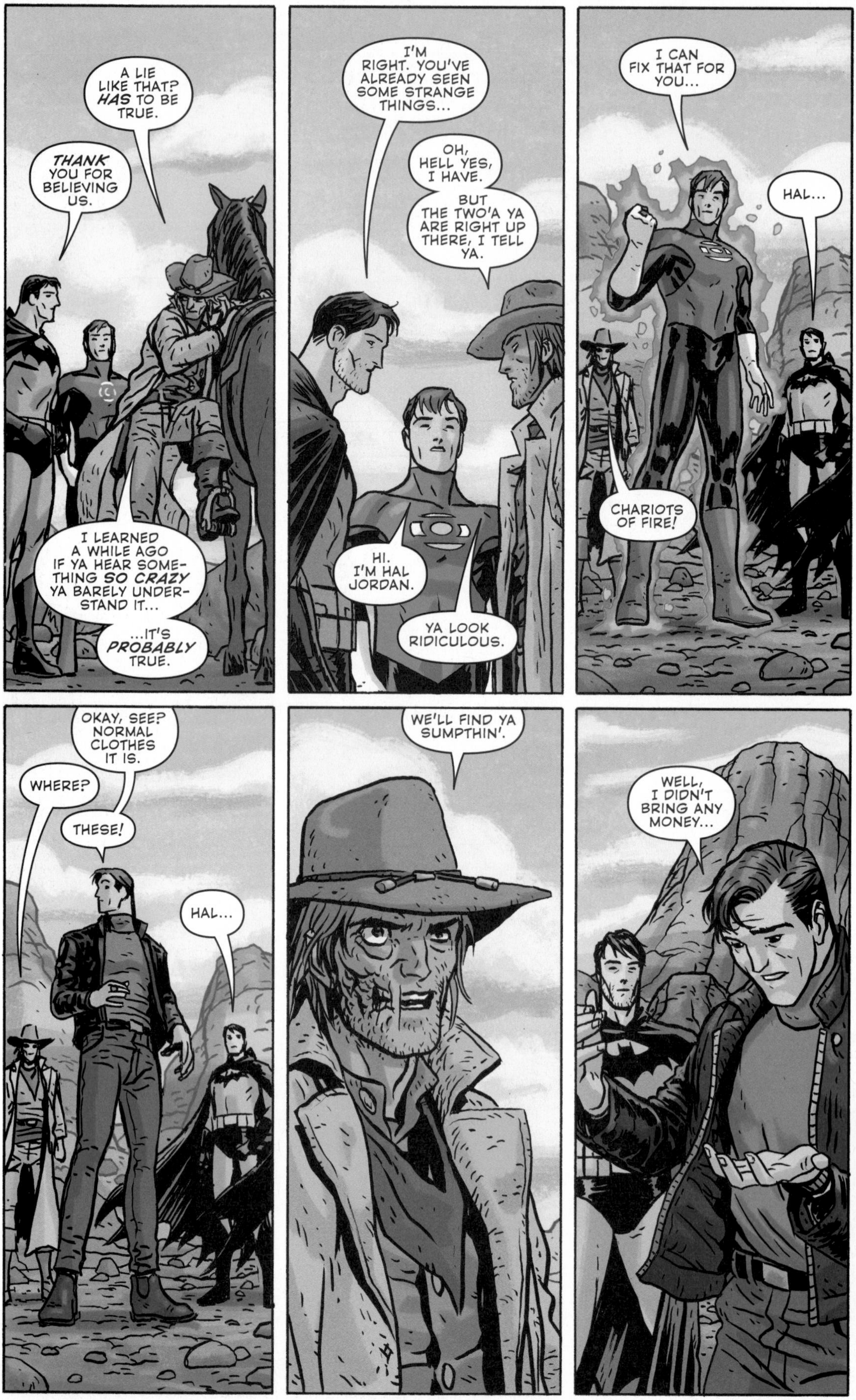
A LIE LIKE THAT? HAS TO BE TRUE.
THANK YOU FOR BELIEVING US.
I LEARNED A WHILE AGO IF YA HEAR SOMETHING SO CRAZY YA BARELY UNDERSTAND IT...
...IT'S PROBABLY TRUE.
I'M RIGHT. YOU'VE ALREADY SEEN SOME STRANGE THINGS...
OH, HELL YES, I HAVE.
BUT THE TWO'A YA ARE RIGHT UP THERE, I TELL YA.
HI. I'M HAL JORDAN.
YA LOOK RIDICULOUS.
I CAN FIX THAT FOR YOU...
HAL...
CHARIOTS OF FIRE!
OKAY, SEE? NORMAL CLOTHES IT IS.
WHERE?
THESE!
HAL...
WE'LL FIND YA SUMPTHIN'.
WELL, I DIDN'T BRING ANY MONEY...

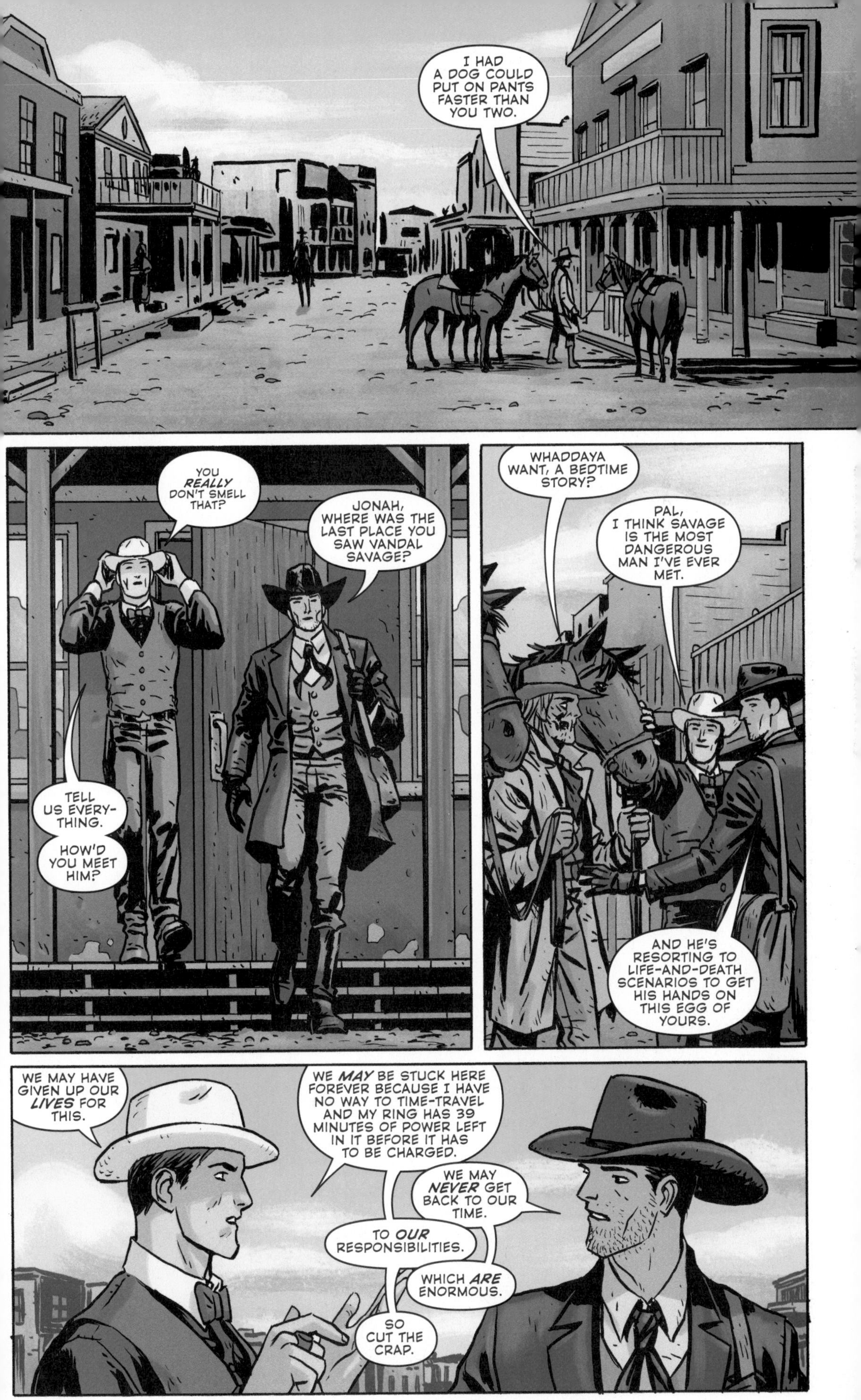
I HAD A DOG COULD PUT ON PANTS FASTER THAN YOU TWO.
YOU *REALLY* DON'T SMELL THAT?
JONAH, WHERE WAS THE LAST PLACE YOU SAW VANDAL SAVAGE?
TELL US EVERY-THING.
HOW'D YOU MEET HIM?
WHADDAYA WANT, A BEDTIME STORY?
PAL, I THINK SAVAGE IS THE MOST DANGEROUS MAN I'VE EVER MET.
AND HE'S RESORTING TO LIFE-AND-DEATH SCENARIOS TO GET HIS HANDS ON THIS EGG OF YOURS.
WE MAY HAVE GIVEN UP OUR *LIVES* FOR THIS.
WE *MAY* BE STUCK HERE FOREVER BECAUSE I HAVE NO WAY TO TIME-TRAVEL AND MY RING HAS 39 MINUTES OF POWER LEFT IN IT BEFORE IT HAS TO BE CHARGED.
WE MAY *NEVER* GET BACK TO OUR TIME.
TO *OUR* RESPONSIBILITIES.
WHICH *ARE* ENORMOUS.
SO CUT THE CRAP.

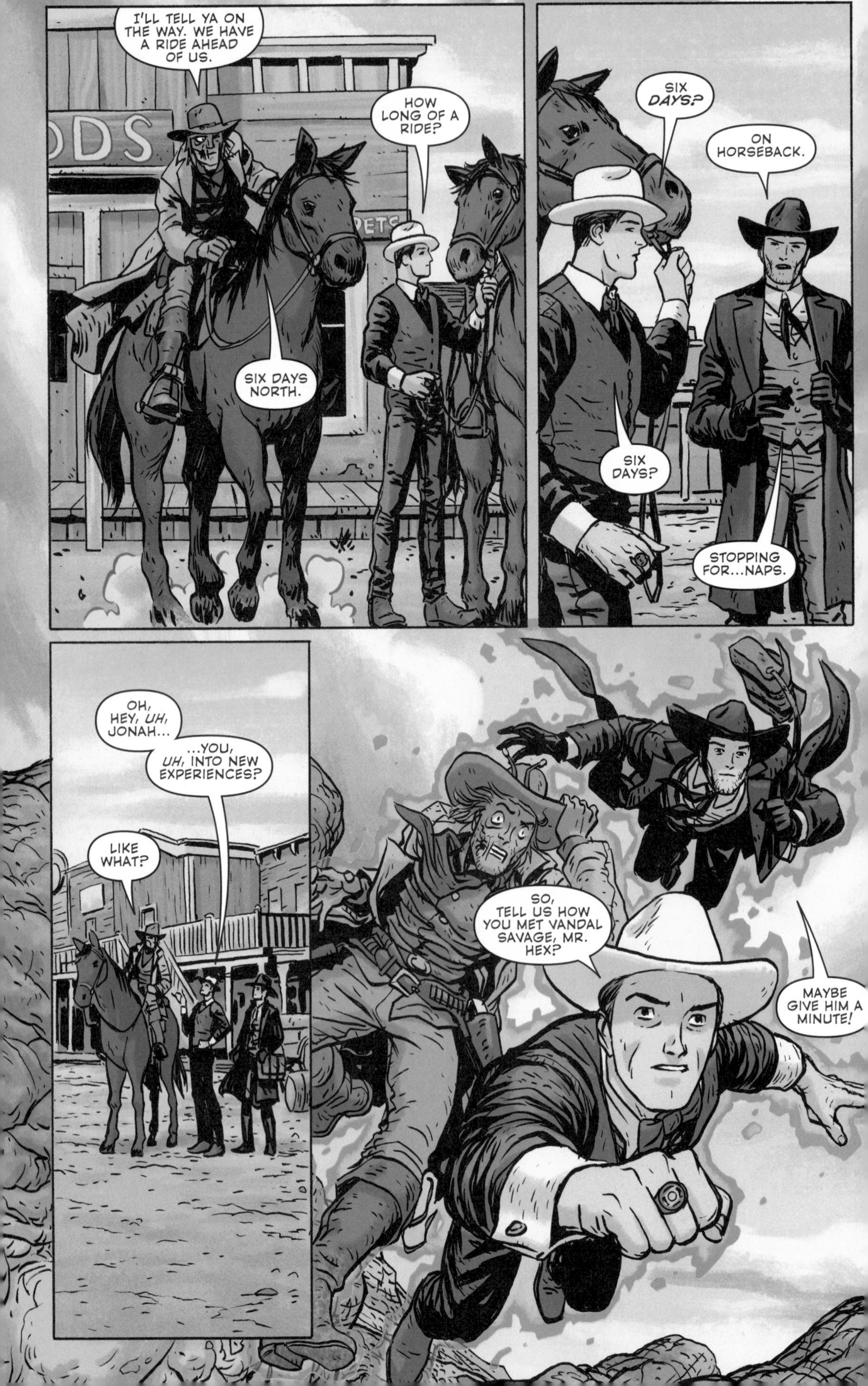

I'LL TELL YA ON THE WAY. WE HAVE A RIDE AHEAD OF US.
HOW LONG OF A RIDE?
SIX DAYS NORTH.
SIX *DAYS?*
ON HORSEBACK.
SIX DAYS?
STOPPING FOR...NAPS.
OH, HEY, *UH,* JONAH...
...YOU, *UH,* INTO NEW EXPERIENCES?
LIKE WHAT?
SO, TELL US HOW YOU MET VANDAL SAVAGE, MR. HEX?
MAYBE GIVE HIM A MINUTE!

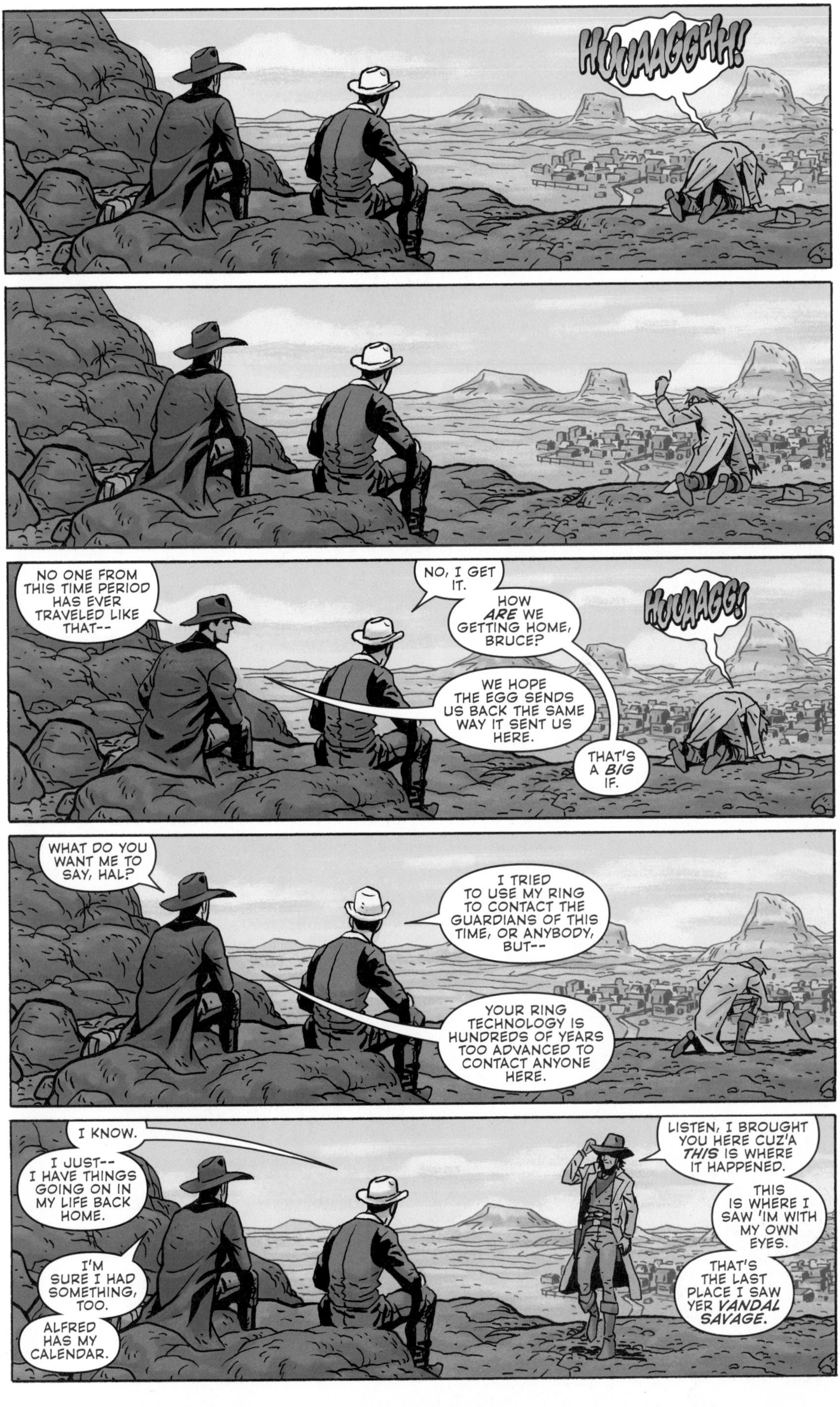
HUUAAGGHH!
NO ONE FROM THIS TIME PERIOD HAS EVER TRAVELED LIKE THAT--
NO, I GET IT.
HOW *ARE* WE GETTING HOME, BRUCE?
HUUAAGG!
WE HOPE THE EGG SENDS US BACK THE SAME WAY IT SENT US HERE.
THAT'S A *BIG* IF.
WHAT DO YOU WANT ME TO SAY, HAL?
I TRIED TO USE MY RING TO CONTACT THE GUARDIANS OF THIS TIME, OR ANYBODY, BUT--
YOUR RING TECHNOLOGY IS HUNDREDS OF YEARS TOO ADVANCED TO CONTACT ANYONE HERE.
I KNOW.
I JUST-- I HAVE THINGS GOING ON IN MY LIFE BACK HOME.
I'M SURE I HAD SOMETHING, TOO.
ALFRED HAS MY CALENDAR.
LISTEN, I BROUGHT YOU HERE CUZ'A *THIS* IS WHERE IT HAPPENED.
THIS IS WHERE I SAW 'IM WITH MY OWN EYES.
THAT'S THE LAST PLACE I SAW YER *VANDAL SAVAGE.*

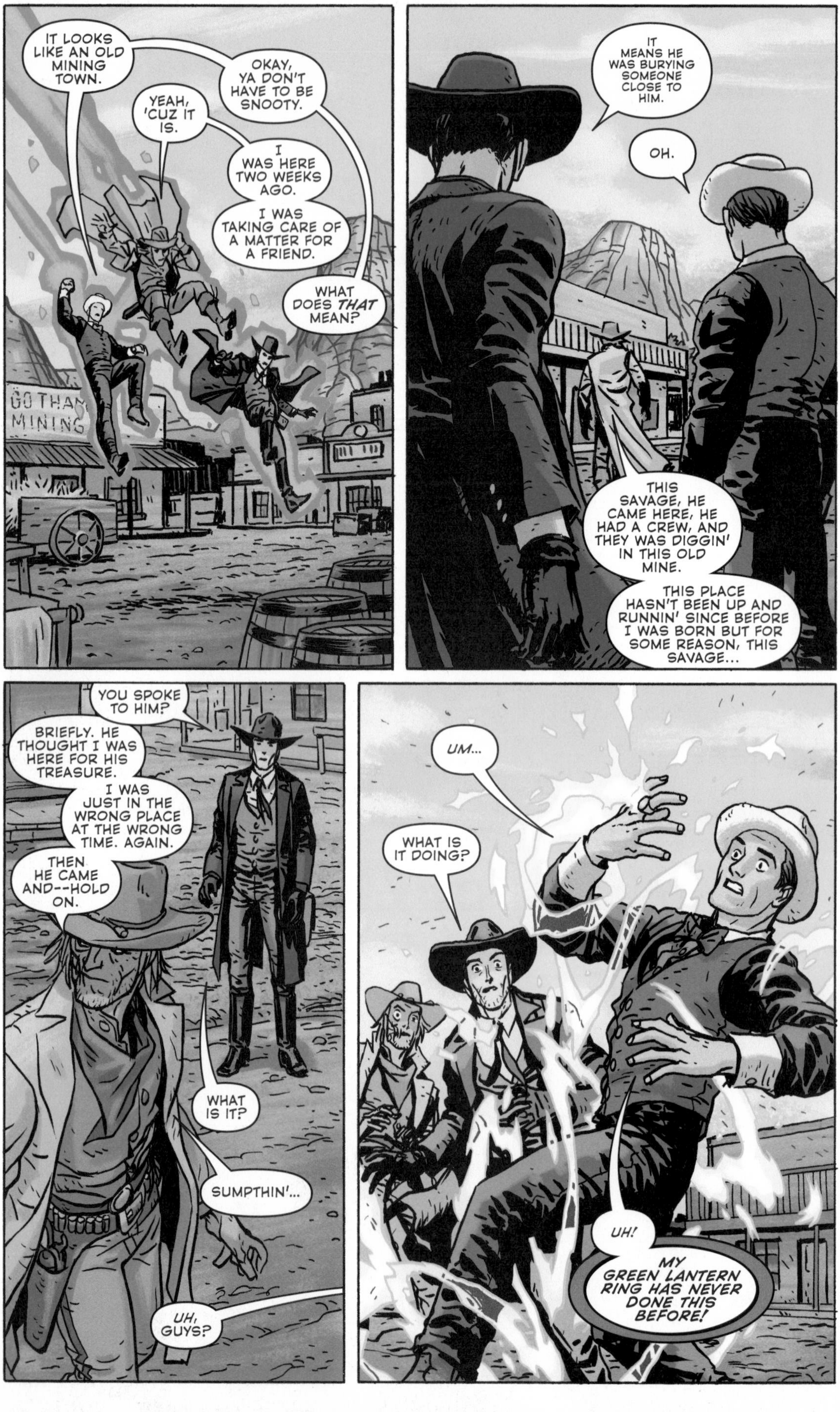
IT LOOKS LIKE AN OLD MINING TOWN.
OKAY, YA DON'T HAVE TO BE SNOOTY.
YEAH, 'CUZ IT IS.
I WAS HERE TWO WEEKS AGO.
I WAS TAKING CARE OF A MATTER FOR A FRIEND.
WHAT DOES *THAT* MEAN?
GOTHAM MINING
IT MEANS HE WAS BURYING SOMEONE CLOSE TO HIM.
OH.
THIS SAVAGE, HE CAME HERE, HE HAD A CREW, AND THEY WAS DIGGIN' IN THIS OLD MINE.
THIS PLACE HASN'T BEEN UP AND RUNNIN' SINCE BEFORE I WAS BORN BUT FOR SOME REASON, THIS SAVAGE...
YOU SPOKE TO HIM?
BRIEFLY. HE THOUGHT I WAS HERE FOR HIS TREASURE.
I WAS JUST IN THE WRONG PLACE AT THE WRONG TIME. AGAIN.
THEN HE CAME AND--HOLD ON.
WHAT IS IT?
SUMPTHIN'...
UH, GUYS?
UM...
WHAT IS IT DOING?
UH!
MY GREEN LANTERN RING HAS NEVER DONE THIS BEFORE!

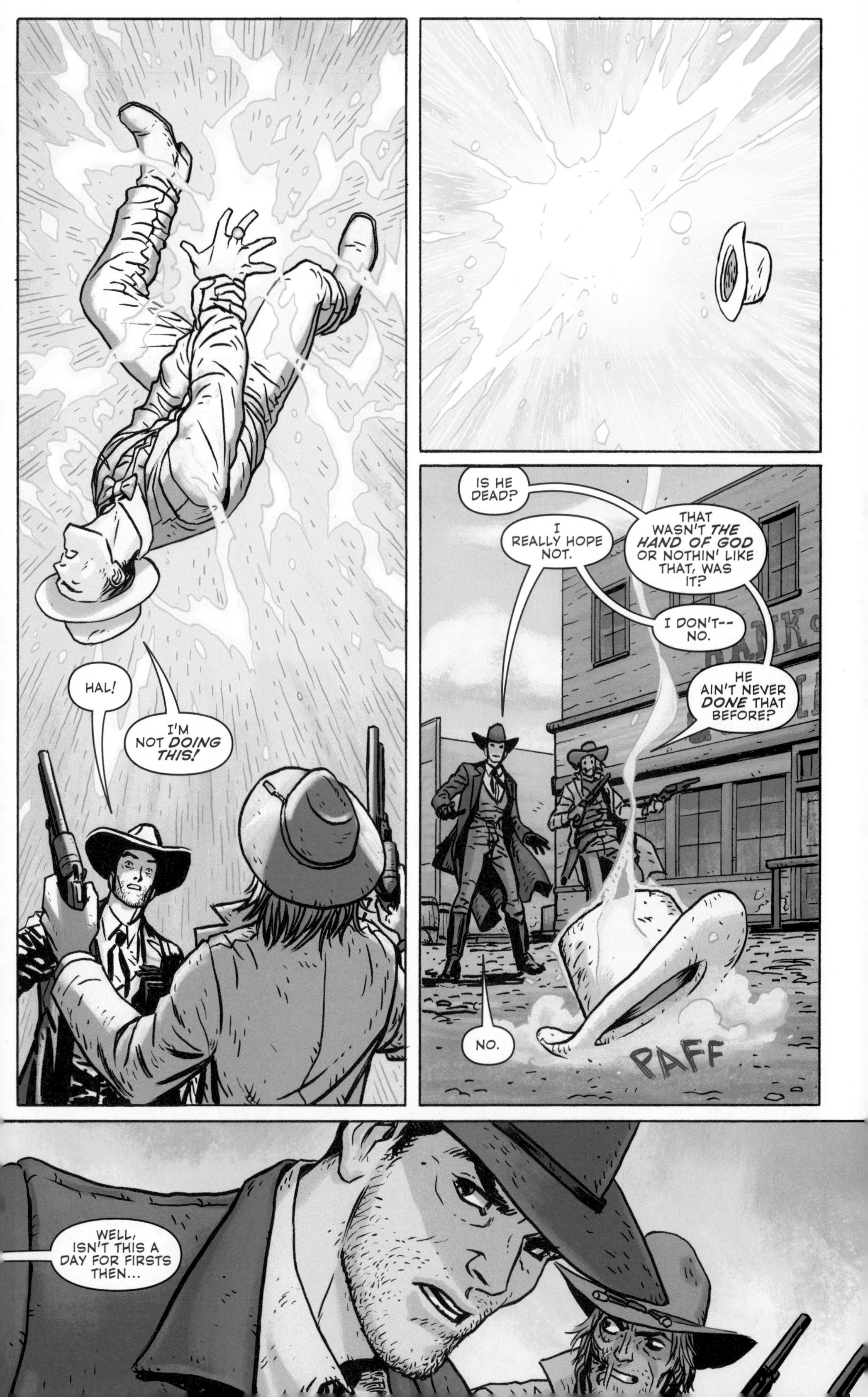
HAL!
I'M NOT DOING THIS!
IS HE DEAD?
I REALLY HOPE NOT.
THAT WASN'T THE HAND OF GOD OR NOTHIN' LIKE THAT, WAS IT?
I DON'T-- NO.
HE AIN'T NEVER DONE THAT BEFORE?
NO.
PAFF
WELL, ISN'T THIS A DAY FOR FIRSTS THEN...

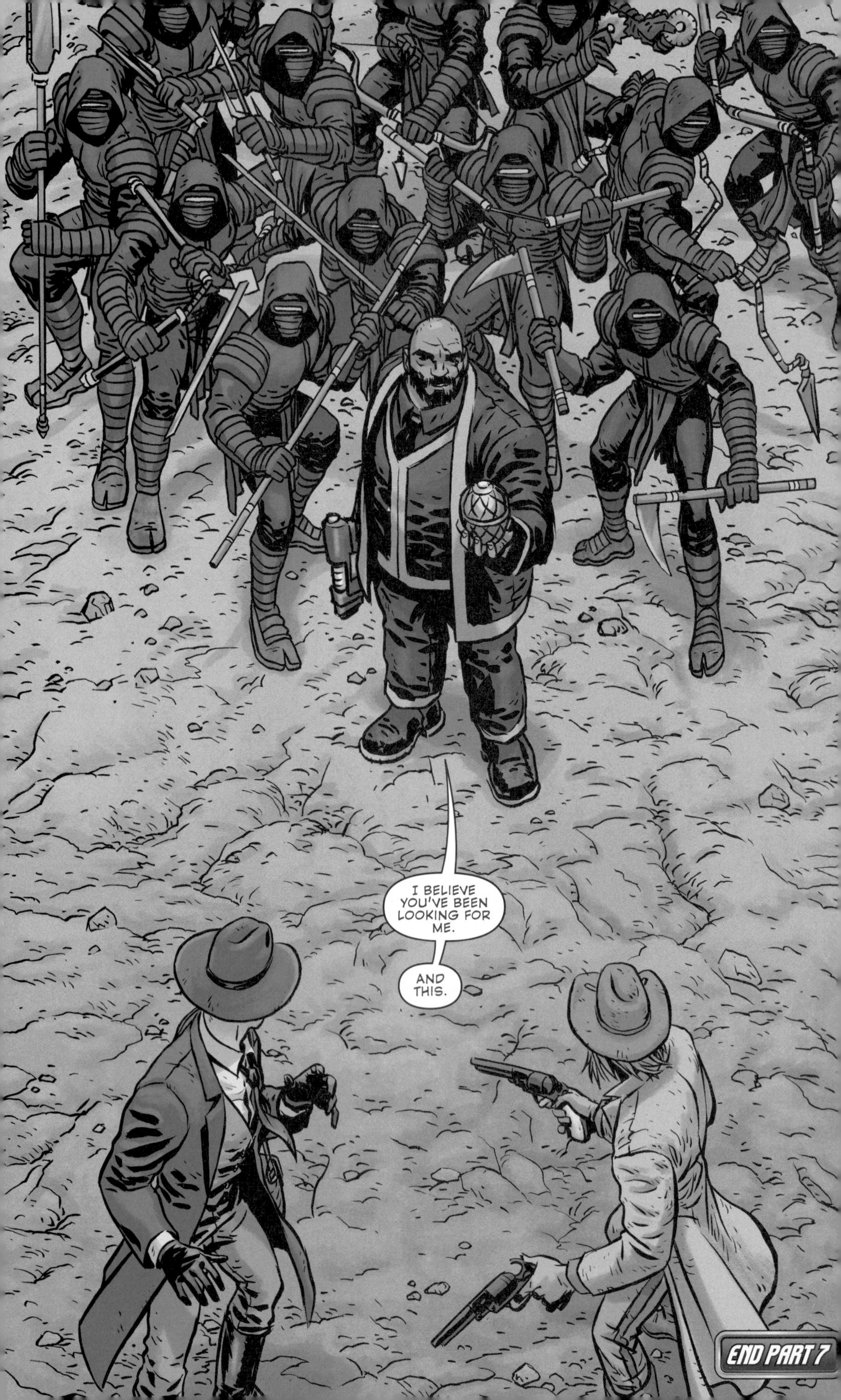
I BELIEVE YOU'VE BEEN LOOKING FOR ME.
AND THIS.
END PART 7

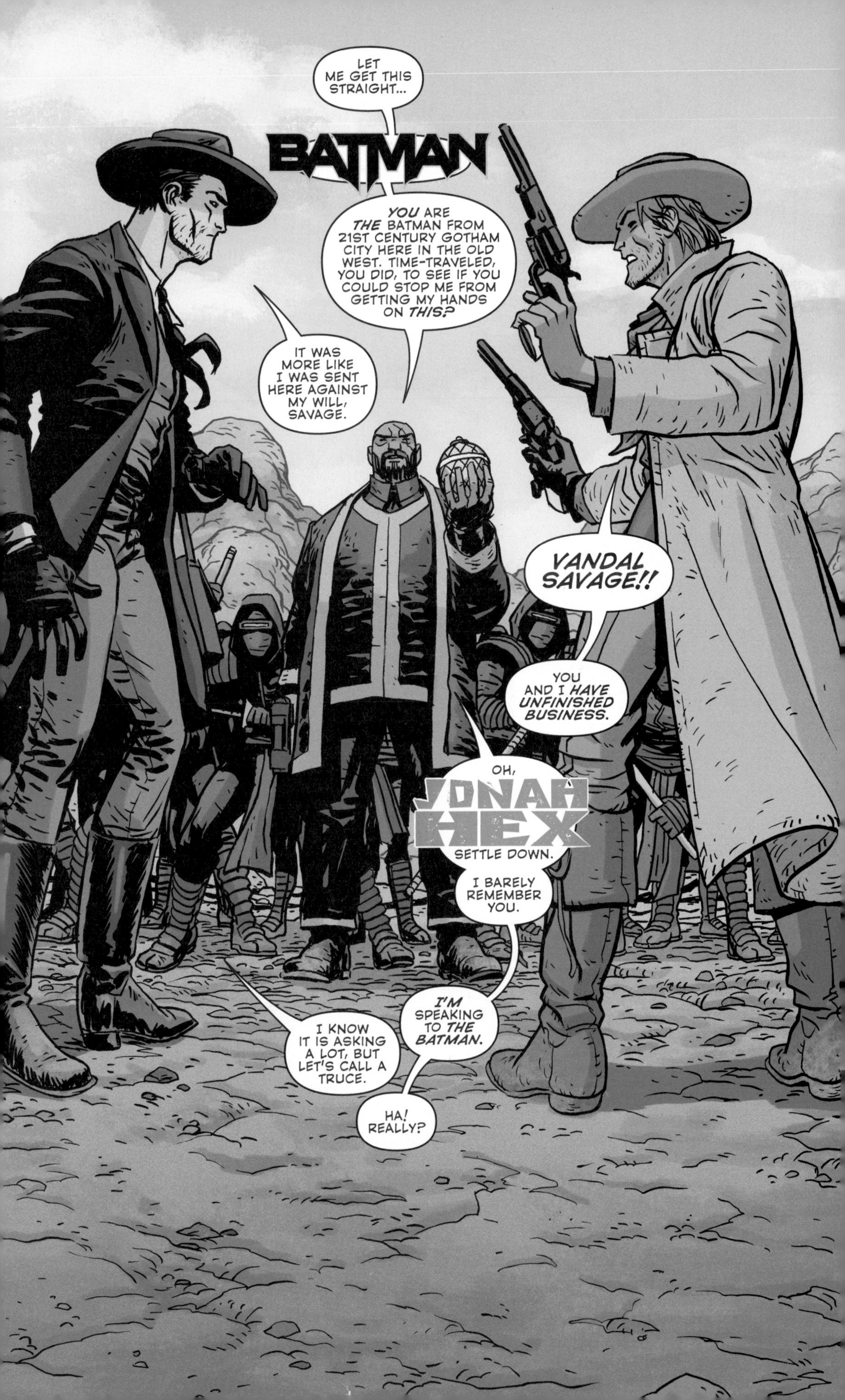
LET ME GET THIS STRAIGHT...
BATMAN
YOU ARE THE BATMAN FROM 21ST CENTURY GOTHAM CITY HERE IN THE OLD WEST. TIME-TRAVELED, YOU DID, TO SEE IF YOU COULD STOP ME FROM GETTING MY HANDS ON THIS?
IT WAS MORE LIKE I WAS SENT HERE AGAINST MY WILL, SAVAGE.
VANDAL SAVAGE!!
YOU AND I HAVE UNFINISHED BUSINESS.
OH, JONAH HEX SETTLE DOWN.
I BARELY REMEMBER YOU.
I'M SPEAKING TO THE BATMAN.
I KNOW IT IS ASKING A LOT, BUT LET'S CALL A TRUCE.
HA! REALLY?

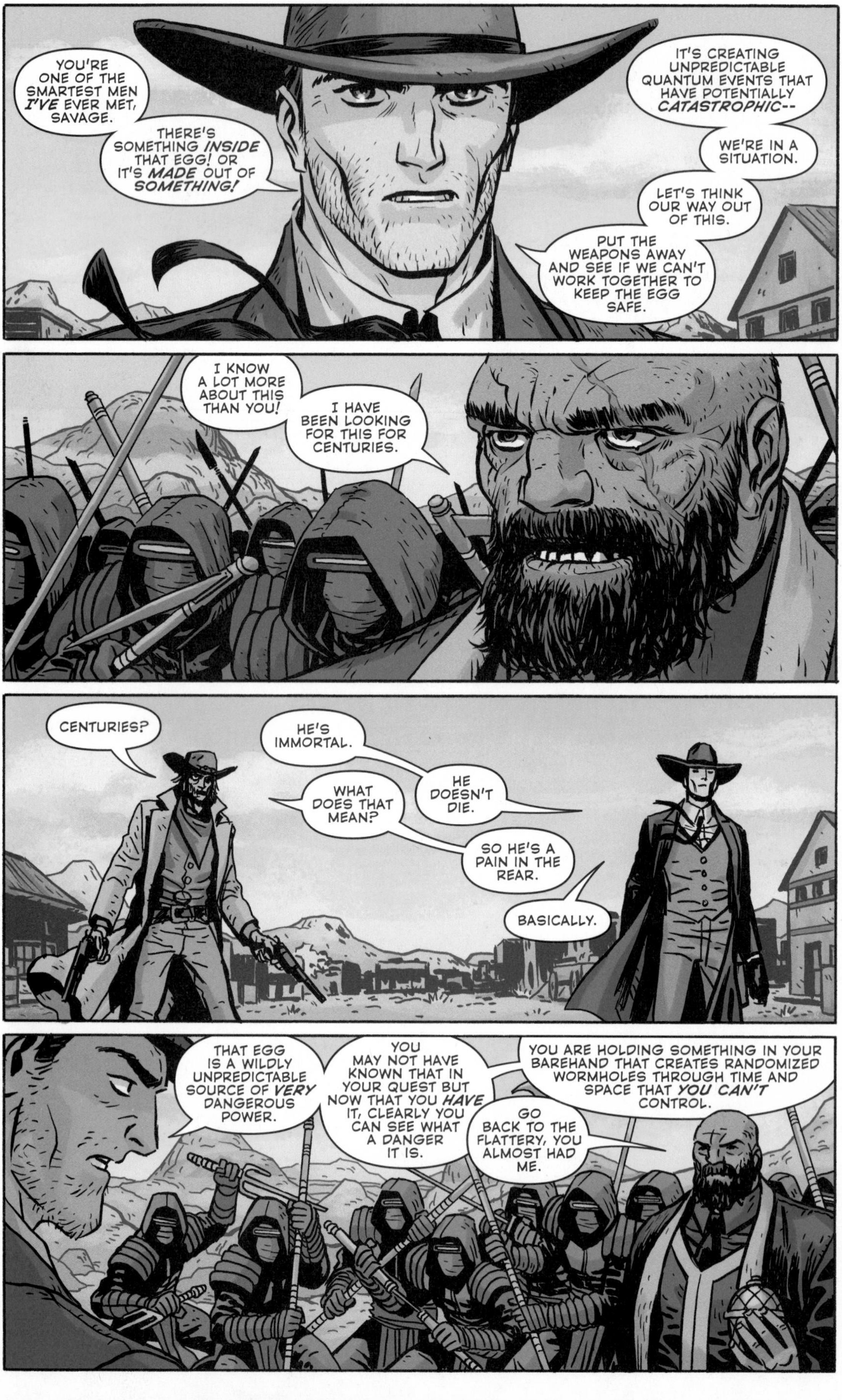
YOU'RE ONE OF THE SMARTEST MEN *I'VE* EVER MET, SAVAGE.
THERE'S SOMETHING *INSIDE* THAT EGG! OR IT'S *MADE* OUT OF *SOMETHING!*
IT'S CREATING UNPREDICTABLE QUANTUM EVENTS THAT HAVE POTENTIALLY *CATASTROPHIC*--
WE'RE IN A SITUATION.
LET'S THINK OUR WAY OUT OF THIS.
PUT THE WEAPONS AWAY AND SEE IF WE CAN'T WORK TOGETHER TO KEEP THE EGG SAFE.
I KNOW A LOT MORE ABOUT THIS THAN YOU!
I HAVE BEEN LOOKING FOR THIS FOR CENTURIES.
CENTURIES?
HE'S IMMORTAL.
HE DOESN'T DIE.
WHAT DOES THAT MEAN?
SO HE'S A PAIN IN THE REAR.
BASICALLY.
THAT EGG IS A WILDLY UNPREDICTABLE SOURCE OF *VERY* DANGEROUS POWER.
YOU MAY NOT HAVE KNOWN THAT IN YOUR QUEST BUT NOW THAT YOU *HAVE* IT, CLEARLY YOU CAN SEE WHAT A DANGER IT IS.
YOU ARE HOLDING SOMETHING IN YOUR BAREHAND THAT CREATES RANDOMIZED WORMHOLES THROUGH TIME AND SPACE THAT *YOU CAN'T* CONTROL.
GO BACK TO THE FLATTERY, YOU ALMOST HAD ME.

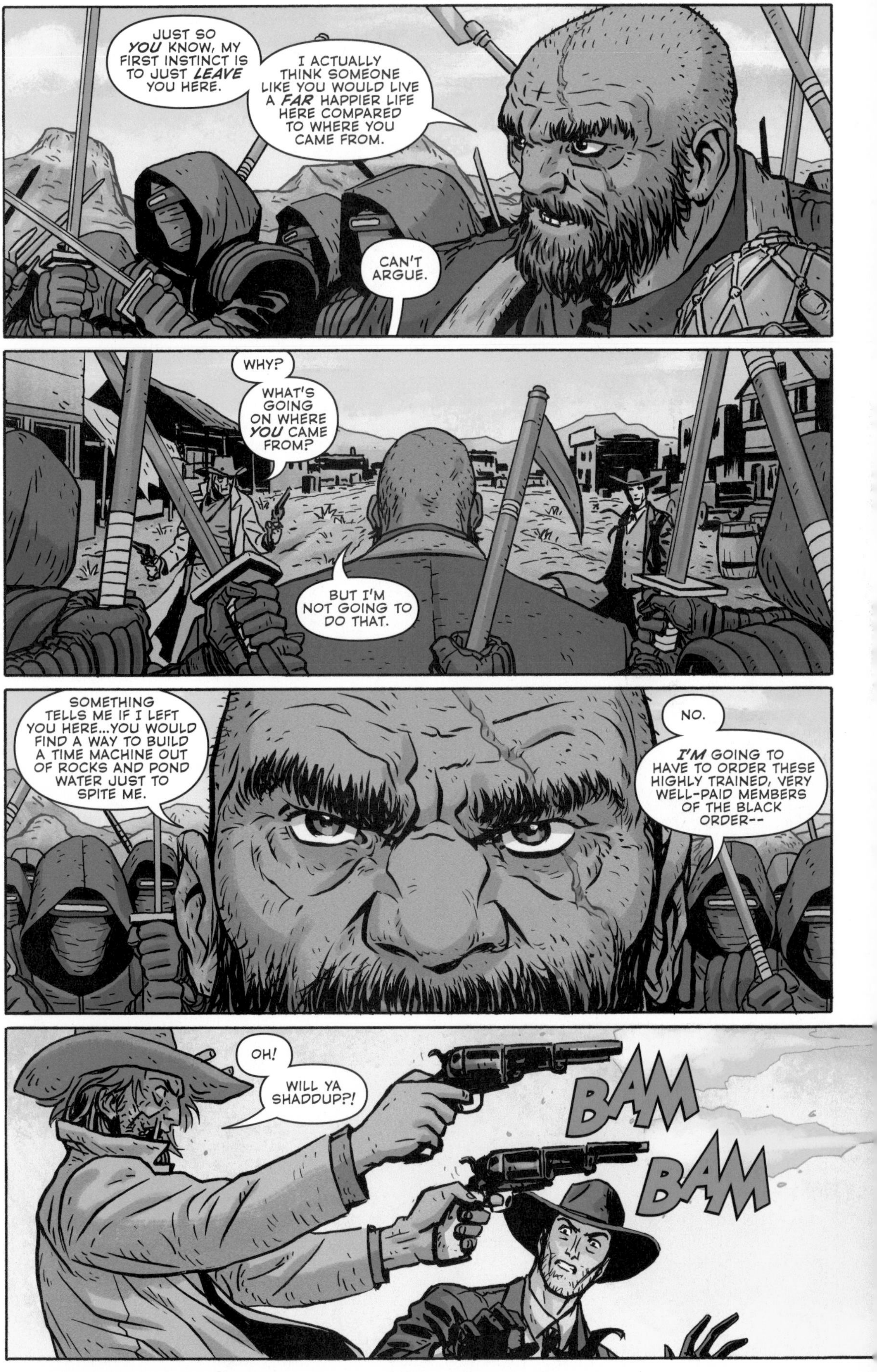
JUST SO *YOU* KNOW, MY FIRST INSTINCT IS TO JUST *LEAVE* YOU HERE.
I ACTUALLY THINK SOMEONE LIKE YOU WOULD LIVE A *FAR* HAPPIER LIFE HERE COMPARED TO WHERE YOU CAME FROM.
CAN'T ARGUE.
WHY?
WHAT'S GOING ON WHERE *YOU* CAME FROM?
BUT I'M NOT GOING TO DO THAT.
SOMETHING TELLS ME IF I LEFT YOU HERE...YOU WOULD FIND A WAY TO BUILD A TIME MACHINE OUT OF ROCKS AND POND WATER JUST TO SPITE ME.
NO.
I'M GOING TO HAVE TO ORDER THESE HIGHLY TRAINED, VERY WELL-PAID MEMBERS OF THE BLACK ORDER--
OH!
WILL YA SHADDUP?!
BAM
BAM

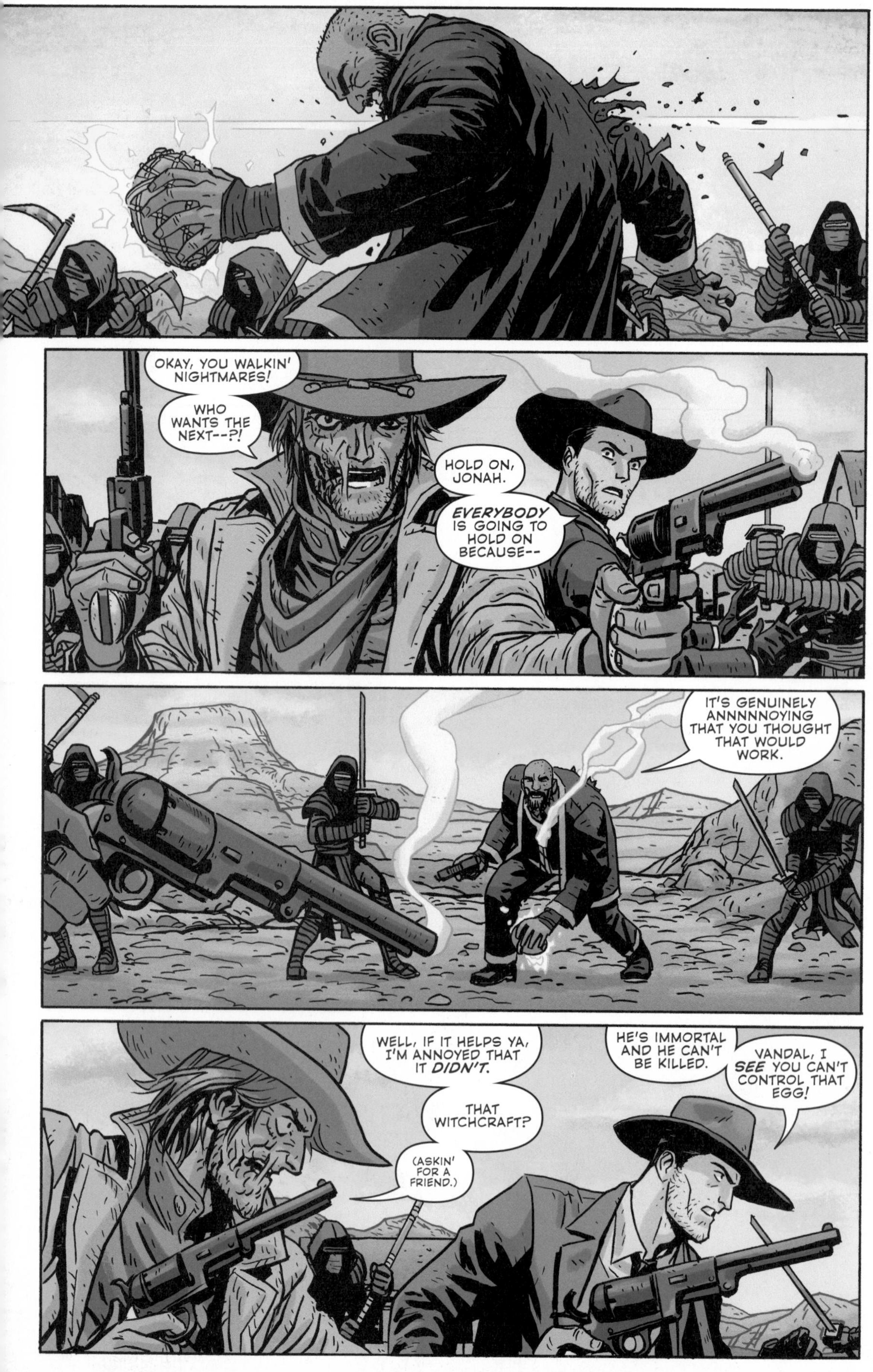
OKAY, YOU WALKIN' NIGHTMARES!
WHO WANTS THE NEXT--?!
HOLD ON, JONAH.
EVERYBODY IS GOING TO HOLD ON BECAUSE--
IT'S GENUINELY ANNNNNOYING THAT YOU THOUGHT THAT WOULD WORK.
WELL, IF IT HELPS YA, I'M ANNOYED THAT IT DIDN'T.
THAT WITCHCRAFT?
(ASKIN' FOR A FRIEND.)
HE'S IMMORTAL AND HE CAN'T BE KILLED.
VANDAL, I SEE YOU CAN'T CONTROL THAT EGG!

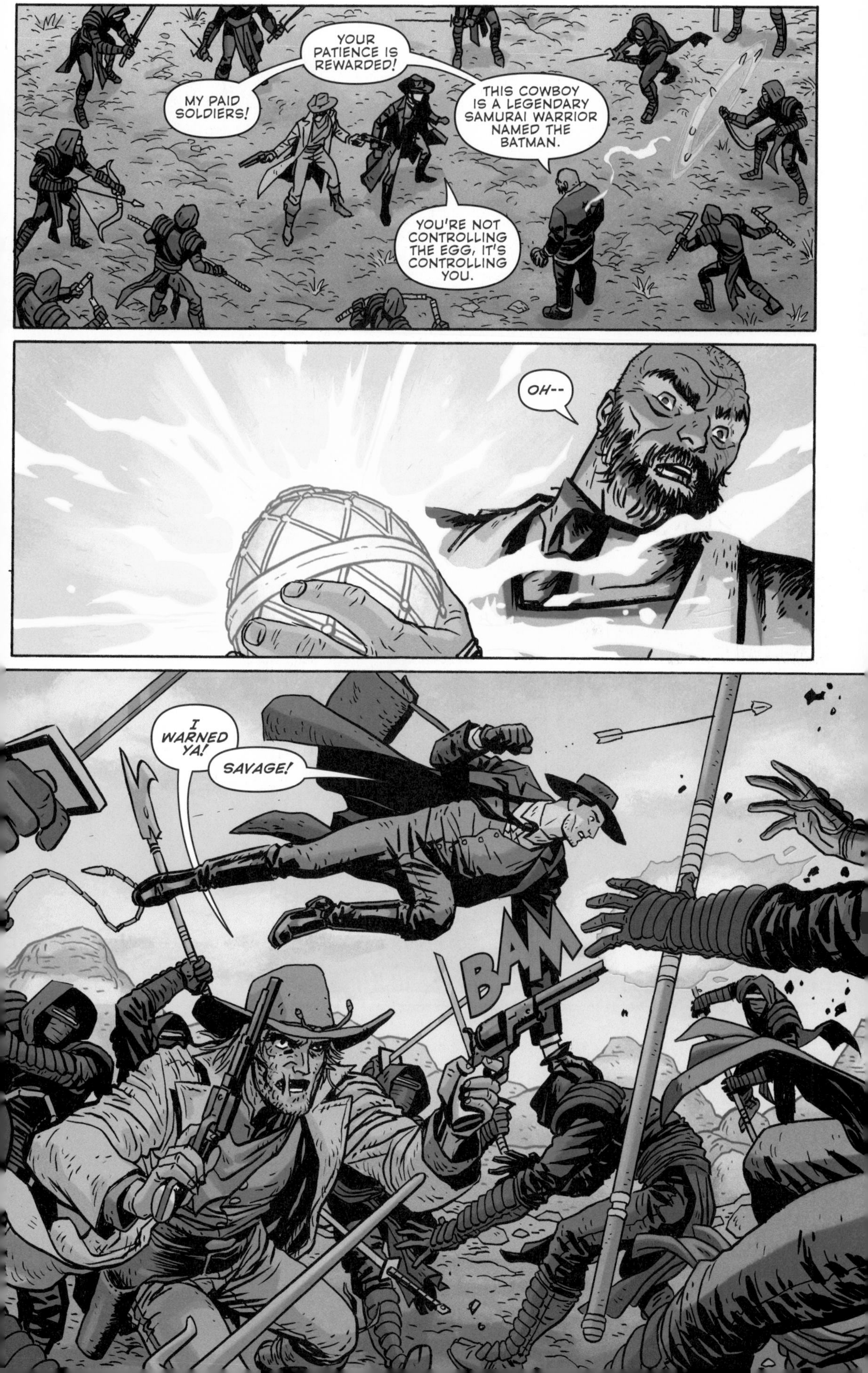
MY PAID SOLDIERS!
YOUR PATIENCE IS REWARDED!
THIS COWBOY IS A LEGENDARY SAMURAI WARRIOR NAMED THE BATMAN.
YOU'RE NOT CONTROLLING THE EGG, IT'S CONTROLLING YOU.
OH--
I WARNED YA!
SAVAGE!
BAM

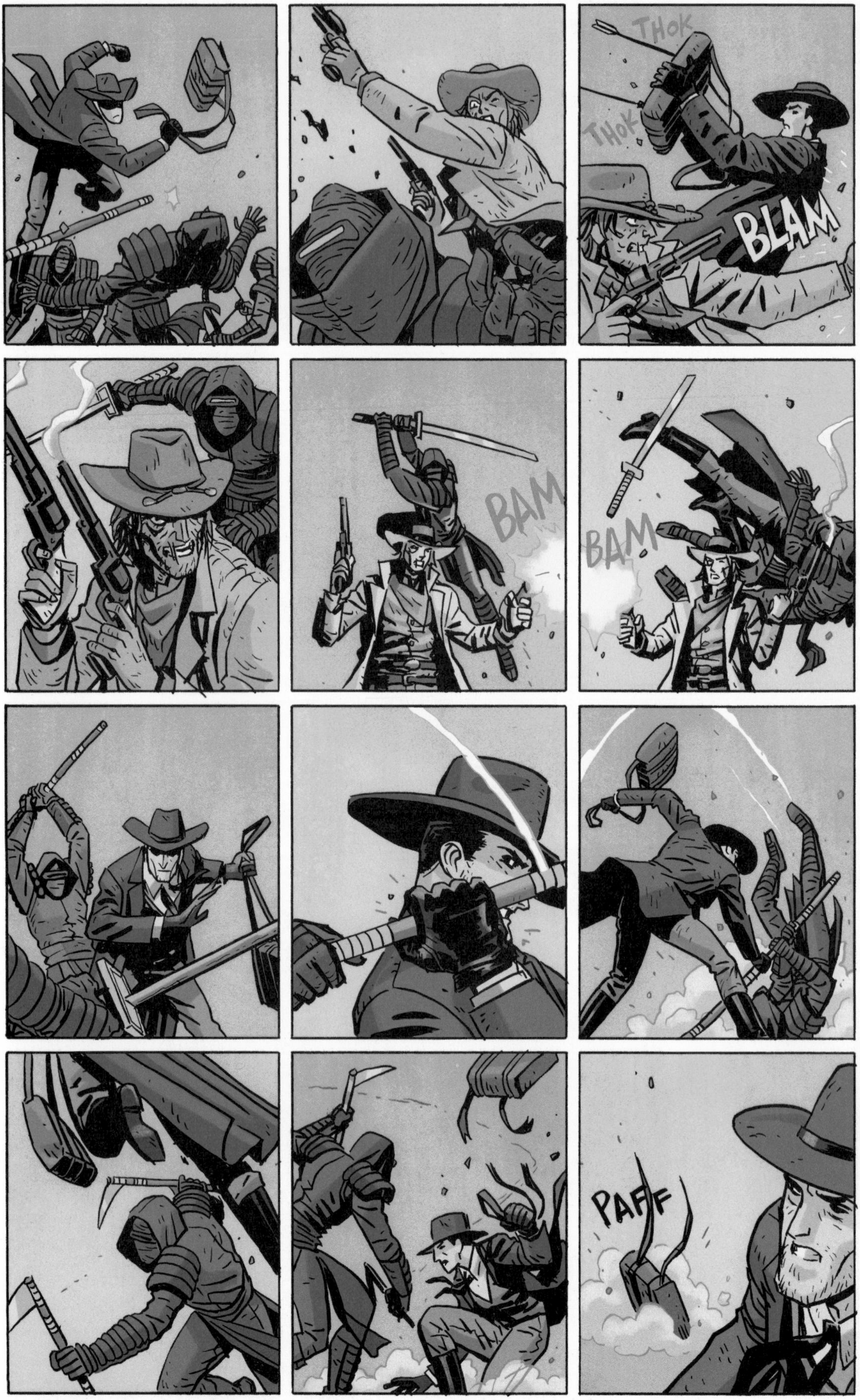
THOK
THOK
BLAM
BAM
BAM
PAFF

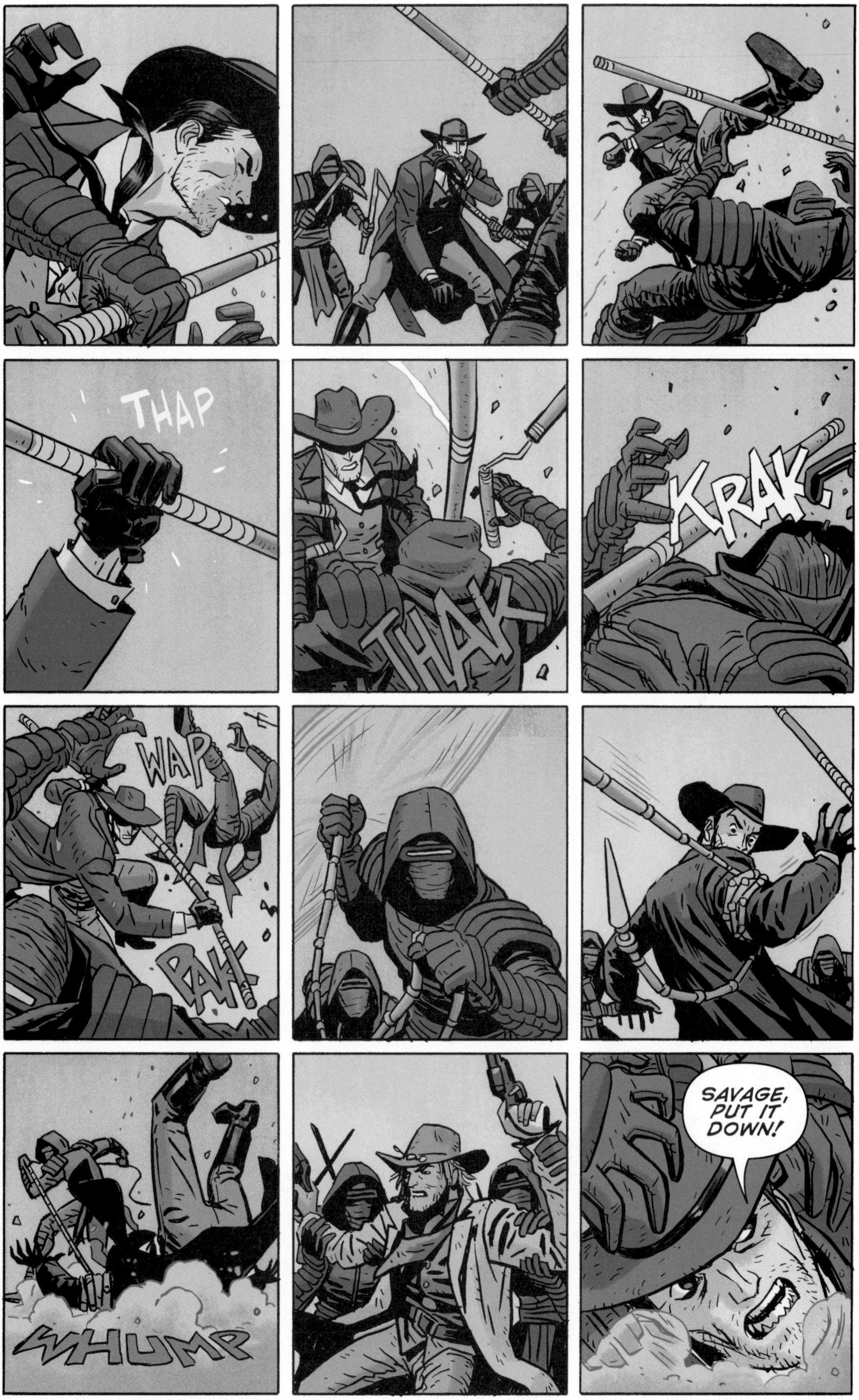
THAP
THAK
KRAK
WAP
PAK
WHUMP
SAVAGE, PUT IT DOWN!

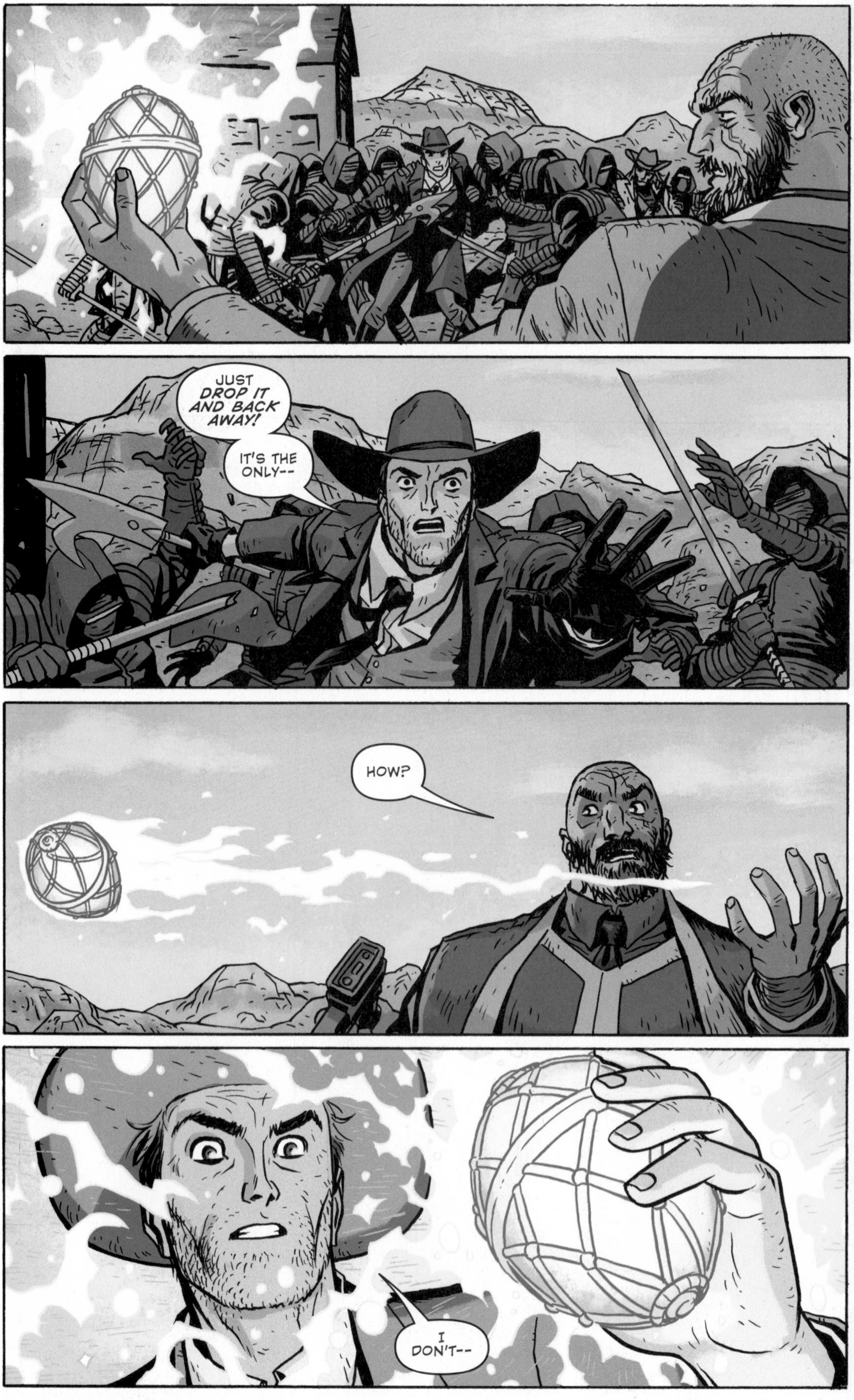

JUST *DROP IT AND BACK AWAY!*
IT'S THE ONLY--
HOW?
I DON'T--

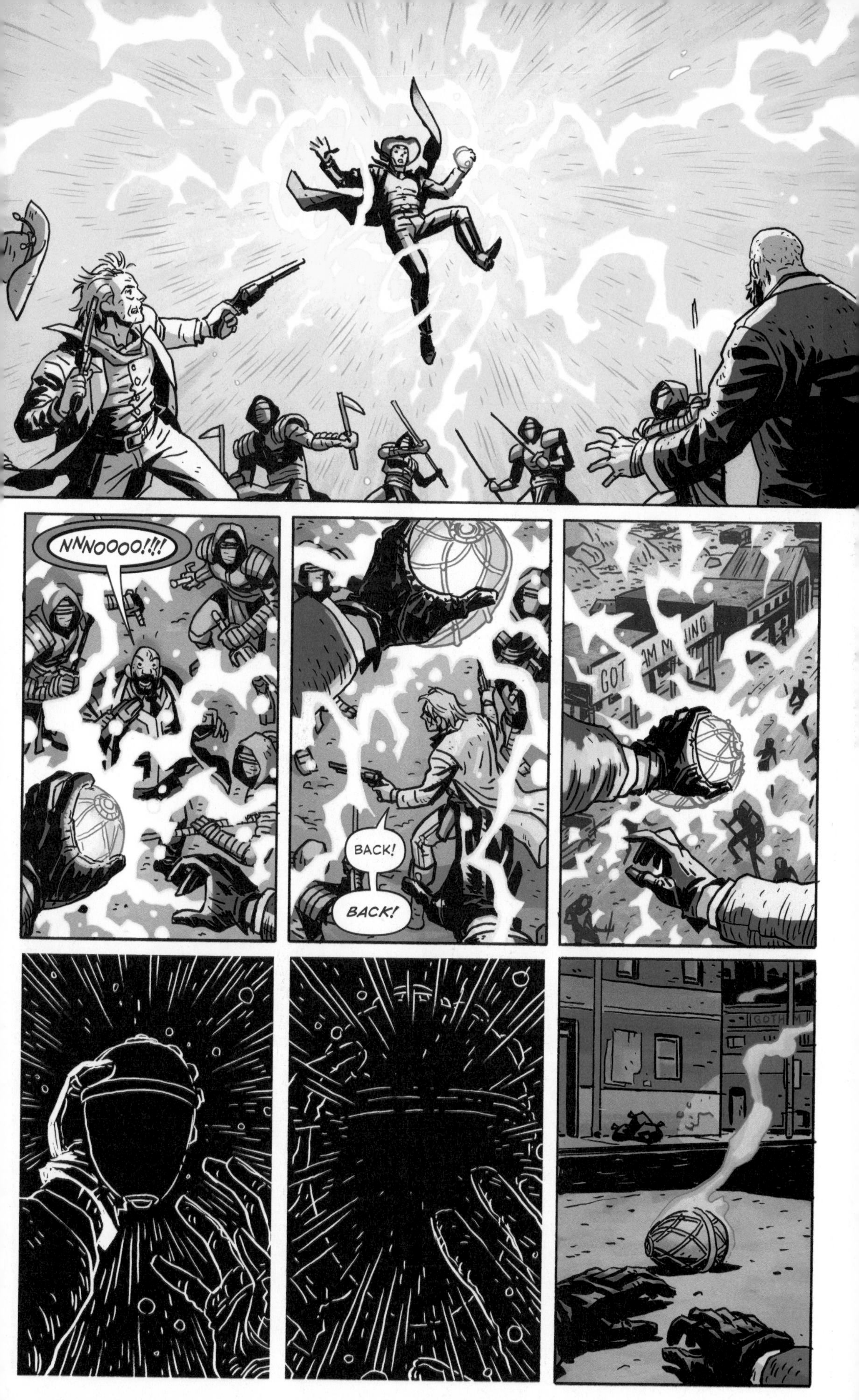
NNNOOOO!!!!
BACK!
BACK!
GOT
AM M
ING
GOTH M

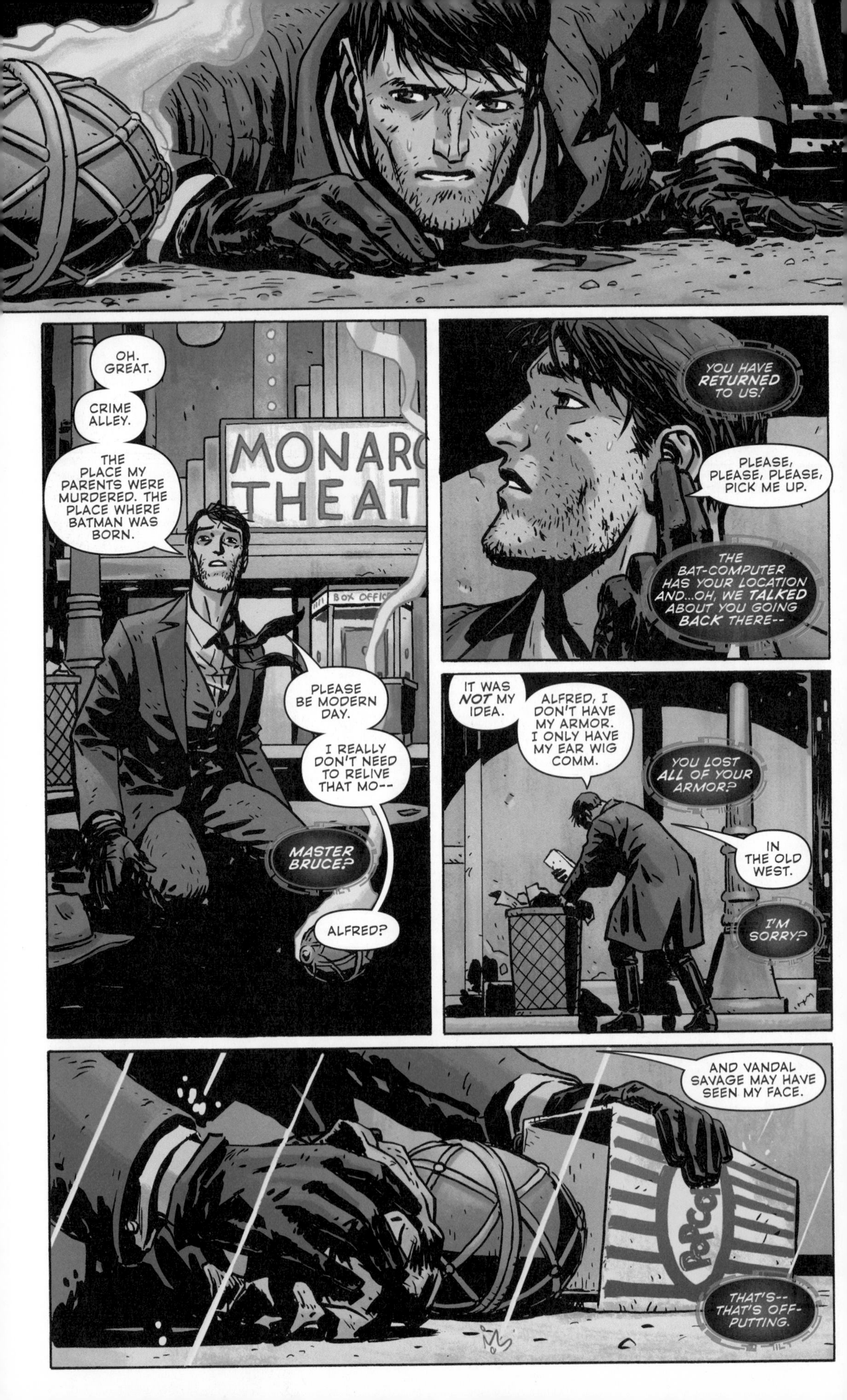

OH. GREAT.
CRIME ALLEY.
THE PLACE MY PARENTS WERE MURDERED. THE PLACE WHERE BATMAN WAS BORN.
MONARC THEAT
BOX OFFICE
PLEASE BE MODERN DAY.
I REALLY DON'T NEED TO RELIVE THAT MO--
MASTER BRUCE?
ALFRED?
YOU HAVE RETURNED TO US!
PLEASE, PLEASE, PLEASE, PICK ME UP.
THE BAT-COMPUTER HAS YOUR LOCATION AND...OH, WE TALKED ABOUT YOU GOING BACK THERE--
IT WAS NOT MY IDEA.
ALFRED, I DON'T HAVE MY ARMOR. I ONLY HAVE MY EAR WIG COMM.
YOU LOST ALL OF YOUR ARMOR?
IN THE OLD WEST.
I'M SORRY?
AND VANDAL SAVAGE MAY HAVE SEEN MY FACE.
THAT'S-- THAT'S OFF-PUTTING.

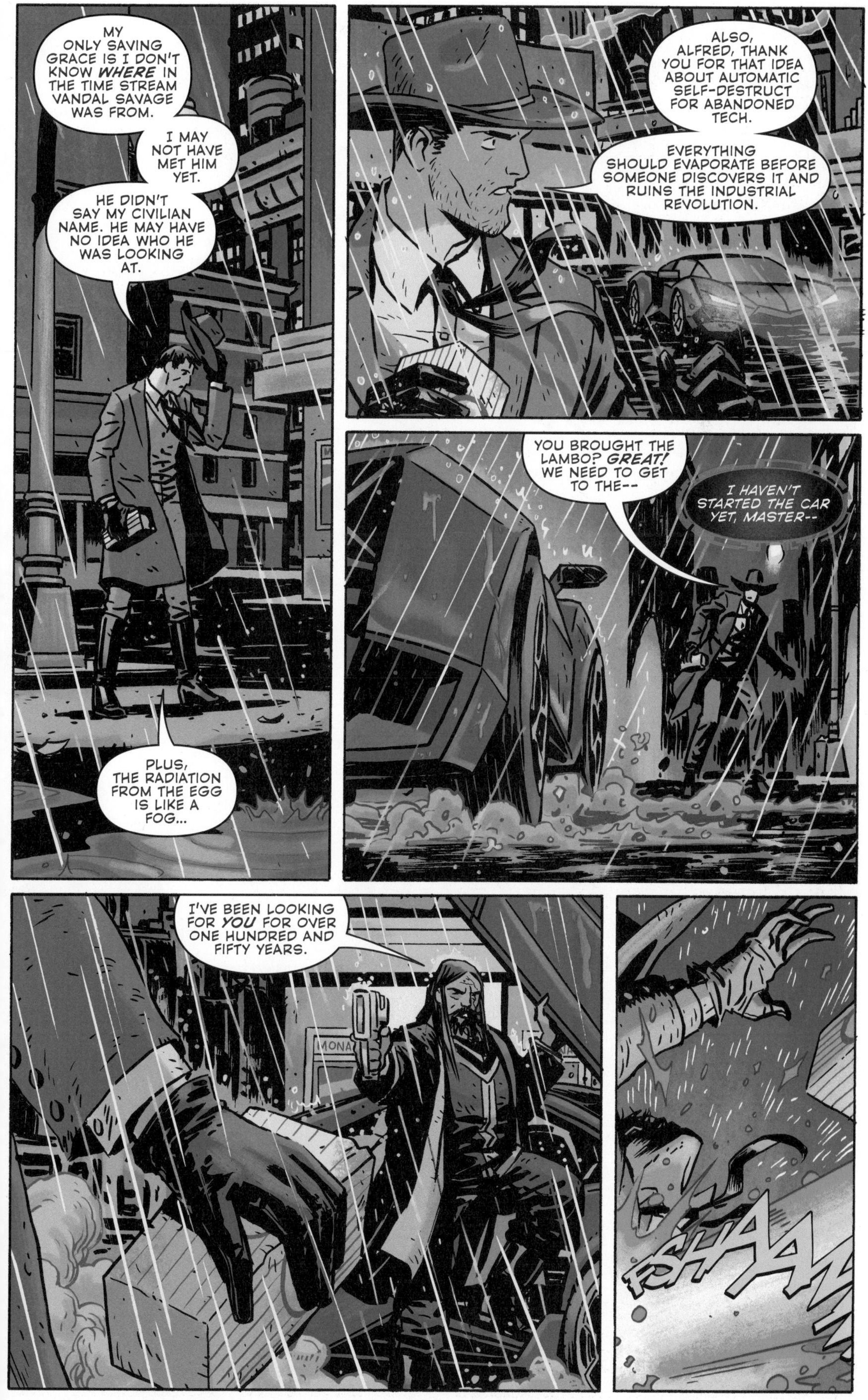
MY ONLY SAVING GRACE IS I DON'T KNOW *WHERE* IN THE TIME STREAM VANDAL SAVAGE WAS FROM.
I MAY NOT HAVE MET HIM YET.
HE DIDN'T SAY MY CIVILIAN NAME. HE MAY HAVE NO IDEA WHO HE WAS LOOKING AT.
PLUS, THE RADIATION FROM THE EGG IS LIKE A FOG...
ALSO, ALFRED, THANK YOU FOR THAT IDEA ABOUT AUTOMATIC SELF-DESTRUCT FOR ABANDONED TECH.
EVERYTHING SHOULD EVAPORATE BEFORE SOMEONE DISCOVERS IT AND RUINS THE INDUSTRIAL REVOLUTION.
YOU BROUGHT THE LAMBO? *GREAT!* WE NEED TO GET TO THE--
I HAVEN'T STARTED THE CAR YET, MASTER--
I'VE BEEN LOOKING FOR *YOU* FOR OVER ONE HUNDRED AND FIFTY YEARS.
FSHAAM

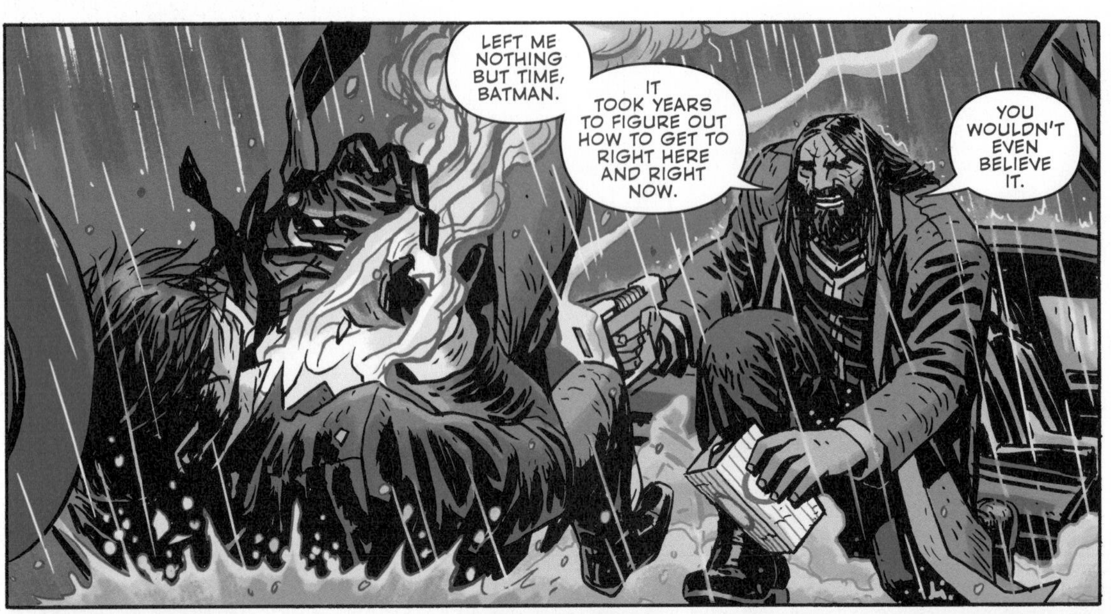
LEFT ME NOTHING BUT TIME, BATMAN.
IT TOOK YEARS TO FIGURE OUT HOW TO GET TO RIGHT HERE AND RIGHT NOW.
YOU WOULDN'T EVEN BELIEVE IT.

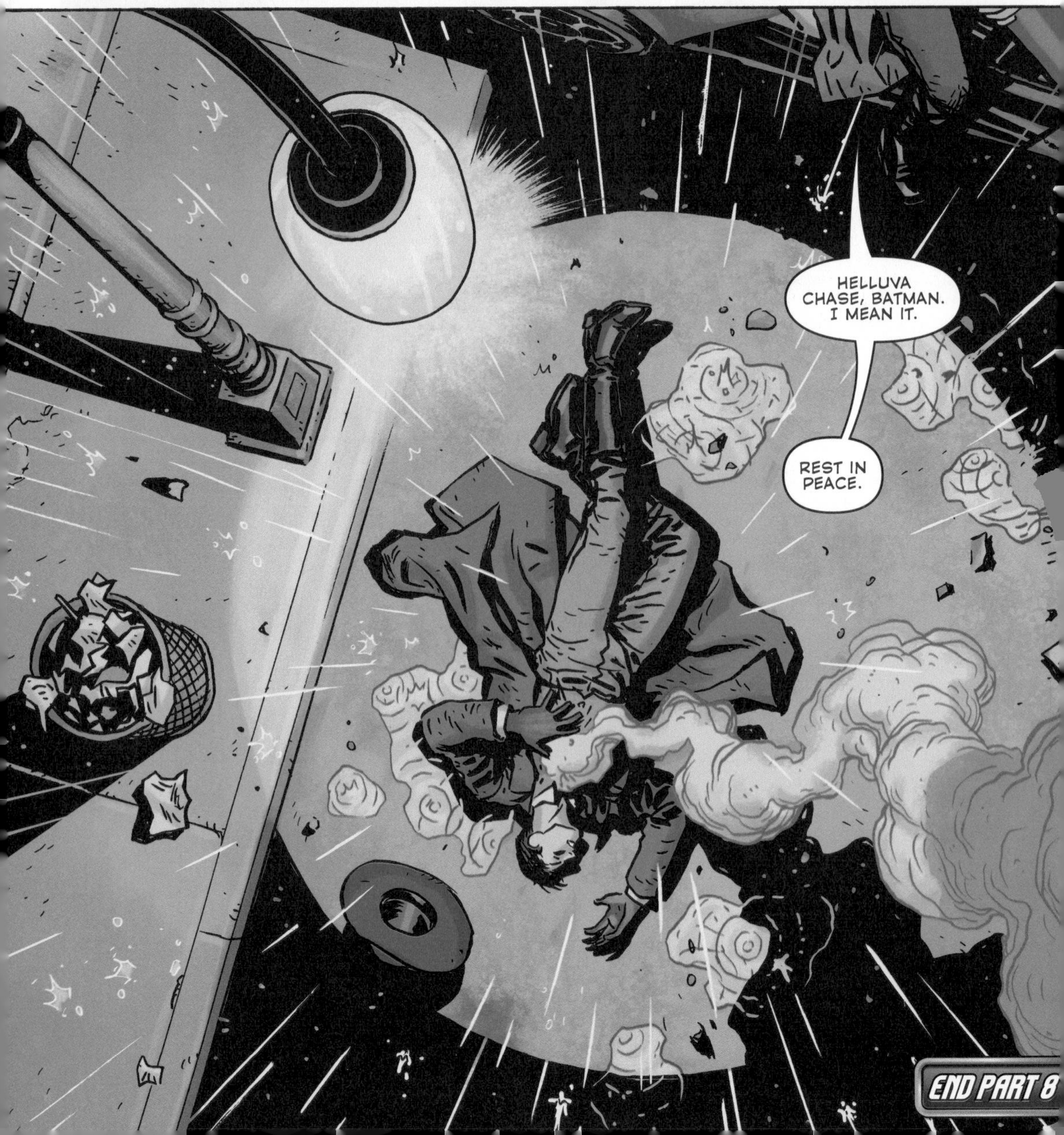
HELLUVA CHASE, BATMAN. I MEAN IT.
REST IN PEACE.
END PART 8

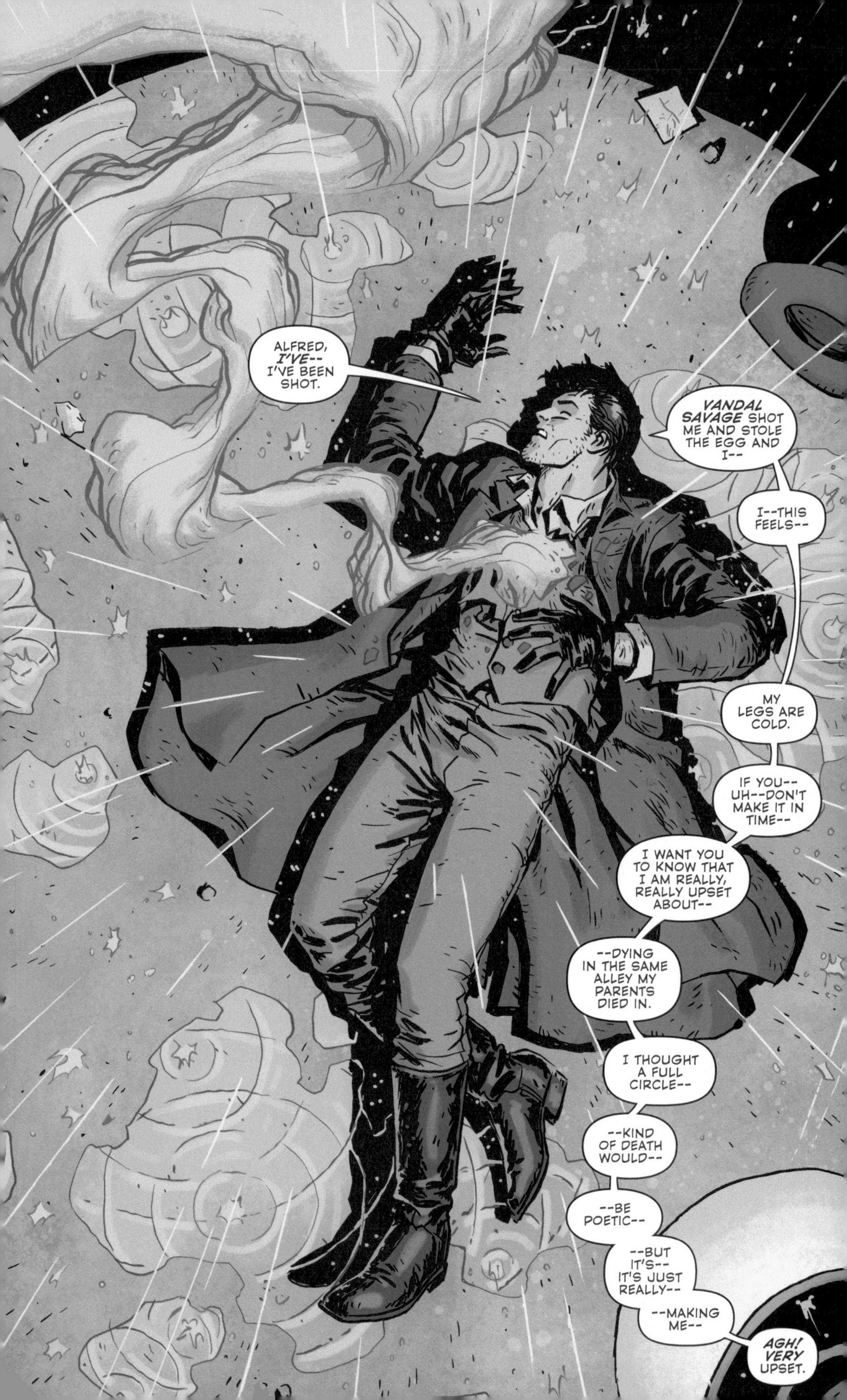
ALFRED, *I'VE*-- I'VE BEEN SHOT.
VANDAL SAVAGE SHOT ME AND STOLE THE EGG AND I--
I--THIS FEELS--
MY LEGS ARE COLD.
IF YOU-- UH--DON'T MAKE IT IN TIME--
I WANT YOU TO KNOW THAT I AM REALLY, REALLY UPSET ABOUT--
--DYING IN THE SAME ALLEY MY PARENTS DIED IN.
I THOUGHT A FULL CIRCLE--
--KIND OF DEATH WOULD--
--BE POETIC--
--BUT IT'S-- IT'S JUST REALLY--
--MAKING ME--
AGH! VERY UPSET.

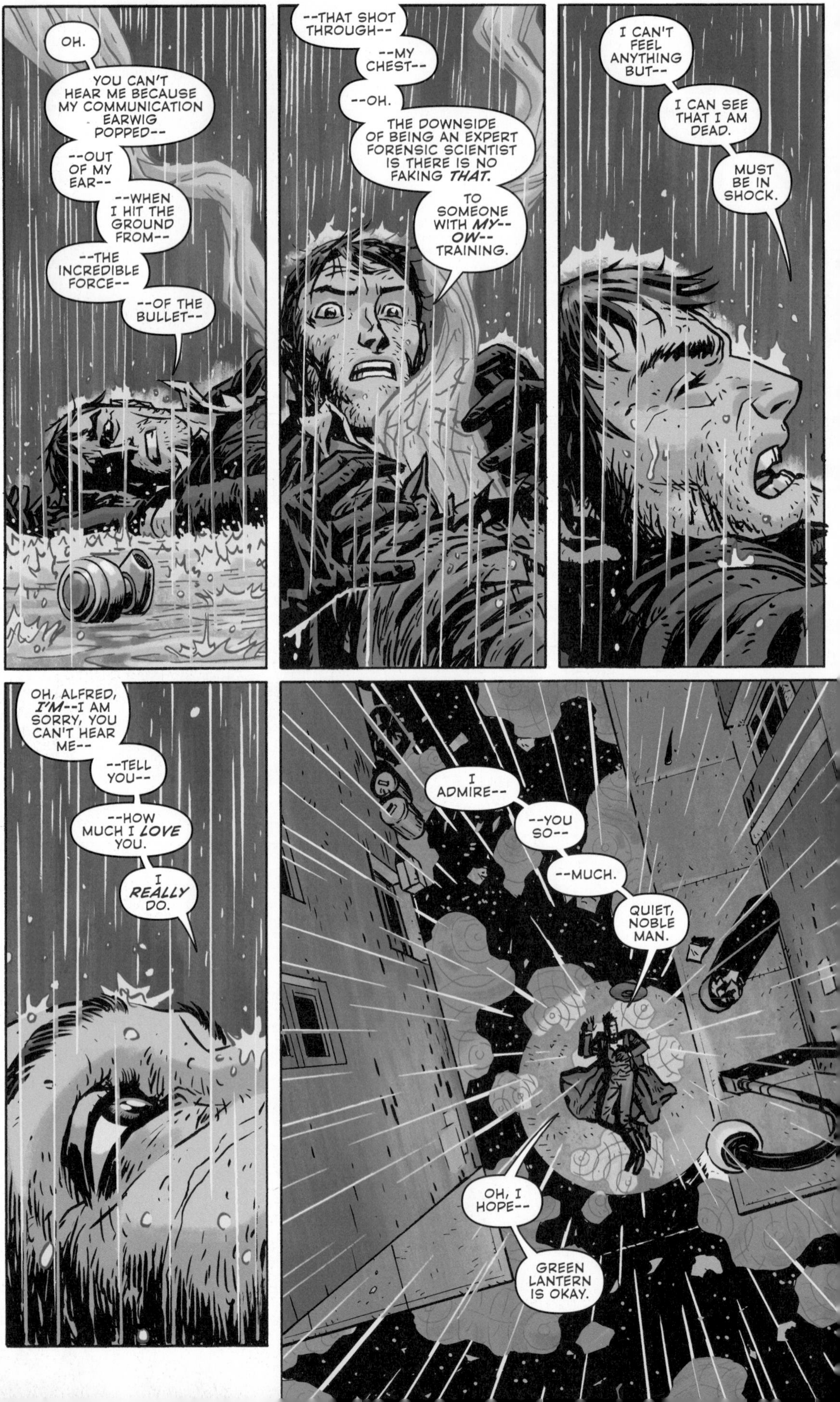
OH.
YOU CAN'T HEAR ME BECAUSE MY COMMUNICATION EARWIG POPPED--
--OUT OF MY EAR--
--WHEN I HIT THE GROUND FROM--
--THE INCREDIBLE FORCE--
--OF THE BULLET--
--THAT SHOT THROUGH--
--MY CHEST--
--OH.
THE DOWNSIDE OF BEING AN EXPERT FORENSIC SCIENTIST IS THERE IS NO FAKING *THAT.*
TO SOMEONE WITH *MY--* *OW--* TRAINING.
I CAN'T FEEL ANYTHING BUT--
I CAN SEE THAT I AM DEAD.
MUST BE IN SHOCK.
OH, ALFRED, *I'M*--I AM SORRY, YOU CAN'T HEAR ME--
--TELL YOU--
--HOW MUCH I *LOVE* YOU.
I *REALLY* DO.
I ADMIRE--
--YOU SO--
--MUCH.
QUIET, NOBLE MAN.
OH, I HOPE--
GREEN LANTERN IS OKAY.

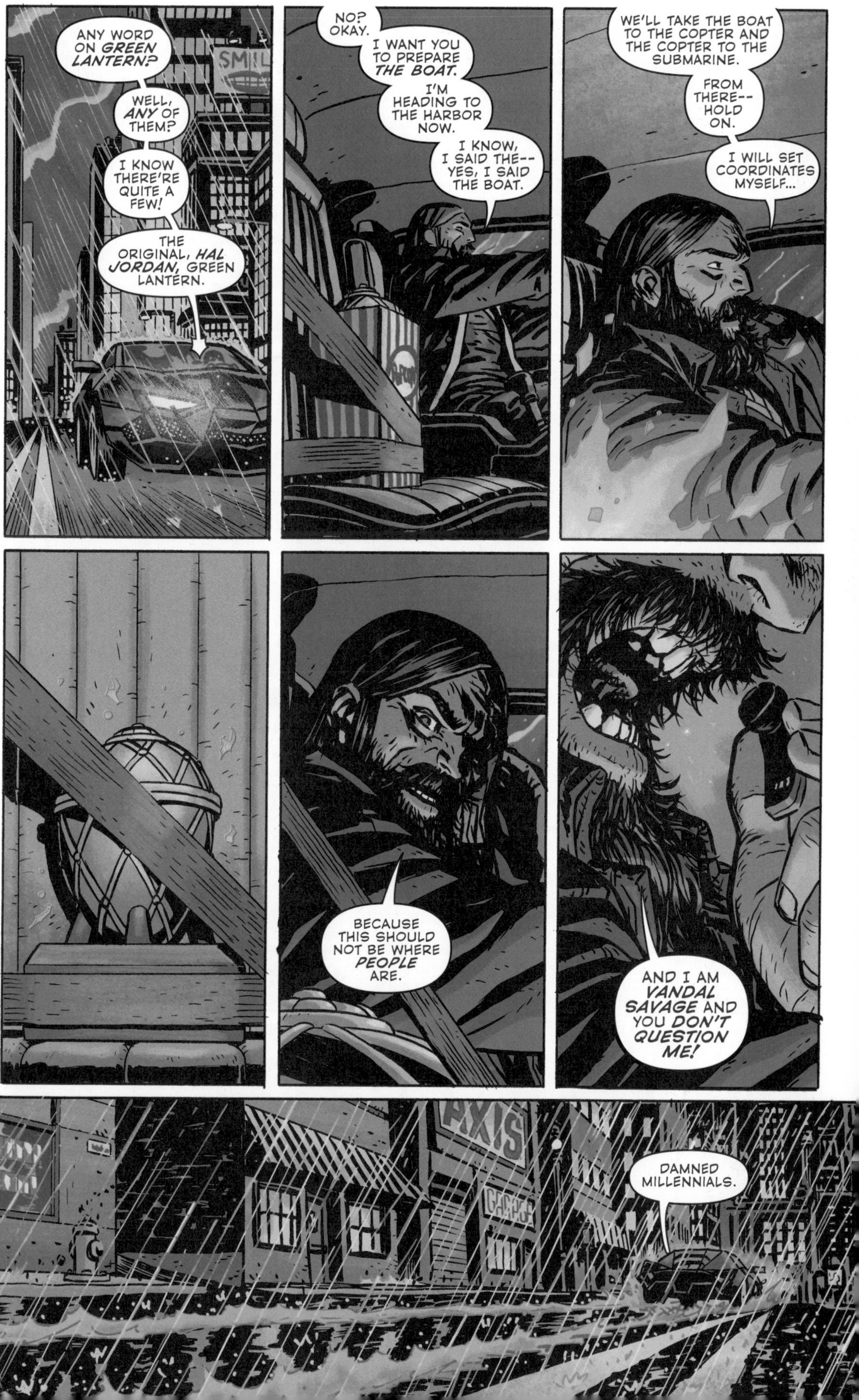

ANY WORD ON GREEN LANTERN?
WELL, ANY OF THEM?
I KNOW THERE'RE QUITE A FEW!
THE ORIGINAL, HAL JORDAN, GREEN LANTERN.
NO? OKAY.
I WANT YOU TO PREPARE THE BOAT.
I'M HEADING TO THE HARBOR NOW.
I KNOW, I SAID THE-- YES, I SAID THE BOAT.
WE'LL TAKE THE BOAT TO THE COPTER AND THE COPTER TO THE SUBMARINE.
FROM THERE-- HOLD ON.
I WILL SET COORDINATES MYSELF...
BECAUSE THIS SHOULD NOT BE WHERE PEOPLE ARE.
AND I AM VANDAL SAVAGE AND YOU DON'T QUESTION ME!
DAMNED MILLENNIALS.

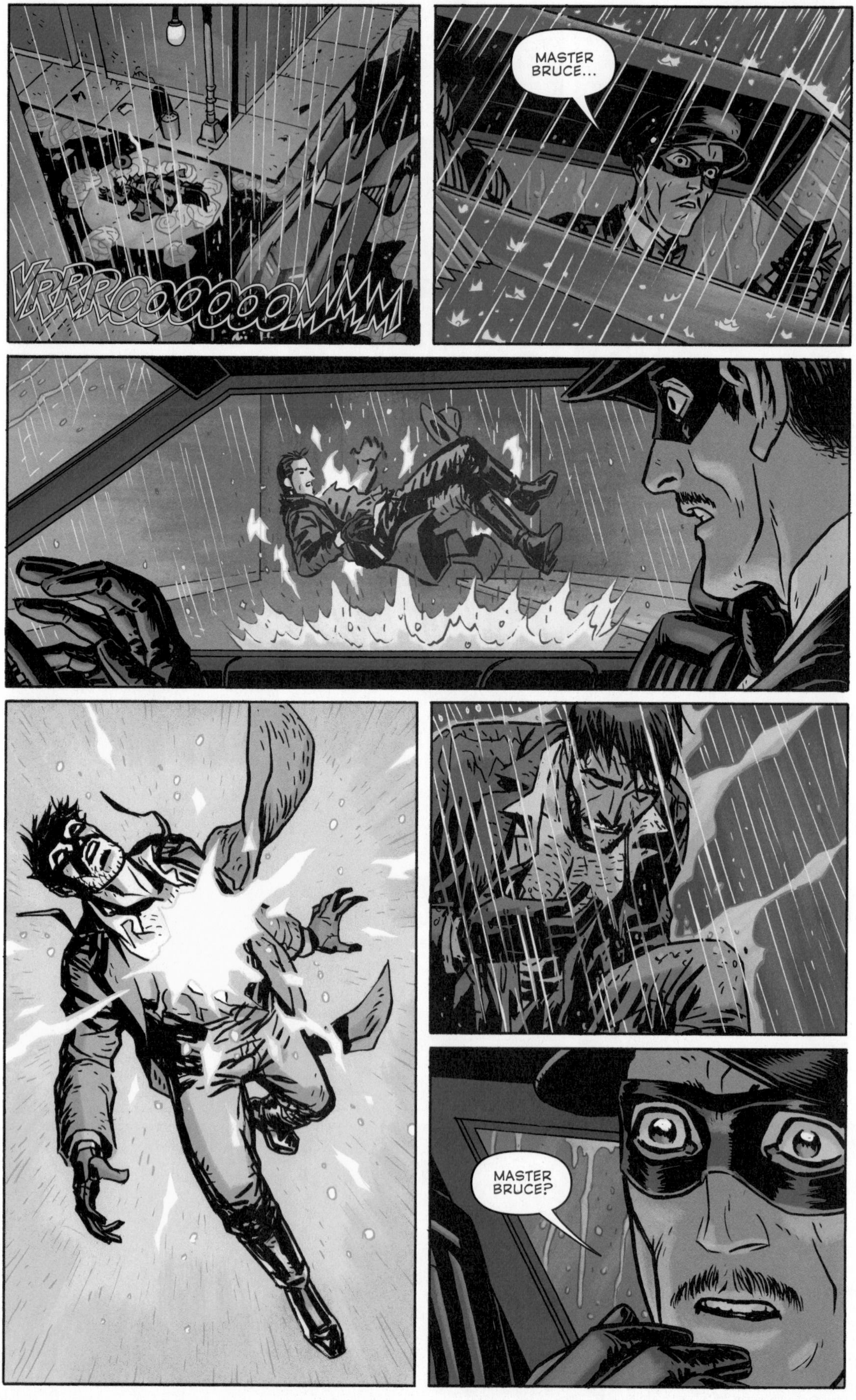
VRRROOOOOOOMMM
MASTER BRUCE...
MASTER BRUCE?

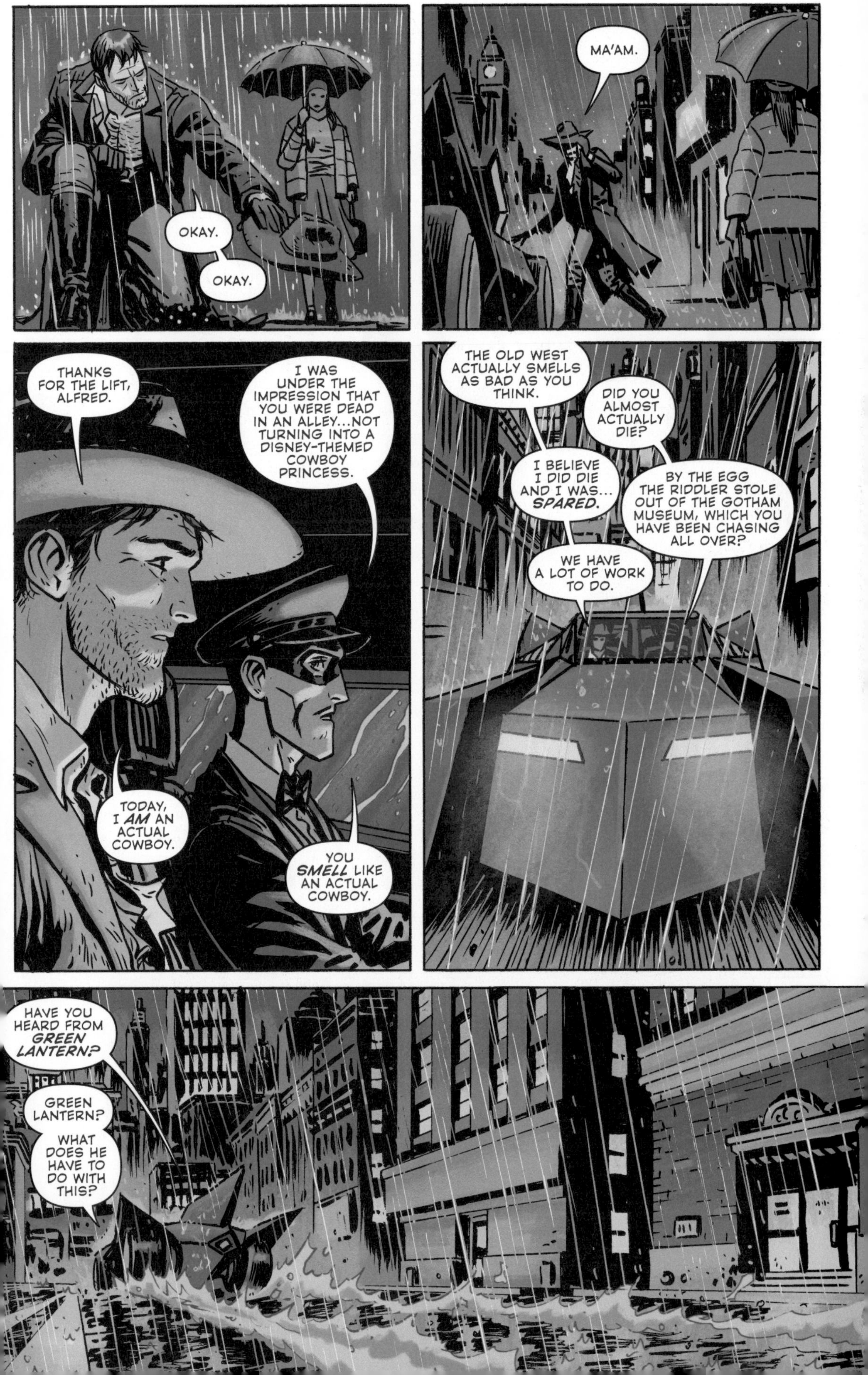
OKAY.
OKAY.
MA'AM.
THANKS FOR THE LIFT, ALFRED.
I WAS UNDER THE IMPRESSION THAT YOU WERE DEAD IN AN ALLEY...NOT TURNING INTO A DISNEY-THEMED COWBOY PRINCESS.
TODAY, I *AM* AN ACTUAL COWBOY.
YOU *SMELL* LIKE AN ACTUAL COWBOY.
THE OLD WEST ACTUALLY SMELLS AS BAD AS YOU THINK.
DID YOU ALMOST ACTUALLY DIE?
I BELIEVE I DID DIE AND I WAS... *SPARED.*
BY THE EGG THE RIDDLER STOLE OUT OF THE GOTHAM MUSEUM, WHICH YOU HAVE BEEN CHASING ALL OVER?
WE HAVE A LOT OF WORK TO DO.
HAVE YOU HEARD FROM *GREEN LANTERN?*
GREEN LANTERN?
WHAT DOES HE HAVE TO DO WITH THIS?

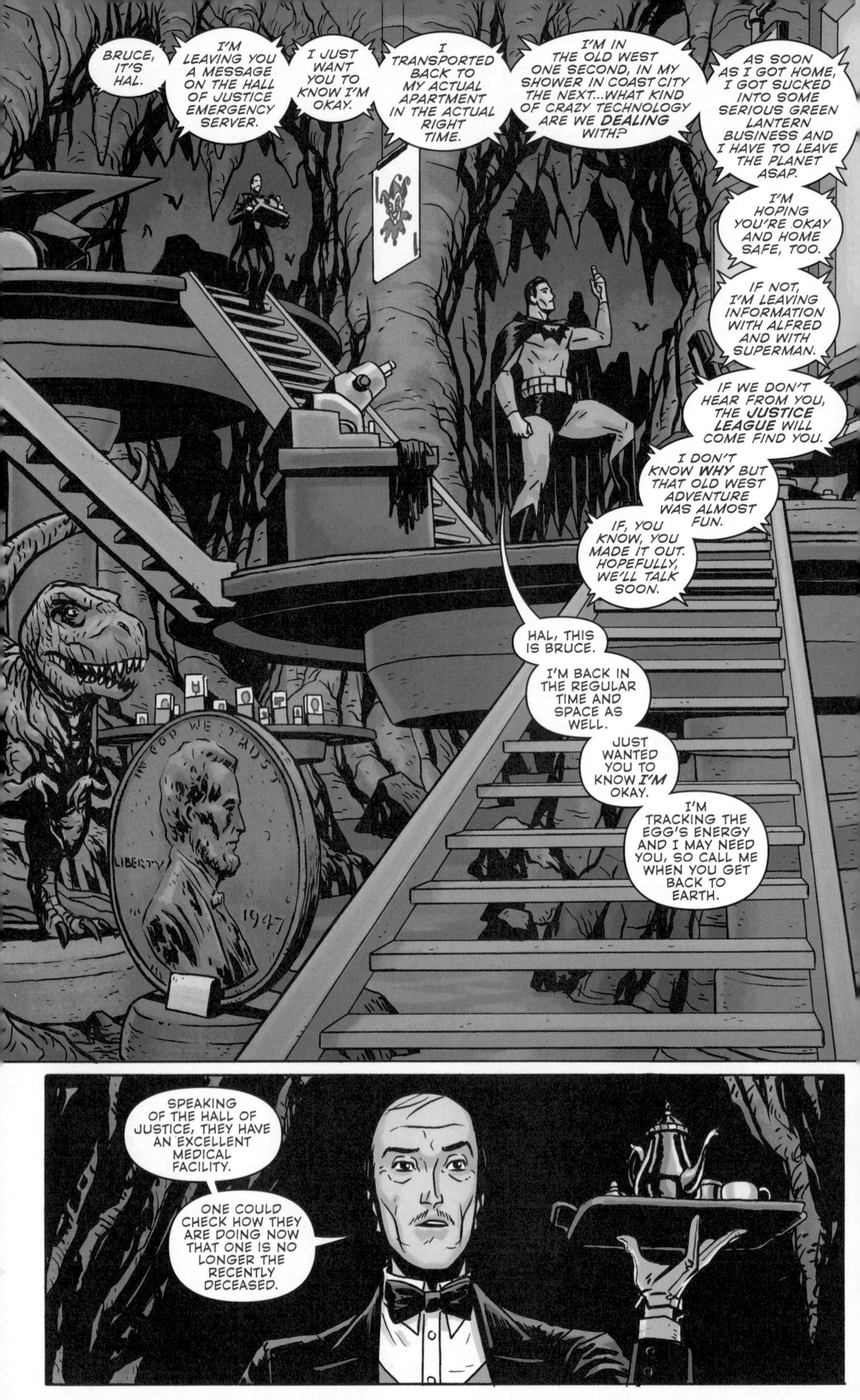
BRUCE, IT'S HAL.
I'M LEAVING YOU A MESSAGE ON THE HALL OF JUSTICE EMERGENCY SERVER.
I JUST WANT YOU TO KNOW I'M OKAY.
I TRANSPORTED BACK TO MY ACTUAL APARTMENT IN THE ACTUAL RIGHT TIME.
I'M IN THE OLD WEST ONE SECOND, IN MY SHOWER IN COAST CITY THE NEXT...WHAT KIND OF CRAZY TECHNOLOGY ARE WE **DEALING** WITH?
AS SOON AS I GOT HOME, I GOT SUCKED INTO SOME SERIOUS GREEN LANTERN BUSINESS AND I HAVE TO LEAVE THE PLANET ASAP.
I'M HOPING YOU'RE OKAY AND HOME SAFE, TOO.
IF NOT, I'M LEAVING INFORMATION WITH ALFRED AND WITH SUPERMAN.
IF WE DON'T HEAR FROM YOU, THE **JUSTICE LEAGUE** WILL COME FIND YOU.
I DON'T KNOW **WHY** BUT THAT OLD WEST ADVENTURE WAS ALMOST FUN.
IF, YOU KNOW, YOU MADE IT OUT. HOPEFULLY, WE'LL TALK SOON.
IN GOD WE TRUST
LIBERTY
1947
HAL, THIS IS BRUCE.
I'M BACK IN THE REGULAR TIME AND SPACE AS WELL.
JUST WANTED YOU TO KNOW ***I'M*** OKAY.
I'M TRACKING THE EGG'S ENERGY AND I MAY NEED YOU, SO CALL ME WHEN YOU GET BACK TO EARTH.
SPEAKING OF THE HALL OF JUSTICE, THEY HAVE AN EXCELLENT MEDICAL FACILITY.
ONE COULD CHECK HOW THEY ARE DOING NOW THAT ONE IS NO LONGER THE RECENTLY DECEASED.

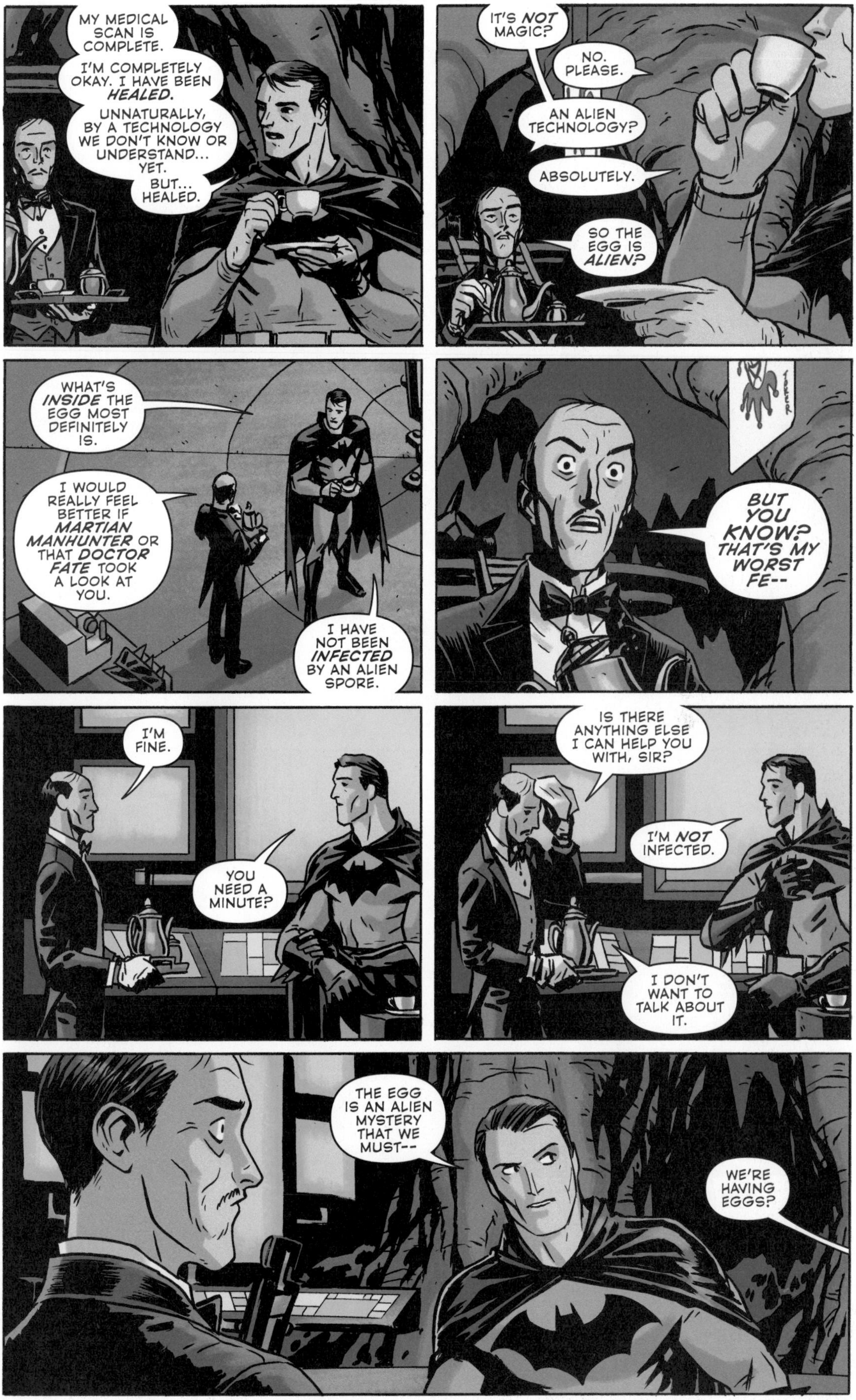
MY MEDICAL SCAN IS COMPLETE.
I'M COMPLETELY OKAY. I HAVE BEEN *HEALED.*
UNNATURALLY, BY A TECHNOLOGY WE DON'T KNOW OR UNDERSTAND... YET.
BUT... HEALED.
IT'S *NOT* MAGIC?
NO. PLEASE.
AN ALIEN TECHNOLOGY?
ABSOLUTELY.
SO THE EGG IS *ALIEN?*
WHAT'S *INSIDE* THE EGG MOST DEFINITELY IS.
I WOULD REALLY FEEL BETTER IF *MARTIAN MANHUNTER* OR THAT *DOCTOR FATE* TOOK A LOOK AT YOU.
I HAVE NOT BEEN *INFECTED* BY AN ALIEN SPORE.
BUT YOU KNOW? THAT'S MY WORST FE--
I'M FINE.
YOU NEED A MINUTE?
IS THERE ANYTHING ELSE I CAN HELP YOU WITH, SIR?
I'M *NOT* INFECTED.
I DON'T WANT TO TALK ABOUT IT.
THE EGG IS AN ALIEN MYSTERY THAT WE MUST--
WE'RE HAVING EGGS?

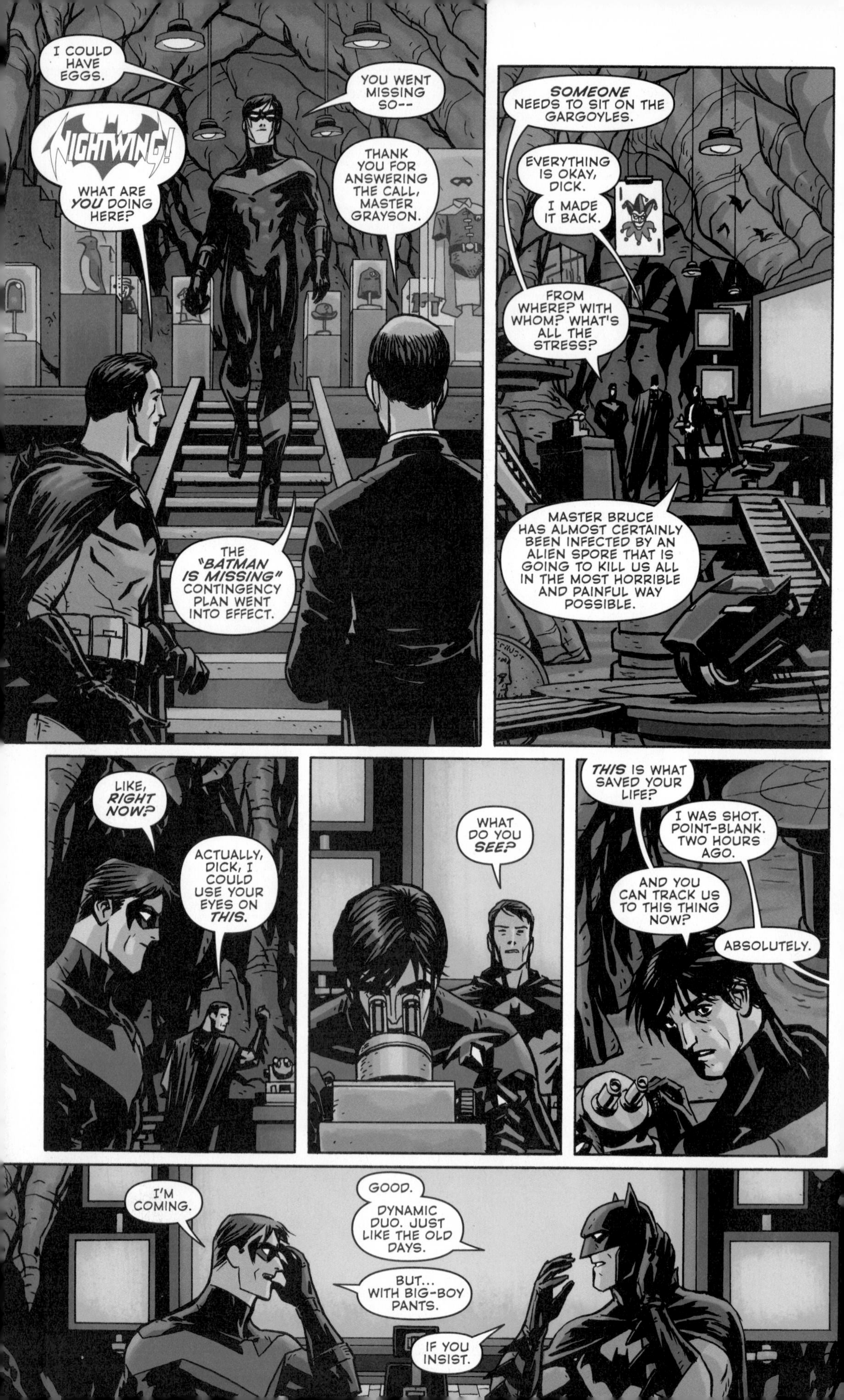
I COULD HAVE EGGS.
YOU WENT MISSING SO--
NIGHTWING! WHAT ARE YOU DOING HERE?
THANK YOU FOR ANSWERING THE CALL, MASTER GRAYSON.
THE "BATMAN IS MISSING" CONTINGENCY PLAN WENT INTO EFFECT.
SOMEONE NEEDS TO SIT ON THE GARGOYLES.
EVERYTHING IS OKAY, DICK.
I MADE IT BACK.
FROM WHERE? WITH WHOM? WHAT'S ALL THE STRESS?
MASTER BRUCE HAS ALMOST CERTAINLY BEEN INFECTED BY AN ALIEN SPORE THAT IS GOING TO KILL US ALL IN THE MOST HORRIBLE AND PAINFUL WAY POSSIBLE.
LIKE, RIGHT NOW?
ACTUALLY, DICK, I COULD USE YOUR EYES ON THIS.
WHAT DO YOU SEE?
THIS IS WHAT SAVED YOUR LIFE?
I WAS SHOT. POINT-BLANK. TWO HOURS AGO.
AND YOU CAN TRACK US TO THIS THING NOW?
ABSOLUTELY.
I'M COMING.
GOOD.
DYNAMIC DUO. JUST LIKE THE OLD DAYS.
BUT... WITH BIG-BOY PANTS.
IF YOU INSIST.

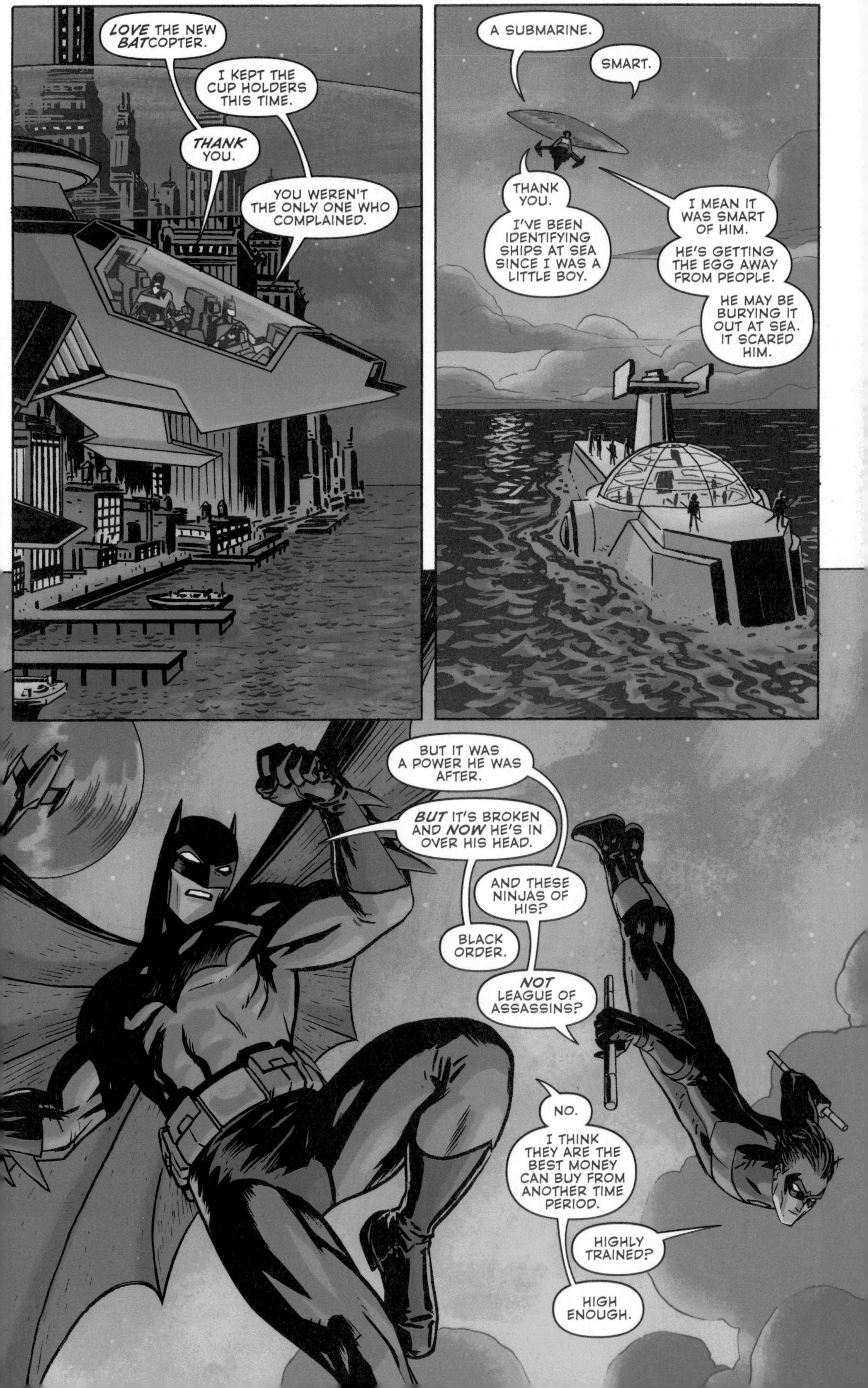

LOVE THE NEW BATCOPTER.
I KEPT THE CUP HOLDERS THIS TIME.
THANK YOU.
YOU WEREN'T THE ONLY ONE WHO COMPLAINED.
A SUBMARINE.
SMART.
THANK YOU.
I'VE BEEN IDENTIFYING SHIPS AT SEA SINCE I WAS A LITTLE BOY.
I MEAN IT WAS SMART OF HIM.
HE'S GETTING THE EGG AWAY FROM PEOPLE.
HE MAY BE BURYING IT OUT AT SEA. IT SCARED HIM.
BUT IT WAS A POWER HE WAS AFTER.
BUT IT'S BROKEN AND NOW HE'S IN OVER HIS HEAD.
AND THESE NINJAS OF HIS?
BLACK ORDER.
NOT LEAGUE OF ASSASSINS?
NO.
I THINK THEY ARE THE BEST MONEY CAN BUY FROM ANOTHER TIME PERIOD.
HIGHLY TRAINED?
HIGH ENOUGH.

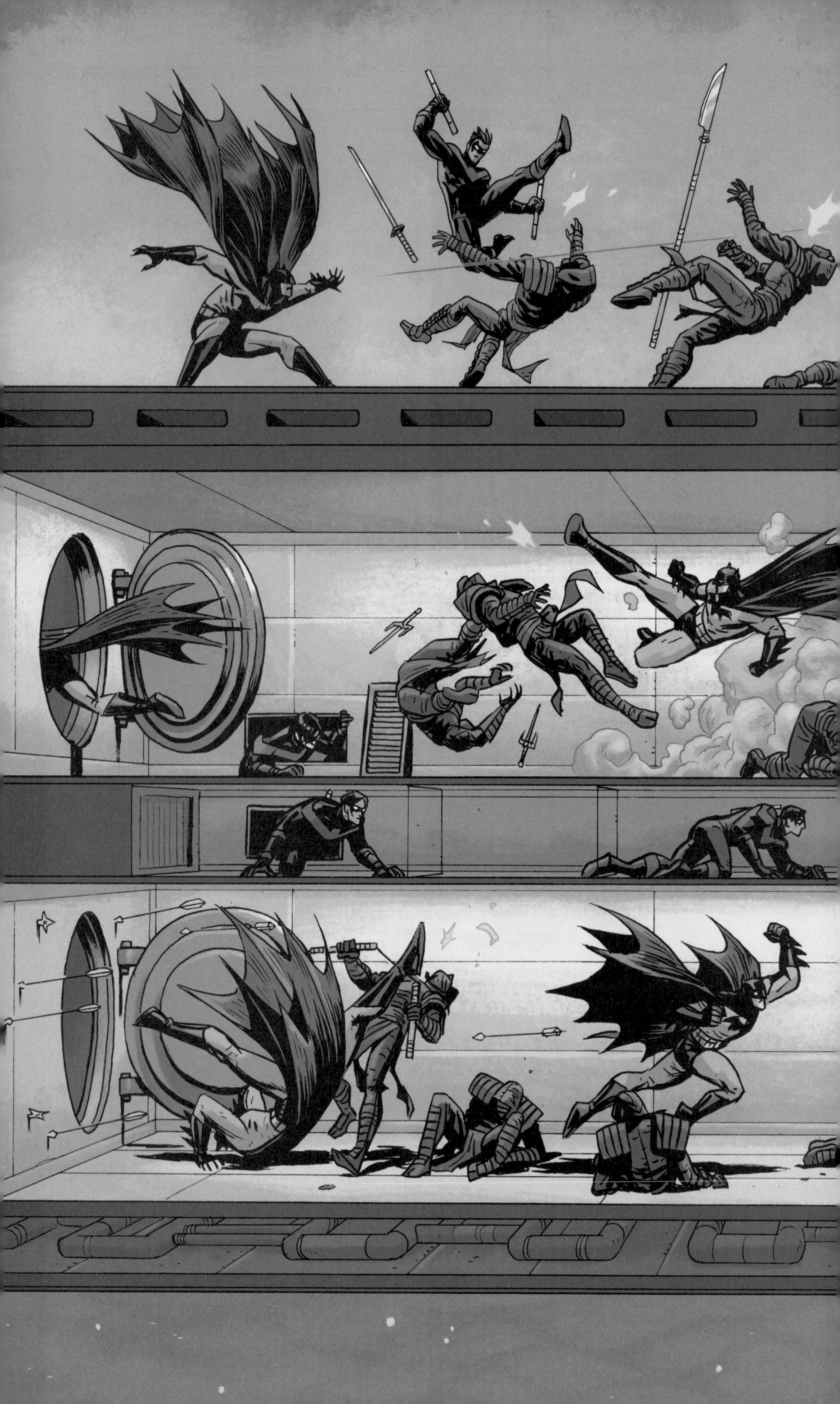

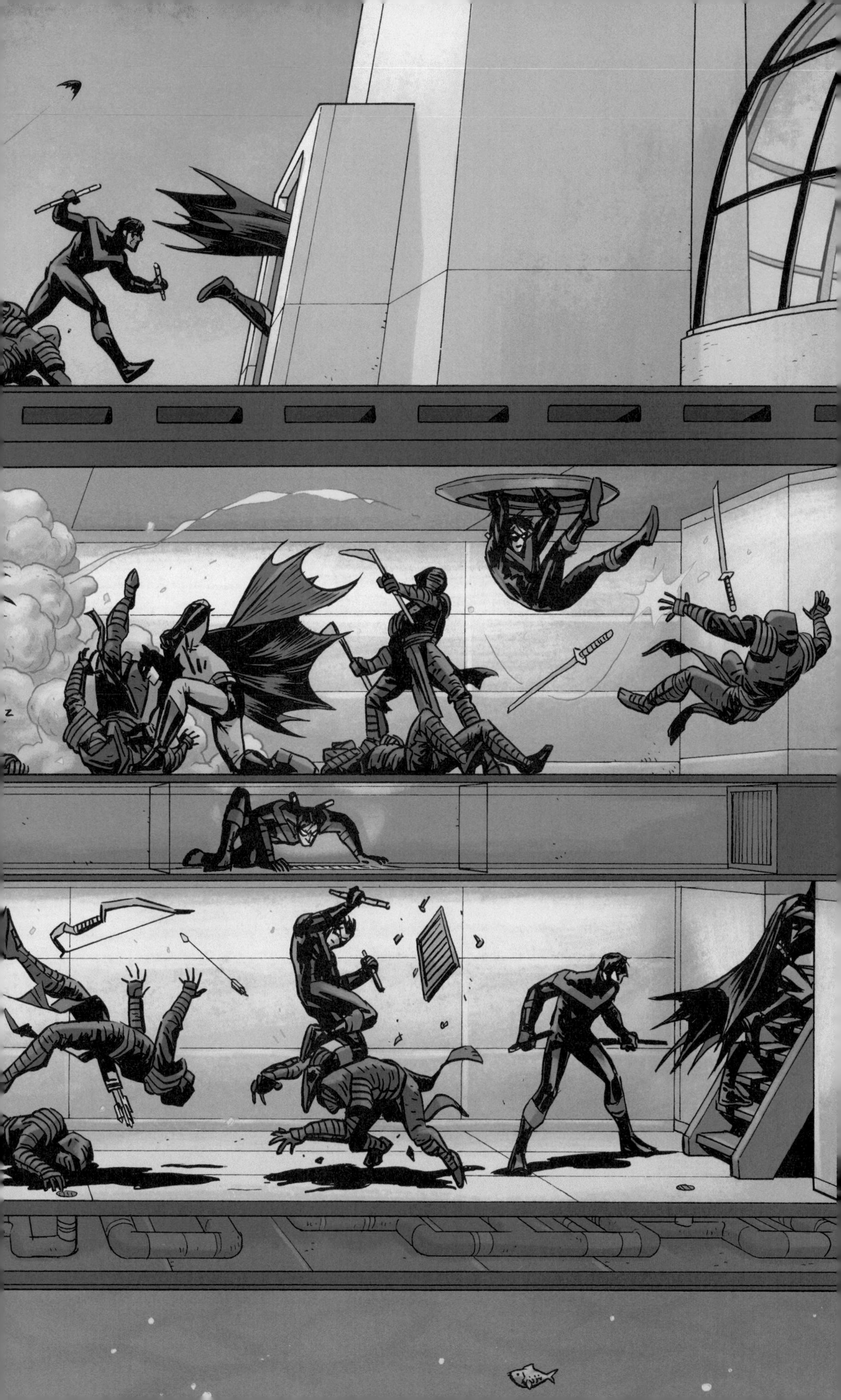

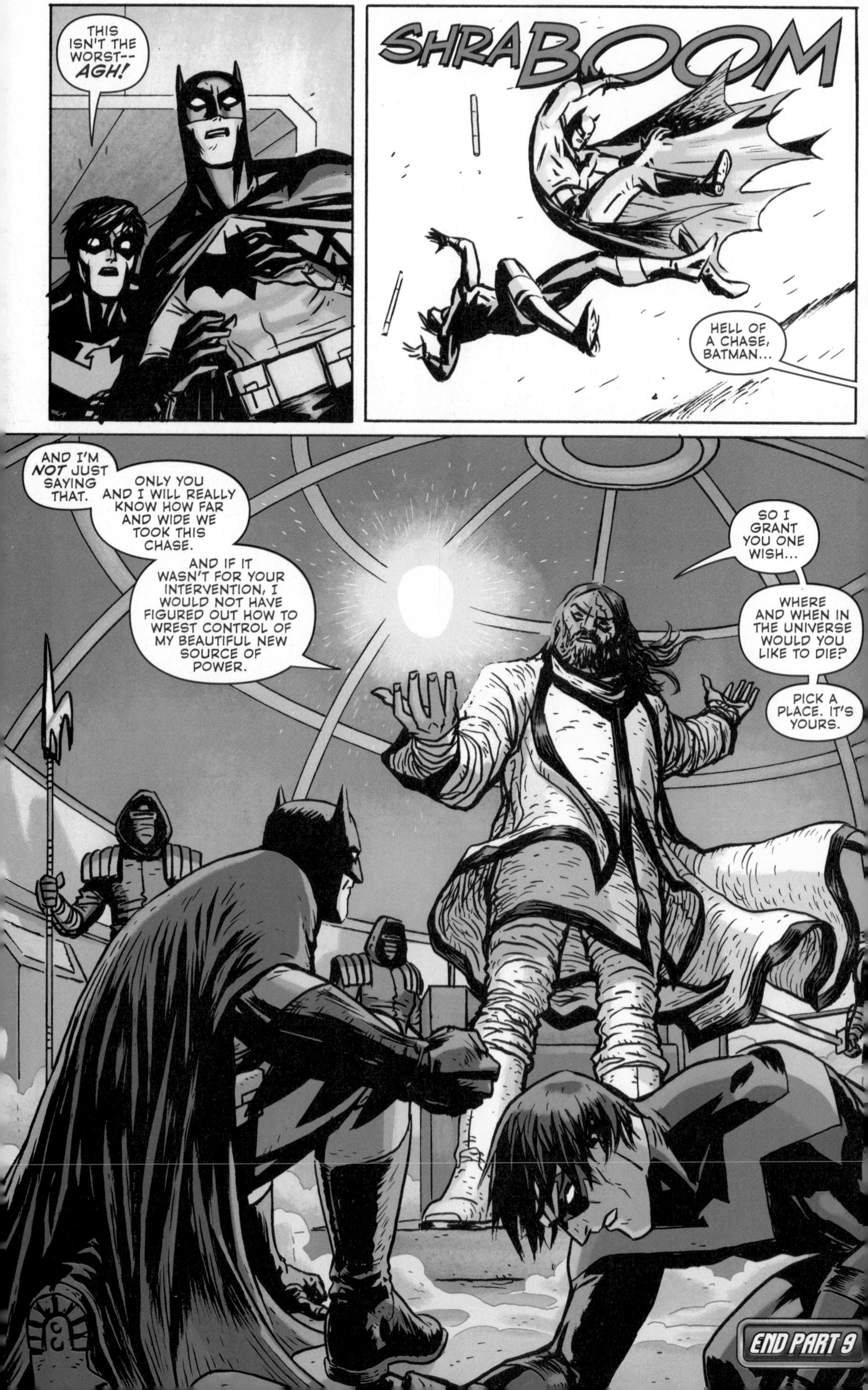

THIS ISN'T THE WORST-- AGH!
SHRABOOM
HELL OF A CHASE, BATMAN...
AND I'M NOT JUST SAYING THAT.
ONLY YOU AND I WILL REALLY KNOW HOW FAR AND WIDE WE TOOK THIS CHASE.
AND IF IT WASN'T FOR YOUR INTERVENTION, I WOULD NOT HAVE FIGURED OUT HOW TO WREST CONTROL OF MY BEAUTIFUL NEW SOURCE OF POWER.
SO I GRANT YOU ONE WISH...
WHERE AND WHEN IN THE UNIVERSE WOULD YOU LIKE TO DIE?
PICK A PLACE. IT'S YOURS.
END PART 9

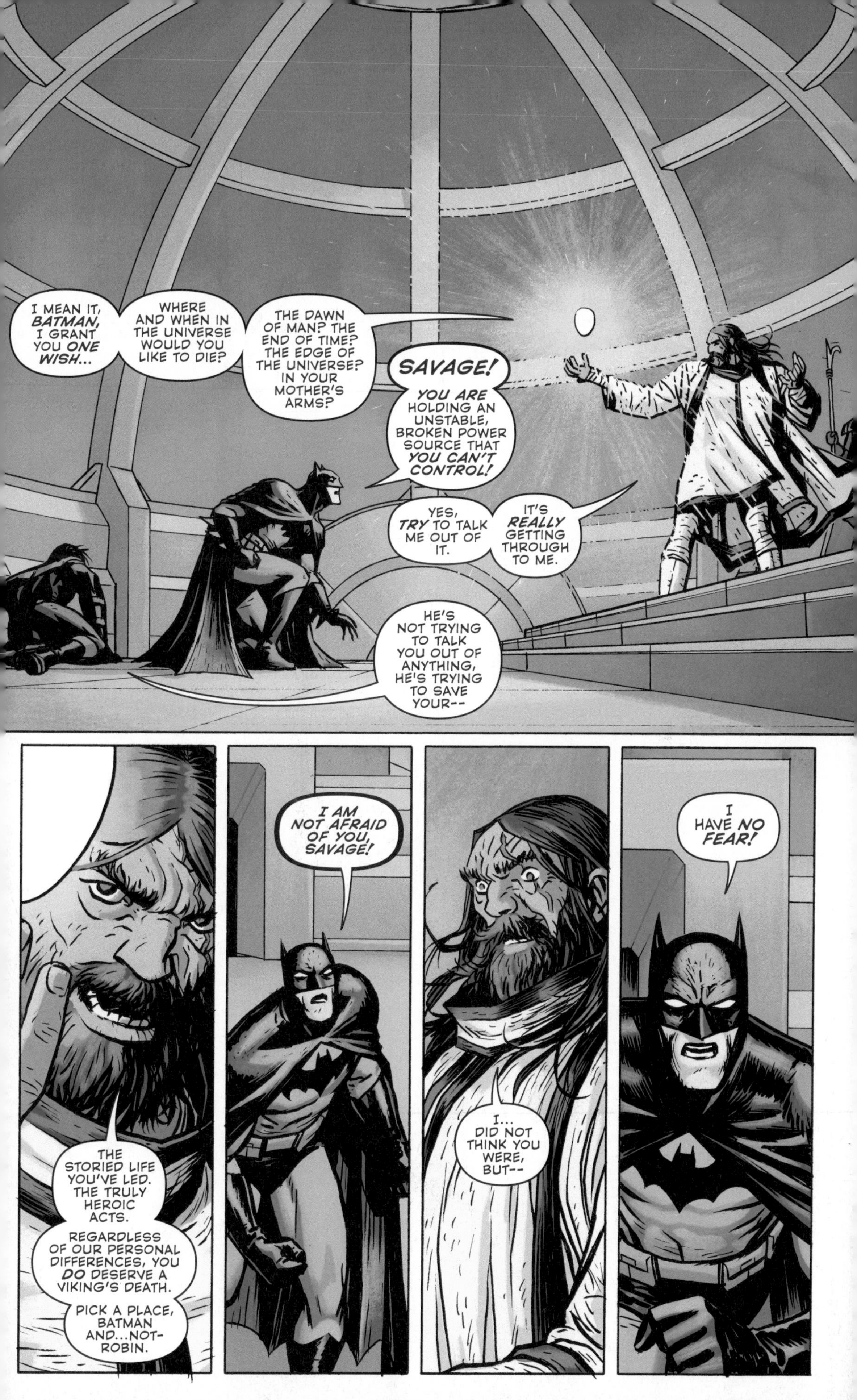
I MEAN IT, BATMAN, I GRANT YOU ONE WISH...
WHERE AND WHEN IN THE UNIVERSE WOULD YOU LIKE TO DIE?
THE DAWN OF MAN? THE END OF TIME? THE EDGE OF THE UNIVERSE? IN YOUR MOTHER'S ARMS?
SAVAGE!
YOU ARE HOLDING AN UNSTABLE, BROKEN POWER SOURCE THAT YOU CAN'T CONTROL!
YES, TRY TO TALK ME OUT OF IT.
IT'S REALLY GETTING THROUGH TO ME.
HE'S NOT TRYING TO TALK YOU OUT OF ANYTHING, HE'S TRYING TO SAVE YOUR--
THE STORIED LIFE YOU'VE LED. THE TRULY HEROIC ACTS.
REGARDLESS OF OUR PERSONAL DIFFERENCES, YOU DO DESERVE A VIKING'S DEATH.
PICK A PLACE, BATMAN AND...NOT-ROBIN.
I AM NOT AFRAID OF YOU, SAVAGE!
I... DID NOT THINK YOU WERE, BUT--
I HAVE NO FEAR!

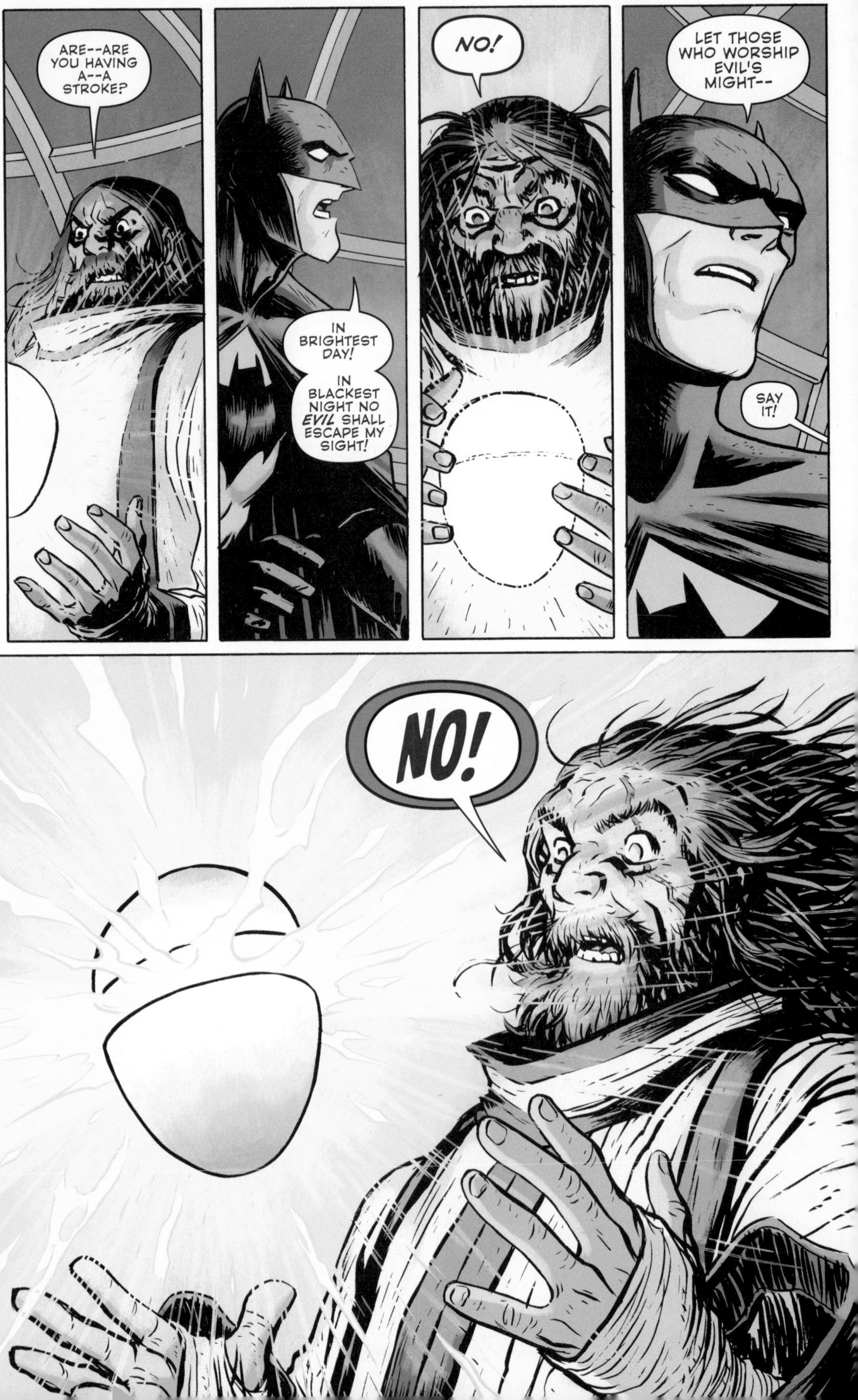
ARE--ARE YOU HAVING A--A STROKE?
IN BRIGHTEST DAY!
IN BLACKEST NIGHT NO EVIL SHALL ESCAPE MY SIGHT!
NO!
LET THOSE WHO WORSHIP EVIL'S MIGHT--
SAY IT!
NO!

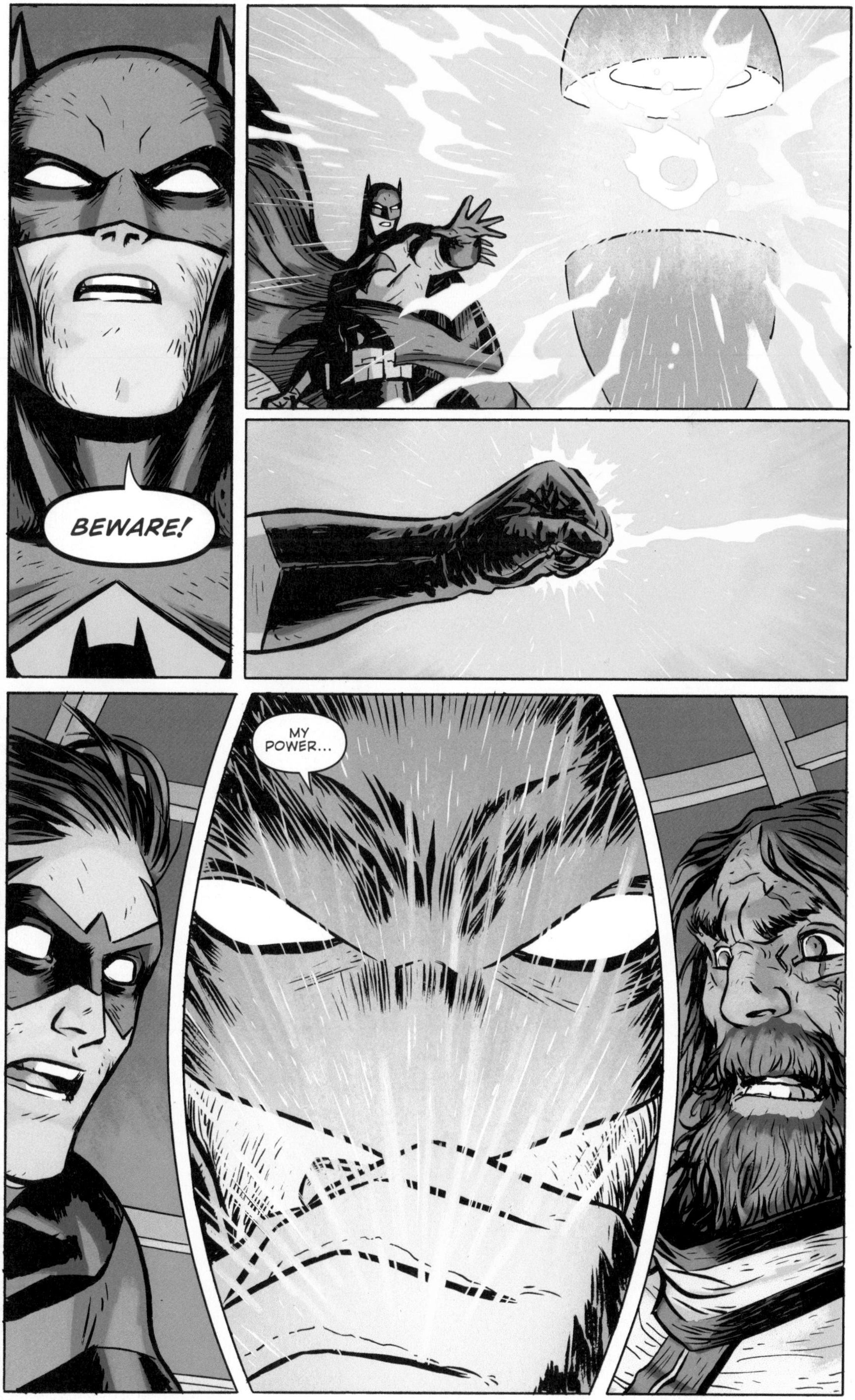

BEWARE!
MY POWER...

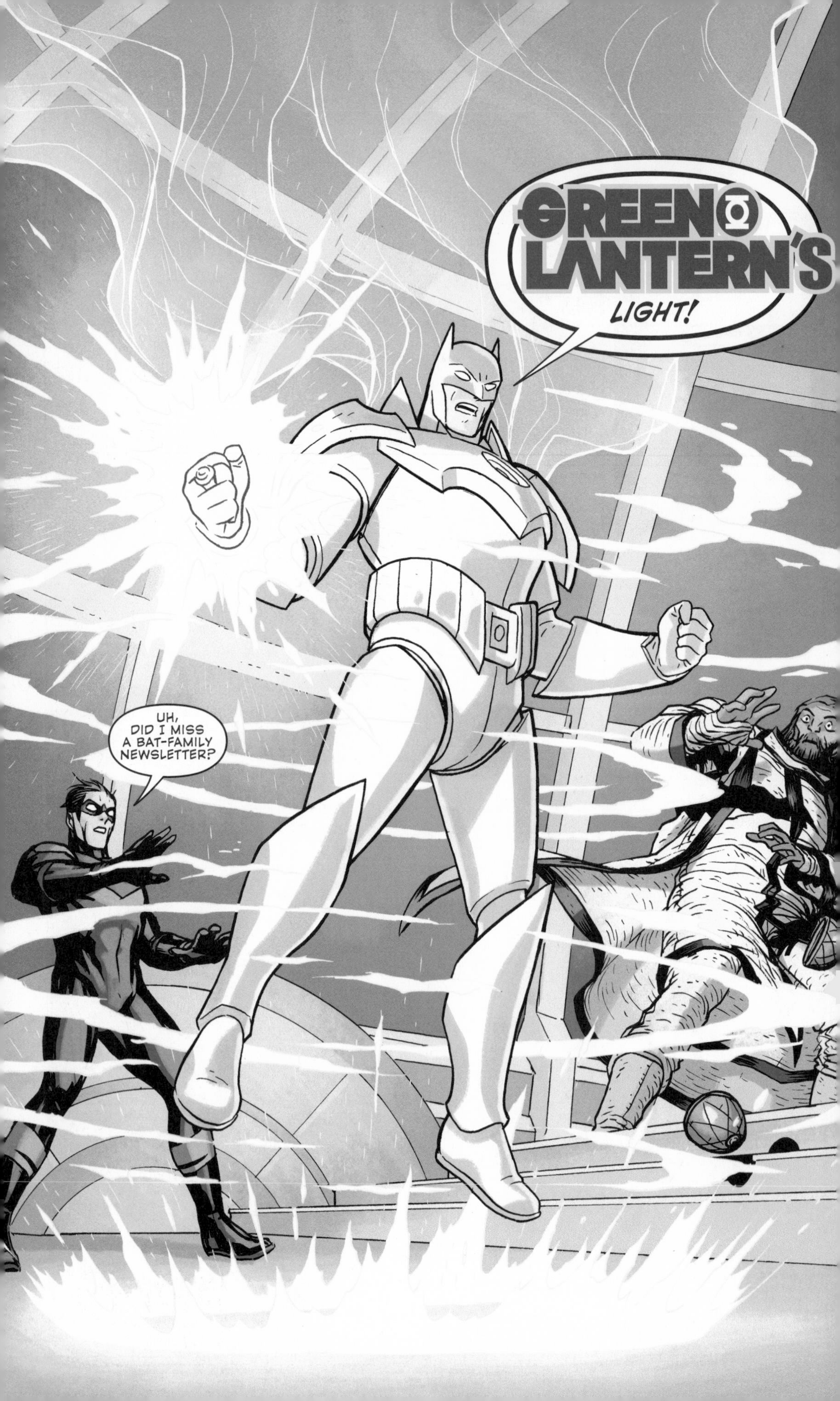
GREEN LANTERN'S LIGHT!
UH, DID I MISS A BAT-FAMILY NEWSLETTER?

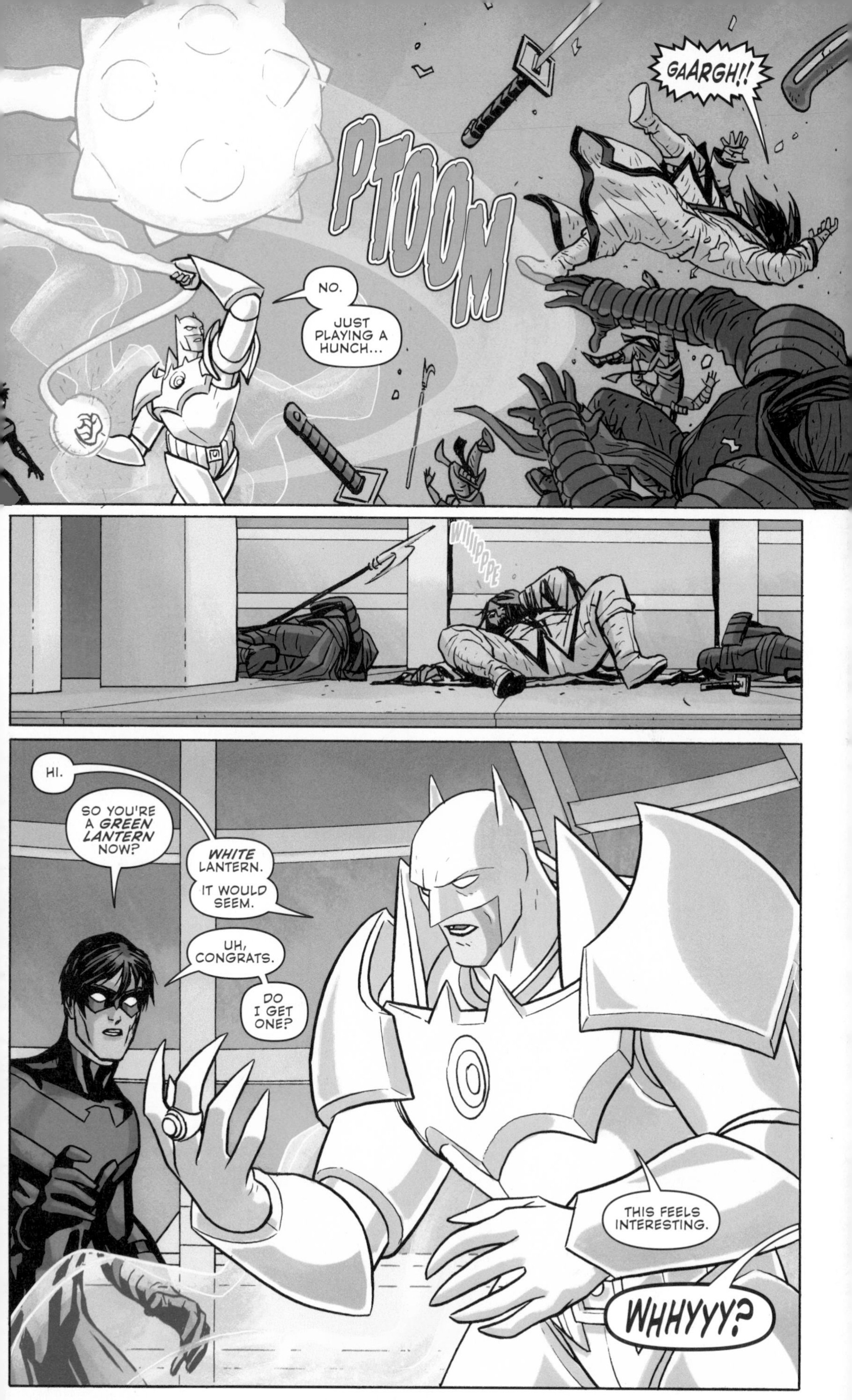
PTOOM
GAARGH!!
NO.
JUST PLAYING A HUNCH...
WIIIPPPE
HI.
SO YOU'RE A *GREEN LANTERN* NOW?
WHITE LANTERN.
IT WOULD SEEM.
UH, CONGRATS.
DO I GET ONE?
THIS FEELS INTERESTING.
WHHYYY?

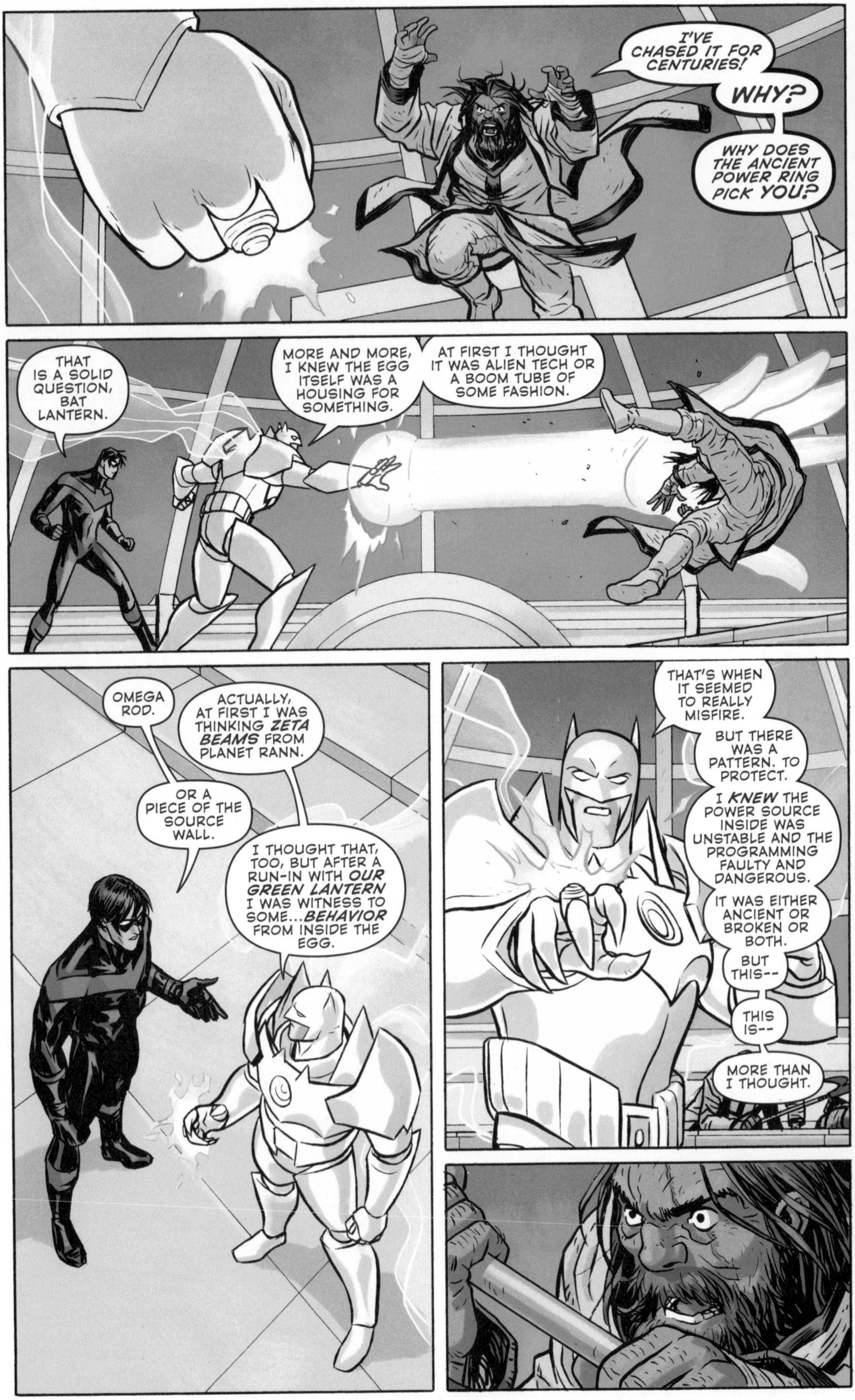
I'VE CHASED IT FOR CENTURIES!
WHY?
WHY DOES THE ANCIENT POWER RING PICK YOU?
THAT IS A SOLID QUESTION, BAT LANTERN.
MORE AND MORE, I KNEW THE EGG ITSELF WAS A HOUSING FOR SOMETHING.
AT FIRST I THOUGHT IT WAS ALIEN TECH OR A BOOM TUBE OF SOME FASHION.
OMEGA ROD.
ACTUALLY, AT FIRST I WAS THINKING ZETA BEAMS FROM PLANET RANN.
OR A PIECE OF THE SOURCE WALL.
I THOUGHT THAT, TOO, BUT AFTER A RUN-IN WITH OUR GREEN LANTERN I WAS WITNESS TO SOME...BEHAVIOR FROM INSIDE THE EGG.
THAT'S WHEN IT SEEMED TO REALLY MISFIRE.
BUT THERE WAS A PATTERN. TO PROTECT.
I KNEW THE POWER SOURCE INSIDE WAS UNSTABLE AND THE PROGRAMMING FAULTY AND DANGEROUS.
IT WAS EITHER ANCIENT OR BROKEN OR BOTH.
BUT THIS--
THIS IS--
MORE THAN I THOUGHT.

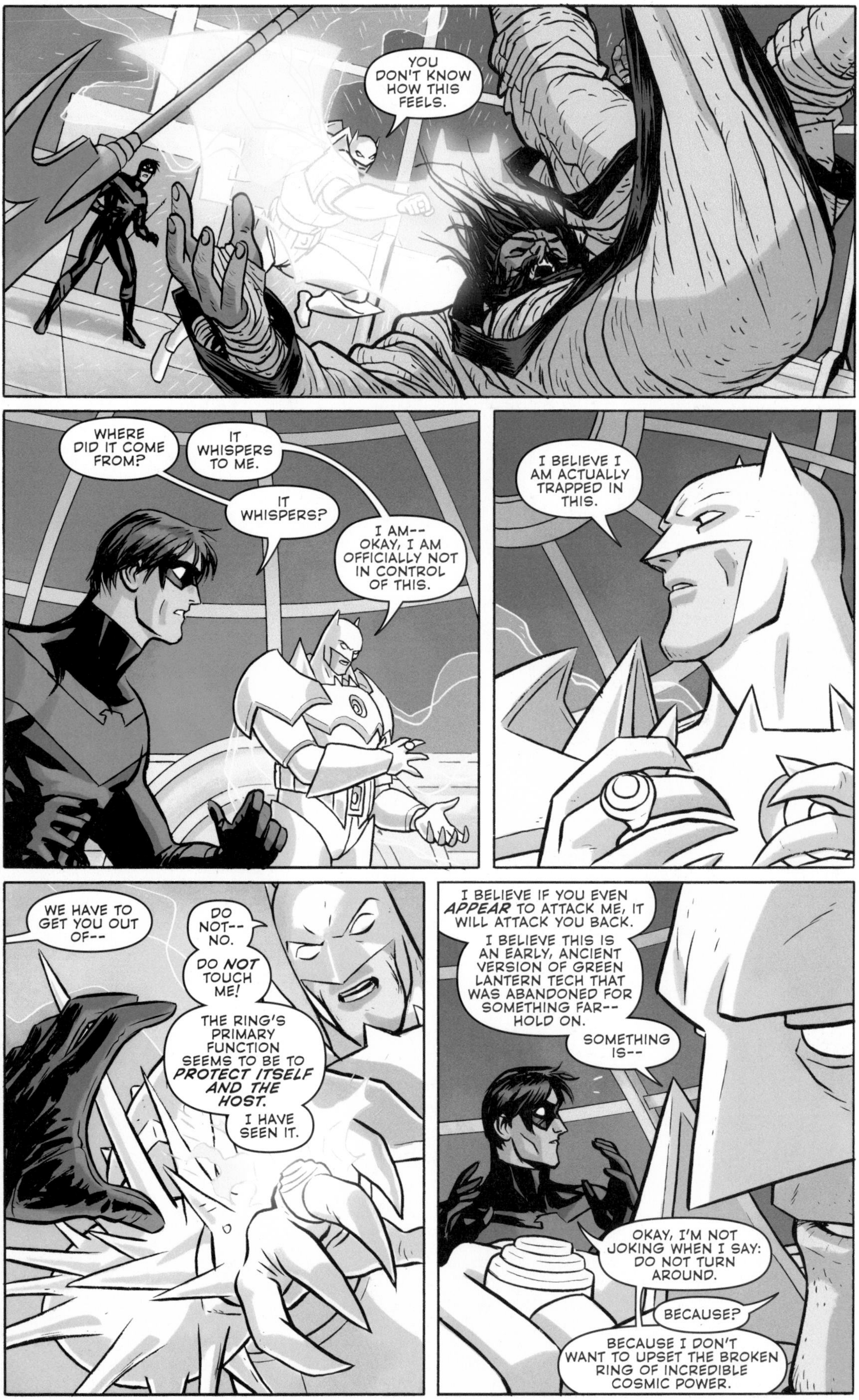
YOU DON'T KNOW HOW THIS FEELS.
WHERE DID IT COME FROM?
IT WHISPERS TO ME.
IT WHISPERS?
I AM-- OKAY, I AM OFFICIALLY NOT IN CONTROL OF THIS.
I BELIEVE I AM ACTUALLY TRAPPED IN THIS.
WE HAVE TO GET YOU OUT OF--
DO NOT-- NO.
DO NOT TOUCH ME!
THE RING'S PRIMARY FUNCTION SEEMS TO BE TO PROTECT ITSELF AND THE HOST.
I HAVE SEEN IT.
I BELIEVE IF YOU EVEN APPEAR TO ATTACK ME, IT WILL ATTACK YOU BACK.
I BELIEVE THIS IS AN EARLY, ANCIENT VERSION OF GREEN LANTERN TECH THAT WAS ABANDONED FOR SOMETHING FAR-- HOLD ON.
SOMETHING IS--
OKAY, I'M NOT JOKING WHEN I SAY: DO NOT TURN AROUND.
BECAUSE?
BECAUSE I DON'T WANT TO UPSET THE BROKEN RING OF INCREDIBLE COSMIC POWER.

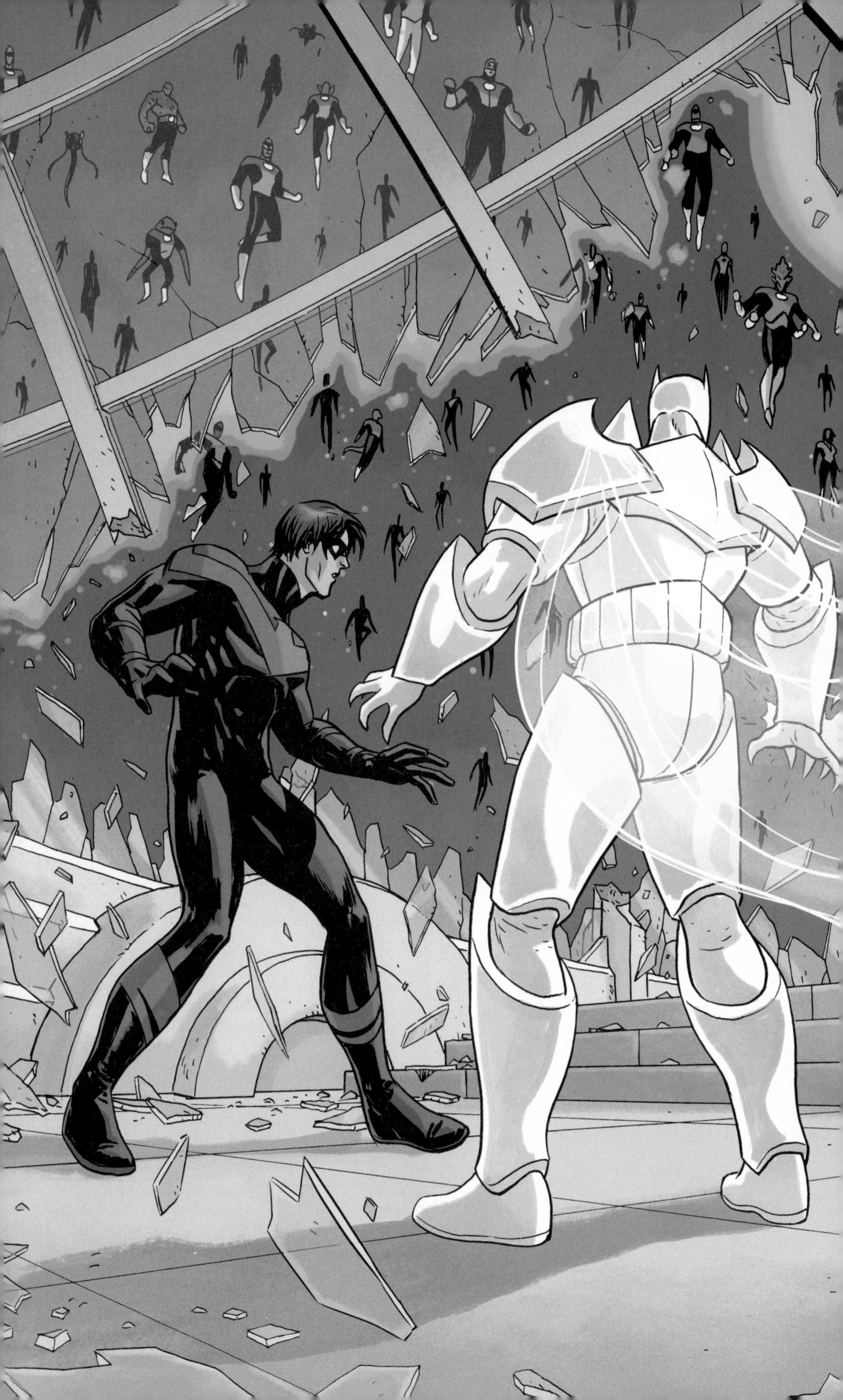

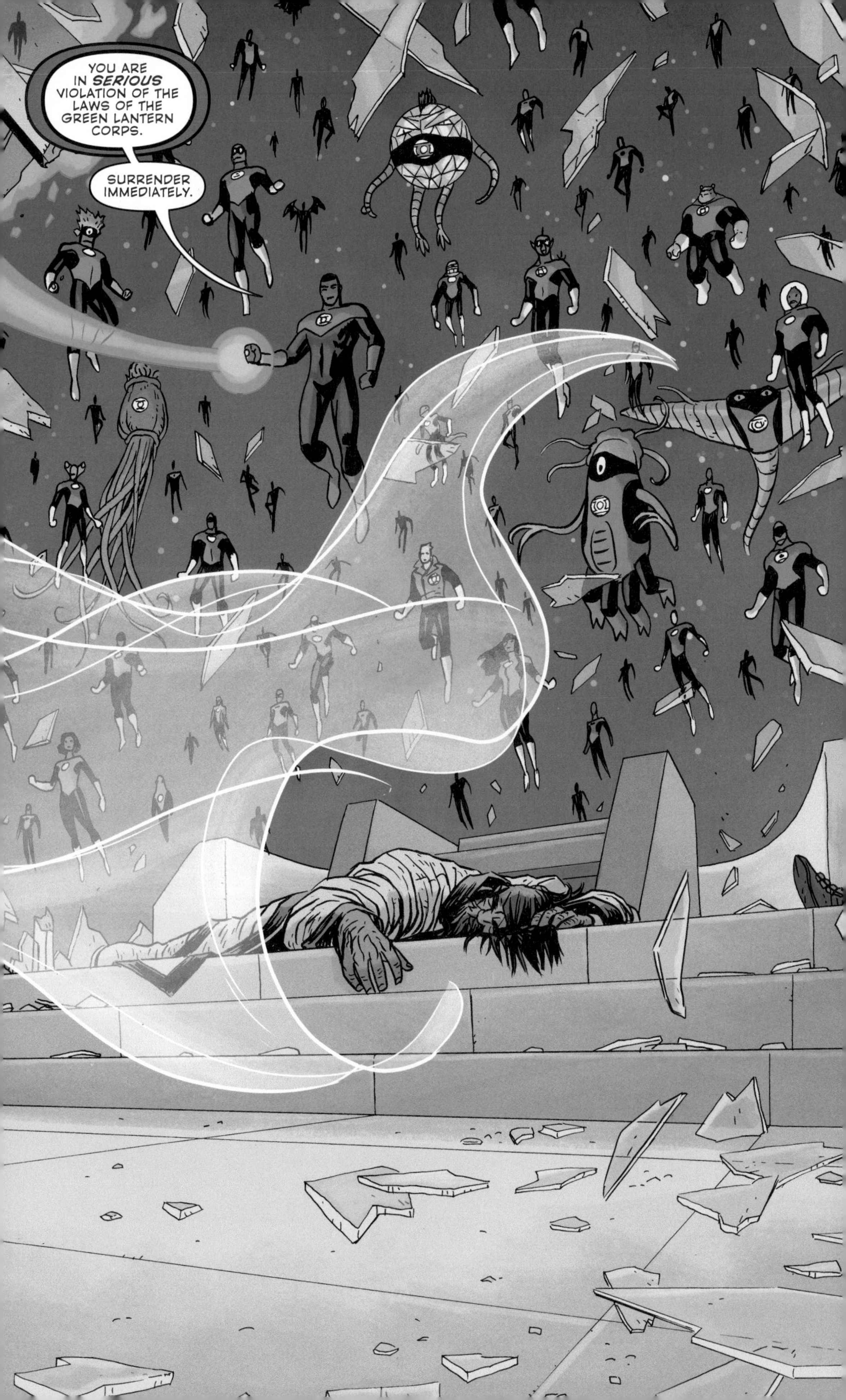

YOU ARE IN SERIOUS VIOLATION OF THE LAWS OF THE GREEN LANTERN CORPS.
SURRENDER IMMEDIATELY.

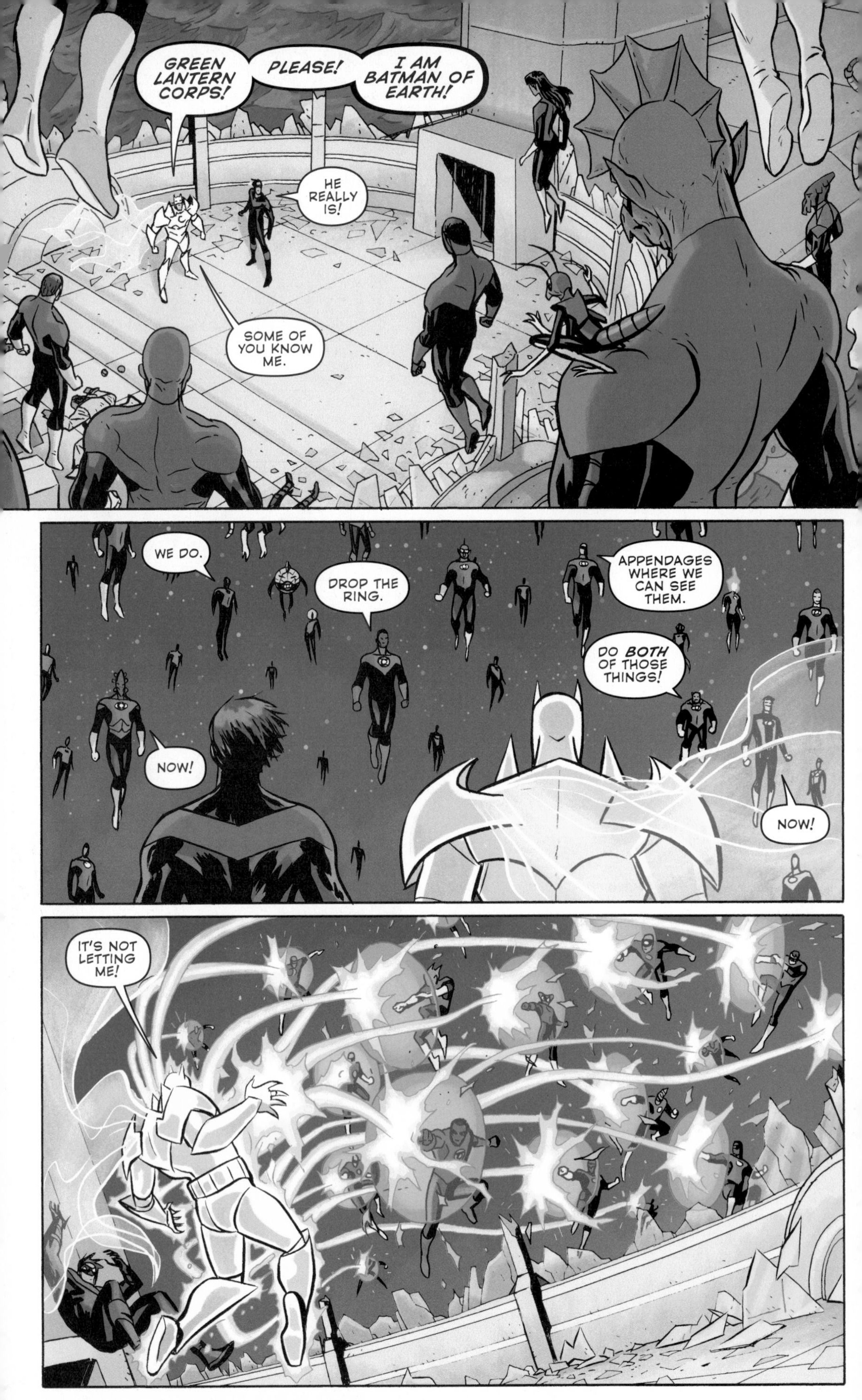
GREEN LANTERN CORPS!
PLEASE!
I AM BATMAN OF EARTH!
HE REALLY IS!
SOME OF YOU KNOW ME.
WE DO.
DROP THE RING.
APPENDAGES WHERE WE CAN SEE THEM.
DO BOTH OF THOSE THINGS!
NOW!
NOW!
IT'S NOT LETTING ME!

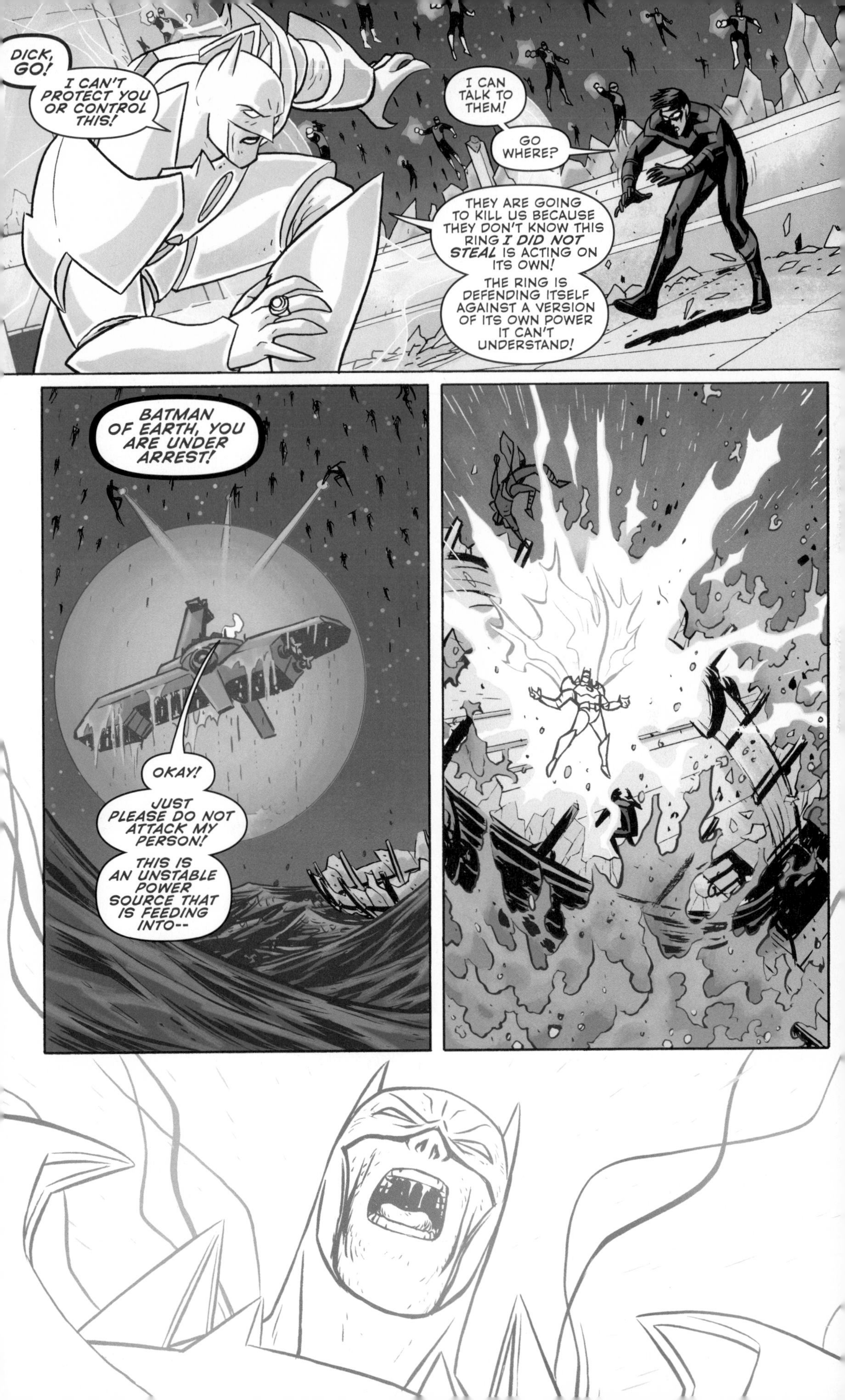
DICK, GO!
I CAN'T PROTECT YOU OR CONTROL THIS!
I CAN TALK TO THEM!
GO WHERE?
THEY ARE GOING TO KILL US BECAUSE THEY DON'T KNOW THIS RING I DID NOT STEAL IS ACTING ON ITS OWN!
THE RING IS DEFENDING ITSELF AGAINST A VERSION OF ITS OWN POWER IT CAN'T UNDERSTAND!
BATMAN OF EARTH, YOU ARE UNDER ARREST!
OKAY!
JUST PLEASE DO NOT ATTACK MY PERSON!
THIS IS AN UNSTABLE POWER SOURCE THAT IS FEEDING INTO--

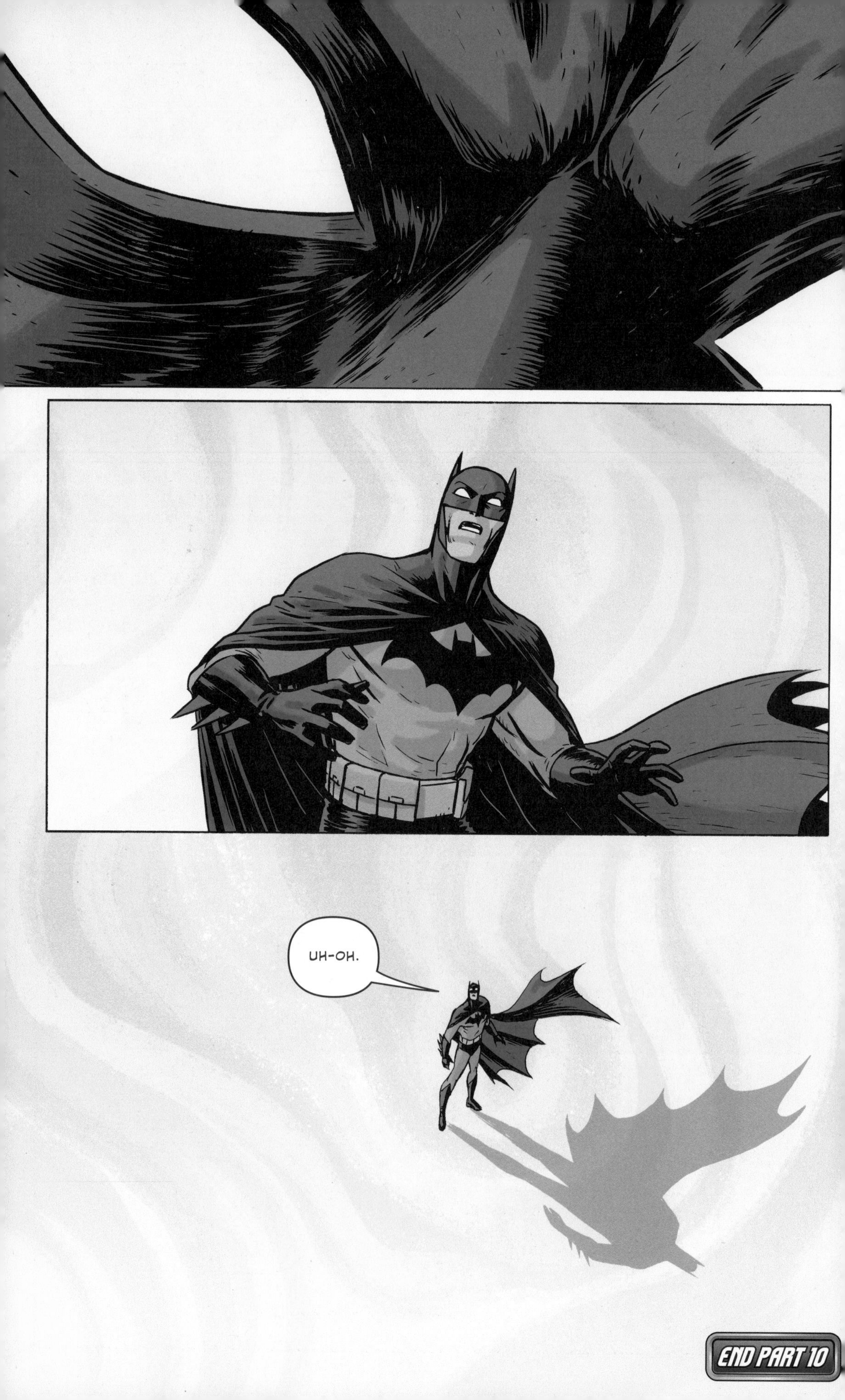
UH-OH.
END PART 10

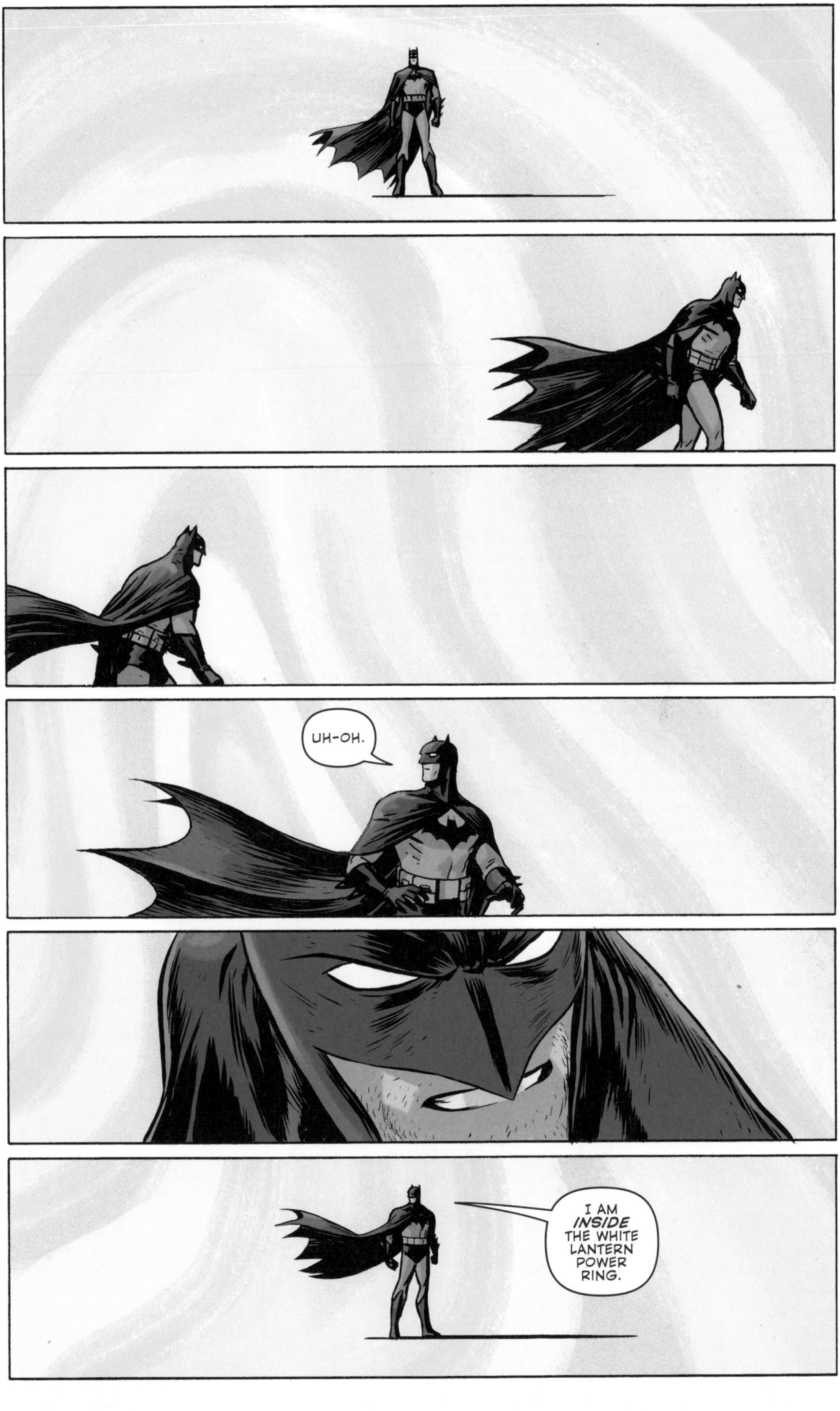
UH-OH.
I AM *INSIDE* THE WHITE LANTERN POWER RING.

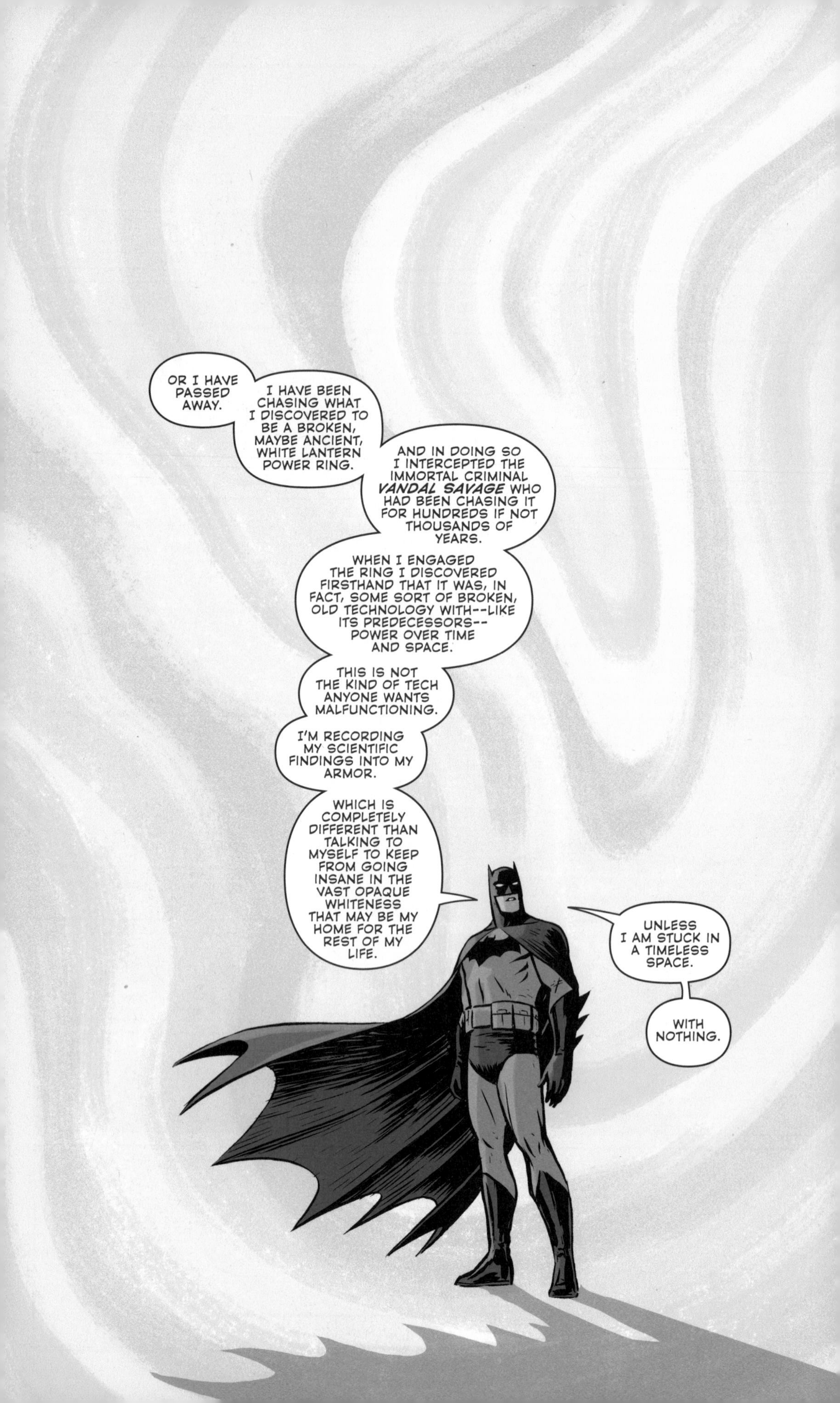
OR I HAVE PASSED AWAY.
I HAVE BEEN CHASING WHAT I DISCOVERED TO BE A BROKEN, MAYBE ANCIENT, WHITE LANTERN POWER RING.
AND IN DOING SO I INTERCEPTED THE IMMORTAL CRIMINAL *VANDAL SAVAGE* WHO HAD BEEN CHASING IT FOR HUNDREDS IF NOT THOUSANDS OF YEARS.
WHEN I ENGAGED THE RING I DISCOVERED FIRSTHAND THAT IT WAS, IN FACT, SOME SORT OF BROKEN, OLD TECHNOLOGY WITH--LIKE ITS PREDECESSORS--POWER OVER TIME AND SPACE.
THIS IS NOT THE KIND OF TECH ANYONE WANTS MALFUNCTIONING.
I'M RECORDING MY SCIENTIFIC FINDINGS INTO MY ARMOR.
WHICH IS COMPLETELY DIFFERENT THAN TALKING TO MYSELF TO KEEP FROM GOING INSANE IN THE VAST OPAQUE WHITENESS THAT MAY BE MY HOME FOR THE REST OF MY LIFE.
UNLESS I AM STUCK IN A TIMELESS SPACE.
WITH NOTHING.

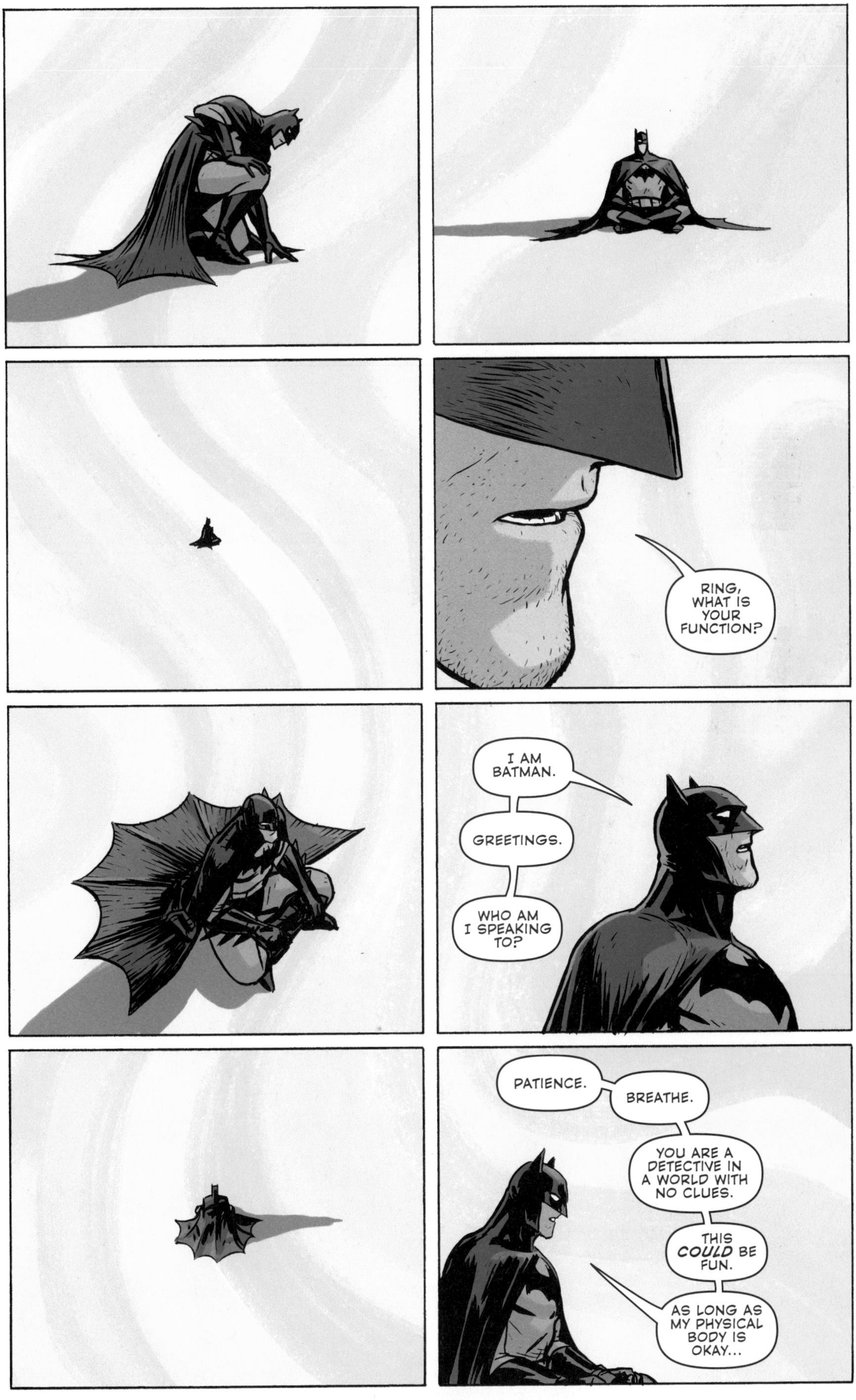
RING, WHAT IS YOUR FUNCTION?
I AM BATMAN.
GREETINGS.
WHO AM I SPEAKING TO?
PATIENCE.
BREATHE.
YOU ARE A DETECTIVE IN A WORLD WITH NO CLUES.
THIS *COULD* BE FUN.
AS LONG AS MY PHYSICAL BODY IS OKAY...

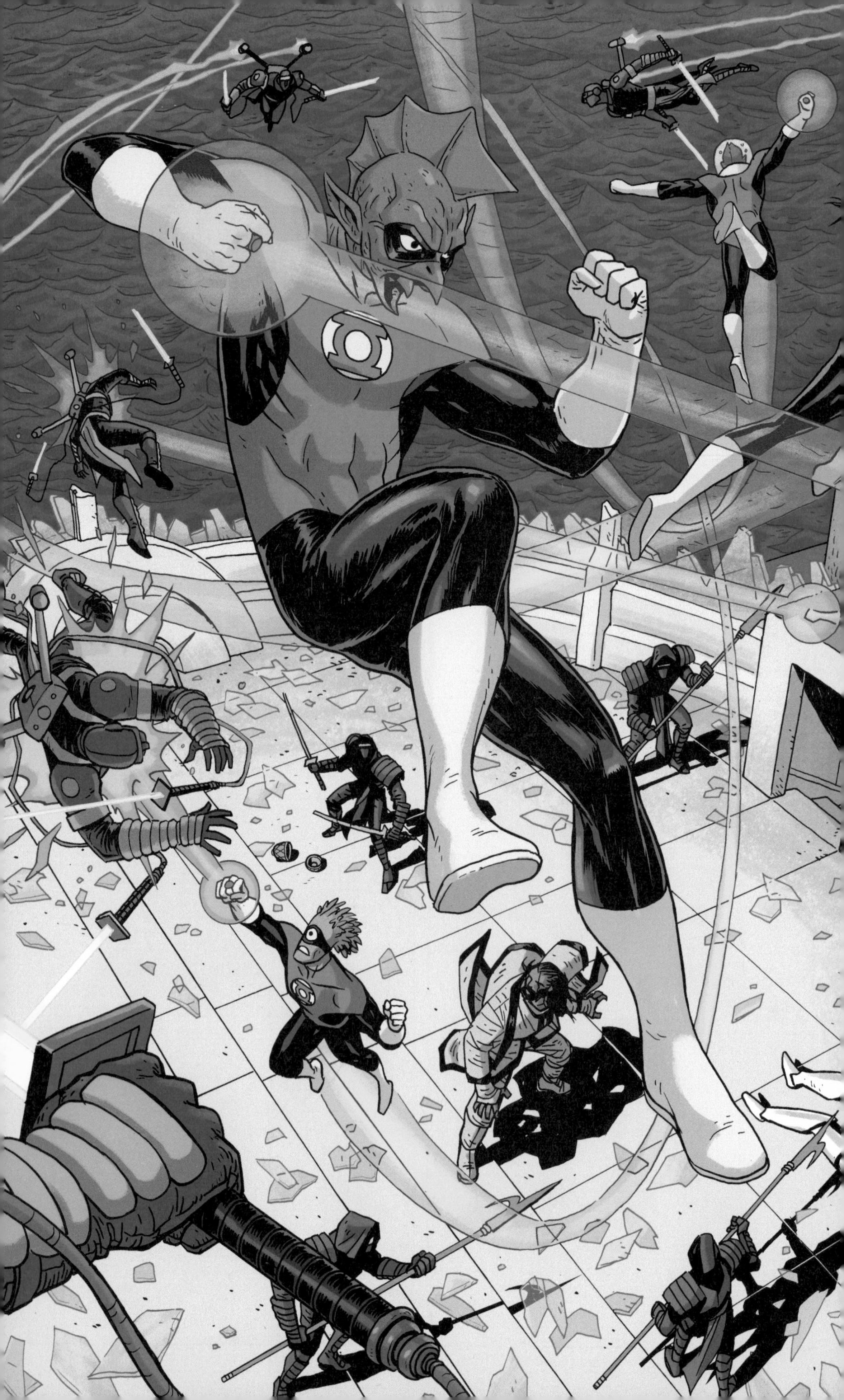

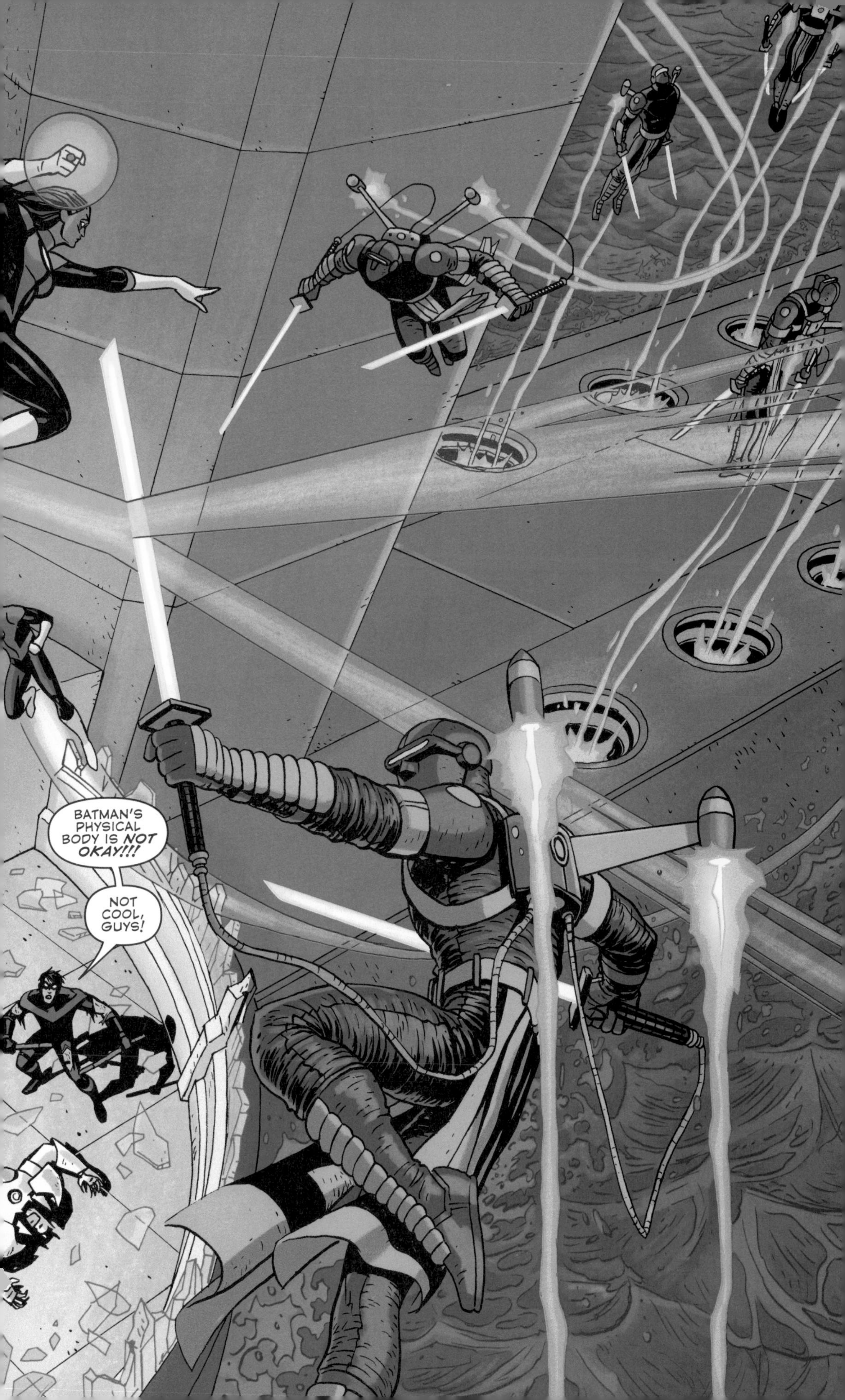
BATMAN'S PHYSICAL BODY IS NOT OKAY!!!
NOT COOL, GUYS!

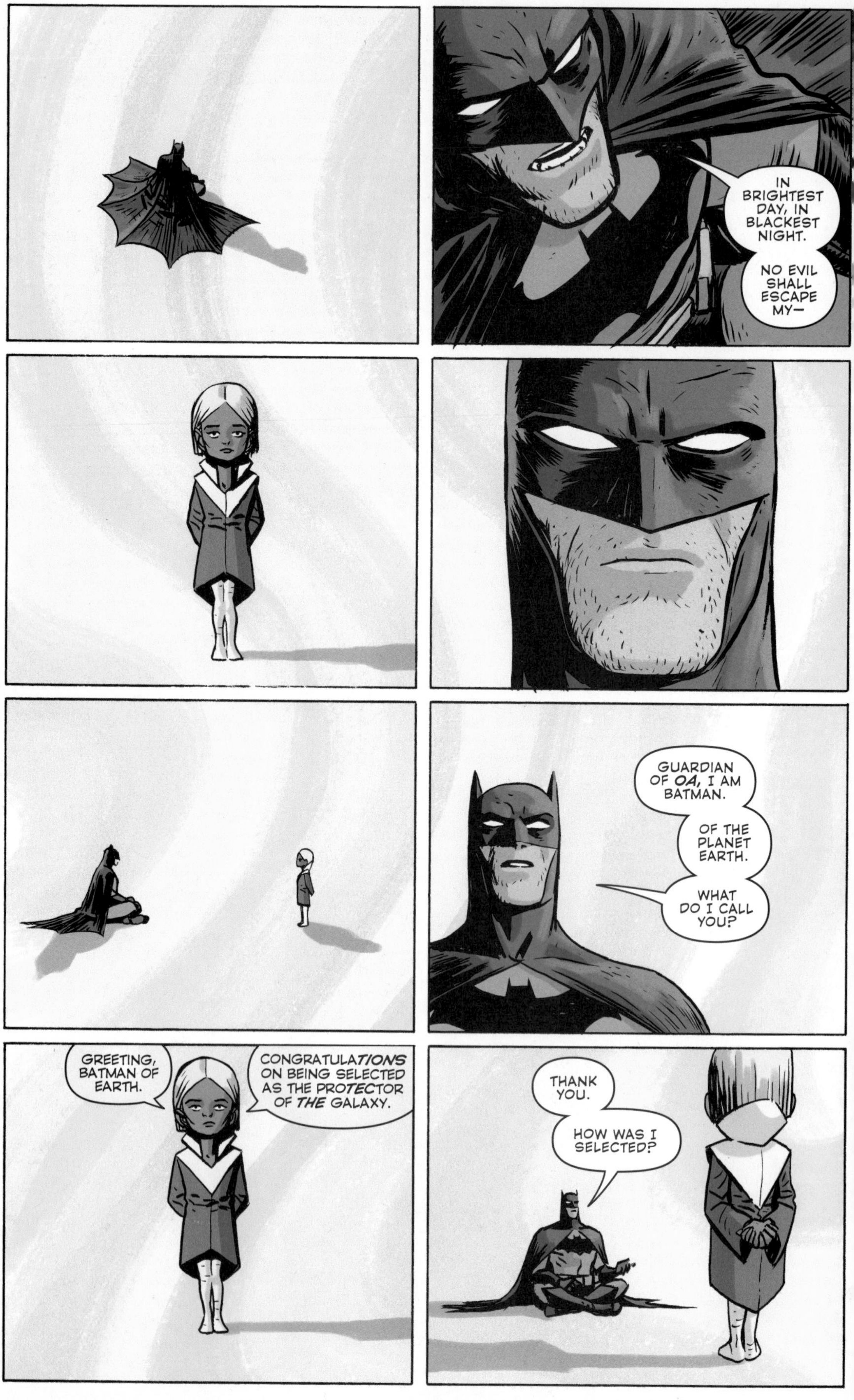
IN BRIGHTEST DAY, IN BLACKEST NIGHT.
NO EVIL SHALL ESCAPE MY—
GUARDIAN OF OA, I AM BATMAN.
OF THE PLANET EARTH.
WHAT DO I CALL YOU?
GREETING, BATMAN OF EARTH.
CONGRATULATIONS ON BEING SELECTED AS THE PROTECTOR OF THE GALAXY.
THANK YOU.
HOW WAS I SELECTED?

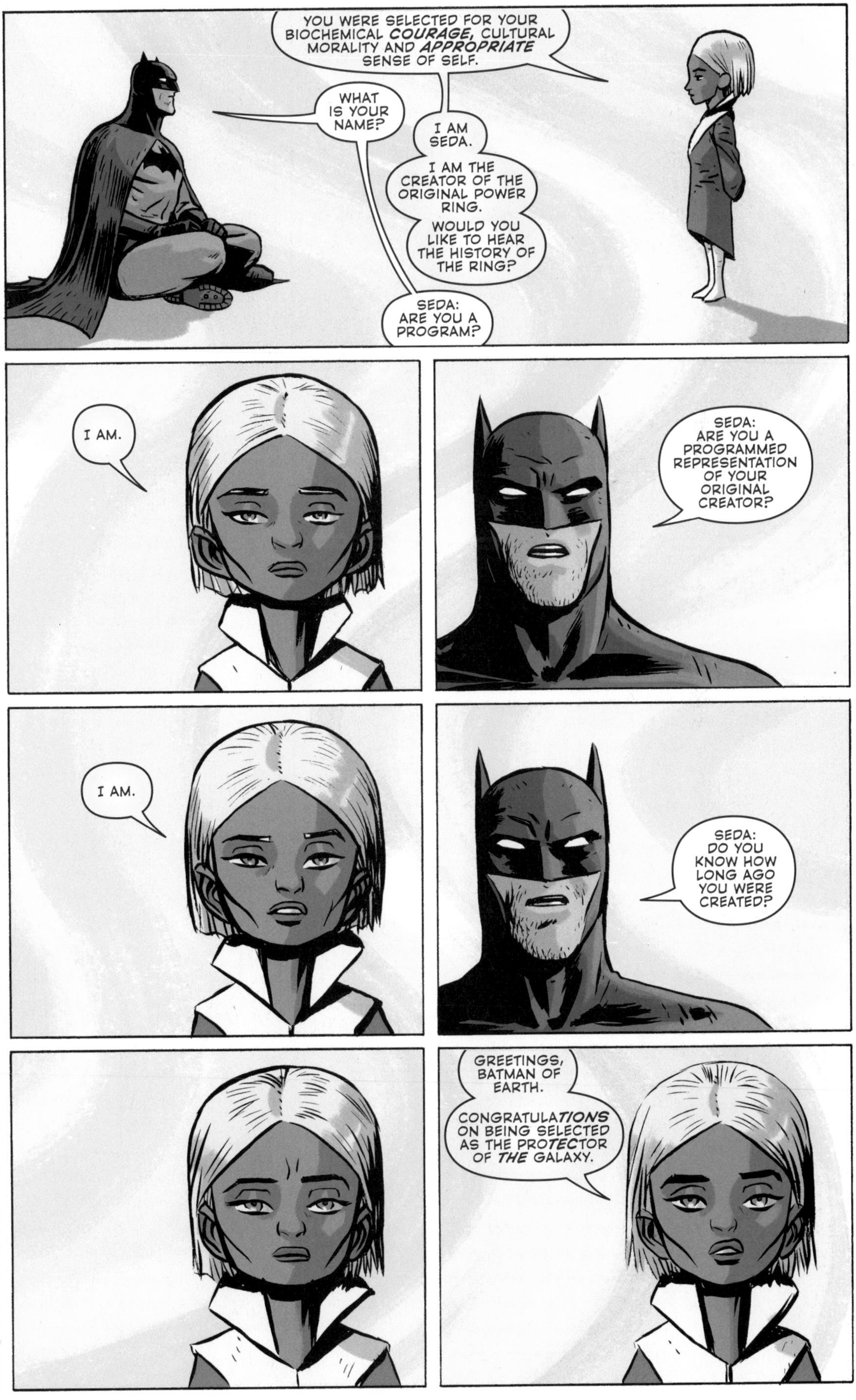
YOU WERE SELECTED FOR YOUR BIOCHEMICAL COURAGE, CULTURAL MORALITY AND APPROPRIATE SENSE OF SELF.
WHAT IS YOUR NAME?
I AM SEDA.
I AM THE CREATOR OF THE ORIGINAL POWER RING.
WOULD YOU LIKE TO HEAR THE HISTORY OF THE RING?
SEDA: ARE YOU A PROGRAM?
I AM.
SEDA: ARE YOU A PROGRAMMED REPRESENTATION OF YOUR ORIGINAL CREATOR?
I AM.
SEDA: DO YOU KNOW HOW LONG AGO YOU WERE CREATED?
GREETINGS, BATMAN OF EARTH.
CONGRATULATIONS ON BEING SELECTED AS THE PROTECTOR OF THE GALAXY.

UH-OH.

BATMAN OF EARTH QUADRANT...

AS A MEMBER OF THE LANTERN CORPS YOU WILL HAVE ACCESS TO A POWER SOURCE BATTERY THAT RELIES ON WILL-POWER AND PERSONAL--

SEDA: YOUR CREATOR CREATED, FROM WHAT I AM GATHERING, THE FIRST VERSION OF THE POWER RING A *VERY* LONG TIME AGO.

NOT ONLY HAS THIS RING PROGRAM AND MODEL BEEN IMPROVED ON OVER THE YEARS...

THE PROGRAM THAT IS YOU--YOUR PROGRAM--HAS BEEN CORRUPTED.

IT IS DAMAGED.

SEDA: THIS RING WAS LOST ON THE PLANET EARTH FOR MANY YEARS AND NOW THAT IT HAS BEEN DISTURBED IT IS A VERY LARGE THREAT TO US.

YOUR RING'S POWER MATRIX OVER TIME AND SPACE IS DANGEROUS *BECAUSE* OF THE DAMAGE TO *YOUR* PROGRAM.

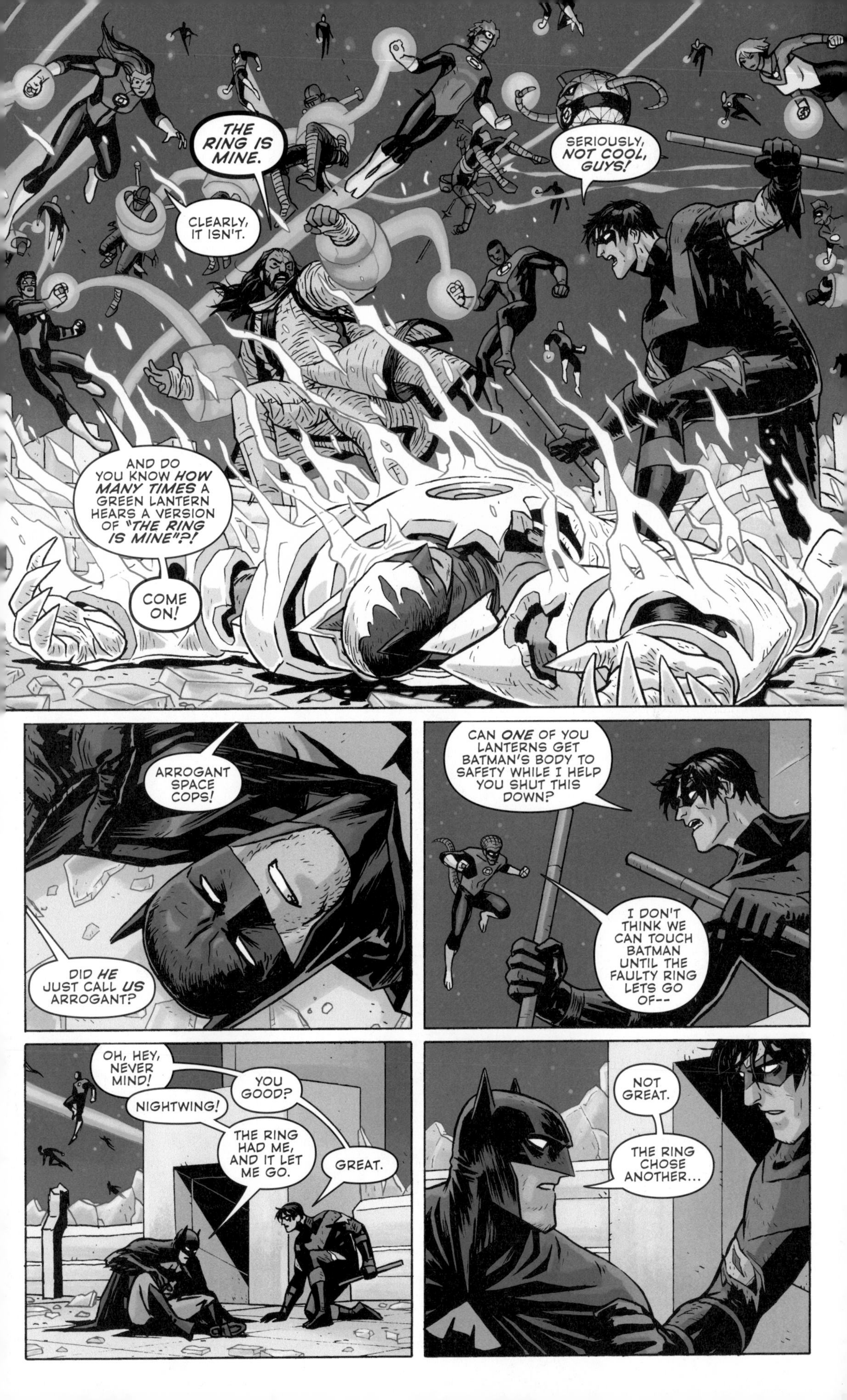

THE RING IS MINE.
CLEARLY, IT ISN'T.
SERIOUSLY, NOT COOL, GUYS!
AND DO YOU KNOW HOW MANY TIMES A GREEN LANTERN HEARS A VERSION OF "THE RING IS MINE"?!
COME ON!
ARROGANT SPACE COPS!
DID HE JUST CALL US ARROGANT?
CAN ONE OF YOU LANTERNS GET BATMAN'S BODY TO SAFETY WHILE I HELP YOU SHUT THIS DOWN?
I DON'T THINK WE CAN TOUCH BATMAN UNTIL THE FAULTY RING LETS GO OF--
OH, HEY, NEVER MIND!
NIGHTWING!
YOU GOOD?
THE RING HAD ME, AND IT LET ME GO.
GREAT.
NOT GREAT.
THE RING CHOSE ANOTHER...

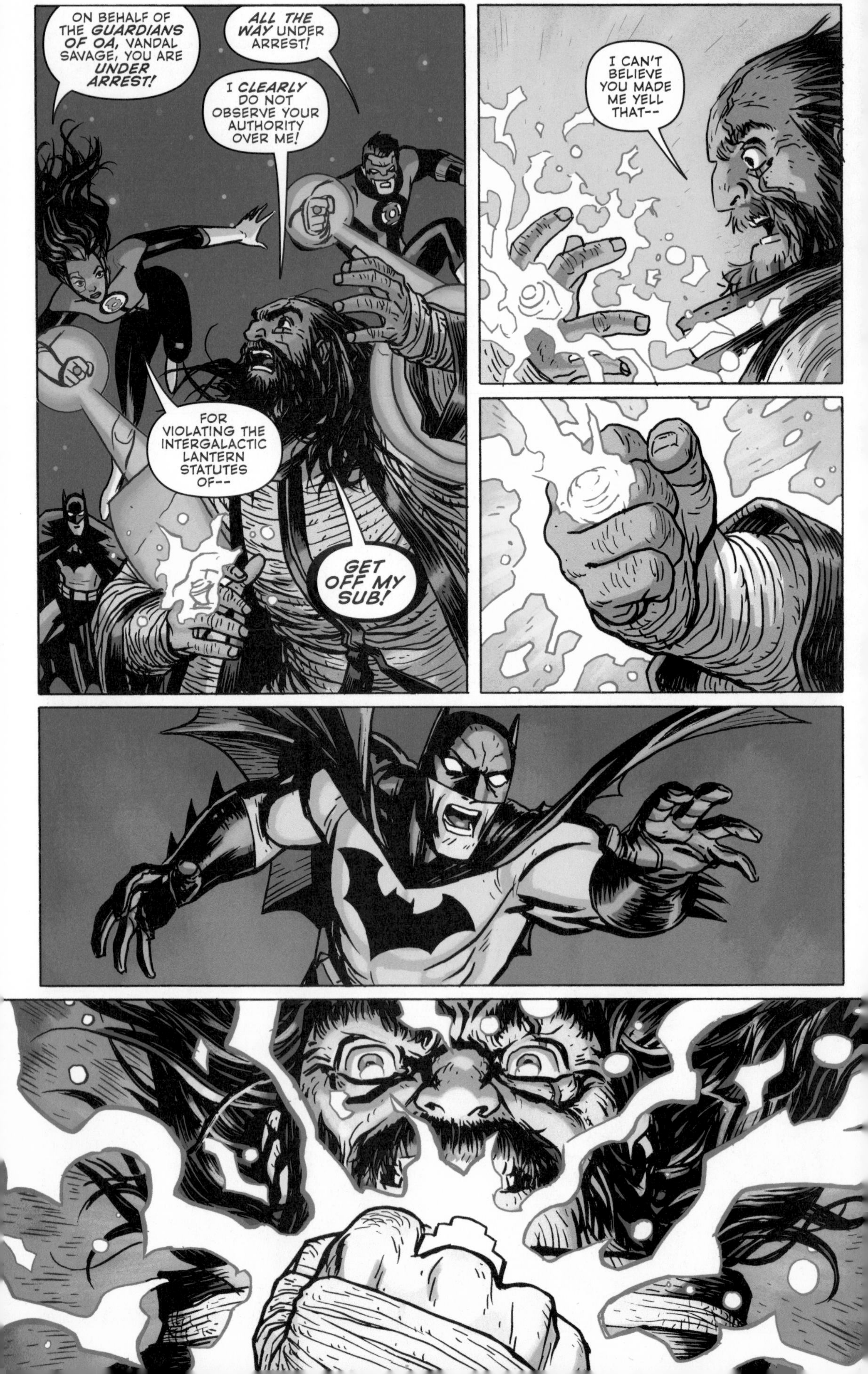
ON BEHALF OF THE GUARDIANS OF OA, VANDAL SAVAGE, YOU ARE UNDER ARREST!
ALL THE WAY UNDER ARREST!
I CLEARLY DO NOT OBSERVE YOUR AUTHORITY OVER ME!
FOR VIOLATING THE INTERGALACTIC LANTERN STATUTES OF--
GET OFF MY SUB!
I CAN'T BELIEVE YOU MADE ME YELL THAT--

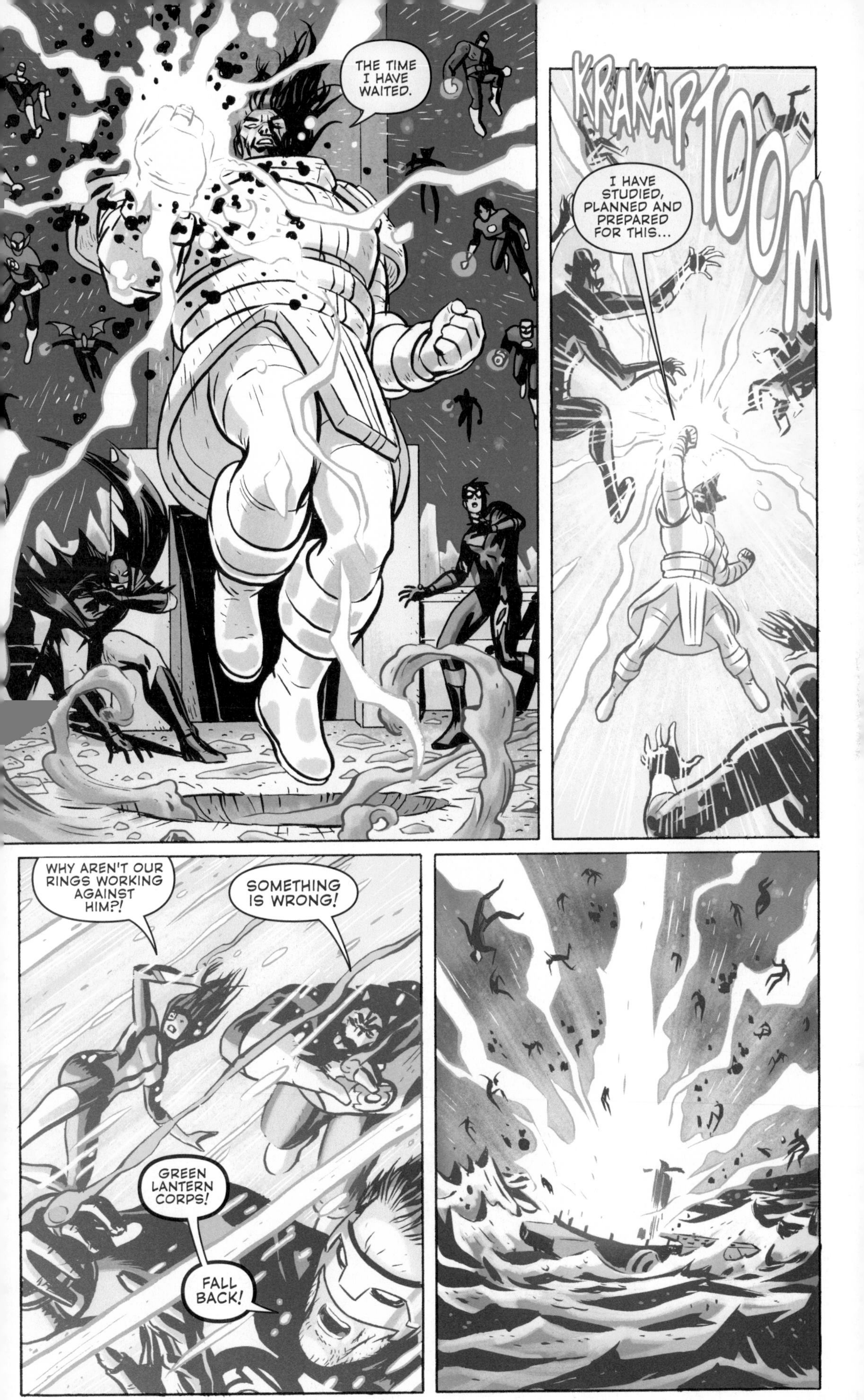
THE TIME I HAVE WAITED.
KRAKAPTOOM
I HAVE STUDIED, PLANNED AND PREPARED FOR THIS...
WHY AREN'T OUR RINGS WORKING AGAINST HIM?!
SOMETHING IS WRONG!
GREEN LANTERN CORPS!
FALL BACK!

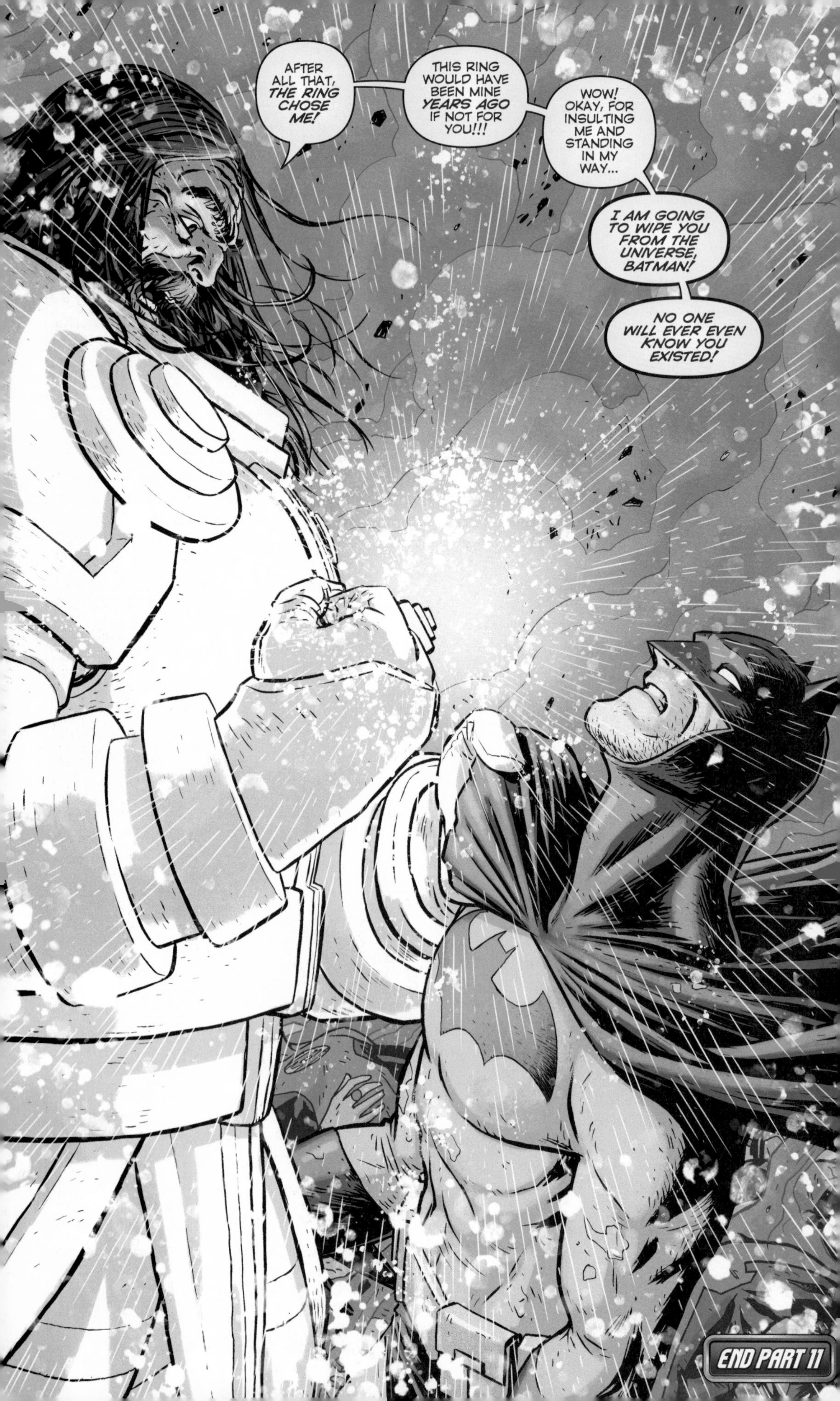

AFTER ALL THAT, THE RING CHOSE ME!
THIS RING WOULD HAVE BEEN MINE YEARS AGO IF NOT FOR YOU!!!
WOW! OKAY, FOR INSULTING ME AND STANDING IN MY WAY...
I AM GOING TO WIPE YOU FROM THE UNIVERSE, BATMAN!
NO ONE WILL EVER EVEN KNOW YOU EXISTED!
END PART 11

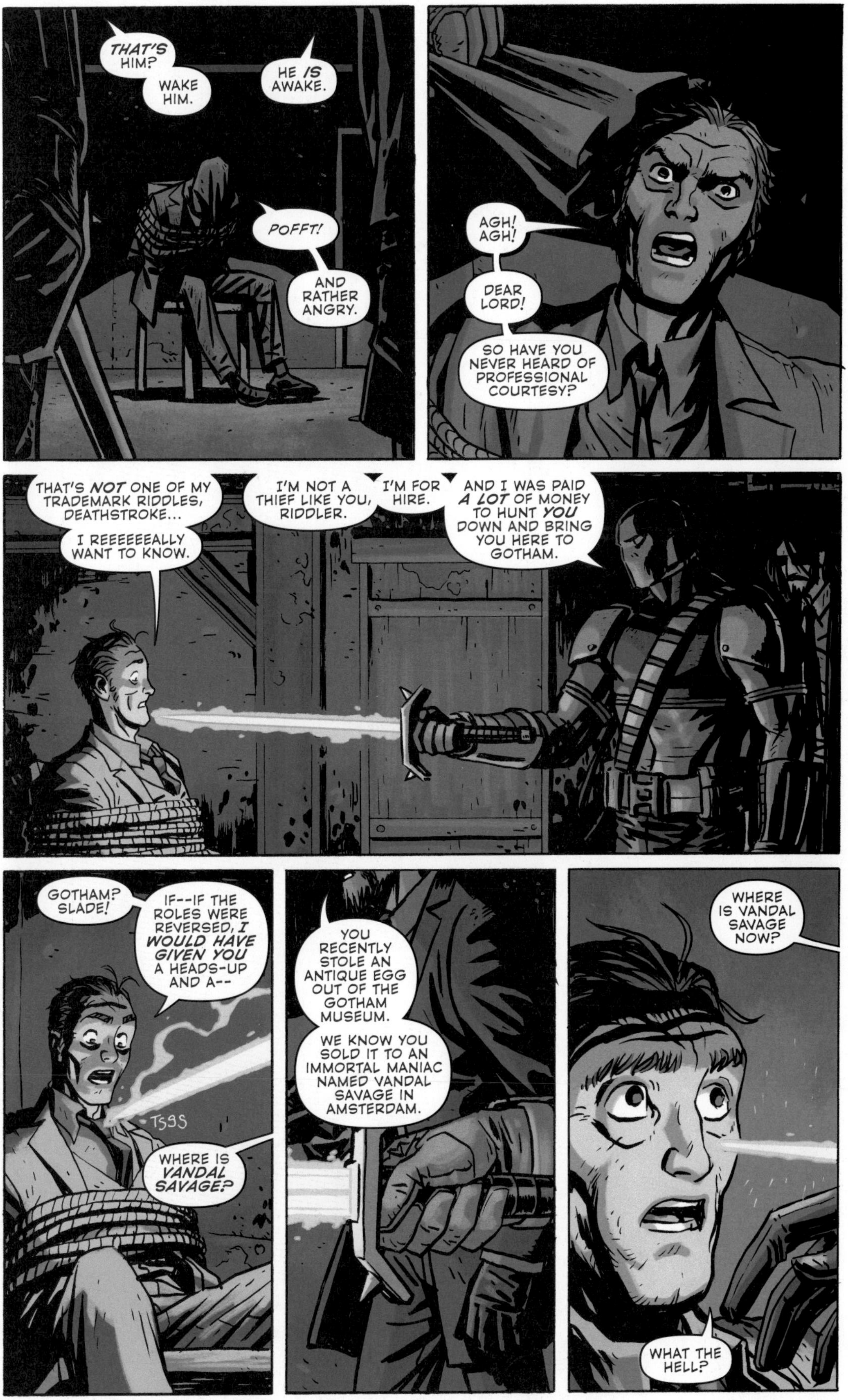
THAT'S HIM?
WAKE HIM.
HE IS AWAKE.
POFFT!
AND RATHER ANGRY.
AGH! AGH!
DEAR LORD!
SO HAVE YOU NEVER HEARD OF PROFESSIONAL COURTESY?
THAT'S NOT ONE OF MY TRADEMARK RIDDLES, DEATHSTROKE...
I REEEEEEALLY WANT TO KNOW.
I'M NOT A THIEF LIKE YOU, RIDDLER.
I'M FOR HIRE.
AND I WAS PAID A LOT OF MONEY TO HUNT YOU DOWN AND BRING YOU HERE TO GOTHAM.
GOTHAM? SLADE!
IF--IF THE ROLES WERE REVERSED, I WOULD HAVE GIVEN YOU A HEADS-UP AND A--
TSSS
WHERE IS VANDAL SAVAGE?
YOU RECENTLY STOLE AN ANTIQUE EGG OUT OF THE GOTHAM MUSEUM.
WE KNOW YOU SOLD IT TO AN IMMORTAL MANIAC NAMED VANDAL SAVAGE IN AMSTERDAM.
WHERE IS VANDAL SAVAGE NOW?
WHAT THE HELL?

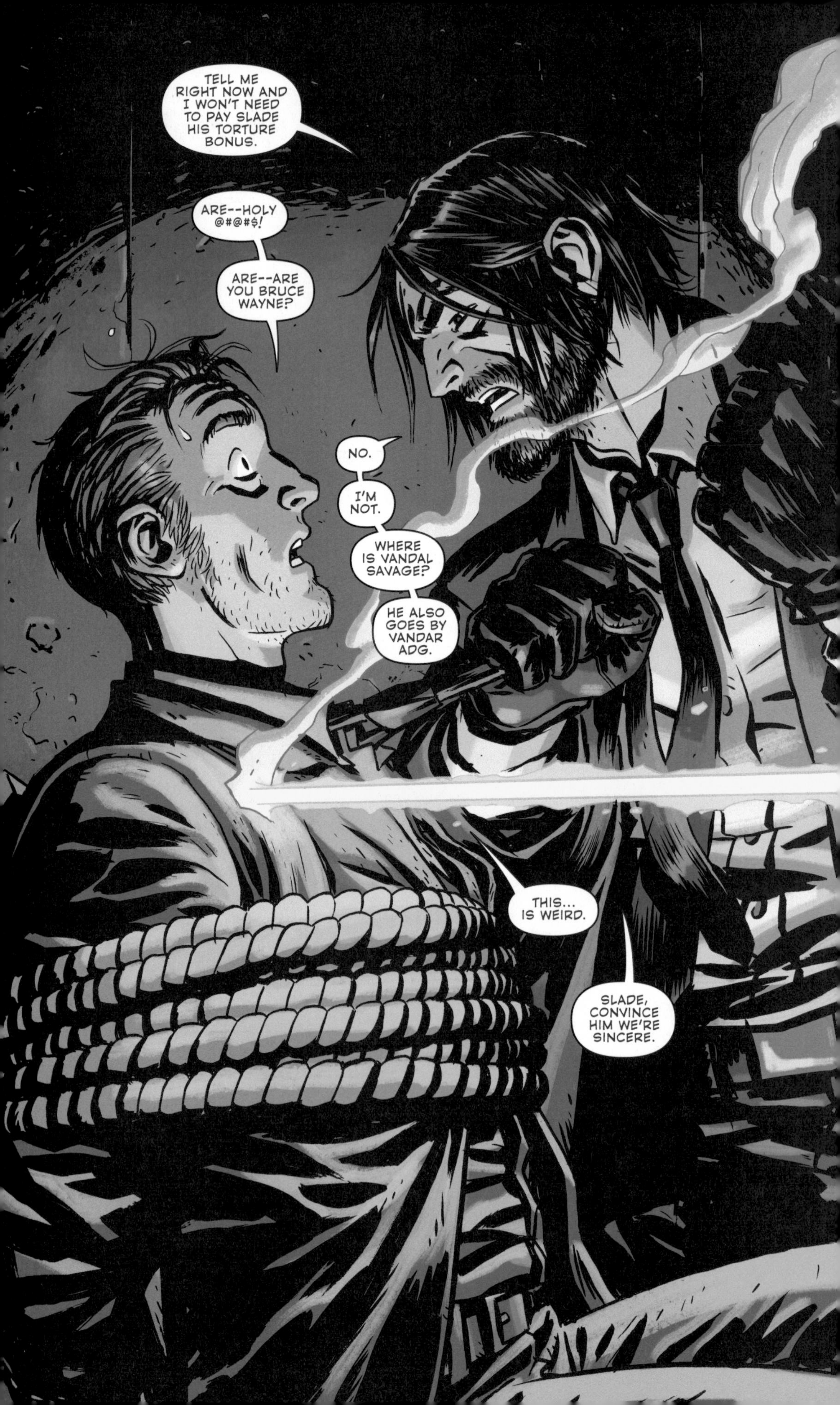

TELL ME RIGHT NOW AND I WON'T NEED TO PAY SLADE HIS TORTURE BONUS.
ARE--HOLY @#@#$!
ARE--ARE YOU BRUCE WAYNE?
NO.
I'M NOT.
WHERE IS VANDAL SAVAGE?
HE ALSO GOES BY VANDAR ADG.
THIS... IS WEIRD.
SLADE, CONVINCE HIM WE'RE SINCERE.

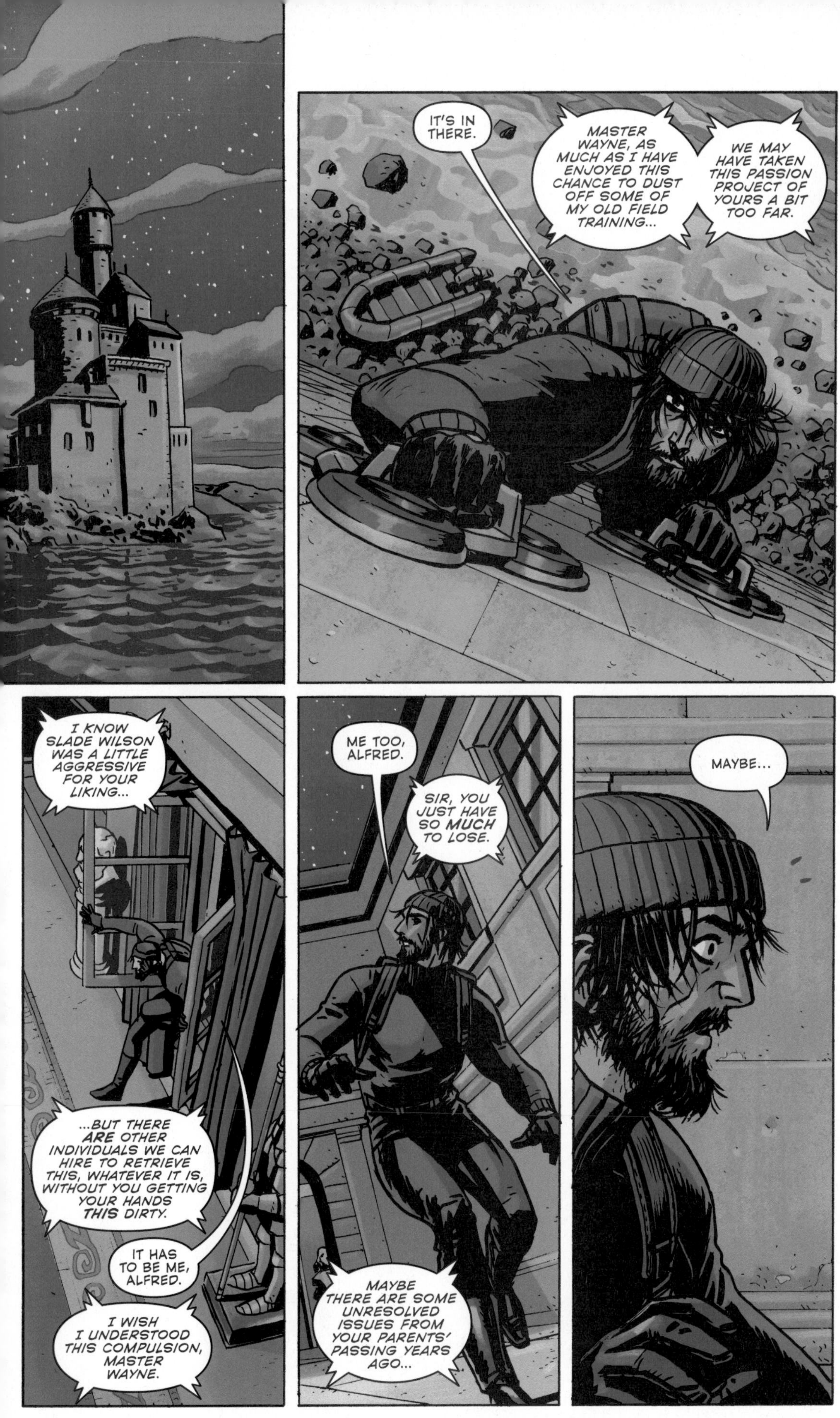
IT'S IN THERE.
MASTER WAYNE, AS MUCH AS I HAVE ENJOYED THIS CHANCE TO DUST OFF SOME OF MY OLD FIELD TRAINING...
WE MAY HAVE TAKEN THIS PASSION PROJECT OF YOURS A BIT TOO FAR.
I KNOW SLADE WILSON WAS A LITTLE AGGRESSIVE FOR YOUR LIKING...
...BUT THERE ARE OTHER INDIVIDUALS WE CAN HIRE TO RETRIEVE THIS, WHATEVER IT IS, WITHOUT YOU GETTING YOUR HANDS THIS DIRTY.
IT HAS TO BE ME, ALFRED.
I WISH I UNDERSTOOD THIS COMPULSION, MASTER WAYNE.
ME TOO, ALFRED.
SIR, YOU JUST HAVE SO MUCH TO LOSE.
MAYBE THERE ARE SOME UNRESOLVED ISSUES FROM YOUR PARENTS' PASSING YEARS AGO...
MAYBE...

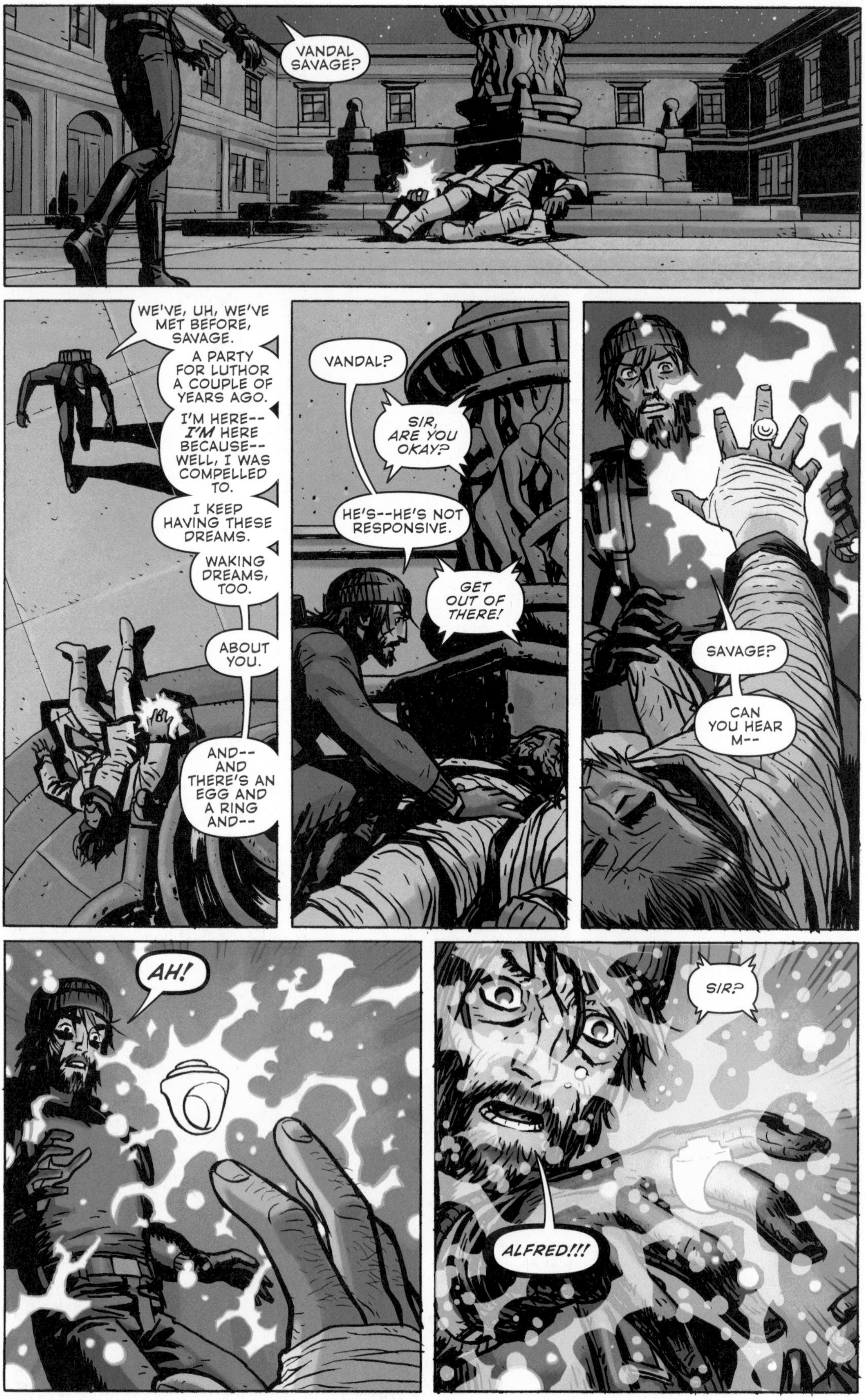
VANDAL SAVAGE?
WE'VE, UH, WE'VE MET BEFORE, SAVAGE.
A PARTY FOR LUTHOR A COUPLE OF YEARS AGO.
I'M HERE-- *I'M* HERE BECAUSE-- WELL, I WAS COMPELLED TO.
I KEEP HAVING THESE DREAMS.
WAKING DREAMS, TOO.
ABOUT YOU.
AND-- AND THERE'S AN EGG AND A RING AND--
VANDAL?
SIR, ARE YOU OKAY?
HE'S--HE'S NOT RESPONSIVE.
GET OUT OF THERE!
SAVAGE?
CAN YOU HEAR M--
AH!
SIR?
ALFRED!!!

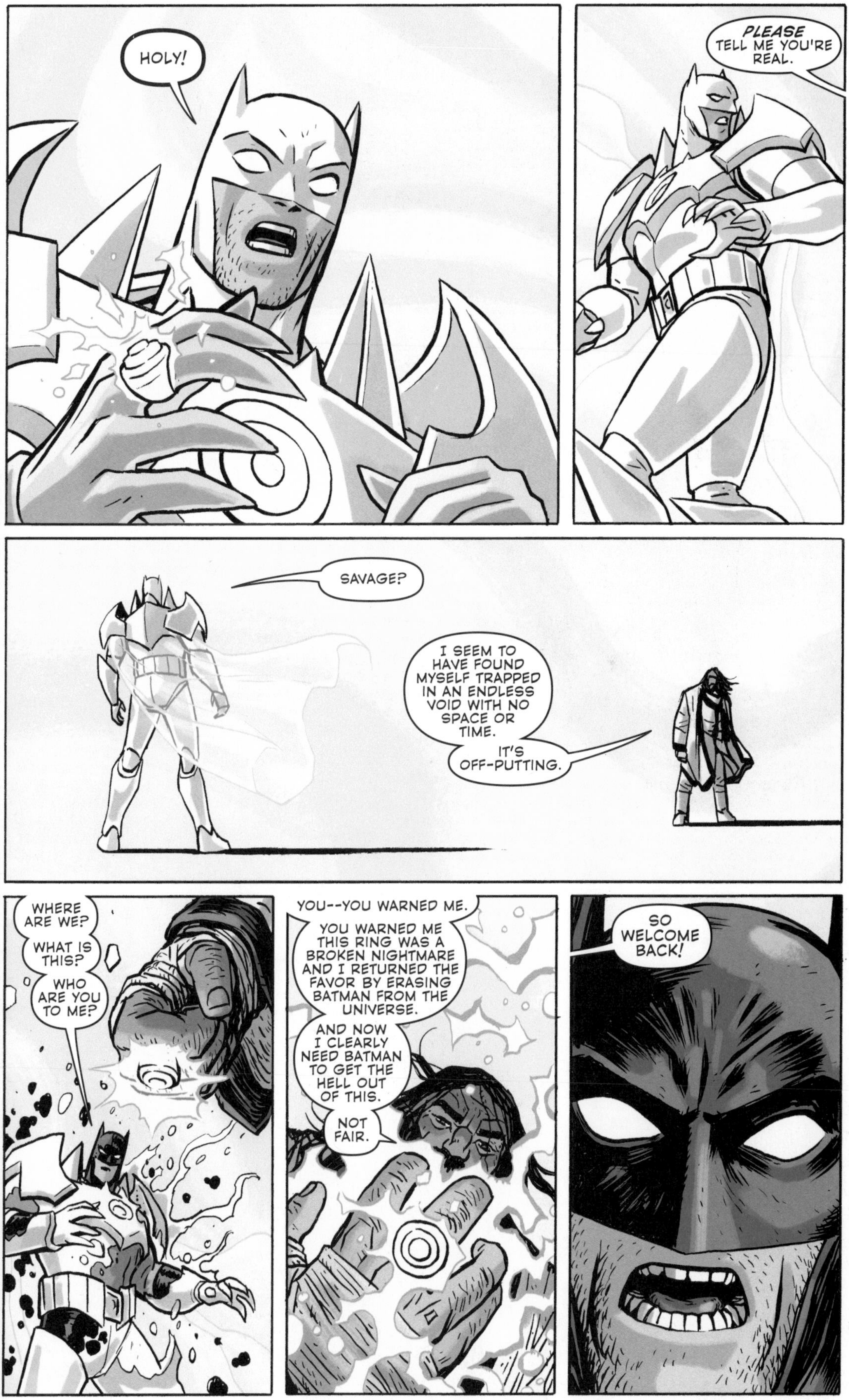
HOLY!
PLEASE TELL ME YOU'RE REAL.
SAVAGE?
I SEEM TO HAVE FOUND MYSELF TRAPPED IN AN ENDLESS VOID WITH NO SPACE OR TIME.
IT'S OFF-PUTTING.
WHERE ARE WE?
WHAT IS THIS?
WHO ARE YOU TO ME?
YOU--YOU WARNED ME.
YOU WARNED ME THIS RING WAS A BROKEN NIGHTMARE AND I RETURNED THE FAVOR BY ERASING BATMAN FROM THE UNIVERSE.
AND NOW I CLEARLY NEED BATMAN TO GET THE HELL OUT OF THIS.
NOT FAIR.
SO WELCOME BACK!

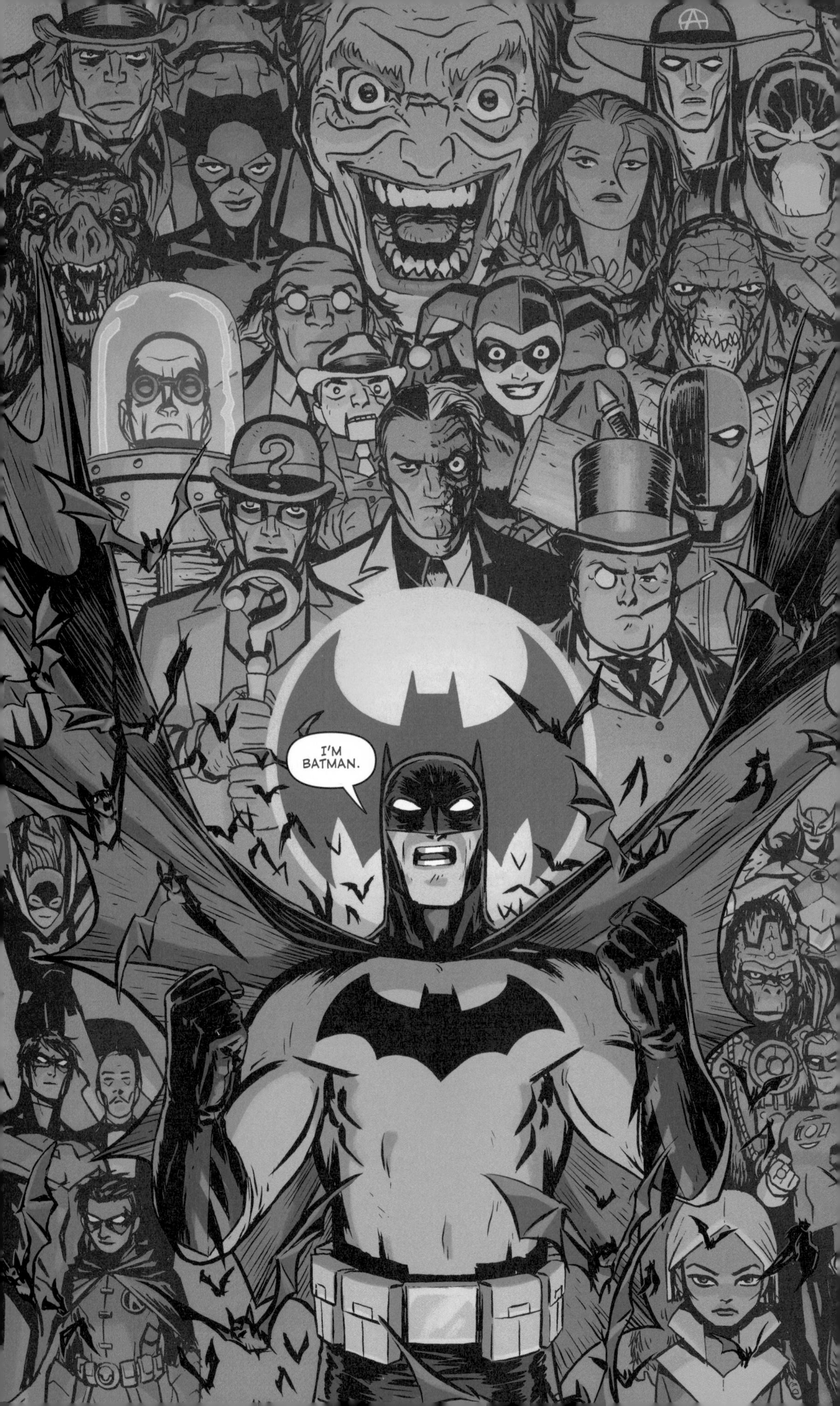
I'M BATMAN.

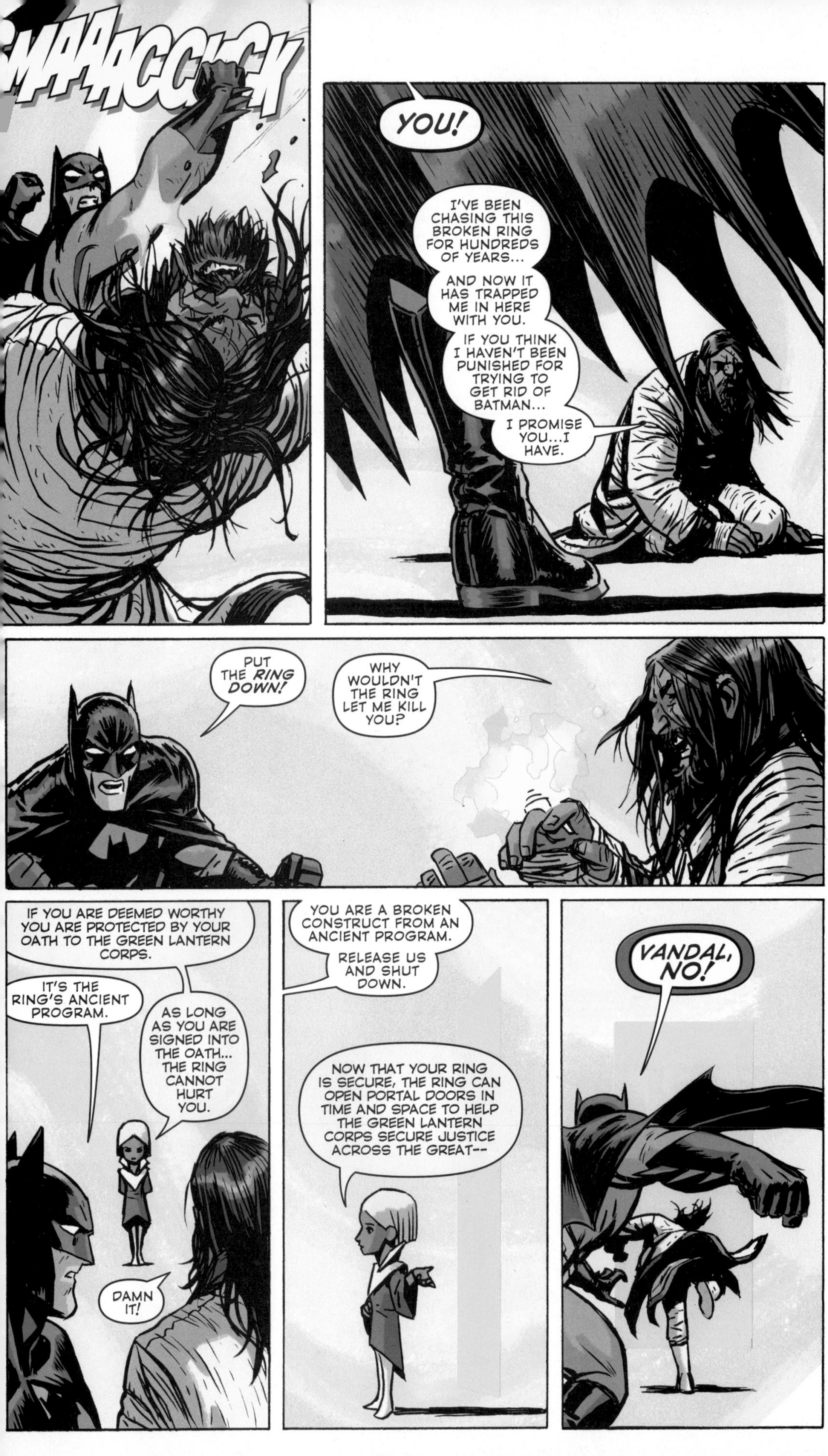
SMAAACCCLCK
YOU!
I'VE BEEN CHASING THIS BROKEN RING FOR HUNDREDS OF YEARS...
AND NOW IT HAS TRAPPED ME IN HERE WITH YOU.
IF YOU THINK I HAVEN'T BEEN PUNISHED FOR TRYING TO GET RID OF BATMAN...
I PROMISE YOU...I HAVE.
PUT THE *RING DOWN!*
WHY WOULDN'T THE RING LET ME KILL YOU?
IF YOU ARE DEEMED WORTHY YOU ARE PROTECTED BY YOUR OATH TO THE GREEN LANTERN CORPS.
IT'S THE RING'S ANCIENT PROGRAM.
AS LONG AS YOU ARE SIGNED INTO THE OATH... THE RING CANNOT HURT YOU.
DAMN IT!
YOU ARE A BROKEN CONSTRUCT FROM AN ANCIENT PROGRAM.
RELEASE US AND SHUT DOWN.
NOW THAT YOUR RING IS SECURE, THE RING CAN OPEN PORTAL DOORS IN TIME AND SPACE TO HELP THE GREEN LANTERN CORPS SECURE JUSTICE ACROSS THE GREAT--
VANDAL, NO!

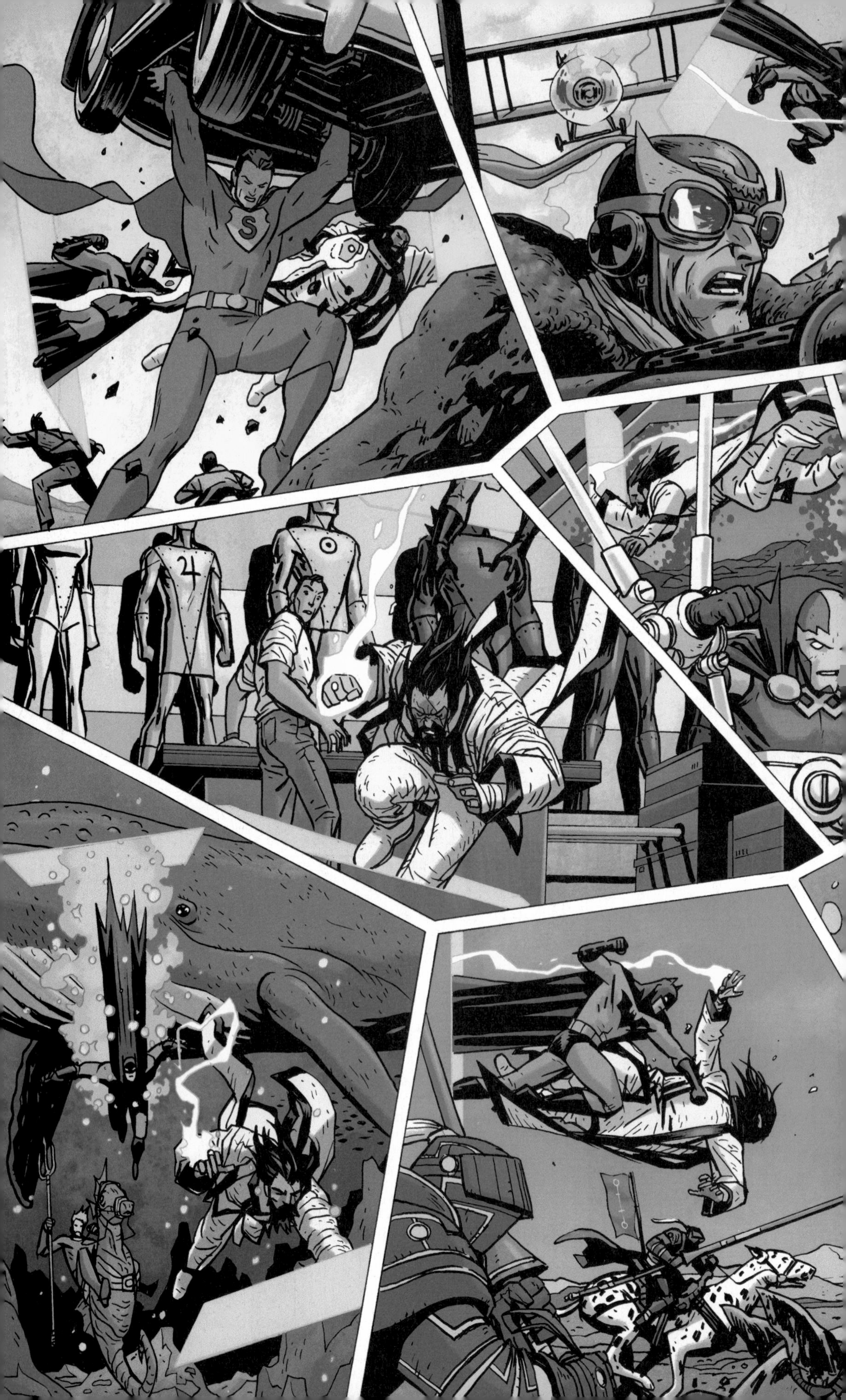

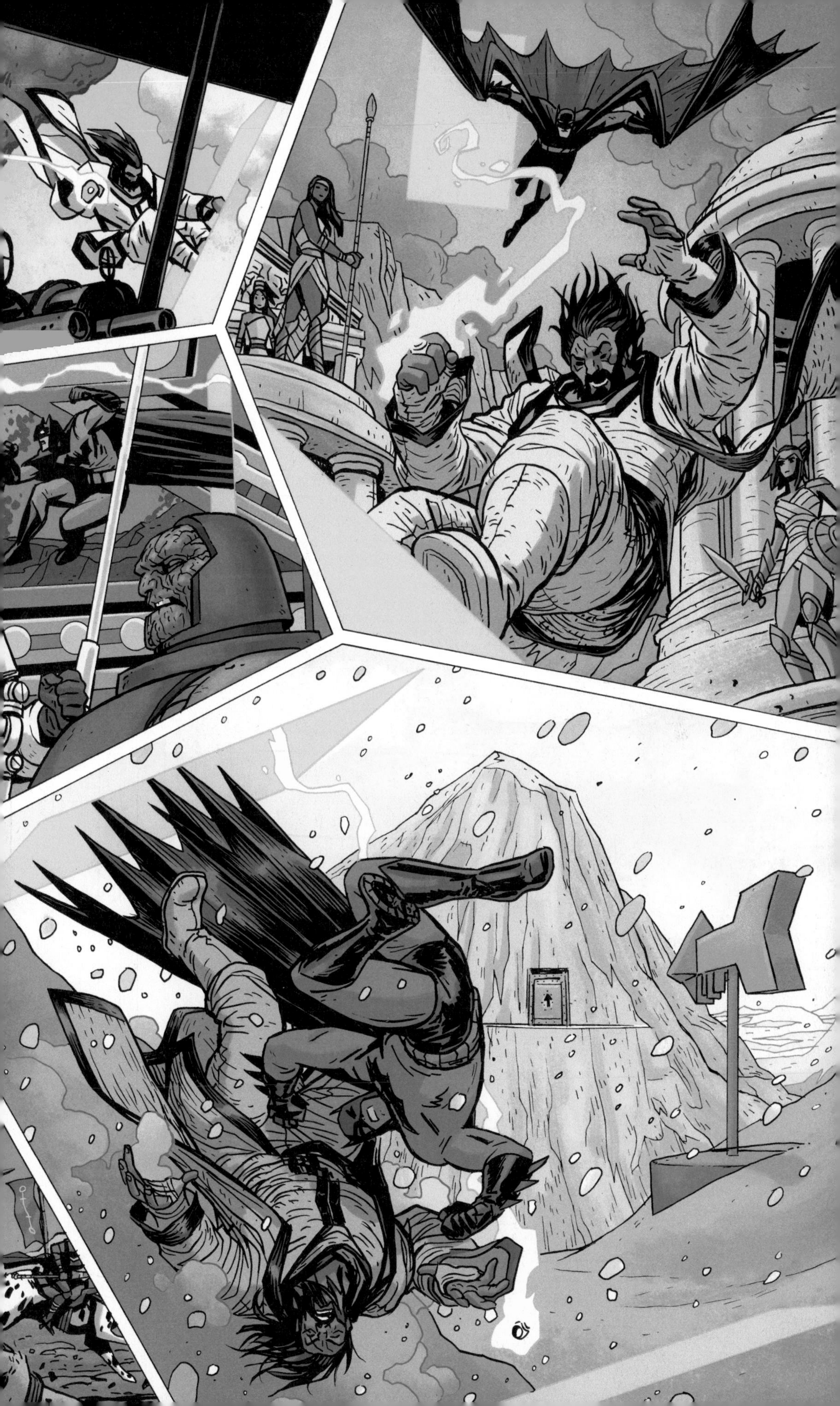

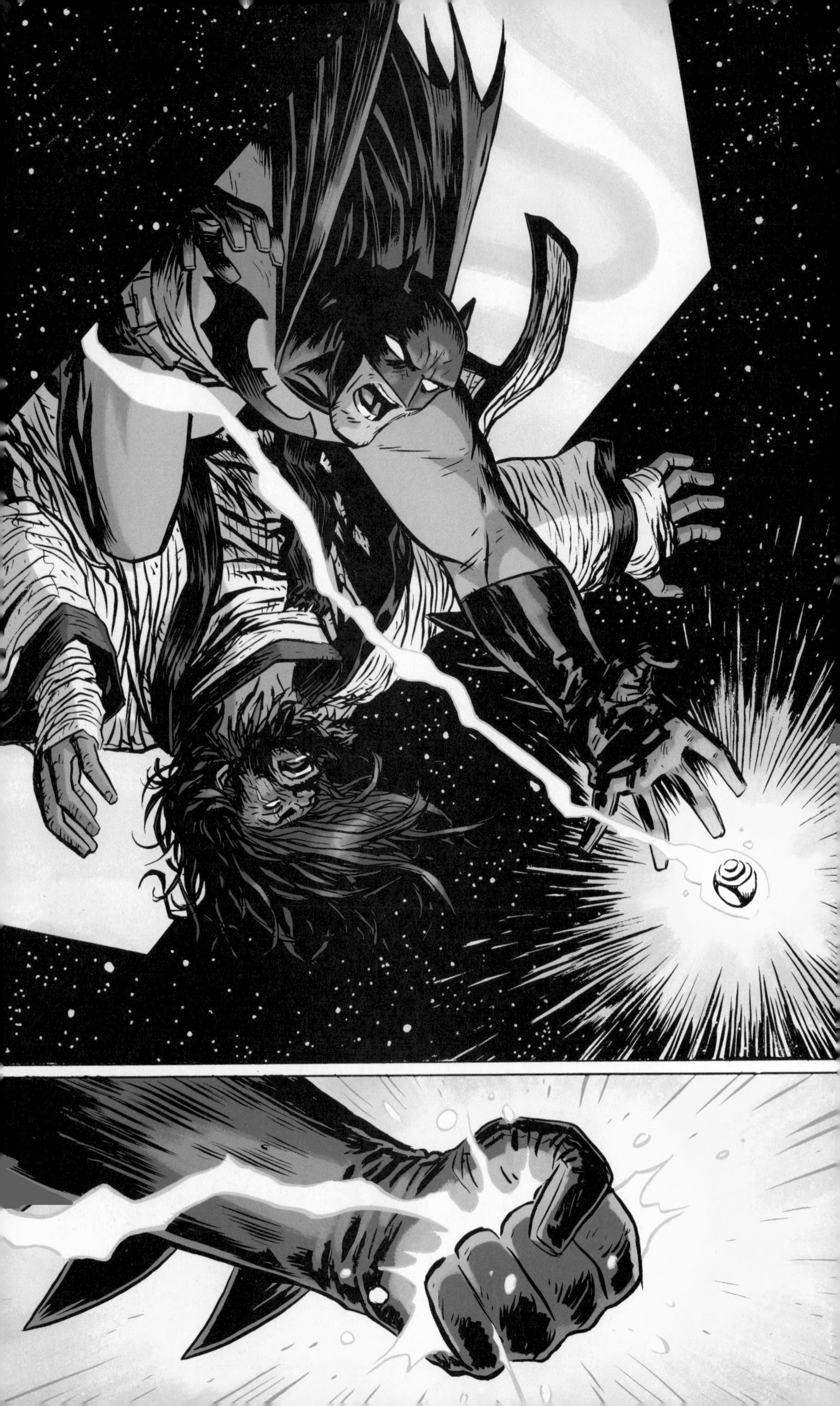

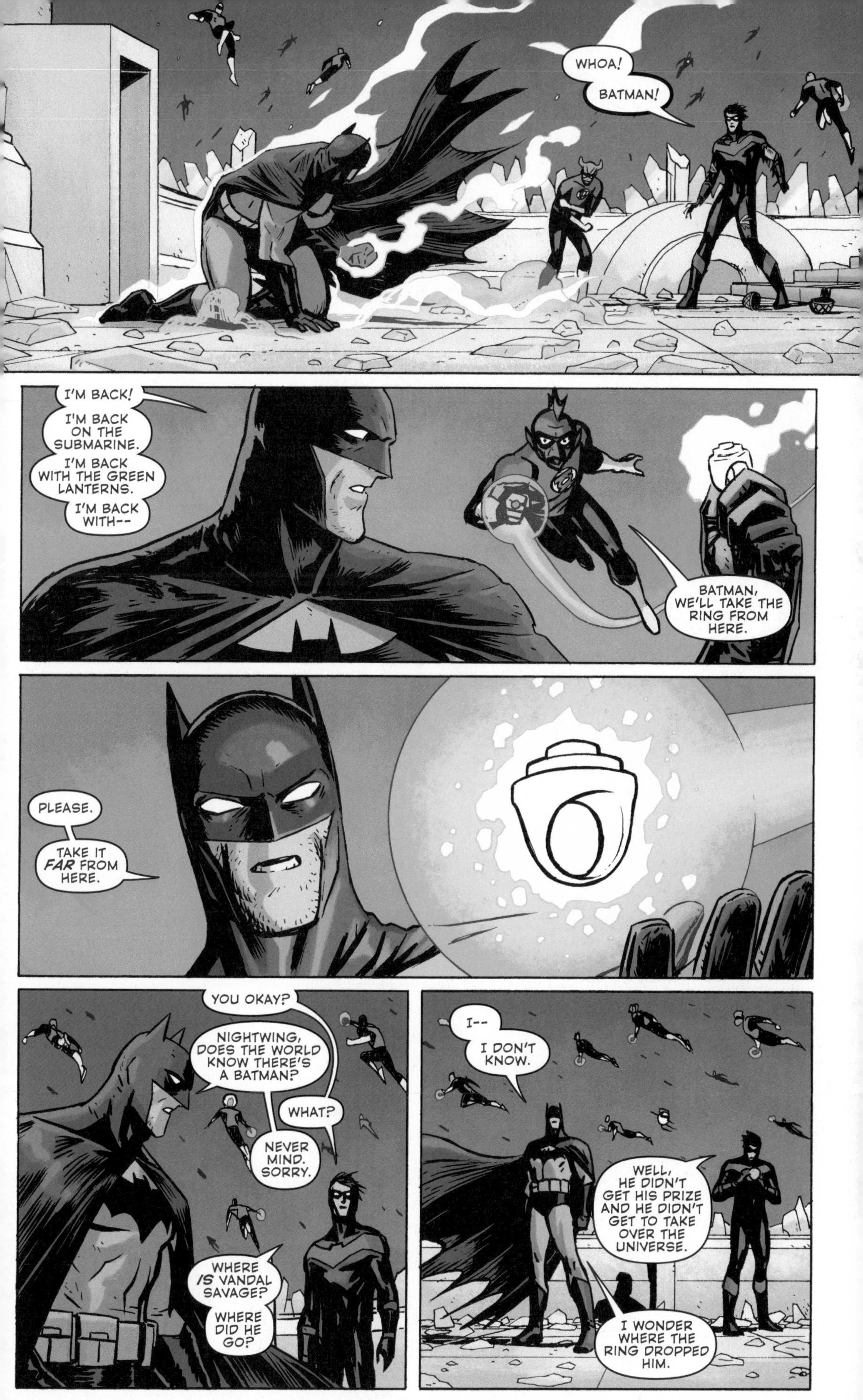
WHOA!
BATMAN!
I'M BACK!
I'M BACK ON THE SUBMARINE.
I'M BACK WITH THE GREEN LANTERNS.
I'M BACK WITH--
BATMAN, WE'LL TAKE THE RING FROM HERE.
PLEASE.
TAKE IT FAR FROM HERE.
YOU OKAY?
NIGHTWING, DOES THE WORLD KNOW THERE'S A BATMAN?
WHAT?
NEVER MIND. SORRY.
WHERE IS VANDAL SAVAGE?
WHERE DID HE GO?
I--
I DON'T KNOW.
WELL, HE DIDN'T GET HIS PRIZE AND HE DIDN'T GET TO TAKE OVER THE UNIVERSE.
I WONDER WHERE THE RING DROPPED HIM.

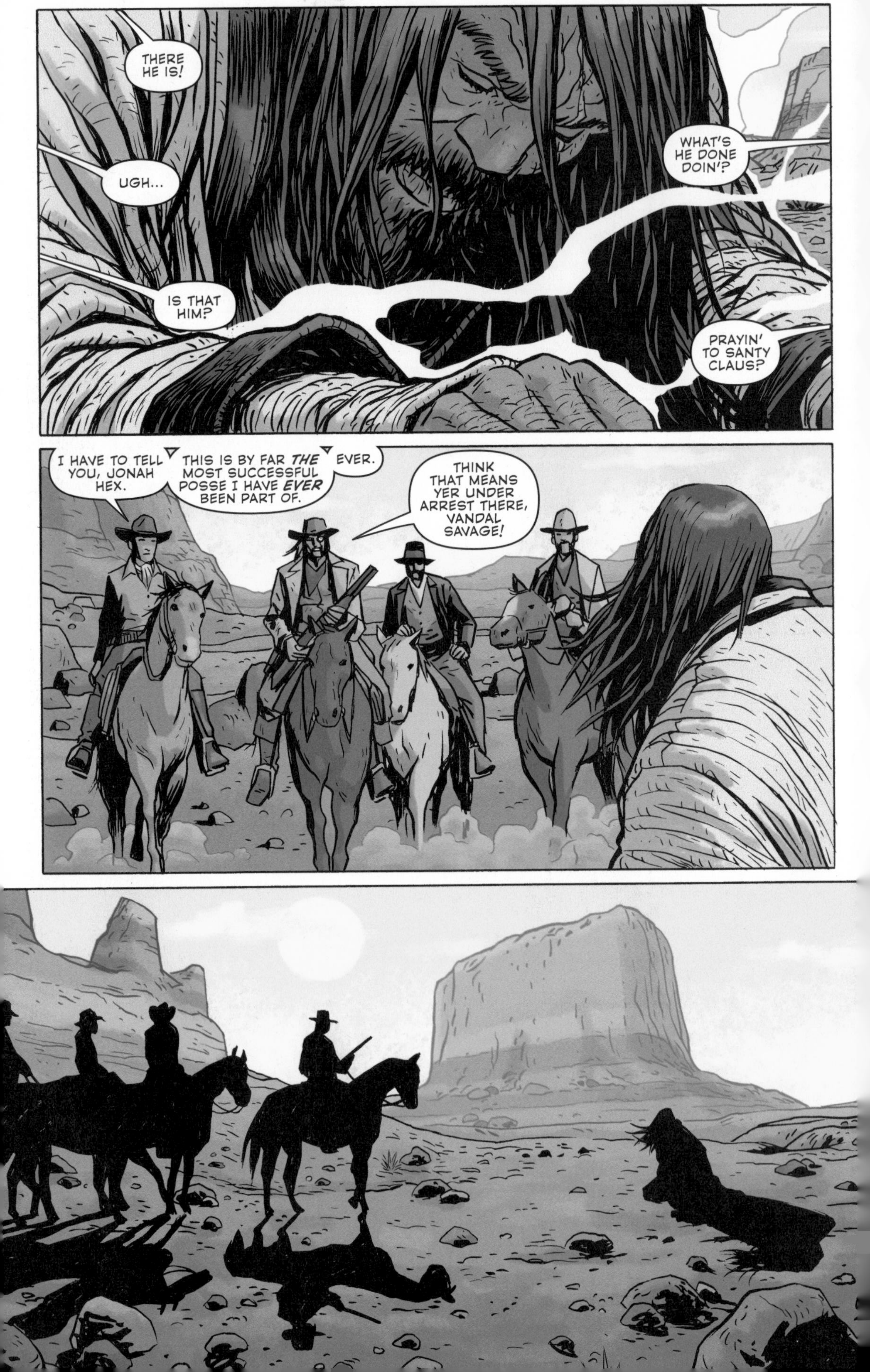
THERE HE IS!
UGH...
IS THAT HIM?
WHAT'S HE DONE DOIN'?
PRAYIN' TO SANTY CLAUS?
I HAVE TO TELL YOU, JONAH HEX.
THIS IS BY FAR THE MOST SUCCESSFUL POSSE I HAVE EVER BEEN PART OF.
EVER.
THINK THAT MEANS YER UNDER ARREST THERE, VANDAL SAVAGE!

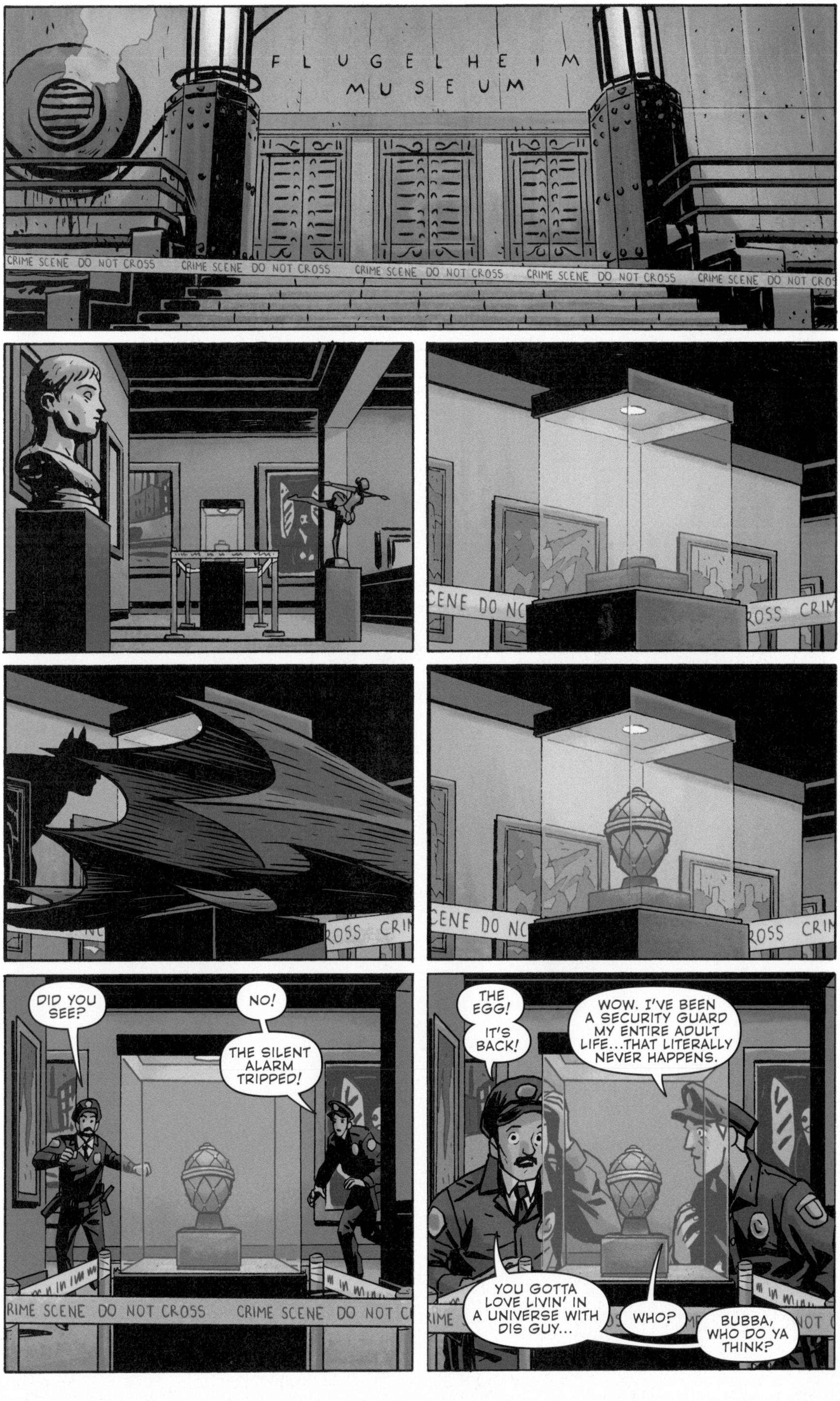
FLUGELHEIM MUSEUM
CRIME SCENE DO NOT CROSS
DID YOU SEE?
NO!
THE SILENT ALARM TRIPPED!
THE EGG! IT'S BACK!
WOW. I'VE BEEN A SECURITY GUARD MY ENTIRE ADULT LIFE...THAT LITERALLY NEVER HAPPENS.
YOU GOTTA LOVE LIVIN' IN A UNIVERSE WITH DIS GUY...
WHO?
BUBBA, WHO DO YA THINK?

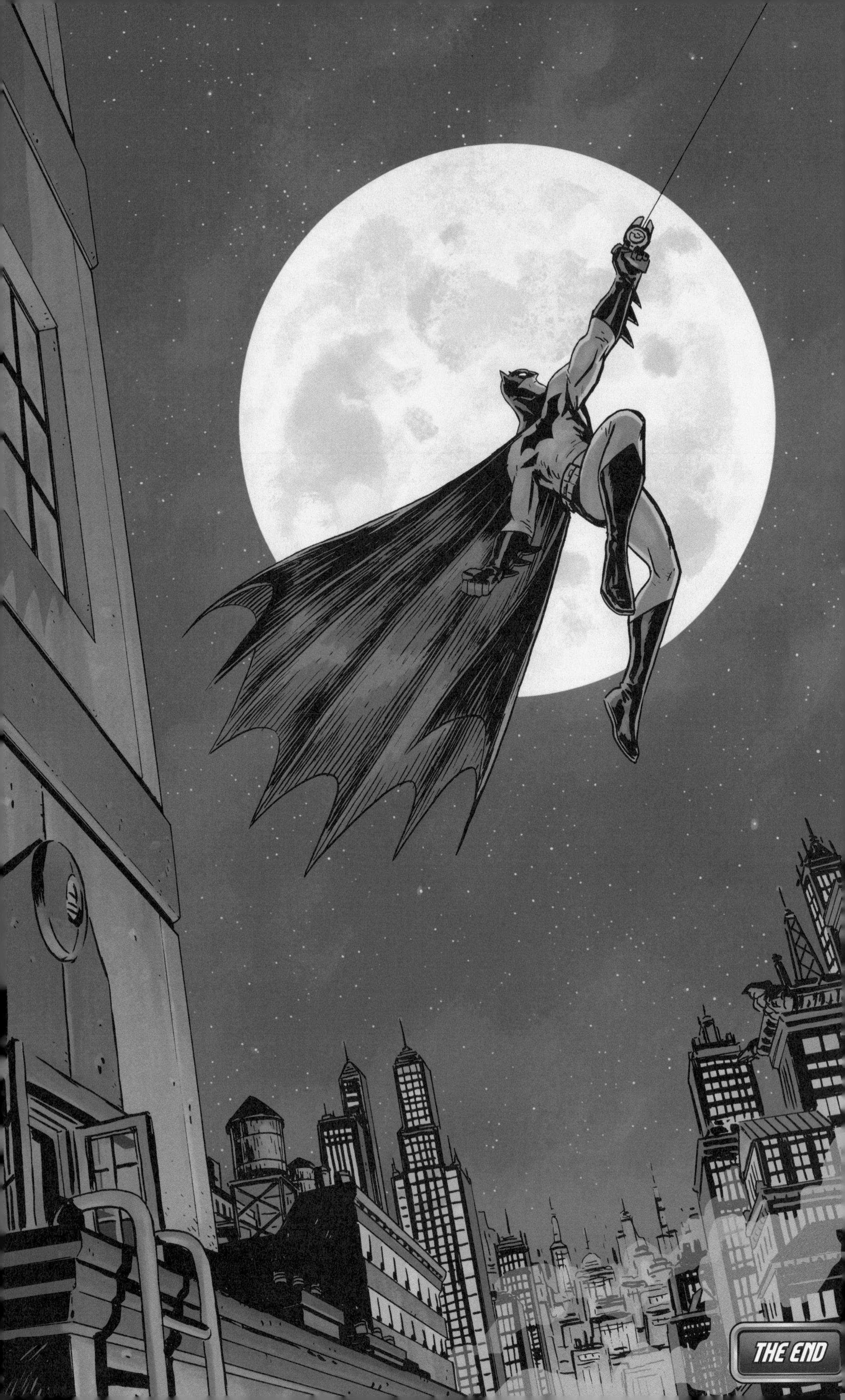
THE END

BATMAN: UNIVERSE COVER GALLERY BY
NICK DERINGTON

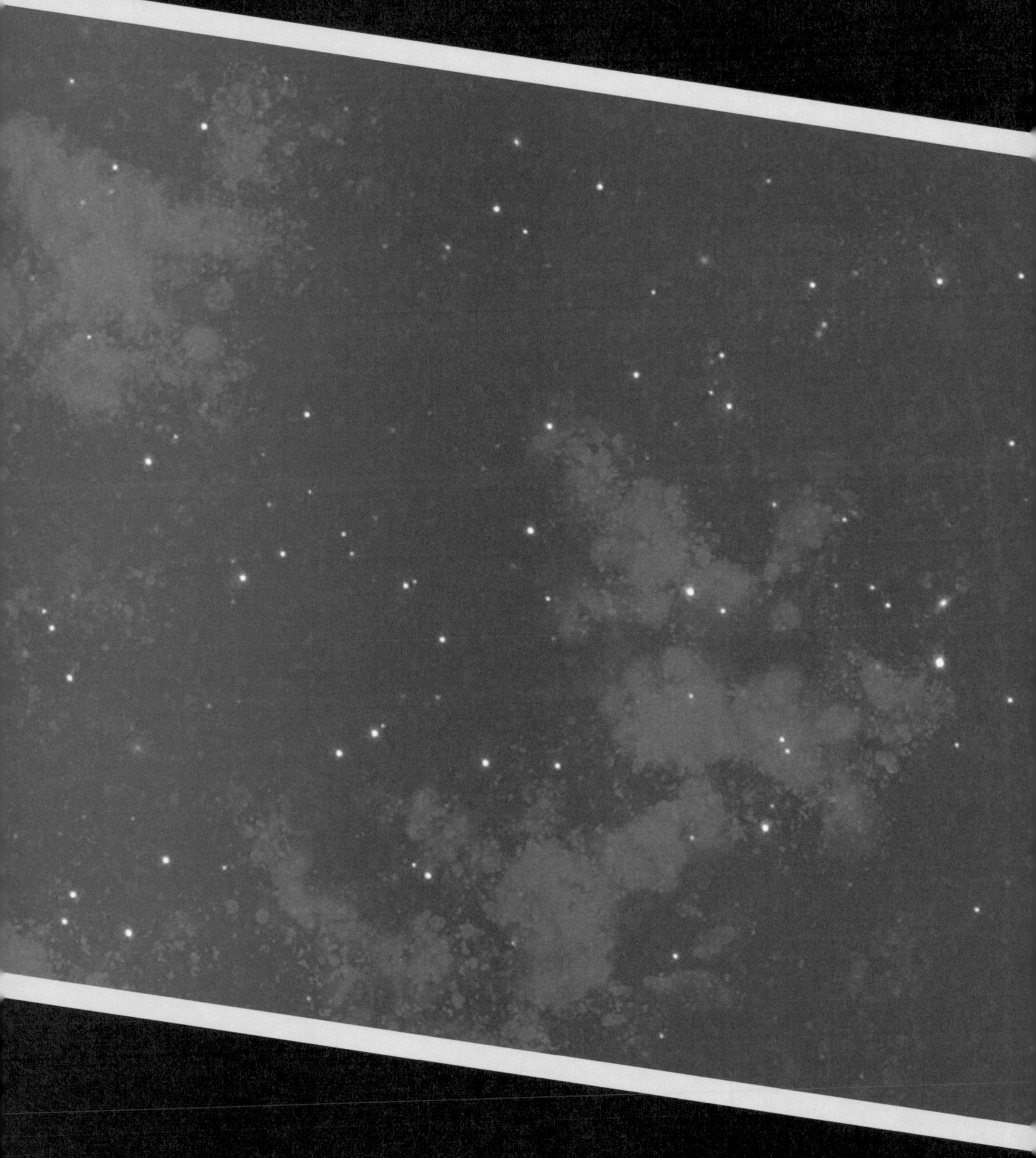

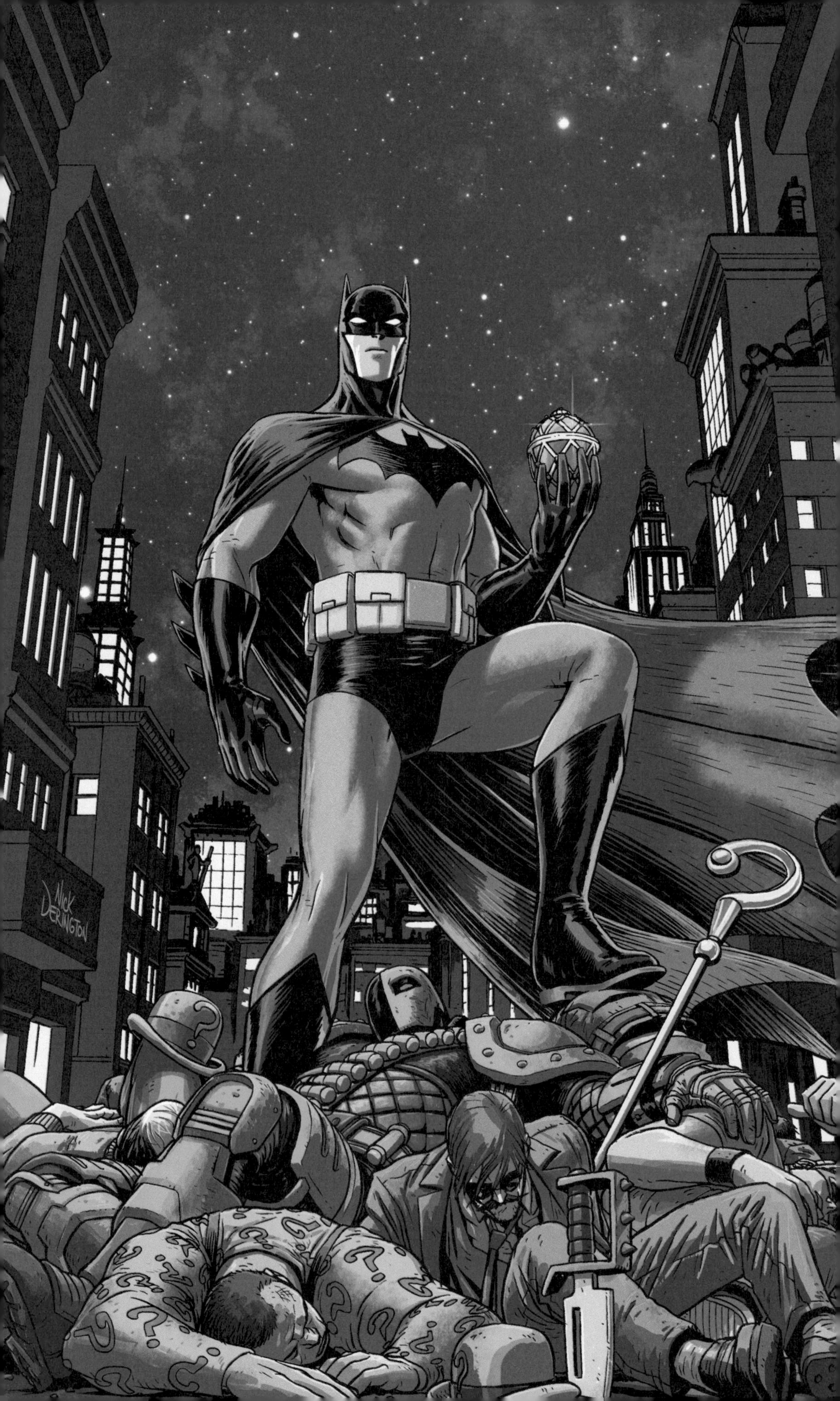
NICK DERINGTON

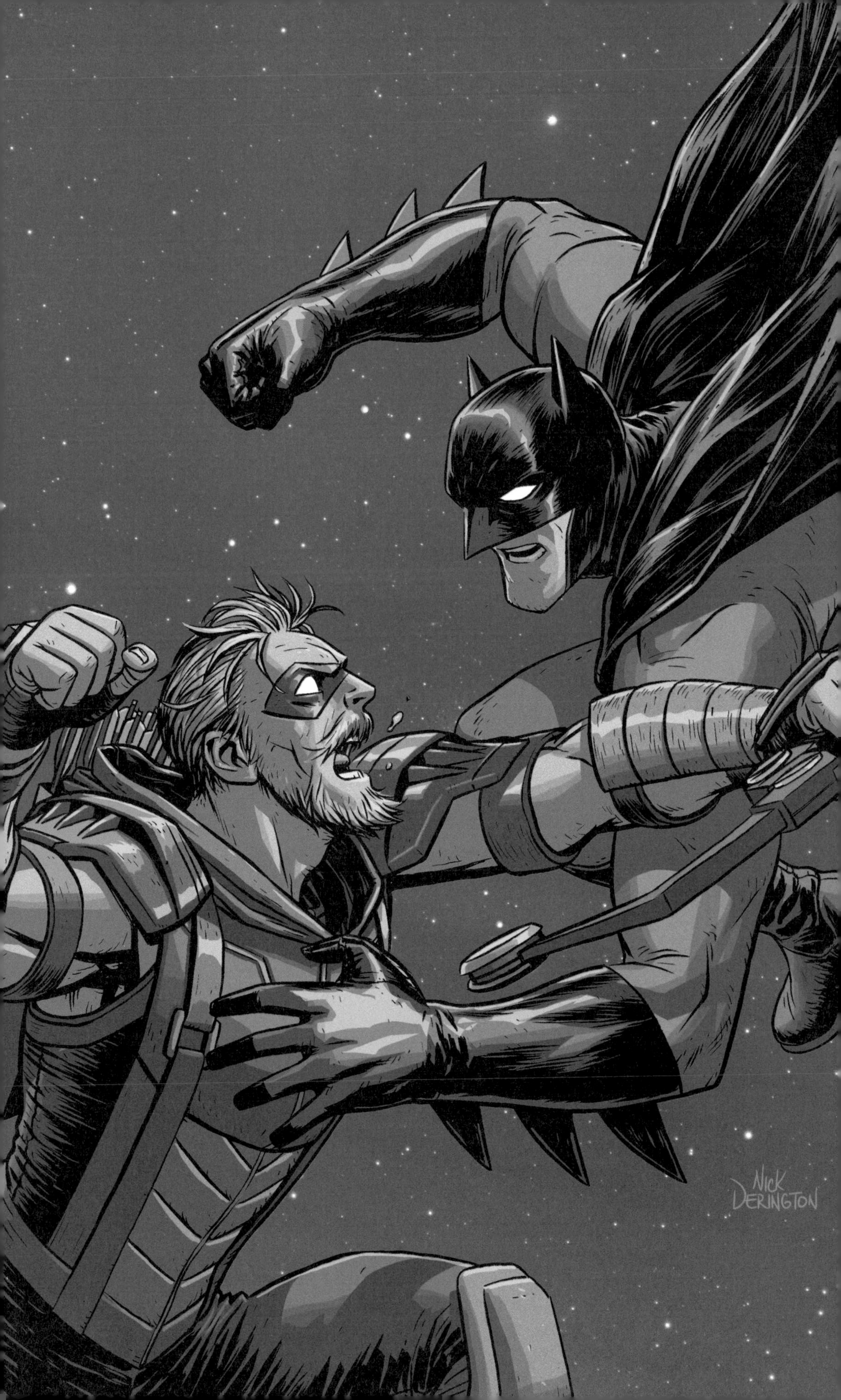
NICK DERINGTON

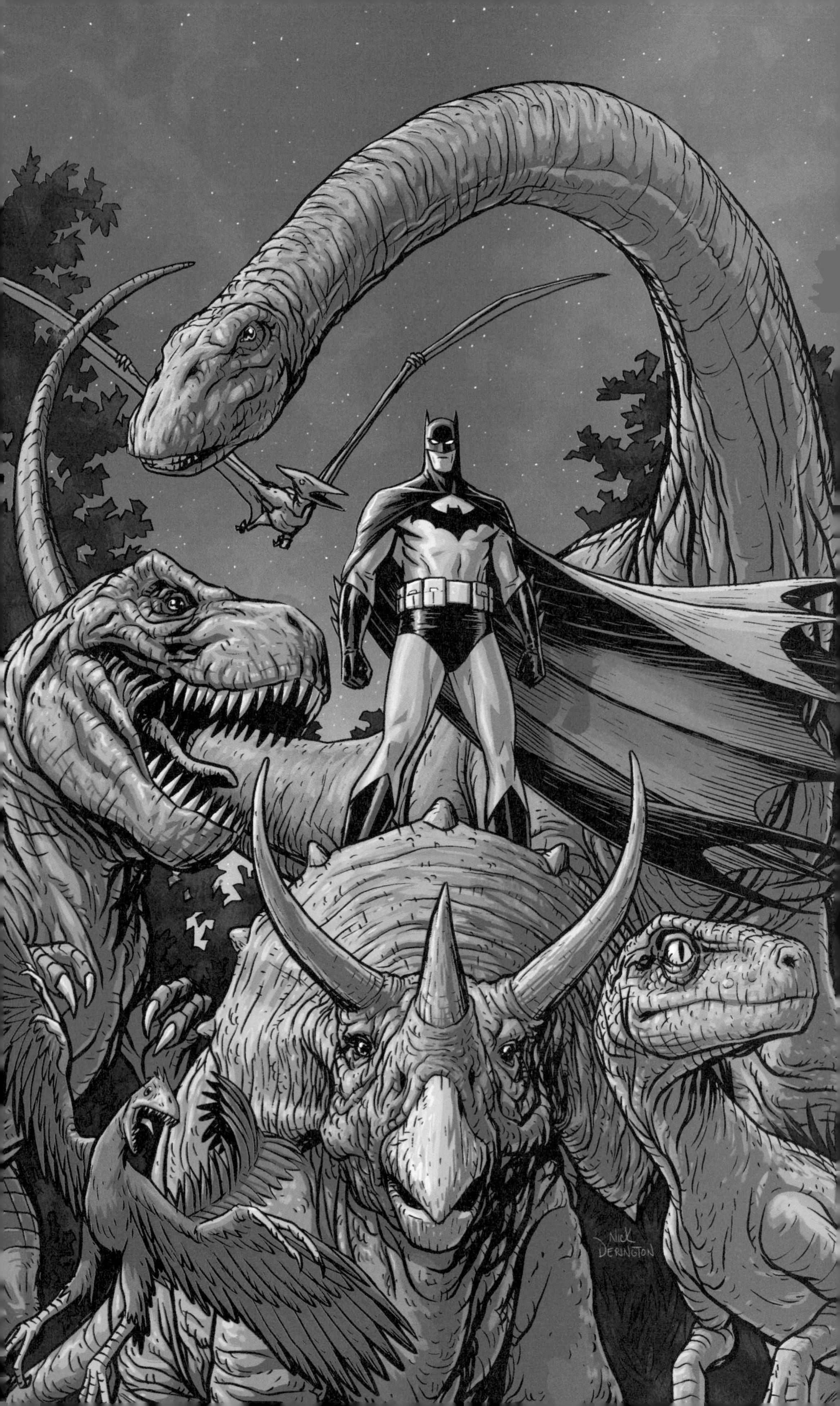
NICK DERINGTON

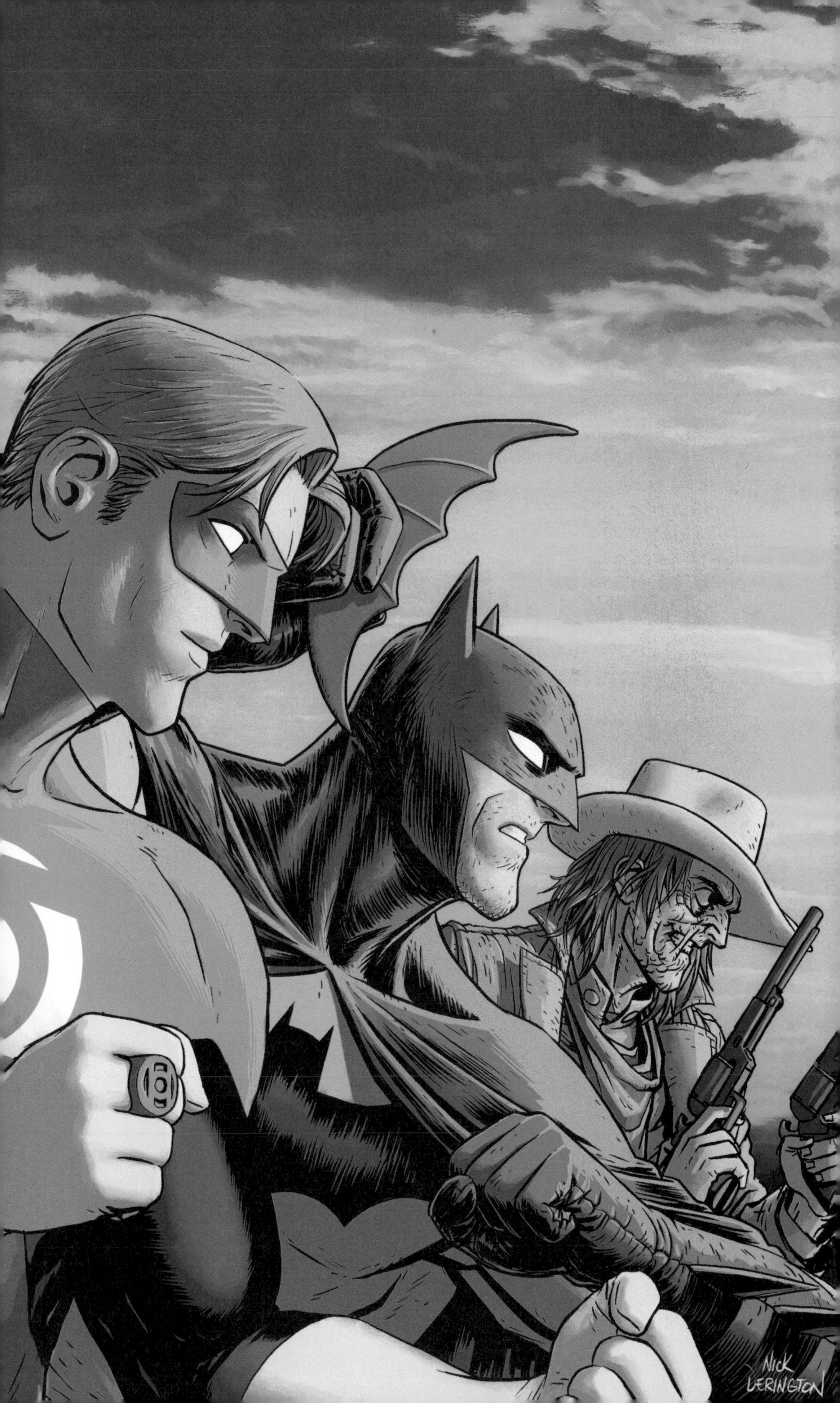
NICK DERINGTON

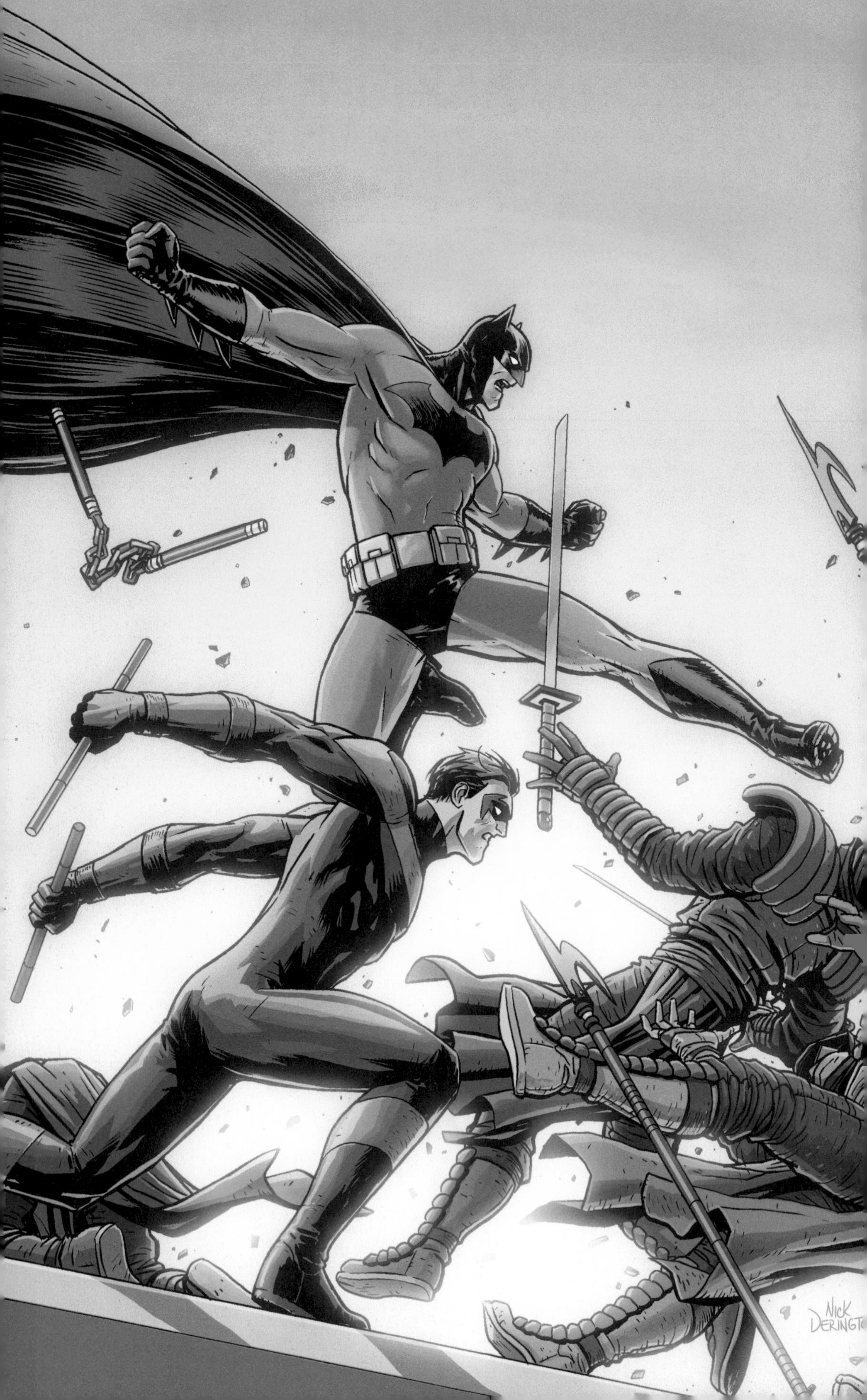
NICK
DERINGTO

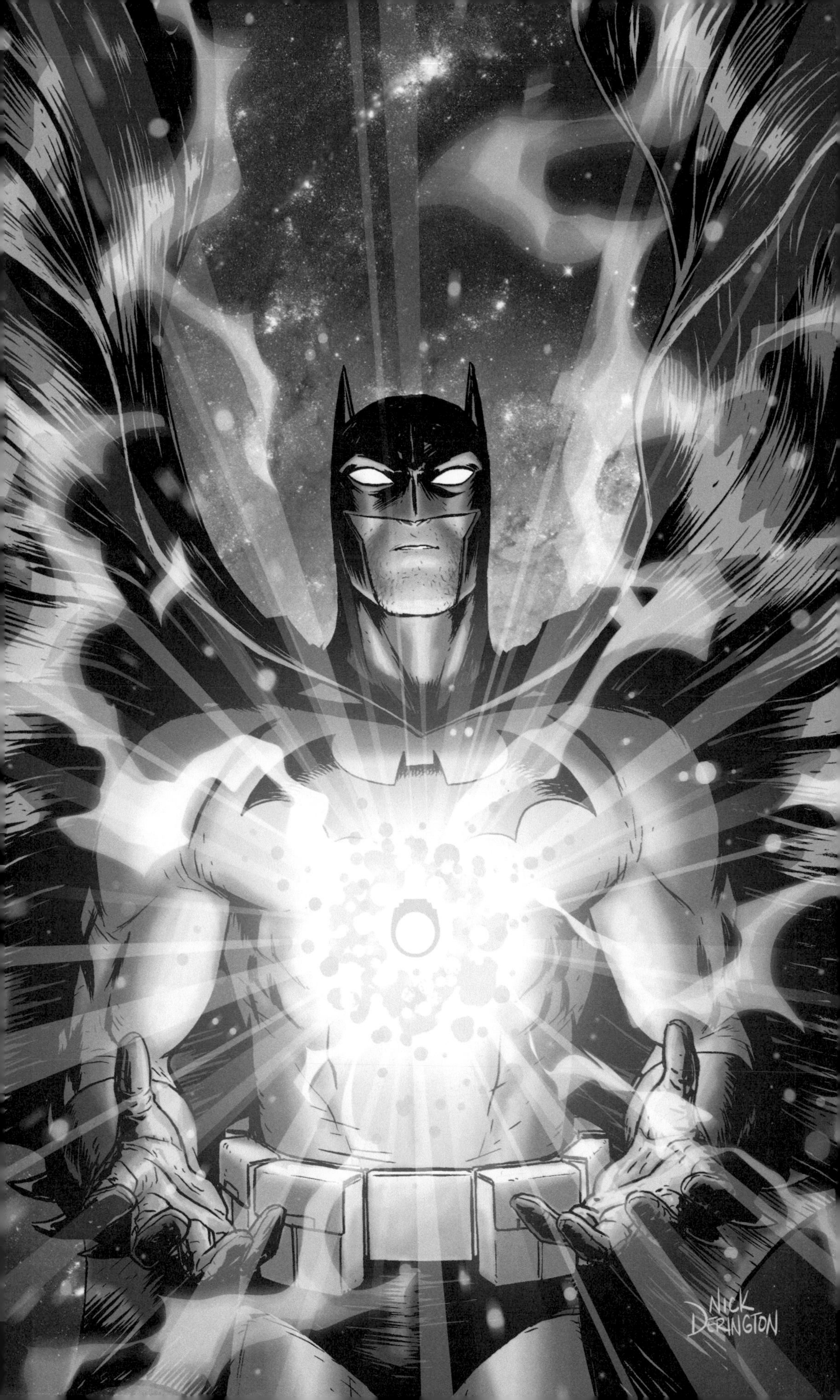
NICK
DERINGTON

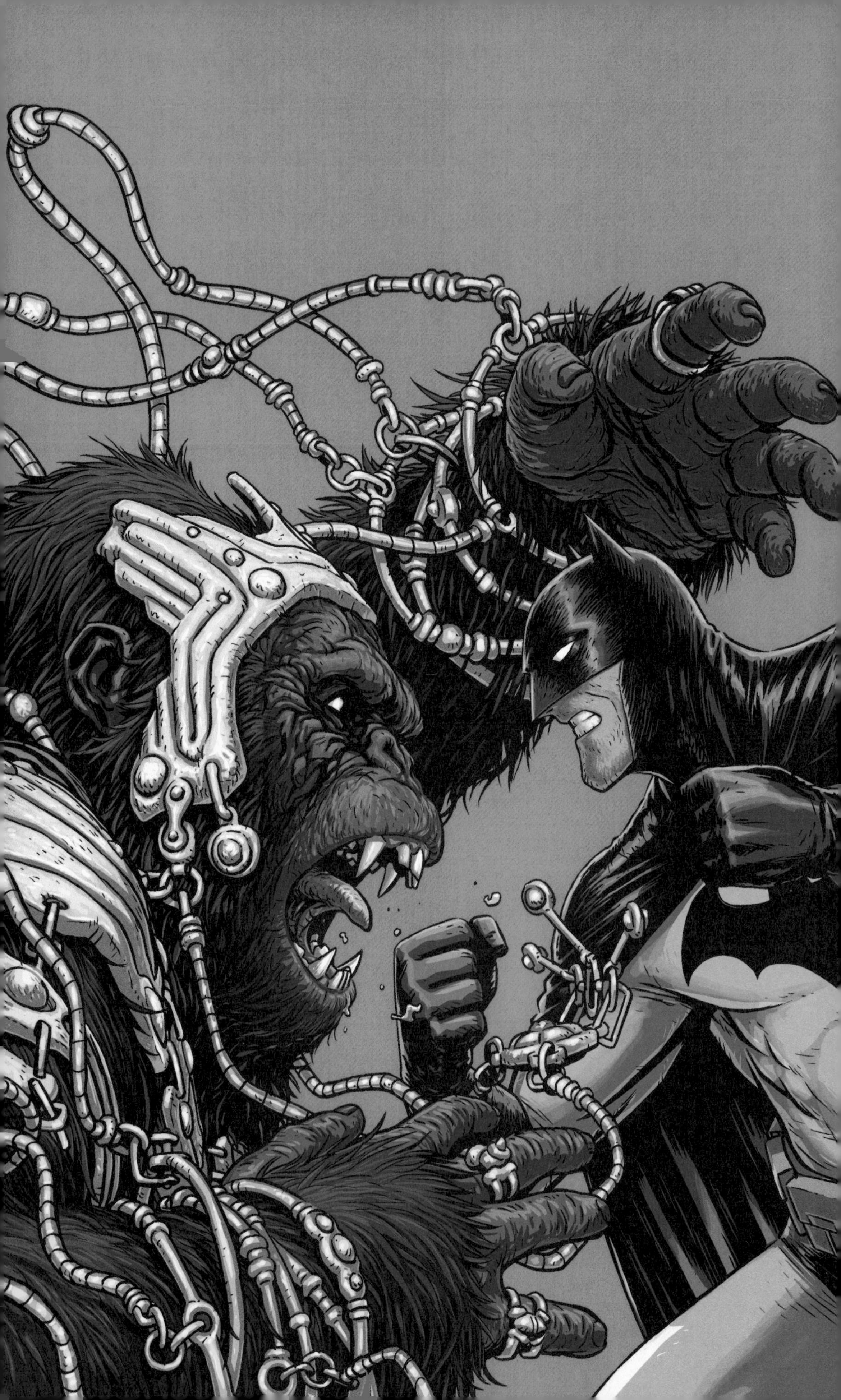

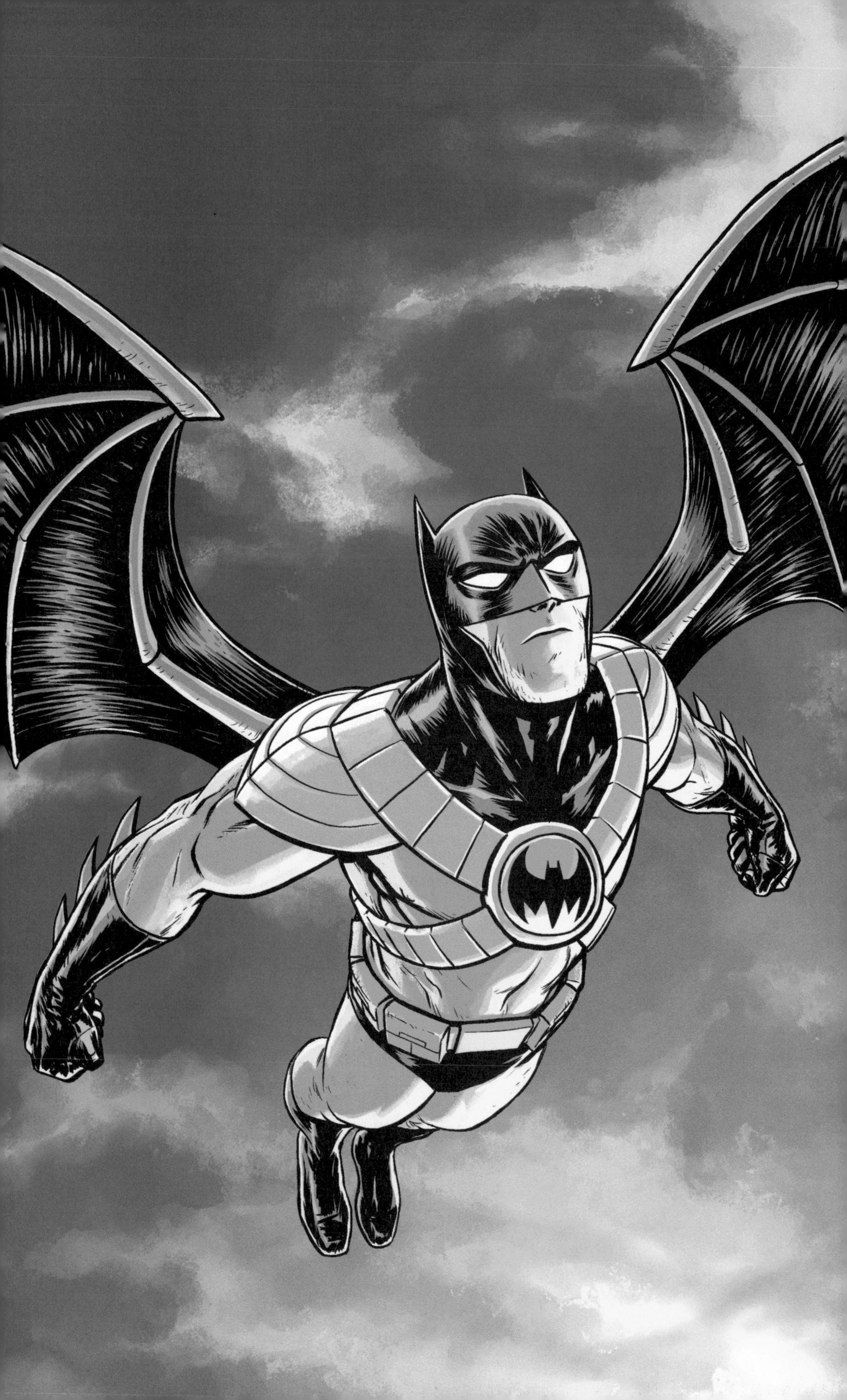

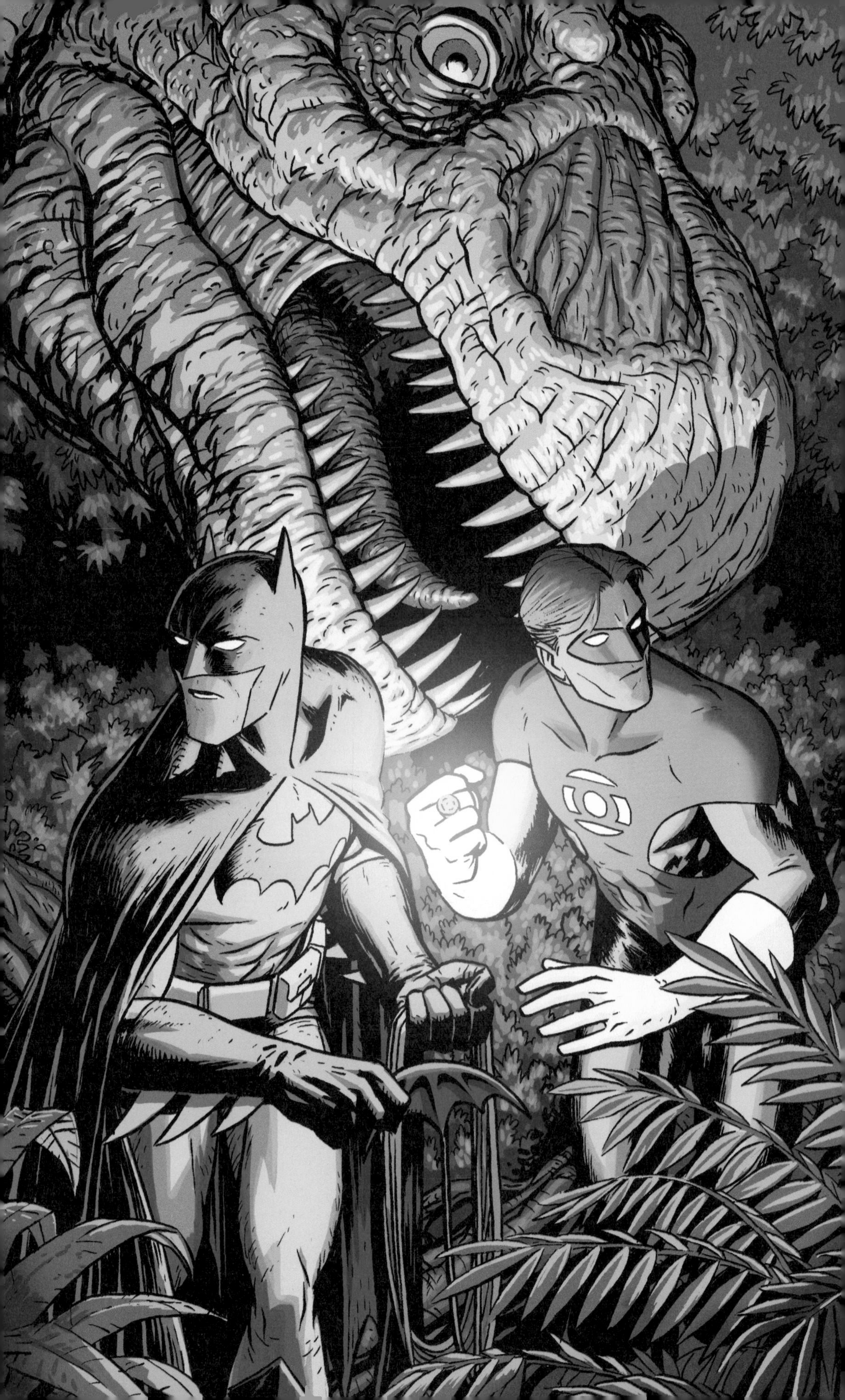

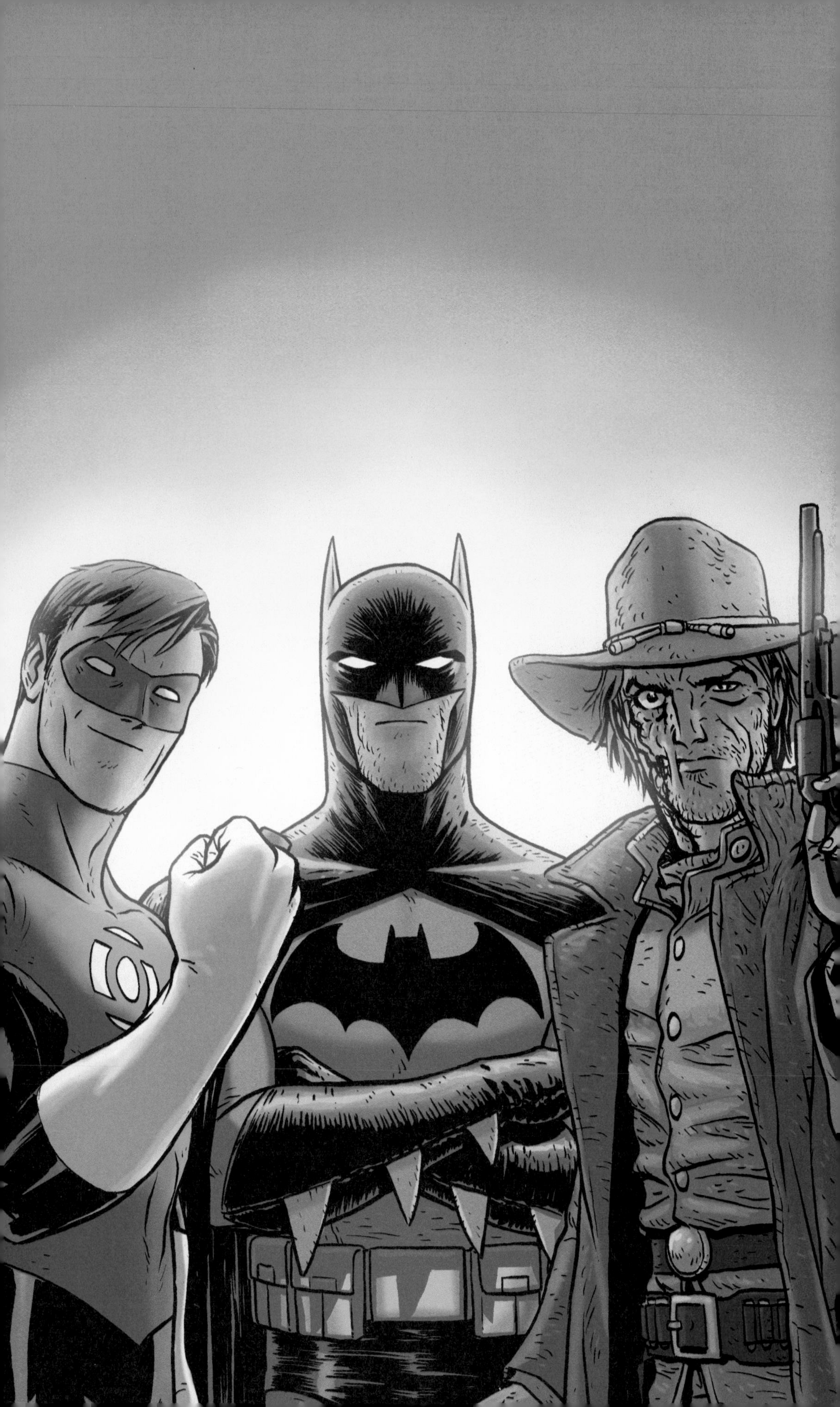

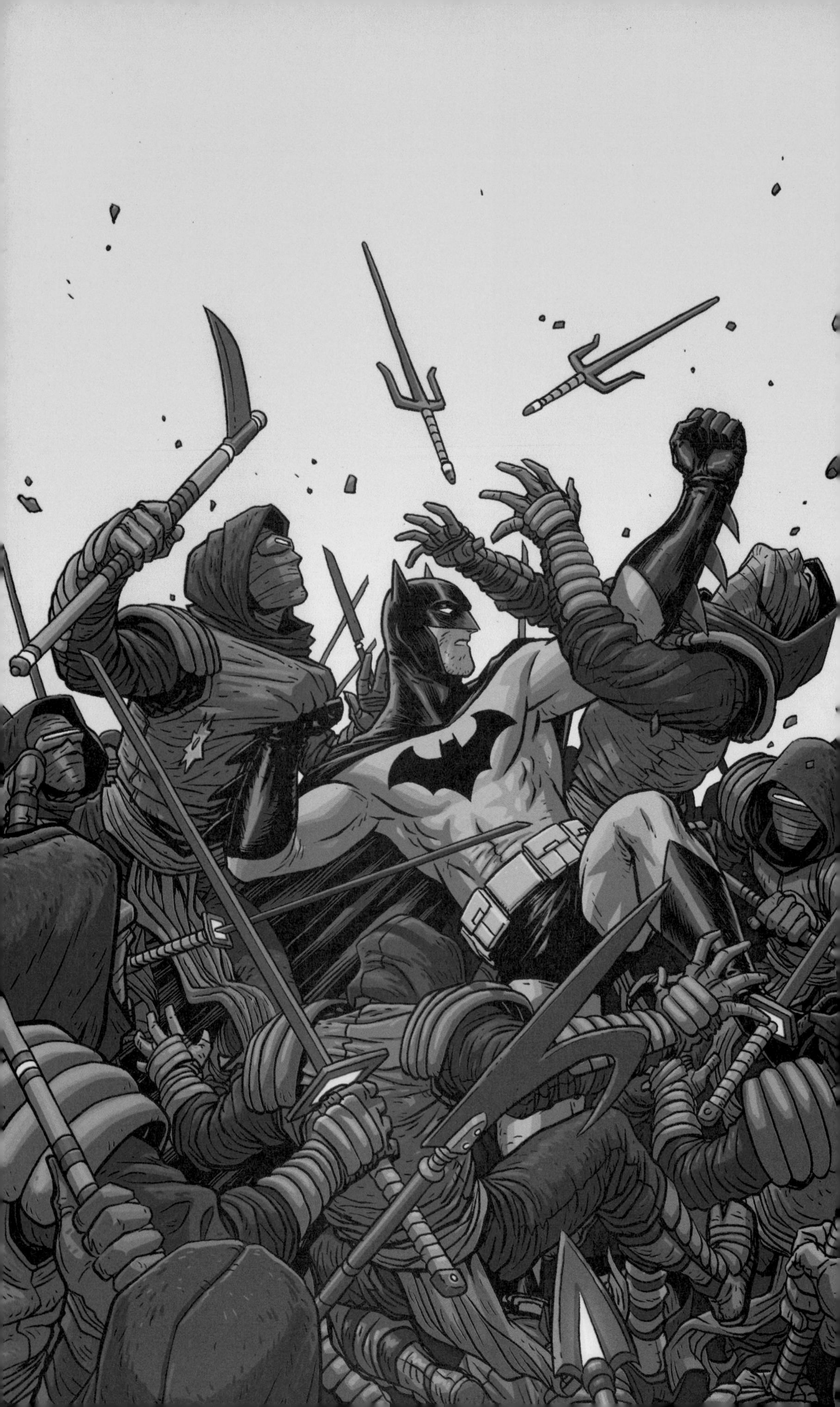

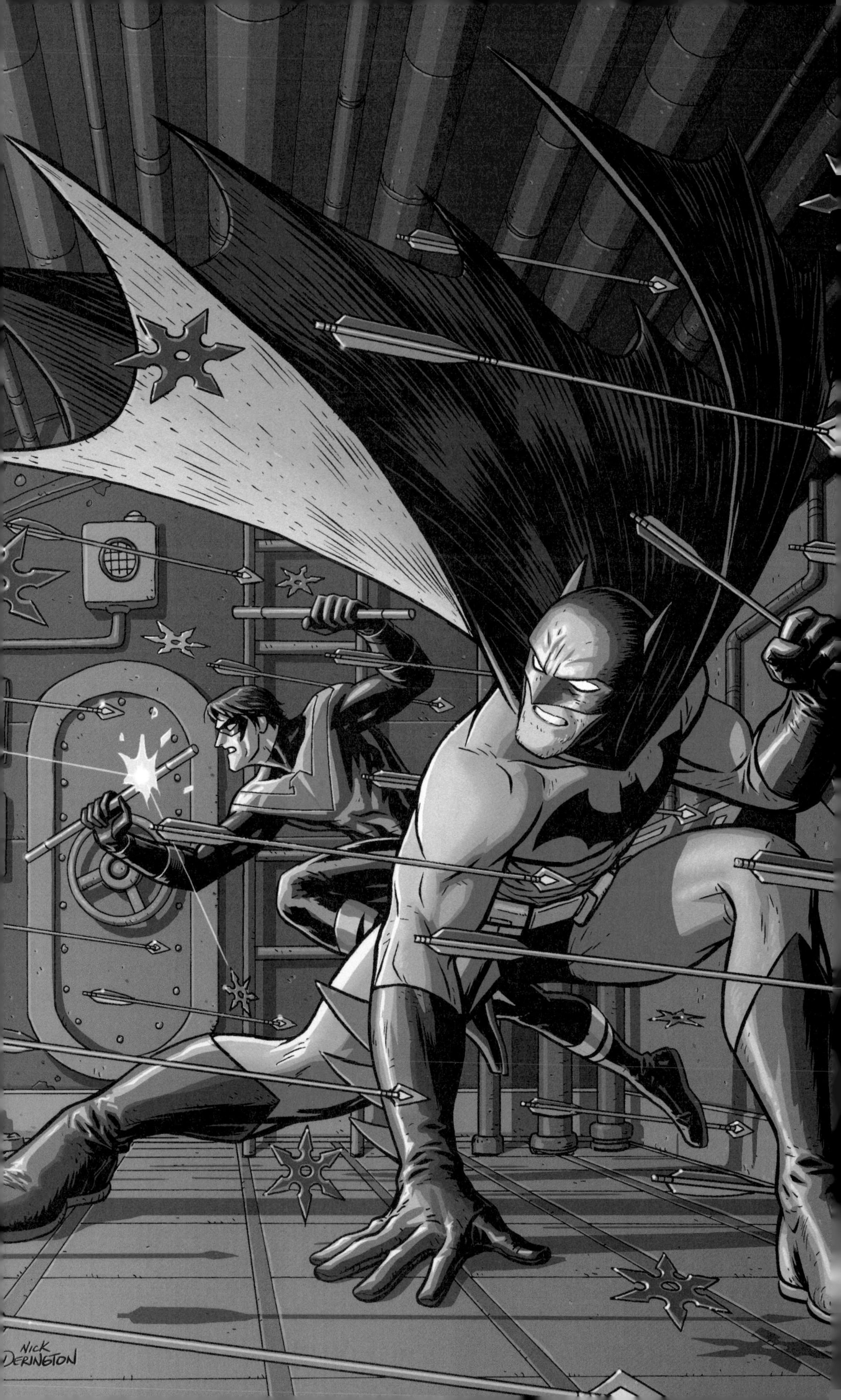
NICK DERINGTON

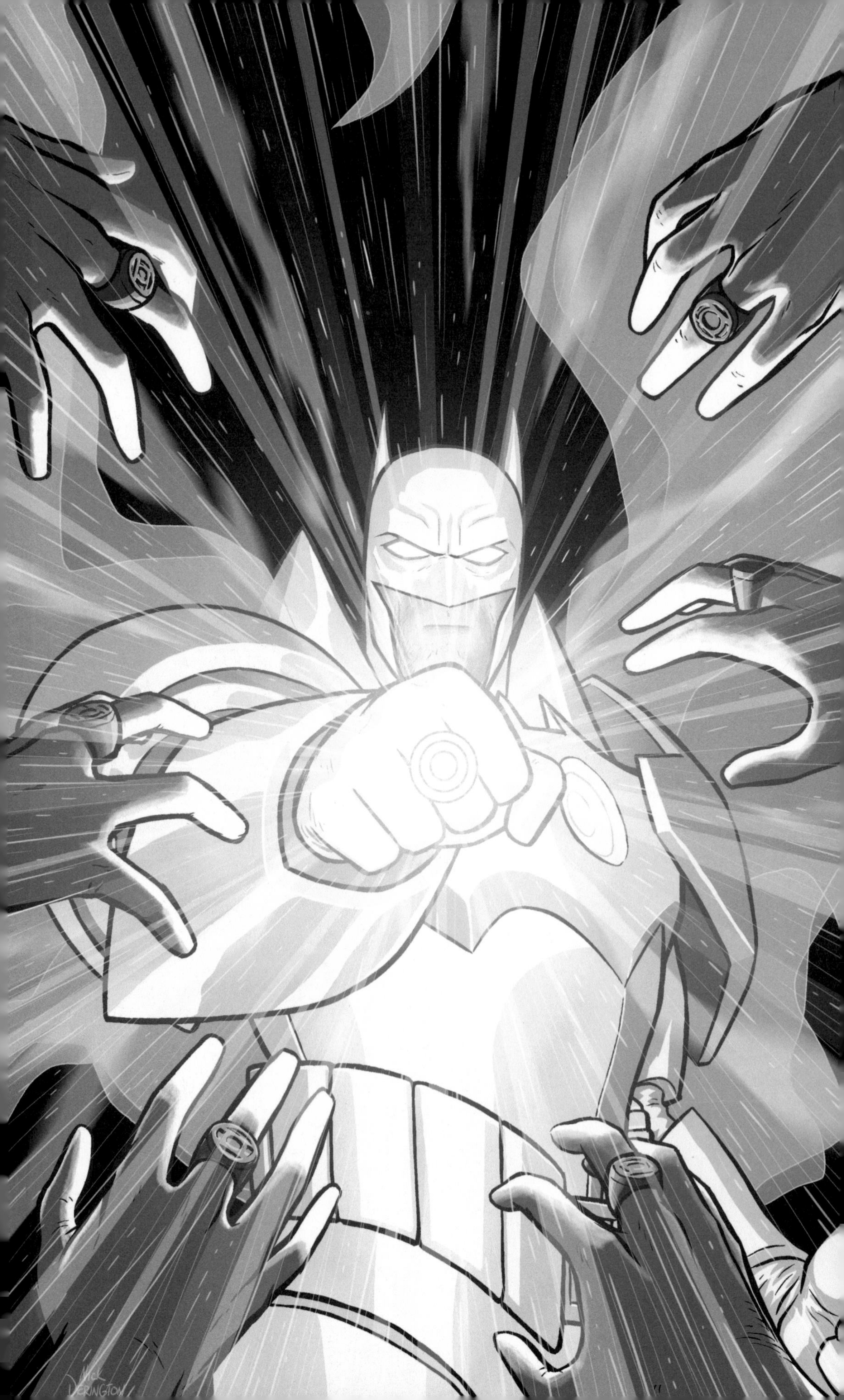

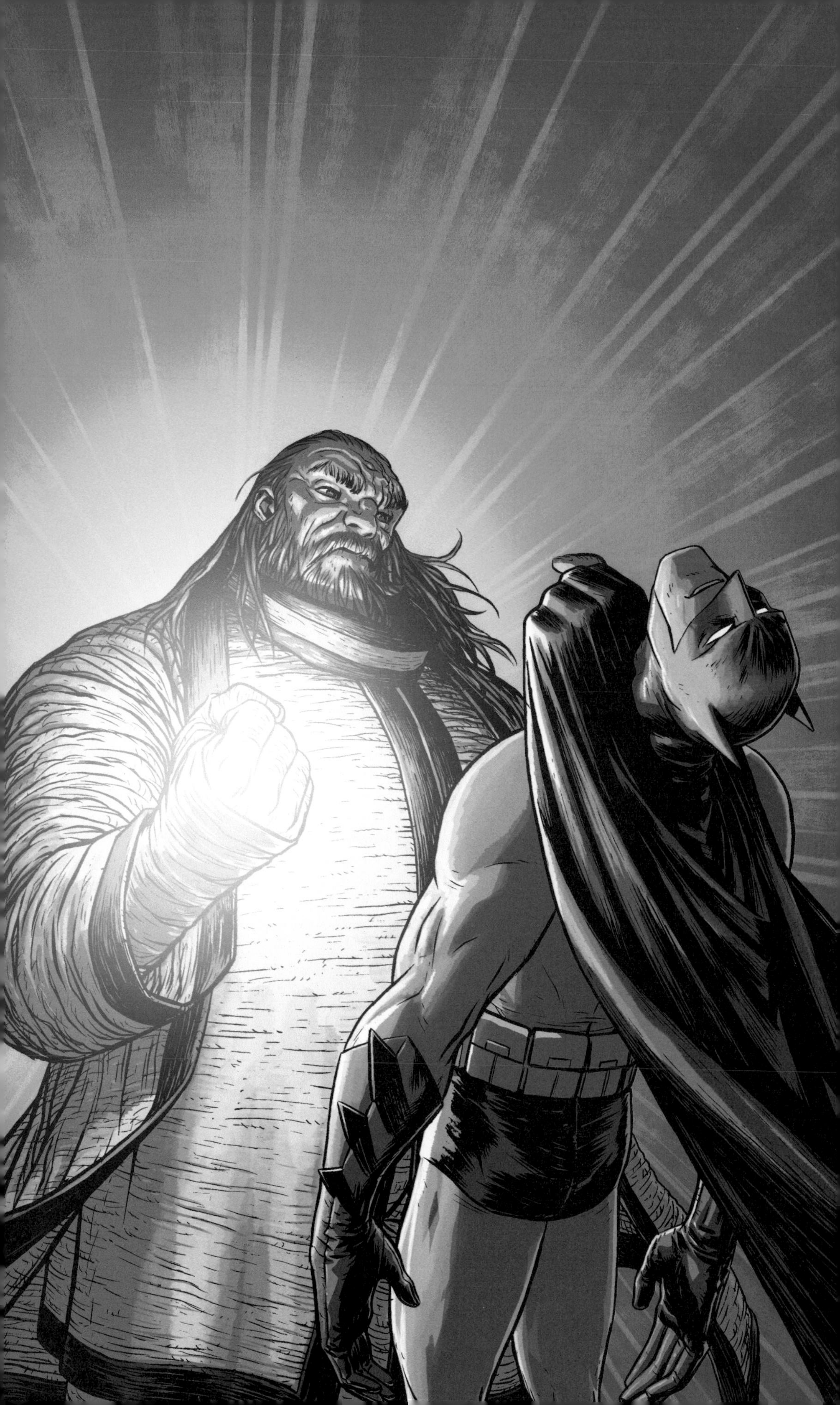

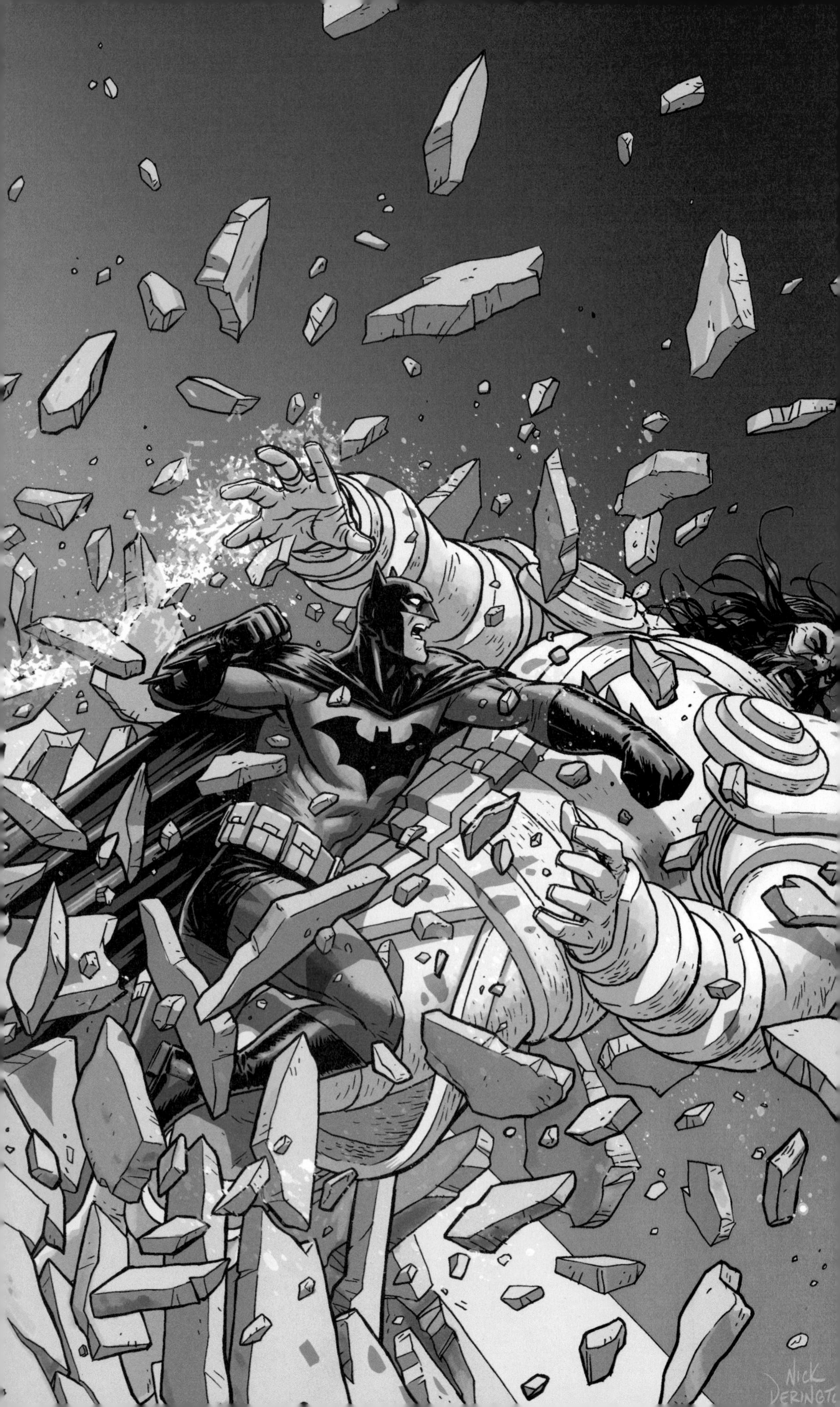
NICK
DERINGT

BATMAN: UNIVERSE SKETCHBOOK BY
NICK DERINGTON

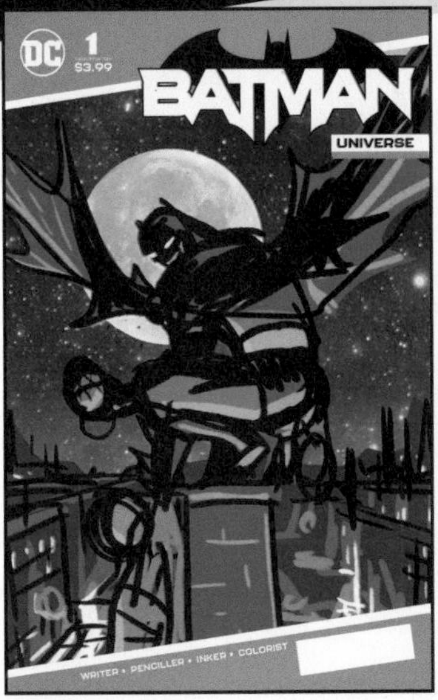
DC
1
$3.99
BATMAN
UNIVERSE
WRITER • PENCILLER • INKER • COLORIST

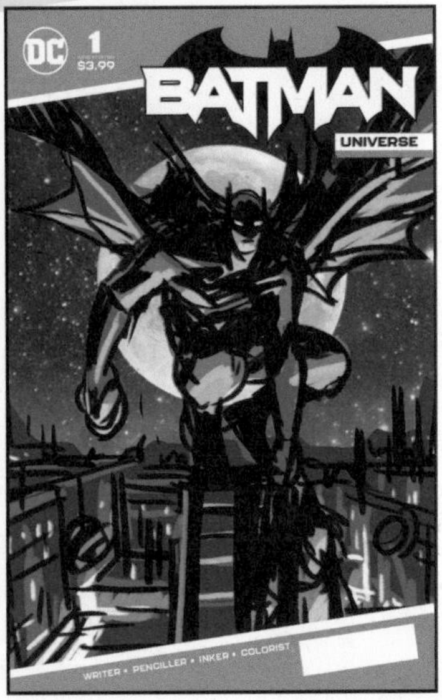
DC
1
$3.99
BATMAN
UNIVERSE
WRITER • PENCILLER • INKER • COLORIST

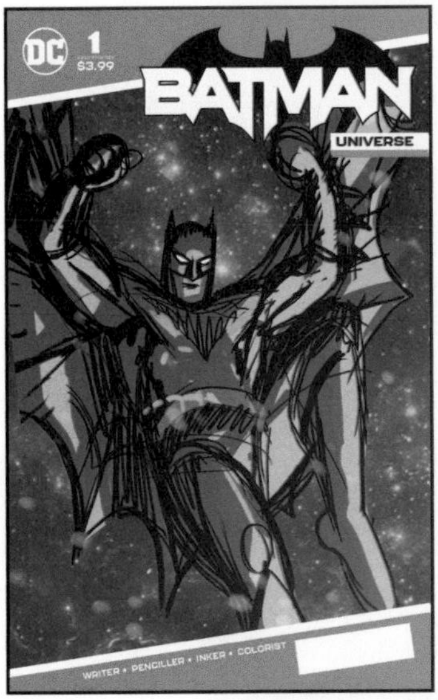
DC
1
$3.99
BATMAN
UNIVERSE
WRITER • PENCILLER • INKER • COLORIST

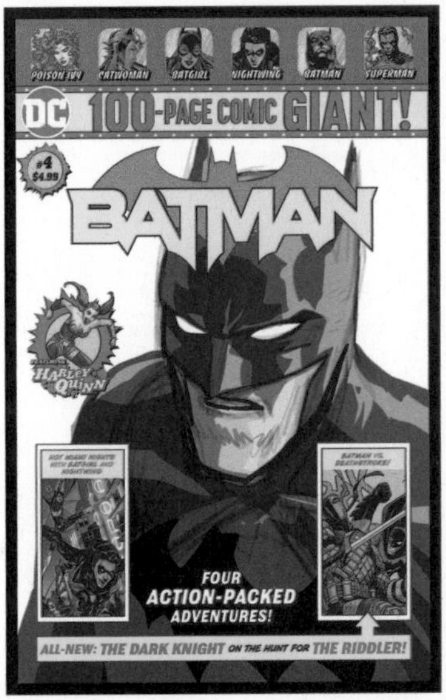
POISON IVY
CATWOMAN
BATGIRL
NIGHTWING
BATMAN
SUPERMAN
DC
100-PAGE COMIC GIANT!
#4
$4.99
BATMAN
FOUR
ACTION-PACKED
ADVENTURES!
ALL-NEW: THE DARK KNIGHT ON THE HUNT FOR THE RIDDLER!

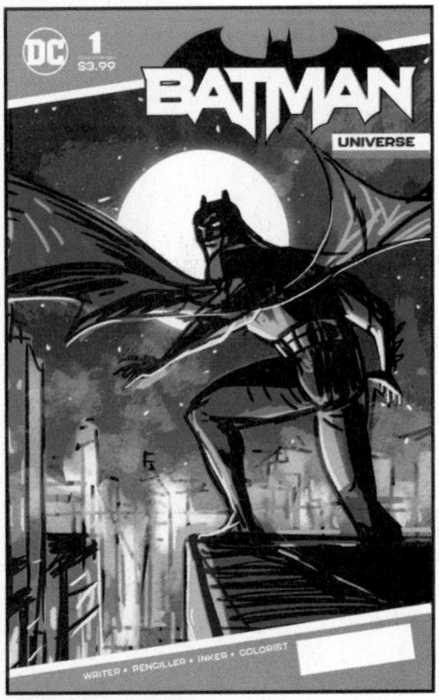
DC
1
$3.99
BATMAN
UNIVERSE
WRITER • PENCILLER • INKER • COLORIST

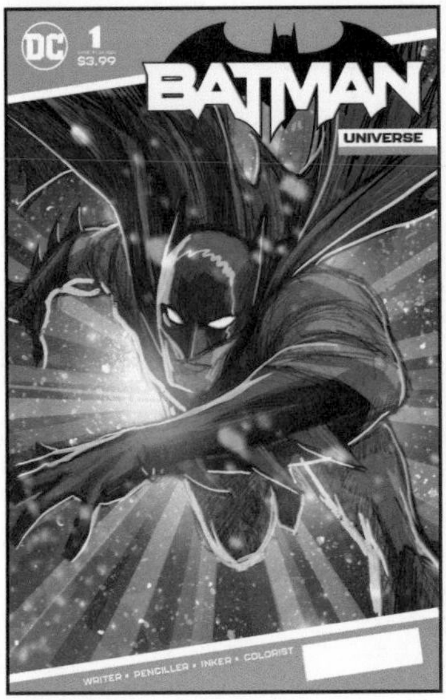
DC
1
$3.99
BATMAN
UNIVERSE
WRITER • PENCILLER • INKER • COLORIST

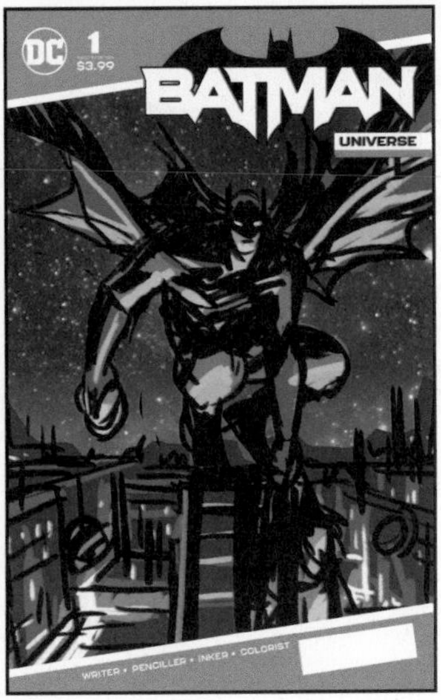
DC
1
$3.99
BATMAN
UNIVERSE
WRITER • PENCILLER • INKER • COLORIST

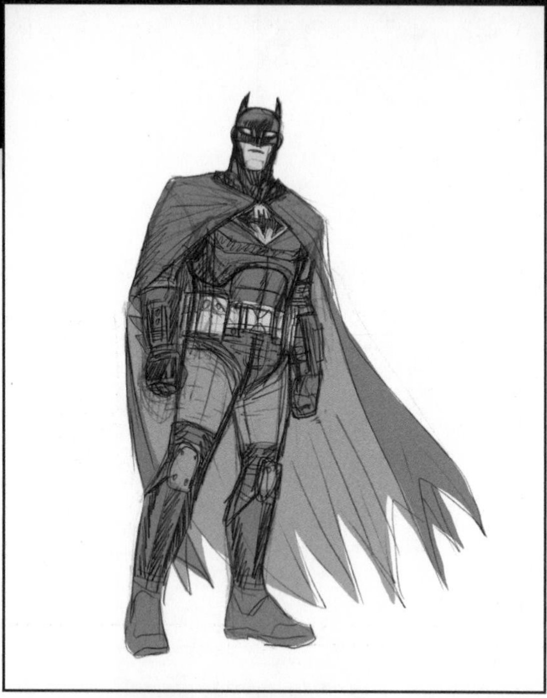

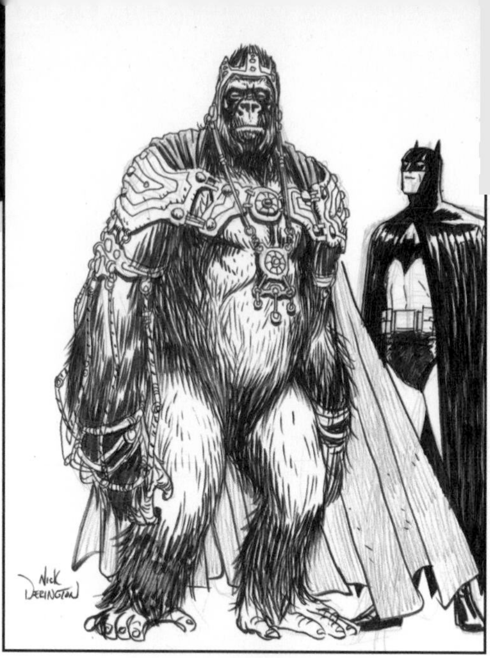
Nick
Derington

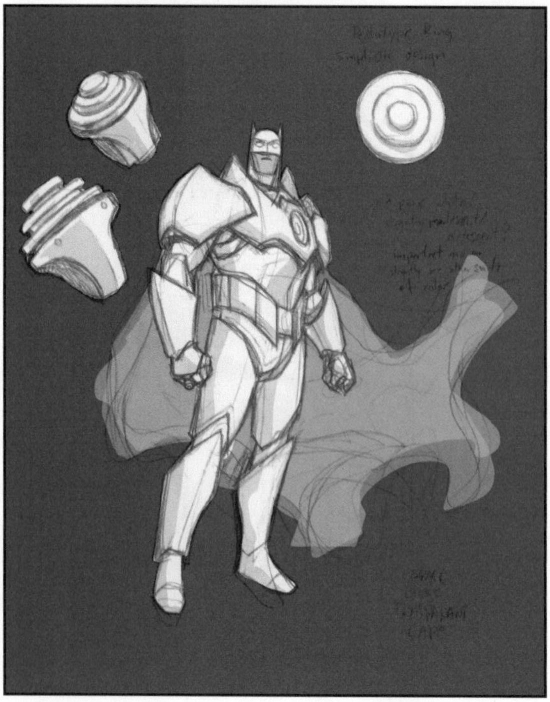

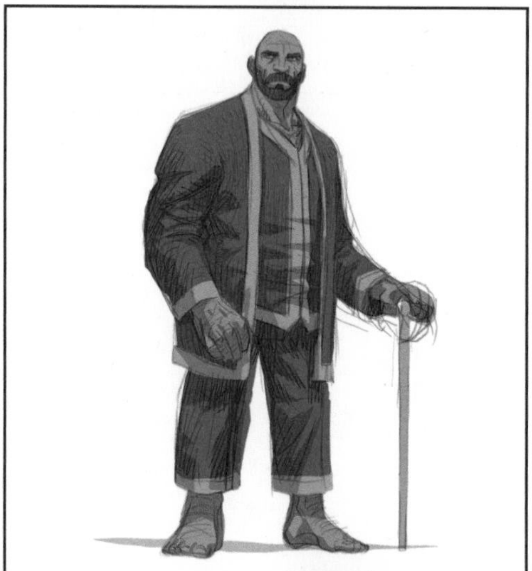

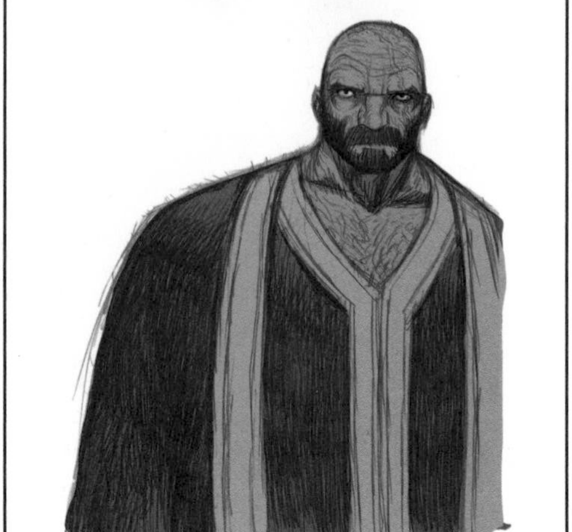

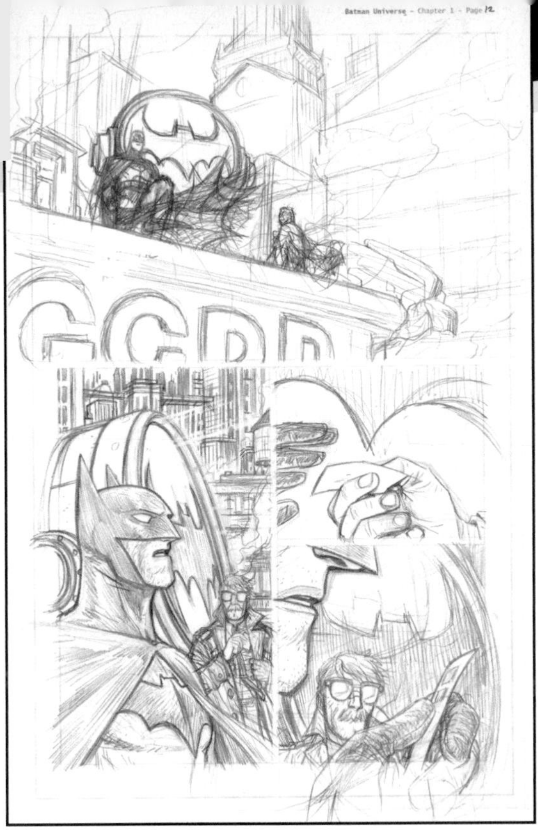
Batman Universe - Chapter 1 - Page 12

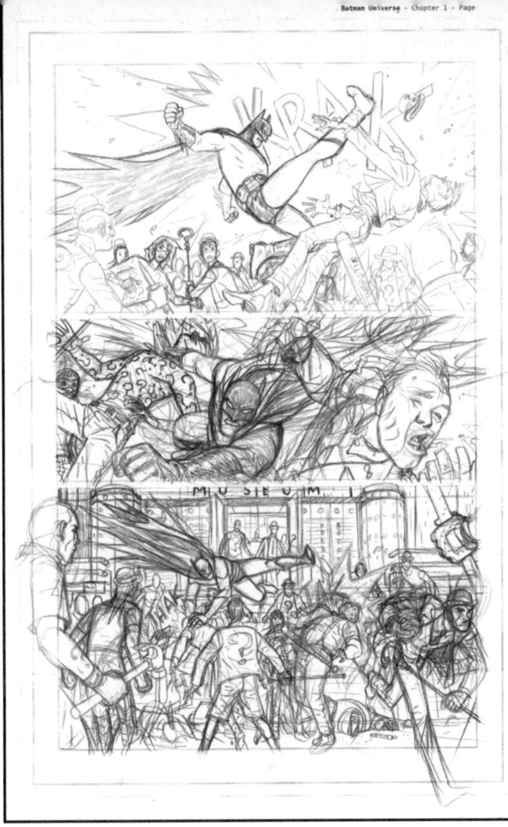
Batman Universe - Chapter 1 - Page
MUSEUM

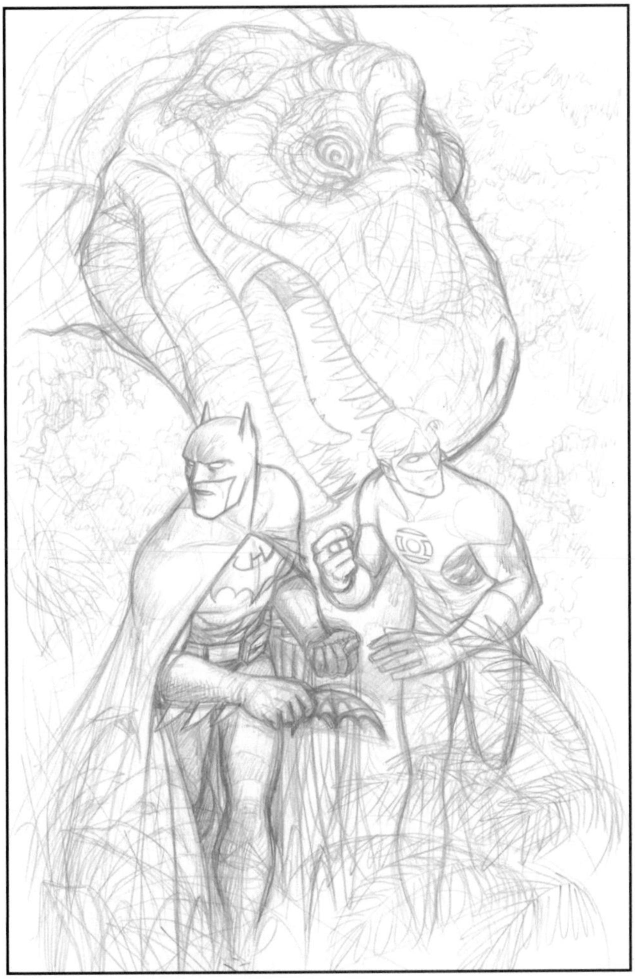

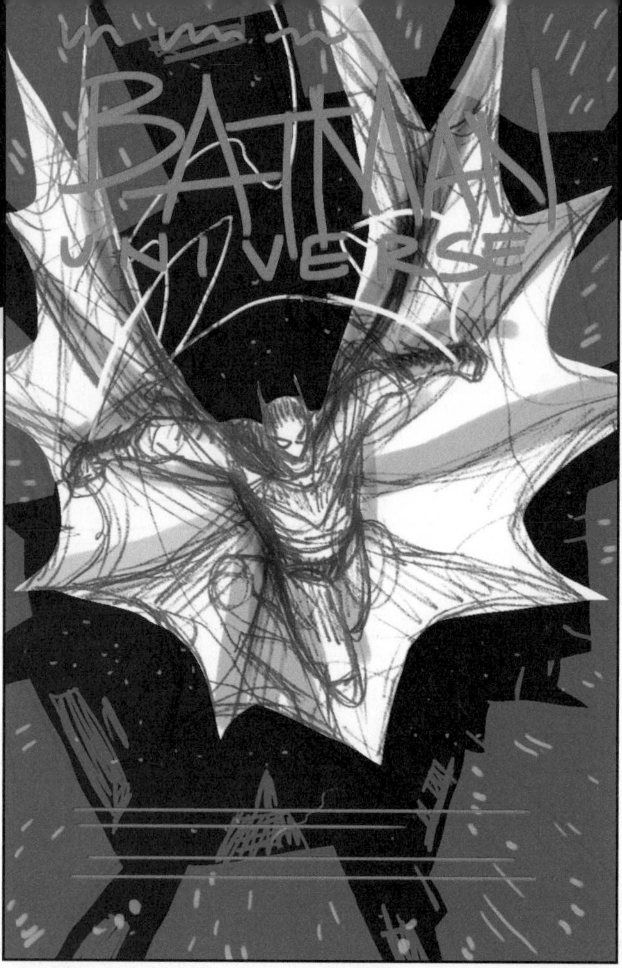
BATMAN
UNIVERSE

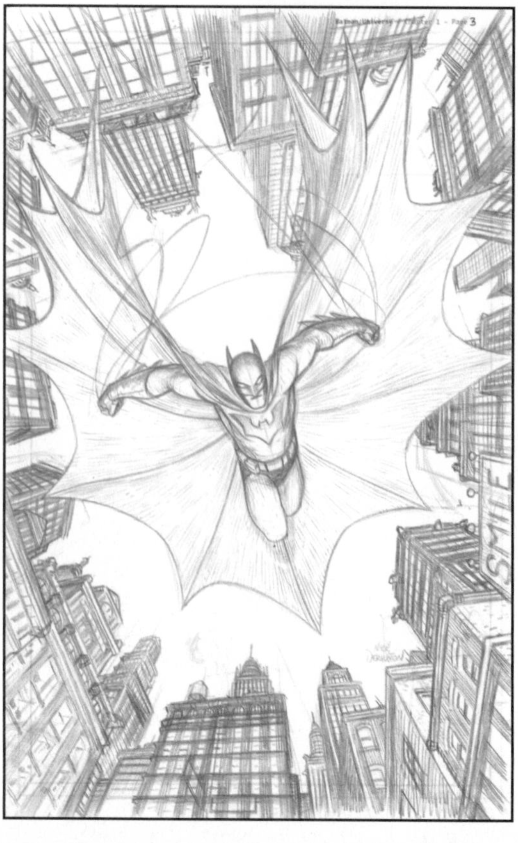
SMILE

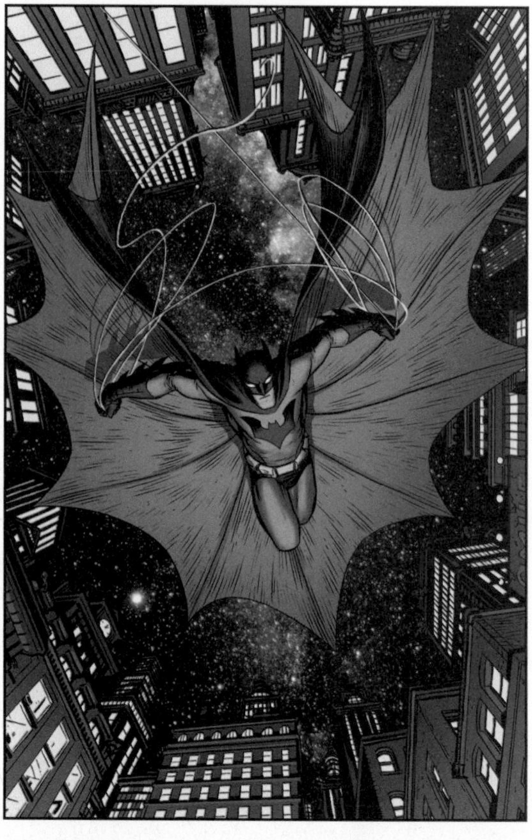

SUPERMAN
VOL. 1: THE UNITY SAGA: PHANTOM EARTH
BRIAN MICHAEL BENDIS AND IVAN REIS

SUPERMAN
VOL. 1 THE UNITY SAGA: PHANTOM EARTH

BRIAN MICHAEL BENDIS

IVAN REIS | JOE PRADO | OCLAIR ALBERT

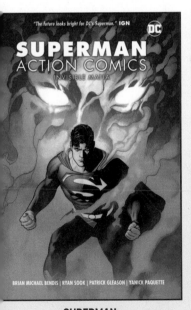

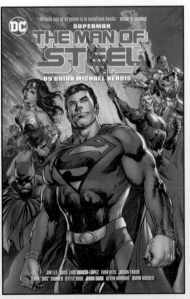

SUPERMAN: ACTION COMICS: INVISIBLE MAFIA

SUPERMAN: THE MAN OF STEEL

ACTION COMICS #1000: DELUXE EDITION

Get more DC graphic novels wherever comics and books are sold!

"[Writer Scott Snyder] pulls from the oldest aspects of the Batman myth, combines it with sinister-comic elements from the series' best period, and gives the whole thing terrific forward-spin."
– ENTERTAINMENT WEEKLY

START AT THE BEGINNING!
BATMAN
VOL. 1: THE COURT OF OWLS
SCOTT SNYDER with GREG CAPULLO

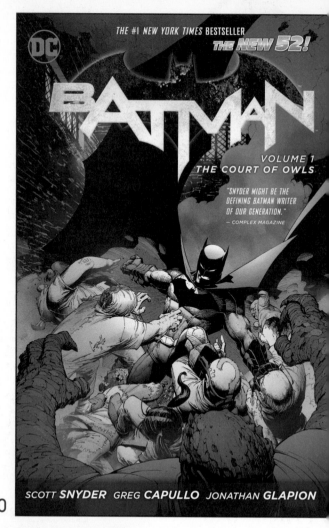

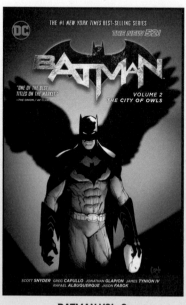

**BATMAN VOL. 2:
THE CITY OF OWLS**

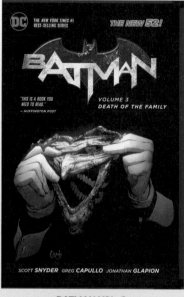

**BATMAN VOL. 3:
DEATH OF THE FAMILY**

READ THE ENTIRE EPIC

BATMAN VOL.
ZERO YEAR – SECRET CIT

BATMAN VOL.
ZERO YEAR – DARK CIT

BATMAN VOL.
GRAVEYARD SHIF

BATMAN VOL.
ENDGAM

BATMAN VOL. 8
SUPERHEAV

BATMAN VOL.
BLOO

BATMAN VOL. 1
EPILOGU

'Brilliantly executed."
-IGN

'Morrison and Quitely have the magic
ouch that makes any book they col-
aborate on stand out from the rest."
-MTV's Splash Page

grant morrison
frank quitely philip tan
BATMAN & ROBIN
"Morrison and Quitely have the magic touch."
— MTV'S SPLASH PAGE
BATMAN REBORN

GRANT MORRISON
with FRANK QUITELY & PHILIP TAN

grant morrison
cameron stewart andy clarke
BATMAN & ROBIN
BATMAN VS. ROBIN

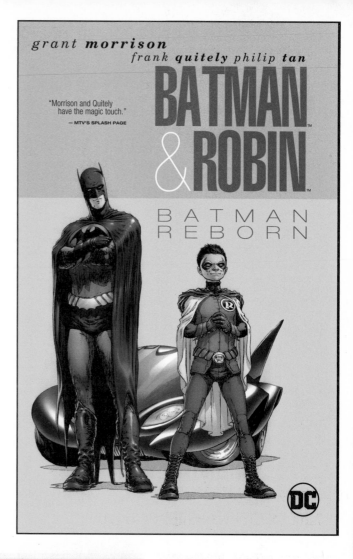

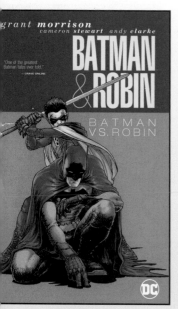

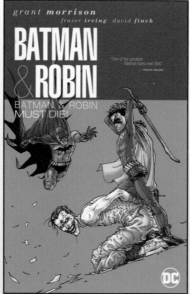

VOL. 2:
BATMAN VS. ROBIN

grant morrison
frazer irving david finch
BATMAN & ROBIN
BATMAN & ROBIN MUST DIE!

VOL. 3:
BATMAN & ROBIN MUST DIE!

"Thrilling and invigorating... Gotham City that has never looked this good, felt this strange, or been this deadly."
–Comic Book Resources

Get more DC graphic novels wherever comics and books are sold!

DC's YOUNG ANIMAL

DOOM PATROL
VOL. 1: BRICK BY BRICK
GERARD WAY with NICK DERINGTON

YOUNG ANIMAL   FOREWORD BY GERARD WAY

DOOM PATROL

VOL. 1:
BRICK BY BRICK
GERARD WAY
NICK DERINGTON
TAMRA BONVILLAIN

**CAVE CARSON HAS A CYBERNETIC EYE
VOL. 1: GOING UNDERGROUND**

**SHADE, THE CHANGING GIRL
VOL. 1: EARTH GIRL MADE EASY**

**MOTHER PANIC
VOL. 1: A WORK IN PROGRESS**